P9-CDN-711

HENRY
THE EIGHTH

HENRY THE EIGHTH

THEODORE MAYNARD

THE BRUCE PUBLISHING COMPANY
MILWAUKEE

TO
CONYERS READ

Contents

HENRY
THE EIGHTH

CHAPTER ONE

Foundations

ON APRIL 21, 1509, the old King died.

He was not really an old man if one measures by years, only fifty-two. But his tall, thin figure, once that of a soldier and sportsman, had been stooped for some time, and for even longer his sparse hair and broken and blackened teeth were among several indications of premature age. The eyes that had once been full of charm, and remained full of intelligence, had a secretive look, accentuated by his sharp features and thin lips. He had been worn down, as on a grindstone, by the cares of office and his own craftiness. Then at last tuberculosis wasted him. It was of this that he died.

For the last six years of his life, since the death of his wife Elizabeth of York – through whom he had his one solid claim to the throne – he had been talking of marrying again. These projects of his – none very dignified and some rather comical, if not disgusting – had as sole justification the fact that, of the seven children Elizabeth had borne him in a loveless marriage all except three died before her. Of these three only one was a boy – a frail thread upon which to hang so doubtful a dynasty as that of the Tudors. Late as the time was, he had wished to marry again so as to obtain, if possible, at least one more son in reserve in case young Henry should die. The boy was certainly far more robust in appearance than his brother Arthur had ever been. Even so it was a constant cause of anxiety to have everything depend on that one life. The projects had come to nothing because the King had been too cautious and calculating about marriage, as about everything else.

The elder Henry had a streak of fantasy in him, shown by his claim to descent from Cadwallader, with hints even at the more or less mythical Arthur. Yet all that was positively known about his descent was that his grandfather Owen Tudor had been clerk of the wardrobe to the widow of Henry V, and was in all probability her lover rather than her husband. Though their son Edward was created Earl of Richmond and married Margaret Beaufort, this lady was great-grand-daughter to John of Gaunt by the illegitimate line. Henry Tudor therefore was not really royal at all and came to the throne mainly because he had undertaken to marry the daughter of Edward IV and so to combine the houses of York and Lancaster against Richard III.

Henry might have claimed the crown by conquest but was careful not to do so, lest he encourage other claimants to use the same methods. Nor would he marry Elizabeth until after his coronation, so as not to appear to be resting his claim upon hers. Even his parliamentary title was insubstantial, as it was recognized by a Parliament summoned and virtually chosen by himself, and with all his opponents in the House of Lords under attainder. His right to be king was therefore very vague and, for good reasons, was never clearly defined.

If Henry VII retained the throne for twenty-four years, this was because he showed himself, in his way, a master at the art of government, building up the national prosperity with one hand while repelling a series of conspiracies and rebellions with the other. But even his energy and dexterity would probably have failed had he not found powerful external support. Pope Innocent VIII had issued on March 27, 1486, so ample a bull in his favor that many years later Henry's son could confide to Sir Thomas More that he owed the "crown imperial" to the Papacy. And he found further support, as against France — from which all invasions must come — in a close alliance with the kingdoms of Castile and Aragon. Aided by them, he gave order to a country that had been torn by sixty years of civil war. One of the least attractive, he was also one of the ablest – perhaps the very ablest – of English kings.

The final consolidation of Henry's rule was the work of the ambassador of Ferdinand and Isabella, Dr. Roderigo Gonzalez de Puebla. This Puebla was a clever little lawyer of Jewish extraction – an unpleasant and (so his enemies said) a disreputable man.* He may have egged Henry on to commit the political crime of executing the Earl of Warwick, who, as the son of the Duke of Clarence, the brother of Edward IV and Richard III, was the true Plantagenet heir. The unfortunate young man had been kept since childhood in the Tower and was sent to the block as much to reassure Ferdinand as to make Henry himself feel secure. But though Puebla wrote to his master that no drop of legitimate royal blood remained in England to challenge the Tudors, this was not quite accurate, for Warwick's sister was alive. She, however, as a girl, was not a serious threat, and none of the several other people who were of royal descent showed any disposition to assert a claim to the throne. Puebla could therefore exult. As for Katherine of Aragon, because of whom this crime had been committed, she mourned to her dying day the fact that her marriage had been made in blood and attributed to this her life of misfortune.

Before she left Spain she was married by proxy to Arthur, Prince of Wales – Dr. Puebla acting as her proxy. And from the moment of her arrival at Plymouth – tired after a three months' journey across Spain (which included a whole night spent in prayer at the shrine of St. James of Compostella) and six weeks at sea – the English people took her to the hearts she was never to lose. They saw in this great-great-grand-daughter of their own

* They gave out that he had lived for several years, while ambassador to England, in a bawdy house. What seems to be true is that because of his poverty he was obliged to lodge with a stonemason, at whose house there also lived some women of ill-repute. It was not Puebla's fault but that of the Ferdinand who treated him so shabbily. Rather it is to his credit that, in spite of such circumstances, he held on to carry through the alliance of England and Spain.

John of Gaunt (but by the legitimate line) and the daughter of the kings of Spain the promise of a king to come about whose right there could be no question. Though even then she was not very good looking, she was, with her fresh complexion and her smiling face, agreeable to look at; and King Henry had stipulated that her ladies-in-waiting must be beautiful. At Plymouth and all the way to London the people roared their welcome.

The King and the Prince of Wales disregarded rigid Spanish etiquette, which forbade the bride being seen before the morning of the wedding and rode down to Dogmersfield in Hampshire to welcome her. Without stopping to change, and still in his riding clothes, the King had insisted on going to her room, saying that he would see the Princess even if she was in bed. Though her duenna was aghast, Katherine did not seem to mind. After supper she sent for her musicians and gave the King and his son, fifteen-year-old Arthur, an exhibition of Spanish dances, after which the Prince led out Lady Guildford in an English dance. Protocol had been dispensed with, the ice broken at once. The King could be very charming when he chose, and the Prince and his bride were able to talk in the Latin in which they had already been corresponding.

In London, as soon as it could be arranged, came the state marriage in St. Paul's, as splendid as the King could make it. Normally parsimonious, he never failed to provide magnificence when the occasion called for it. The chronicler Edward Hall noted "the rich apparel of the Princess, the strange fashion of the Spanish nation, the beauty of the English ladies, the goodly demeanor of the young damsels, the amorous countenance of the lusty bachelors." Another picture shows her as wearing a little hat shaped like that of a cardinal's with a lace of gold to hold it in place. Her auburn hair hung loose over her shoulders – a token of virginity – and she had a coif of carnation color between her head and the hat. Among the crowds that lined the streets that November 15 was a young lawyer only just called to the bar, who thought this future queen of England lacked nothing that the most beautiful girl should have. His fate was to be closely entwined with hers; his name was Thomas More.

Beauty, strictly speaking, Katherine never had. But an evident goodness and nobility shone in her face, and everybody noted that she was always smiling, the smiles of a really kind and affectionate nature. They all felt warmed by those smiles, each man and woman present taking them as personally bestowed. A thrill ran through crowded St. Paul's when, along the wooden ramp erected from the entrance to a platform before the high altar, the Princess from Spain walked with her arm in that of her eleven-year-old brother-in-law, Henry, Duke of York. He it was who presented her to her waiting bridegroom, Arthur, Prince of Wales.

Henry shone, too, at the festivities later in the day at Westminster Hall. In the yard outside a tilting-ring had been set up; inside there was music and dancing. Then the young Duke won more applause than did even the antics of Katherine's Spanish fool when he threw off his heavy cloth-of-gold suit and danced in his small clothes, a big, bounding cherub. He was already almost as tall as, and far sturdier than, the sickly Arthur.

After the official and public bedding of the two children at Baynard's Castle, there was some discussion as to whether they should live together as man and wife. This was regarded with misgivings by some members of the Council. It was also disapproved of by some of the Spaniards at the court, as they remembered that Katherine's brother, Juan the Infante, he in whom had rested the hopes of the kingdoms of Spain, had married while still in his adolescence and had quickly gone from his marriage bed to his grave. All objections on this score were overborne by Alessandro Geraldini, Katherine's learned Italian confessor. He was an officious person, addicted to pluming himself upon his discernment. He used to claim that he was the only one who foretold the success of Columbus, the Captain of the Ocean Sea, when everybody else thought him a fool or a charlatan. So now he took it upon himself to assert that Queen

Isabella would wish her daughter to live with the Prince as his wife. Accordingly they went off together to Ludlow Castle, the official residence of Arthur as Prince of Wales. When four and a half months later Arthur died on April 2, Geraldini again was knowledgeable, for he declared that the marriage had been consummated, something hotly denied by Katherine's duenna, Doña Elvira Manuel, as contrary to her own positive knowledge and that of all the attendant ladies of the little court on the Welsh marches. Queen Isabella believed Doña Elvira, but to cover all possible contingencies Ferdinand asked the Pope to supplement the dispensation that had been given for Katherine's marriage to her brother-in-law. To console Isabella on her death-bed, where she lay worrying about the craftiness of Henry Tudor, this brief was sent.

Arthur's death in his sixteenth year was a shattering blow to England, as it was to his father and mother. Crushed by the news that reached him, the desolate King at once sent for his wife. Then when she had done her best to comfort him and had gone back to her own room, she broke down so completely that her ladies had to send for the King to comfort her. It is almost the only glimpse we get of any tenderness between them.

Arthur was laid to rest in Worcester Cathedral, and ten months later his mother was herself dead, dying after having given birth to a daughter who soon followed her to the grave.

The diplomatic as well as the dynastic interest had at once shifted to Arthur's brother Henry. On the very day that the news of Arthur's death reached Spain, a special envoy was commissioned to go to England to sound the English as to the possibility of a marriage being arranged between the widowed Katherine and the new Prince of Wales. Ferdinand and Isabella were sure that Katherine's dowry – already half paid – would not be disgorged by the English King. It would not be wasted, however, if a new English marriage could be made.

King Henry agreed to the extent of wishing to get the balance of Katherine's dowry. Without rejecting outright the proposals regarding Katherine and his son, he discovered, as soon as Queen Elizabeth died, a better plan. It was that of marrying Katherine himself. There would be several years before the Prince would be of a marriageable age. Why wait until then? He was a widower now, and Katherine was already in England. Let the rest of the dowry be paid and Katherine could be queen of England at once. This happy and ingenious suggestion Katherine was herself induced to make on behalf of her father-in-law to her mother.

Isabella indignantly rejected the proposal. This, however, was not because she was horrified by it, for if Katherine had been, as she believed, married only in name, there could be no more real objection to Katherine's marrying the elder instead of the younger Henry. The disparity of age was considerable – forty-six to eighteen – but it was not a shocking disparity, and in dynastic marriages even a greater disparity was no barrier. Isabella's objection was to an offer that was not a good enough bargain. When the middle-aged King died, he would be succeeded not by any son Katherine might bear but by the younger Henry. Then Katherine would have to live the rest of her life in England as queen dowager. To win that empty honor for her Ferdinand and Isabella had no intention of paying out the other half of her large dowry. They therefore suggested that, if the King of England was looking for another wife, he marry the widowed Queen of Naples. She was twenty-six and Ferdinand's niece; such a marriage would suffice to preserve the Spanish connection.

Henry took this suggestion seriously enough to send envoys to inspect the lady; they were to report on her figure and were to try to discover whether she had a sweet or a bad breath. Henry dropped the idea only when he found that the material returns were not going to be substantial enough. He therefore considered Margaret of Savoy, the daughter of the Emperor Maximilian. At the start the Emperor was willing; in the end Margaret was not.

The project that Henry became most interested in was the

oddest of all. It was that of marrying the insane Queen Joan of Castile, though she was still said to be wandering about with the unburied body of her husband Philip of Burgundy. Henry had been greatly impressed by her beauty when she and her husband had been driven in 1506 into an English port in a storm. She did not seem to him insane at that time, and he believed that the reports about her derangement were fabricated by her father Ferdinand as a pretext for acting as her regent in Castile. Even if the reports were true, he said he had no objection to a little insanity. Perhaps she would recover when married to him. And if she did not recover he was assured that this would not affect her bearing of children. Katherine, who was by now officially accredited as an ambassador by Ferdinand, had to act as negotiator for the preposterous marriage.

Meanwhile Katherine was being held in England as a kind of pawn ticket for the payment of the balance of her dowry; upon that depended the final decision as to what disposal would be made of her. A Hapsburg alliance was coming to seem more and more advantageous to the elder Henry. Though he had formally betrothed the Prince of Wales to Katherine on June 23, 1503, he was exploring other possibilities. If he himself could not get mad Joan, why should not his son marry Joan's daughter Eleanor, and his daughter Mary marry Joan's son, Charles of Ghent? It was already almost a foregone conclusion that Charles would eventually succeed his grandfather Max as emperor. And if Charles should die, Eleanor would become queen of Castile. The young Prince of Wales was therefore taken a few days before his fourteenth birthday to the house of Richard Fox, the Bishop of Winchester, and told to make a formal and written protest against his marriage to Katherine, declaring it null and void on the grounds that the engagement was entered into while he was still a child. The treachery was of course carefully concealed from Ferdinand and Katherine. They remained bound; but now the two Henries were free to seek a better marriage elsewhere if one could be discovered. The boy was merely obeying his father's orders; the only justification for the King is that, now that Isabella was dead, Ferdinand showed no sign of intending to carry out the terms of the marriage contract.

Everything turned on money, the two Kings haggling like cheap-jacks over every ducat each thought to be his due. Poor Katherine lived in solemn state in the palace of the Bishop of Durham on the Strand, surrounded by threadbare attendants whose salaries she could not pay, and needing all her Spanish fortitude and pride to survive. She often wrote to her father begging cash for the mere necessities of life, but never getting it. Ferdinand was not going to throw good money after bad, and as England was virtually holding his daughter as a hostage, he thought that England should at least pay her household bills.

King Henry, when appealed to by Katherine, explained that he was actuated only by the most delicate consideration for her, as this was apparently the only way of inducing her father to pay her marriage portion. But Ferdinand was, if possible, even more avaricious than Henry. Dr. Puebla's salary was paid so irregularly that most of the time he was half starved. When King Henry was asked why the Doctor went to court at all he answered tersely, "To eat!" Fuensalida, a new Spanish ambassador sent to England to see what he could do where Puebla had failed, had to report that the stinking fish he saw on the table of the Princess was such as he would not give his horse-boy. Her entourage were so down-at-heel that they were ready to beg in the streets.

Katherine's father-in-law was at least better than her father. For Ferdinand gave her nothing and would not allow any of the plate she had brought from Spain to be touched until a marriage settlement had been reached, whereas Henry did now and then dole out sums for her support, though they were hardly sufficient for the barest of monthly needs and never removed more than a grain or two from her mountain of bills. Yet in doing even this much he made her poverty all the more galling by never failing to remind her that what he gave was only out of charity. By this time he grew livid with rage at any mention of Ferdinand's name. The King of Aragon exculpated himself by saying that Katherine's dowry was not a charge on his kingdom but on that of Castile.

The young Prince of Wales to whom Katherine was betrothed knew nothing about what was going on. He was kept in the strictest seclusion, never being allowed to see Katherine, even when they were living under the same roof. When he began to emerge from adolescence he was allowed to go nowhere and to do nothing except under close supervision. He even slept in a room opening off his father's, through which was its only entrance.

This probably was due to his grandmother, the Countess of Richmond, usually known as the Lady Margaret. She rather than her son should have occupied the throne, on the supposition that her son had any right to it at all. A famous blue-stocking, a shriveled little ascetic, very learned and alert and pious, she was the patron of the John Fisher whom her grandson was to behead. Admirable woman though she was, she was also, in respect to young Henry, very ill-advised. But she could not fail to see in him, even when he was a boy, a marked resemblance to his maternal grandfather, Edward IV, the handsomest man of his time, until corpulence caught up with him in early middle age, but also the most sensual of English kings. The most famous of his mistresses, Jane Shore, was still alive and was to live many years more. The Lady Margaret could not but fear for the morals and the eternal destiny of her grandson. Fearing as she did, she had him subjected to a discipline that a wiser woman would have seen to be too severe. But the King himself feared, and once when he was whipping the boy and Alcock the Bishop of Ely interposed, the father answered, "Never entreat for him; this child will be the undoing of England."

Too much should not be made of the kind of remark that other irate men have used of their sons. Some blame should rather be attached to the father and grandmother, good as their intentions were. But in other respects the boy got an excellent education, having as his tutor John Skelton, the best poet in England, though perhaps hardly the best of moral mentors. Skelton at all events had some right to boast:

> The honor of England I learned to spell,
> I gave him drink of the sugared well
> Of Helicon's waters crystalline
> Acquainting him with the Muses nine.

Skelton would have been well qualified to introduce young Henry to the Muses. But if the Prince was ever really thought of – while Arthur was alive – as a future cardinal-archbishop of Canterbury and given a training suitable for this office, this must have been under John Fisher, who had him in charge for a while. On the face of it, however, a study of theology does not seem likely in the case of one so young. His education would rather appear to have been along the lines of the humanist fashion then coming into vogue, one that took all knowledge for its province. In this, theology had its part but, in Henry's case, was probably mainly a taste acquired later.

We get in one of the letters of Erasmus an entertaining account of a visit that he and Lord Mountjoy and Thomas More paid in 1499, when Henry was only eight, to the royal children at Eltham Palace. It was designed by Mountjoy, who had been a student under Erasmus in Paris, as a pleasant surprise for his former professor. The three men were received in the great hall by the little Duke of York, with the other children grouped around – Edmund, the youngest, being a babe in arms – and were entertained at dinner. During the meal Duke Henry embarrassed Erasmus a little by sending him – no doubt prompted by his tutor – a note asking why he had not written him a poem. Erasmus concludes, "I went home, and though the Muses, from whom I had been long divorced, were unwilling, I finished the poem in three days." So delicate a compliment had to be responded to in a set of Latin verses. The surveillance over Henry – something from which he naturally recoiled as soon as possible – did not begin until he was emerging into adolescence.

In spite of this, or because of this, one cannot see much of his father in him except his love of music and his love of money.

Henry VII laid the foundations very solidly for his dynasty. His was a contribution to English history that has failed to receive adequate recognition only because of the greater brilliance of his son and grand-daughter. But it must be acknowledged that, able though the first of the Tudors was, he lacked genius and that what are accounted his weaknesses are of the least lovable kind. The chief charge against him is not so much avarice as that he kept careful accounts. It was looked upon as very unseemly in a king that he should put down every shilling won or lost at dice or archery; the proper thing, of course, was to squander ten times more than he did and never give it another thought. But he punctiliously went through his private and the public accounts, annotating them, questioning expenditures, seeking reductions, and passing nothing except after close scrutiny. His sprawling "H" on these may still be seen. It would have been well for the younger Henry had he possessed a larger share of his father's business sense, however understandable it may be that, tired of what he had come to look upon as petty parsimony, he should, when he became king, spend lavishly without much care as to where the money was going and demanding more and more money to spend.

In the case of Henry VII it would be most unjust to sum everything up under the single word *avarice*. Though that was an element in the matter, a still larger element may have been conscientiousness. The theory upon which the English monarchy operated at that time was that the king should "live on his own." This meant that his personal revenues – which included not only manorial holdings but all the sources of revenue that were grouped as the royal "forests," mines and fisheries among them – were expected to suffice not only for his private needs but for all normal national necessities. These had, in his case, been supplemented by the taxes known as tonnage and poundage, and with him they not only sufficed to cover all financial demands but to leave a large surplus. Henry VII was the first, and also the last, of English kings who actually did make ends meet and so was seldom obliged to ask Parliament for supplementary grants.

It was very wise of him to proceed as he did. Parliament would have felt that it had already done enough in granting taxes which brought in over £32,000 at the beginning of the reign and showed an average yearly increase of close on to £500. This alone was sufficient for ordinary expenses. Henry was aware that, since his claim to the throne could be considered as, at best, a parliamentary one, he should avoid further dependence on Parliament. But in his desire to strengthen the monarchy, and in particular his doubtful dynasty, by building up a large financial reserve, he could not refrain from indulging in an odious fiscal policy. This was another reason why he did not wish to lay himself open to parliamentary criticism.

The policy was largely extortionary. First there was the device known as "Morton's Fork," though it was really the invention of Bishop Fox and not of the juster-minded Archbishop Morton, the Chancellor. It based its exactions on the assumption that, if a man was spending little, it was a sign that he must be saving a great deal; whereas if he was spending freely it was a sign that he must be rich. Either way he should be heavily taxed. And after the death of Morton in 1500 the notorious Empson and Dudley took control and managed to extract immense revenues by the devices of attainder and, still more, by the use of obsolete statutes, under which large fines were imposed for offenses which Henry's subjects had never imagined to be such. Francis Bacon, while pointing out that this King was not cruel, commented, "But the less blood he drew the more he took of treasure." It was a state of affairs tolerable only on condition that the accruing money was wisely expended and the country given a strong government.

In line with Henry's custom of exacting all possible feudal dues was his discovery — one made after Arthur's death — that he was entitled to a large parliamentary grant for Arthur's knighting. At the same time he demanded from Parliament a grant for the marriage in 1503 of the Princess Margaret to James IV of Scotland. When these demands were presented to the Parliament of 1504 a new member, the youthful Thomas More, referred to by the King as a "beardless boy," spoke so effectively that the £90,000 asked for had to be scaled down to £40,000.

The King was so angry that, as he could not touch the twenty-four-year-old More, he clapped his father, a newly elected sergeant of law, into the Tower, from which he was released only after the payment of a fine of £100. Bishop Fox tried to trap Thomas More by advising him to sue for the King's pardon. Fortunately Fox's secretary, Richard Whitford, later a monk of Syon and the translator of the *Imitation of Christ*, confidentially advised More to the contrary, saying that this would give the government just the handle it needed against him. "My Lord," Whitford added, "to serve the King's turn, will not stick to agree to his own father's death." Such being the situation, Thomas More found it safer for his health to withdraw for a time to the continent. He had at least succeeded in demonstrating that Parliament was determined to exercise independence in financial matters.

The aristocracy of England, while reduced, had not approached anything like physical extinction as a result of the Wars of the Roses. But it had lost much of its former power, and many of its members lay under attainder, the King seeing to it that the nobility were kept in subjection to the Crown. A bureaucracy of high ecclesiastics and lay officials managed most of the state departments, with the peers retained in the Council mainly as a decorative element. This was not merely to ensure the Crown against conspiracy but to promote trade. Henry's was what may well be called the first of the English business governments. Its policy was to encourage trade, now marvelously flourishing with the Low Countries as a result of the alliance with the House of Burgundy, at the expense of those aristocrats whose factional intrigues had resulted in the Crown of England changing hands five times in a hundred years, with three kings – Richard II and Henry VI and Edward V – murdered, and another, Richard III, killed in battle.

How insecure Henry VII's position was during the early part of his reign was shown by the appearance of a succession of pretenders, all of whom received some backing from abroad, especially from the dowager Duchess of Burgundy, who accepted them all, in turn, as one or other of the two Princes murdered in the Tower by their uncle (her brother) Richard III. Even though Warwick was safely in the Tower, he too was successfully impersonated; if he was executed in the end, this was brought on by the danger of a new rebellion. Lambert Simnel had been spared in a mood of good-natured contempt and had been given a position as scullion in the royal kitchens. The others had been exhibited before London crowds in proof that they were imposters. Poor Warwick ended under the axe to assure the kingdoms of Spain that the new dynasty of England was fully capable of holding what it had snatched at Bosworth. That much had to be done if Spain was to guarantee support to the Tudors by sending Katherine of Aragon to England as its future queen.

That guarantee was given, however, not so much on this account as because Henry had already several times shown himself capable of dealing with all challenges, and also because he was able to exhibit a prosperous country ruled by a very wealthy king.

Henry's idea of prosperity was eminently sound. It was that nobody, except himself, should be too powerful or too rich, but that the profits of trade and industry should be as widely distributed as possible. Though his extortionary methods must be condemned, they were prompted, not so much by the King's personal avarice, as by a policy of drastically repressing anybody who, in the King's opinion, was trying to climb too high for the general good.

His was a remarkable achievement. He had come in 1485 to the throne of a country whose population had dwindled, mainly as a consequence of the Black Death, but partly also because of the civil wars, to probably somewhat less than three millions from close to twice that number during the true Middle Ages. London was smaller than Florence, Venice, Paris, and Milan; and Norwich, the only other considerable English city, had shrunk to half its former size. England's dazzling military history was a thing of the past. Richard the Lion Heart was a legend like the English yeomen archers who had won the astounding victories of Cressy and Agincourt. But England had more recently been looked upon as a turbulent land, incapable of stable government, until Henry Tudor, the right man arriving at the right moment, managed to restrain its nobles, rescue its finances, and build up trade. He gave the English monarchy a new start.

Such defects as he had — his cold calculation, his caution, even his avarice — were put to good use. Had he been brilliant and dashing and adventurous he would almost certainly have failed. As it was, after one tentative experiment with war in France, he withdrew from the continent and settled down to the administration of his estates in England. It was a policy which, if somewhat drab, paid big dividends.

He owed much to the Papacy, yet his was only a conventional piety. As a means of spiritual insurance he founded a monastery or two and burned a few heretics. When he attempted to get Henry VI canonized, he was actuated not so much by devotion as by the idea that this would enhance his own position as a Lancastrian king.

But if England was not a notably religious country, it was more free of heresy than perhaps any other part of Europe. Some oddities of denial were occasionally to be met with — the flotsam and jetsam of the wreck of the Wycliffite and Lollard movements. There was, however, no system of heretical thought, but merely eccentricities. It is nonsensical to see in the recantation made by a Stephen Swallow on July 3, 1489, any adumbration of what is now thought of as Protestantism. For although Swallow denied the Sacrament of the Altar, he also asserted that baptism was not necessary for the offspring of Christians and that marriage was superfluous. Yet Henry felt it incumbent upon himself to suppress such things when they were drawn to his attention. He even actively participated in the conversion of a heretical priest who was, nevertheless, burned at Canterbury, duly repentant, in May, 1498. With the Church the King had no quarrel, nor the Church with him. It would have been quite inconceivable to him, or to anybody else in the country, that England could be anything else but Catholic. Religion was for him an essential part of social stability; it inspired little enthusiasm.

The intellectual movements of the time were encouraged chiefly by the King's mother, the Lady Margaret, though not without some encouragement (at her prompting) by Henry himself. All these movements were entirely orthodox, however critical they were disposed to be of a scholasticism in temporary decline. John Fisher, backed by the Lady Margaret, the patroness also of Caxton, was rejuvenating Cambridge University. Linacre, who had been tutor to Prince Arthur, was to go on to teach Greek at Oxford and to found the Royal College of Physicians. Grocyn and Colet had begun their careers. Polydore Vergil was writing his monumental history. Erasmus had touched the witty talent of Thomas More into the flame of genius and had been saved, perhaps by the winsome piety of his English friends, for the Catholic side in the religious quarrel not far distant. Whatever leaven was at work was not the leaven of the Pharisees but a very typical English thing, full of common sense and kindliness and humour. At any rate it was typical of the time, and developed only because the sober and safe government of Henry VII gave it its chance.

This intellectual ferment was part of Henry VII's rich bequest to his son. That he would have regarded it as of very minor importance is beside the point. Like everything else the first

Tudor left to his successor – a rich treasury, a nobility completely dominated by the monarchy, a Church flourishing though somewhat somnolent – much of it was to be badly handled. Yet these were the assets that made the son's brilliant, showy, and destructive career possible.

And now that Henry VII was dead the feelings of the subjects over whom he had ruled so long were mixed. For the person of the King there was hardly a trace of affection. But his Council was not unmindful of what he had accomplished and so recognized that his funeral ought to be the most splendid that England had ever seen. If that was the dead King's due, it could also be a form of rejoicing that there was now a new king. The pomp of feudalism was largely extinct, but Henry had accustomed them to pomp of an even more opulent sort. It was fitting that he should have this for his burial. The bulging treasury made it all the more permissible.

The preparations for this took time; not until May 8, eighteen days after the King's death, did they remove his body from Richmond to Westminster. It was a Tuesday when, as evening fell, the procession arrived at the southern end of London Bridge. At the head of everything rode the sword-bearer and the vice-chamberlain, with the King's trumpeters behind, followed by the officials of the court. The sheriffs and aldermen of the city of London carried roses in their hands, and behind them rode two heralds at arms and a knight all in black bearing the royal standard. Then came the bishops and abbots, followed by chanting friars, their voices augmented by those of the canons of St. Paul's and the choir of the chapel royal. A knight followed carrying a steel helmet crowned, and another with the King's armour, its visor open and in his hand the King's battle-axe, its head resting upon his stirrup. At last there came the funeral car – drawn by seven horses in trappings of black velvet – with a wax effigy of Henry resting upon the coffin. It was clad in the King's robes of state, crowned and with the sceptre and ball in its hands. Over this was carried a canopy of cloth of gold. At the side of each horse marched a knight, and the four lords at the side of the car each carried a banner.

The Knights of the Garter, headed by the young Duke of Buckingham, came next, and after them gentlemen carrying the swords and caps given the King by three successive popes. The procession went on slowly and interminably across London Bridge towards St. Paul's.

There, where the Bishop of London, Richard Fitzjames, was waiting, twelve men of the guard lifted up the coffin, and thence under a canopy and amid clouds of incense carried it, with the noblest of England's aristocracy touching it as official pall-bearers. So it was laid to repose for the night before the high altar.

The next day, after three Masses had been said, and the Bishop of Rochester, John Fisher, had preached, the procession, keeping the same order as on the previous day, went down Fleet Street to Charing Cross. There the Abbot of Westminster, accompanied by his monks and three other abbots, incensed the coffin on the car before it rolled on its way to the Abbey, where it was received by the archbishops of Canterbury and York, William Warham and Christopher Bainbridge. In the dim interior, lighted with thousands of candles, it again lay in state guarded by knights.

Not until Thursday, May 10, was the King's body buried at last beside that of his wife in the exquisite unfinished chapel which bears his name. After three Low Masses a solemn requiem was sung by Bishop Warham. The usual offerings were made; as four heralds bore the King's armour, his shield, his sword, and his crowned helmet. Then into the Abbey rode Sir Edward Howard in mail but unhelmeted. Dismounting, he was led into the sacristy and there clad in a black robe. Meanwhile the Duke of Buckingham and the Knights of the Garter, pacing with solemn steps, spread palls over the catafalque. The Bishop of London having preached, the image of the King was lifted from the coffin to repose in the Abbey; and while the choir chanted

Circumcederunt me gemitus mortis the corpse received a final censing, and the insignia were removed. Now there lay nothing over the King but black velvet marked with a cross in white satin.

So was the founder of the Tudors borne to his vault. The last absolution was given, and the Primate threw the first handful of earth on the coffin, while the royal officers broke their staves of office and cast them into the vault. When it had been closed a pall of cloth of gold was spread over it. The heralds hung their tabards round the empty catafalque and cried in French, "The noble King Henry the Seventh is dead!"

One more bit of ceremony remained. The heralds put on their tabards again and cried, this time with loud rejoicing voices, "Long live the noble King Henry the Eighth!"

CHAPTER TWO

"Heaven Laughs and the Earth Rejoices"

SHORTLY after Henry VIII's accession to the throne William Blount, Lord Mountjoy, the same man who had taken Erasmus and Thomas More to see the royal children at Eltham ten years earlier, and who was almost the only man among the English nobility who had much interest in letters, wrote enthusiastically to Erasmus, urging his return. In England the great Dutch scholar had made many friends during his previous visits, but he had been disappointed with the extent of the patronage he had received. Mountjoy wished him to know that things would be different under the new King. "Heaven laughs and the earth rejoices," he wrote; "everything is full of milk and honey and nectar. Avarice has fled the country. Our King is not after gold or gems or precious metals, but virtue, glory, immortality." He went on to record a conversation he had had with Henry. The King had expressed a wish that he were more learned. To this Mountjoy had answered: "That is not what we want from you but that you should foster and encourage learned men."

"Why of course," Henry had politely agreed, "for without them life would be hardly life."

This brought Erasmus hurrying to England, to the tossing off of his *Praise of Folly* in a few weeks in More's house at Bucklersbury and a professorship at Cambridge. Even so Erasmus was again disappointed in the results of his visit, though it included a benefice in Kent given him by Archbishop Warham, a sinecure for which he had to do no work. He was to find that Henry, however much he liked to pose as a patron of learned men, did little for them. As for the King's learning, Erasmus, while recognizing that it was respectable, rated the accomplishments of Katherine of Aragon much more highly.

Mountjoy's opinion of Henry was, however, that of all Englishmen, though few of them would have used Mountjoy's flowery terms or advanced Mountjoy's reasons. The youth who had been an unknown quantity until his father's death, because of the strict seclusion in which he had been kept, now appeared under the public sun and at once blossomed gorgeously. In place of a king who could be accorded nothing higher than a wry respect, there was this new Henry, eighteen, handsome, already over six feet tall and still growing, golden haired, robust in frame, and with the most hearty and affable manners anyone had ever seen. England was instantly captivated.

As we look at his features in the little-known colored terracotta bust of him made by Pietro Torregiano at this time – Torregiano had come only because Benvenuto Cellini had refused an invitation to England – we are reminded somewhat of Oscar Wilde at thirty, florid, a little too florid, assured, humorous, but already with a touch of self-indulgence and even of arrogance under the good humour. We may perhaps also infer that this young man was likely to develop into the fearsome creature, bearded and corpulent, with which the painting that passes for Holbein's has made us familiar. But no, it would be impossible to imagine that Henry of later days did we not know that he came to exist. Certainly none of his adoring subjects could imagine such a person. Not then.

It is nevertheless a little hard for us to understand why so many of the descriptions that have come down to us of the young King stress his angelic or feminine good looks. That bull neck, those powerful shoulders, that beefy body indicate instead an immense masculine force. Kept in the background though he had been, under the watchful eye of his father and grandmother, it was already well known that this was an athlete, possessing far more than that degree of virtuosity with horse and lance that was drilled into every young prince. Now Henry came out into the gaze of his people, frankly reveling in their delighted admiration of his prowess at archery and tennis and wrestling. However large a deduction may be made from the praise he was given for his skill – for we may suspect that some of his subjects found it politic to allow him to win, and we hear a little later of Frenchmen, who were not under this necessity, beating him at tennis and even throwing him in wrestling – there can be no doubt that he was extremely proficient in sports and martial exercises.

His intellectual gifts, which will be touched on later, had perhaps not as yet been discovered, and these were not the things that would have won the highest admiration of the mass of the people or even of his courtiers. What they deliriously applauded was a knight unhorsing all opponents in the tilting-yard, a smashing drive in the tennis court, or seeing the champion archer of the royal guard outshot at the butts. Never was there a man who came to the English throne in a greater blaze of popularity. It was all the greater because the new reign promised a brilliance and gaiety and freedom lacking under the sly tyranny and extortion of the King England had just buried with so few regrets.

If anything was needed to add to Henry's popularity it was soon provided by his marriage and the execution of Empson and Dudley.

To deal briefly with the less important of these matters first: on April 25, 1509, only four days after his father's death, Henry issued a proclamation that anyone who felt himself to have suffered any injustice at the hands of the fiscal commissioners might make application to the Crown for redress. There proved to be hundreds of such applications from nobles and abbots and rich city merchants. To pacify their wrath Empson and Dudley were arrested and, after an absurd charge that they had conspired to seize the government, were condemned to death.

When the first Parliament assembled in the new year the two men were also attainted, thereby implicating the whole nation in this judicial but highly approved murder.

As Edmund Dudley was being led out to the block on Tower Hill he met Thomas More, who had been a member of the 1504 Parliament of which Dudley was the Speaker. More ventured to refer to the advice that Bishop Fox had given that he should apologize to the King for having opposed the demanded grants. "In the matter of the exactions was I not right?" he asked. "Oh, Mr. More," came the reply, "it was by God's guidance that you did not acknowledge your fault to the King, for if you had done so you would certainly have lost your head."

One must be careful not to condone any act of injustice, and the particular grounds of the condemnation of Empson and Dudley were certainly unjust. Yet in a broad sense they may be said to have been guilty of treason against the whole English people. All England rejoiced in their downfall. In so willingly sending them to their doom Henry gave the first of many proofs of his keen perception of public sentiment. Without this he would never have been able to steer himself through the shoals that lay ahead.

The same perception of public sentiment was shown in Henry's marriage to Katherine of Aragon, though this, so far from being merely a politic move, was something he did because he very much wished to do it. But while capitalizing on the marriage at home, he gave another explanation when writing to Margaret of Savoy. He told her that he was marrying Katherine because his father had requested this on his death-bed.* Henry VII may indeed have urged this course as a means of making belated reparation to Katherine, but it is not necessary to believe that Henry VIII was really actuated by filial piety. If so, it was the only indication he gave of any such sentiment.

It was astonishing how what had for six years proved insuper-

---

*On April 27 Fuensalida wrote to Ferdinand to say that two members of the Council had told him that Henry had said on his death-bed that his son could marry whomever he wished.

able difficulties were now cut through at a single stroke. The haggling was over. And Eleanor, Katherine's young niece, for whose marriage to Henry negotiations had been going on, was unceremoniously ditched. Henry naturally had to find some plausible explanation when writing to Margaret, her other aunt, even though he was marrying Eleanor's aunt Katherine, instead.

The ordinary formalities for a royal wedding were dispensed with. Nor was the death of Lady Margaret permitted to cause postponement. The marriage was celebrated, not as in the case of Arthur in a crowded St. Paul's, but very quietly in the chapel of the Observant Friars at Greenwich. If Warham was asked to officiate this was probably not so much because he was Archbishop of Canterbury — for Henry never bothered in any of his other five marriages to receive his bride from the hands of the Primate — but because the Archbishop had formerly expressed some doubts as to whether it was within the Pope's competence to give a dispensation for the marriage of a widow to her brother-in-law. As he had raised that doubt, he should now lay it to rest for ever. Henry insisted that the dispensation was valid; in any event it was only a matter of form, as Katherine had been his brother's wife merely in name. Warham's objections, which had never been more than of a mild uncertainty, were overborne — probably after he had received from Katherine herself an assurance that her previous marriage had been no more than nominal — and on June 11th, just a month after Henry VII's burial, his son and the girl he had so shamefully mistreated were married in the friars' little chapel.

To make up for the semi-private marriage the coronation was carried out in full splendor. With a generous gesture Henry insisted that Katherine be crowned with him, something not at all necessary in the case of a queen consort. Moreover, as this was her first public appearance, Henry had her carried from the state apartments in the Tower in a litter of cloth of gold. Furthermore, she was gowned in white satin and with her hair unbound, both of which were tokens of her virginity. They were not lost upon the crowds, indicating that the King was intending to proclaim what, to do him justice, he never later expressly denied, however unscrupulously he encouraged what might be the contrary supposition. It was an age when declarations of this sort were made by medium of allegory. To enforce others, page boys rode on horseback representing Henry's possessions – England itself, the Duchy of Cornwall, the Principality of Wales, the Lordship of Ireland, and his officially retained pretensions to Normandy, Gascony, and Guienne. The French ambassador may have smiled indulgently at this, yet he knew that there was always a possibility of the revival of English claims under a warlike English king. He was aware that there was all the more danger of this now that Henry had married the daughter of the King of Aragon.

The Council remained for the most part unchanged, with Warham as chancellor, assisted by three other bishops – Fox, West, and Ruthall. Thomas Howard, who had lost his dukedom by fighting on the wrong side at Bosworth but who had partially rehabilitated himself and was now Earl of Surrey, and the Earl of Shrewsbury represented the old aristocracy. With them in charge there was no immediate change in England's foreign policy. Instead the treaties that were in force when Henry VII died were renewed. There was no reason why the son should find it any more necessary than the father had done to embroil himself in the rivalries of the continent. The Channel justified isolationism far more completely than the whole width of the Atlantic and Pacific could justify it four centuries later.

Not even when Julius II formed the Holy League was there any need for England to be dragged in. The first Tudor, after a little not too fortunate dabbling in international affairs, had wisely decided that he had quite enough to attend to at home. A true statesmanship called for the development of English commerce, with an eye kept open to the possibilities of exploiting the vast New World. Though this unfortunately was not quite the view taken by his ambitious son, under the guidance of the royal almoner, Thomas Wolsey, now beginning to come into his own, yet for a whole year there was no overt move in any other direction, and still another year was to pass before any preparations were made for a war.

Henry came to the throne with a longing to add to his glory by conquest. But for a while he was content to enjoy the kingdom God had given him, with all the endless opportunities for amusement that were now opening. While Katherine was writing to her father to tell him, "We spend our time in continual festival," Henry was assuring him, "If I were still free, I would choose her for a wife before all others." Though he was given to saying much the same thing twenty years later when he was moving to divorce her, he was at least sincere in that early outburst.

That she was five and a half years older than himself probably was to her advantage at this time, whatever disadvantages encroaching time brought. Katherine was only twenty-three, or not much more, fresh and kind and large-hearted, eager to praise and finding her brilliant and handsome husband worthy of all praise. She entered into his pleasures – hunting all day and dancing all night – with enthusiasm. It did everybody's heart good to see how much the King and Queen were in love.

Henry was in fact, at this time, a most uxorious husband. He was proud of his wife, as well he might be, as he had married the kindest and best of women. In the lists he entered himself under the title of Sir Loyal Heart, wearing his wife's favour on his sleeve. Banquet and song – everything was arranged for her in a touching fashion which would have been slightly comical had it not remained touching. Probably his poetry came a little later, but it was assuredly inspired by those starry or morning-gilded skies.

> Green groweth the holly, so doth the ivy.
> Though winter blasts blow never so high,
> Green groweth the holly.
> As the holly groweth green
> And never changeth hue,
> So am I, and ever hath been,
> Unto my lady true.

Whatever mockery later events made of such sentiments, at the time they were uttered they were genuine. And though better poems have been written, no poet would be ashamed to own such verses. They were written by a young man in love, one who was a true poet.

So also with what some have rated, probably correctly, as an even better poem:

Pastance with good company
I love and shall until I die.
Grudge who will, but none deny,
So God be pleased this life will I
  For my pastance
  Hunt, sing and dance.
  My heart is set:
  All goodly sport
  To my comfort
  Who shall me let.

King Henry's authorship of these songs has been questioned, though on no sufficient grounds. It is not denied that he wrote the charming airs that went to the words, and the only argument has been as to whether somebody else did not provide the lyrics. One may reasonably ask, who could this have been? Skelton, the King's old tutor, was the only poet of the time capable of producing anything so good. But much of Skelton fell below this level, though of course Skelton at his best surpassed the best that Henry could do. In any event, as these songs are not in Skelton's vein, we must allow Henry to have written them.

As to Henry's musical compositions there can be no doubt. It is not questioned that those attributed to him are really by him. We also hear of compositions no longer in existence, including a couple of Masses. To produce them called for a stronger wing than that needed for the brief lyric flight. Even when we judge him from what probably are only fragments of his work—his songs and that noble anthem still sometimes sung in English cathedrals, "O Lord, the Maker of all thing," and the chamber music of his which is occasionally performed—he has a high place among the English composers of the sixteenth century, and also a place among its poets.

There are those who have accounted for these gifts on the ground that the Tudors were of Welsh origin. Henry VII, though enjoying no creative powers of this sort, was passionately fond of music, one of the few things on which he spent money freely, seeking out not merely what might be called the best local talent but paying high salaries to French and Italian lutanists and choristers. From all this his son must have derived stimulation, and he was carefully trained in a number of musical instruments, ranging from the recorder to the organ. But the Welsh part of the matter need not be stressed; nearly everybody in sixteenth-century England sang part songs, every family of culture constituting itself, with the aid of the servants, an orchestra and a glee club. By these means and by the dancing that usually went with the singing, the long winter evenings were whiled away. The larger and richer the household the more facilities for such delightful amusements; and of course no household could begin to compete with the court in this respect. But though Henry's advantages were, in regard to music, as well as much else, very great, he must also be credited with considerable natural talents.

This artistic side of Henry was one of the many manifestations of a superabundant energy. The young men who began to gather round their young King had, as a rule, little more than a crude physical force. It was so, for example, with Charles Brandon and William Compton, who, though not without intelligence, were mainly good for sport and heavy eating and drinking. Henry, while fully holding his own with them, had something left over that demanded another outlet. As time went on he dabbled in architecture and engineering and the designing of boats and the improvement of artillery, revealing qualities much finer than those possessed by his boon companions, while also showing a sheer physical energy beyond their comprehension. People were astounded at the way he could rise early in the morning—at four or five—and after hearing Mass (sometimes, in an excess of piety, three Masses), go out to his furious riding in the tilting-ring. Moreover, then or a little later, he made himself into a good amateur theologian, reading fairly widely if not deeply. The Queen's tastes ran rather to devotional works, and she grew more and more pious with the years, rising at midnight when she was at Greenwich to attend Matins at midnight in the chapel of the Observant Friars and becoming a Franciscan tertiary. Though as time went on she showed a disposition to regard it as waste of time to pay too much attention to her dress, which was a mistake in the case of a woman in her position, she always wore expensive clothes, however hastily she threw them on. In these early days of her marriage, however, she took the pains over her appearance she should never have ceased to take.

She also was, so far as this was possible, Henry's companion in his sports. After a dinner, often taken at ten in the morning, and rarely later than noon, she would at least watch from a safe distance with her admiring heart in her mouth, while her impetuous husband leaped the widest ditches on his long pole to retrieve his bird and its quarry while hawking. And she was there to applaud while her champion, Sir Loyal Heart, challenged all comers in the lists. Tilting was, at this time, something very different from what it had been in the days of real chivalry. The trappings and the code were preserved, but carefully padded armour, blunted swords and lances designed to snap at too hard an impact, made such mimic battles relatively safe. Even so, the way Henry rode and laid about him was a bit dangerous for his opponents, even for beefy, bull-necked Brandon, even for Henry himself, as his raging onset resulted in a number of bad falls from his horse. Katherine was always a little anxious at these spectacles.

Then day would end with a supper even larger than the dinner that had been stowed under the belts of the hunters and knightly contestants. Pork and venison and fat swans were washed down with flagons of French wine. After which the inexhaustible Henry, as like as not, would call for the tables to be cleared out of the great hall, and there, under the light of sconces, he would exhibit his skill in throwing the javelin, or shooting at a mark, or, if nothing else served, in long or high jumps that were the marvel of all beholders. No half hour seemed to pass without amusement of some sort, even if it was only playing at dice, or watching the baiting of a bull or a couple of cocks put up to fight.

It was the day of new men round a new king. The older aristocracy, what was left of it, put in a perfunctory appearance at court as an assurance of loyalty and good will; but some of the bluest-blooded – the Courtenays, the Talbots, the Howards, and the Staffords, headed by the slightly aloof and supercilious Duke of Buckingham – gazed with hardly concealed disdain at the gyrations of these sweaty young fellows, whose furious antics they could not hope to emulate, and which they considered rather vulgar. Though they were relieved of the oppressive hand of Henry VII, they were a little apprehensive as to where the younger Henry was going to lead them. The old King had found time for sport and music, for he was not always buried in his accounts, but the young King was acting in such a way that they feared he could not be attending to public business. It was one thing to be a skinflint, and they were glad that the miser and his extortioners were gone; but this was something else again, a lavish expenditure that knew no limits, that supposed there could be no bottom to the royal coffers.

Especially was this true of the sober-sided Warham, the Chancellor, and that wily Bishop of Winchester who was so appropriately named Fox. They were getting old and weary and a little apprehensive of the future. Already they were beginning to think that it was about time they retired from politics and paid some attention to their dioceses. Men such as they, rather than nobles, had been in charge of most of the important affairs of state. Their wintry wisdom seemed out of place in the riot of spring.

It is not quite true, however, as is sometimes said, that Warham and Fox were deliberately ousted by the most remarkable — indeed, the only remarkable — man among the new men. But as they witnessed the swift advance of the King's Almoner, Thomas Wolsey, the Dean of Lincoln, they could not but recognize that a driving power and intelligence were arriving that would not for long brook the sedate and unadventurous control they had exercised. The time was at hand when they had better retire gracefully.

Much was afterwards made by Wolsey's enemies of his humble origin. It was obvious enough that he was not a "gentleman." His father had been a fairly well-to-do grazier — the unkind said a butcher — in Ipswich, and there was nothing in his son's early career that suggested the prominence he would obtain. That he graduated precociously at Oxford at fifteen might easily have resulted in the usual fate of precocity, nonentity. That he became a fellow of Magdalen College and a master of the school connected with it pointed to his sinking down into the donnish and the humdrum. Then, through two of his pupils, the sons of the Marquis of Dorset, he attracted the attention of the Marquis and so obtained an appointment to a living in Somerset. With that achieved, one might have expected him to disappear quietly and comfortably. Almost the only detail that emerges from this period of his life is that, because of somewhat unclerical conduct at a country fair, he was put in the stocks by Sir James Pawlet, a county magnate, an indignity Wolsey never forgot and for which he exacted revenge many years later.

Of such a man, judging merely from things of this sort, one would not look for a great deal. Nor, for that matter, when the Dorset influence got him an appointment as chaplain to the Governor of Calais, was anything very notable indicated. England swarmed with ecclesiastics of this type, those who obtained a fat sinecure and were content. Not so with Wolsey. In 1507 he became one of Henry VII's chaplains and showed what he could do when, entrusted with a letter to the Emperor in the Low Countries, he contrived by a combination of energy and good luck — what might be described as "making every green light" — to reach the Emperor and to get back to the King at

Richmond so quickly that Henry, on seeing him, upbraided him for having delayed his departure so long. Such efficiency and dispatch were rewarded with the deanery of Lincoln and the position of royal almoner. From that moment he was on his way upwards, and yet, had Henry VII lived, it was a way that probably would not have led further than to one of the less opulently endowed bishoprics after years of diligent service.

His great chance came with the accession of Henry VIII. He was still young enough, only thirty-four, to be a boon companion to the young King, pouring out floods of amusing and knowledgeable talk, being the life of Henry's parties, and providing parties of his own at which he could make the company forget his cloth by regaling them with story and jest and even dancing for their entertainment.

But there was of course much more in Wolsey than that. Had this been all, he might have been regarded as a superior buffoon. It may well have been that there were other young clerics who attempted to worm their way into Henry's good graces by using the same methods. But Wolsey added to his bonhomie first-class brains and extraordinary efficiency. A large full-blooded man, he gave an immediate impression of physical force, and when the honors started raining upon him he supported them with a majestic presence. Those who had seen Pope Alexander VI and saw Wolsey as Cardinal used to say that only he could compare with the Borgia Bull in this regard. In him was no touch of the pomposity that so often makes ecclesiastical (and other) dignitaries slightly absurd. Though arrogance increased in him, it was a studied arrogance, assumed to put in their place all those who aspired to equality with him. To those above him – to Henry and to Katherine (though Katherine soon came to distrust him) – he showed a respectful affability. To those below him – servants and poor suitors – he was kindly, knowing how to unbend without losing any particle of his dignity. But towards the nobles and the bishops his calculated insolence grew with the years, so that in the end he was the man they most venomously hated.

About this he cared less than nothing, so sure he was of the favour of the King. All was done by calculation, and all his calculations were perfectly correct until an unforeseen accident occurred to bring him to ruin. It was in calculation, too, that he took at this time what was euphemistically termed an uncanonical wife, a woman named Larke, by whom he had a son and a daughter. About this connection he made no secret, and though the pious Katherine disapproved, Henry was willing to overlook this little matter, even when Wolsey loaded his son, who passed under the name of Winter, with ecclesiastical benefices and appointed Miss Larke's brother his chaplain and then to the headship of an Oxford college. A mode of life of this sort, while not very common among the higher ecclesiastics of England at that time, was not quite unknown. So it was accepted by the world in which this man was the worldliest of souls, until it provided his enemies with another handle against him at the time of his downfall.

All that was very far off, and quite inconceivable to Wolsey or, perhaps, to anybody else. His energy and ability and capacity for prolonged and detailed work were without a parallel in sixteenth-century England, and have hardly been equalled in history. Henry had a boundless liking and admiration for him and even, as his powers were again and again triumphantly proved, a kind of awe. Though he was not appointed to the Council until 1511, from the outset unofficially, as plain Mr. Almoner, he exercised an immense influence.

It was wonderful to have such a man available, one whose mind could cut through at a stroke to the pith of every problem that arose, whom no emergency could daunt, for whom no amount of complicated business was too much. The young and inexperienced King was more than willing to delegate all the troublesome details of administration to this miraculously efficient man, who was also the best of good fellows and the most amusing person in the world. Accordingly the King was able to give himself to his hunting and his music and his hundred other pleasures, quite sure that all the bothersome burden of business would be taken off his shoulders by Wolsey. So at least it seemed to observers, though it is evident from the marginal notes that are in the King's hand on a number of state documents that he must have worked by fits and starts and was not altogether the play-boy he appeared to be.

Henry had in Katherine another adviser upon whom he relied a good deal during these early years of his reign. She had learned much about diplomacy in a hard school during the seven years since Arthur's death, and had actually been officially credited as Ferdinand's ambassador during the previous reign. She continued to act as such until 1514, many of the more confidential dispatches passing through her hands rather than those of the other Spanish envoy. It put her in a somewhat anomalous position, but Henry completely trusted her judgement and her loyalty to England.

For Katherine, however, in the end this proved to be unfortunate. For though she believed that her advice was always in the English interest, even when it happened also to accord with that of Spain, she was in a position that was to get her blamed when things went wrong. Yet her egging on of Henry against France fully accorded with his secret ambitions, as with those of such members of the Council – the old Earl of Surrey, for instance – whose talents were military and who hoped to extract personal glory from a European war. An ominous note was struck quite early in the reign when the new French ambassador, upon presenting his credentials in September, 1509, made the innocent remark that he wished to acknowledge the letter sent to Louis XII expressing a wish for continued peace with France. Henry roared in reply, "Who wrote that letter? *I* ask peace of the King of France! He would not dare to look me in the face, still less make war on me." He was already dreaming of repeating the exploits of the Fifth Henry, and was deterred only by the caution of Ferdinand who wrote to tell him that the time for this was not yet ripe. Indeed it was not, after the French victory the previous May over the Venetians at Agnadello. It had made Louis master of all northern Italy.

This was not anything that need have disturbed Henry, but it inflamed his jealousy. He could never bear to hear of any other king's military success, and had a way of justifying his envy by bringing himself to believe that his kingdom was put in danger. When the wiser members of his Council, such as Warham and Fox, advised peace, he set them down as timorous old men and turned to listen instead to those who gave what he considered more bold and brilliant counsel. And if Henry VIII was thinking of Henry V, Katherine was thinking of that English great-great-grand-uncle of hers, the Black Prince, not to mention her own father and mother with the victory they had patiently built up against the Moors. Both the King and Queen seem to have overlooked the trifling circumstance that there were five or six times as many Frenchmen as Englishmen.

Though the speech reported by Lord Herbert, Henry's first biographer, as having been delivered in the Council may be partly fictitious, it no doubt represents fairly enough the views of the strong peace party in England. It ran: "In God's name let us leave off our attempts on *terra firma*. The natural situation of islands seems not to comport with conquests in that kind. England alone is a just empire. Or when we enlarge ourselves, let it be in that way we can and to which it seems the eternal providence hath destined us, which is the sea." The authenticity of such sentiments has been questioned on the ground that England's maritime period had hardly begun. But it should be remembered that Henry VII had already entertained colonizing projects in commissioning the Cabots. And that such ideas remained in the air is shown not only by the passage in the *Utopia* which tells us that the Utopians "count this the just cause for war, when any people holdeth a piece of ground void and vacant to no good nor profitable use, keeping others from the use and possession of it"; but also by the fact that John and Thomas More helped to finance a colonizing project promoted by their connection by marriage, John Rastell. It came to nothing largely because it was merely a private venture. Henry VIII did have a golden opportunity in North America which he neglected to exploit, after his father had pointed the way. Instead he allowed himself to be engrossed during the early years of his reign in expensive and utterly profitless French wars.

Those first two years passed in peace, if not in what Henry considered glory. He and Katherine lived in a radiant happiness, full of revelry and song and love. The King was Adonis and Apollo and Achilles – at least he was going to be Achilles – all rolled into one. To the sacredness that was coming to be attached to the person of the monarch – something very different from the mediaeval concept of the King as feudal overlord – he enjoyed an adoration peculiar to himself, something which can only be faintly conveyed by the word *popularity*. It was something compounded of reverence and pride and loyalty and passionate attachment and (in Henry's case) an admiration passing all bounds.

That he was such a good husband to the Queen, long beloved by the English people for her own sake and looked on with indignant pity for what she had suffered from her father-in-law, further endeared Henry to the whole nation. If he indulged in any gallantries at this time, they were of a casual kind not to be taken seriously, even by Katherine. But probably he really was as faithful as he proclaimed himself to be in his poems, as faithful as he announced himself when riding in the lists as Sir Loyal Heart, as faithful as he made a point of indicating when, by weaving or carving his own and Katherine's initials everywhere, he boasted his uxoriousness to the world.

They had a disappointment when their first child, a girl, was prematurely born, dead, on January 31, 1510. But Katherine bore again just eleven months later, this time a live boy whom they named Henry. The King and Queen rejoiced, and England rejoiced with them. To offer his thanks for the heir who was to make the Tudor dynasty safe forever Henry rode to the shrine of Our Lady of Walsingham, later to be despoiled by him. The court celebrated the fortunate occurrence with a specially splendid tournament. Wine flowed in the palace fountains; at the bonfires in the streets, kegs of beer were broached. The country was delirious with delight.

The joy did not last long. The child was sickly and died in less than eight weeks. While its life was flickering, Henry went again to Walsingham, this time in secret and barefoot, to pray to our Lady for his little son. When, in spite of this, the baby died, Henry could not understand why such a blow could have been given to one so favored by heaven. He brooded on this so darkly that those near him had to be careful how they condoled with him in his sorrow. Any expression of sympathy coming from the French ambassador would have struck his acerbated mind as a veiled jeer; it was therefore unuttered. He had to be left alone in his angry gloom.

His was, however, an ebullient nature; he rebounded quickly. After all, he could console himself with the reflection that two children had been born in less than two years. He was still not quite twenty; Katherine was not much more than twenty-five; there was a lot of time ahead. Children would come; God was merely trying His elect. Henry was soon revelling as lightheartedly as ever.

CHAPTER THREE

Meteor in the Sky

THOUGH the wealth that Henry VII left has been grossly exaggerated – contemporary estimates placed it at figures that ranged from £1,800,000 to £4,500,000 (and it need hardly be said that there was not that amount of gold and silver currency in the whole country) – it was incomparably larger than the surplus left by any previous English king.* The truth is that by far the

* This might be a good place to make a few monetary comments. Very little money was in circulation in any European country until the great flood of precious metals from the New World began. Much of the payment of rent and wages was in kind. The coins used were the noble (six shillings and eight pence), the angel (a ten-shilling piece), the mark (which was double the value of the noble), and the pound. The rough and ready rule for reckoning comparative values used to be that one should count a penny as worth a shilling in its purchasing power. Historians, however, who are not expert in political economy have often been very vague. Thus Cardinal Gasquet in his otherwise invaluable *Henry VIII and the English Monasteries* gives a ratio of 1 to 20 on pages 5 and 10 of his first volume, raising this absent-mindedly to 1 to 30 on page 42, dropping to 1 to 12 on pages 406 and 414, but giving only a 1 to 10 ratio throughout his second volume. Belloc in one of the appendices to his *Wolsey,* which was published in 1930, argues that the true ratio should be 1 to 20 or 25, thinking even that conservative. This would probably be sound on most staple commodities; on the other hand a certain number of articles were expensive. I would be inclined to accept the lower ratio for working purposes, if only to be on the safe side, were it not within everybody's experience that since the first World War and, still more, after the second, prices have risen astronomically. But a billion pounds gold reserve, for that is what the higher contemporary estimate comes to in modern values, would be unthinkable for any small country. England then had not much more than three million inhabitants, the vast majority of whom earned their living on the land. The merchant class alone needed much in the way of currency, and that class in Henry's time was small,

larger part of this wealth was in the form of paper obligations, uncollectable in cash (if they were to be demanded at once) and payable only if spread over a number of years. These obligations were probably never thought of as being much more than a device for keeping powerful people under the King's thumb. His son, initiating a new policy – not so much out of generosity as because nothing else would have been tolerated from him – cancelled most of these "debts" to the Crown.

Nevertheless Lingard is correct in saying: "The immense treasure which [Henry VIII] inherited from his father was perhaps a misfortune; because it engendered habits of expense not to be supported from the ordinary revenues of the crown." Henry could see no reason, nor (to do him justice) could most of his subjects, why, when there was so much treasure in the royal vaults it should not be spent freely. His personal extravagance, in building, in sumptuous furnishings and feasts, in rich clothes and fabulous jewels, no doubt did some good by putting money into circulation, though far less good than would be obtained now. A habit of extravagance is always bad, and leads to progressive demoralization. To keep up with the King many of his courtiers had to run heavily into debt. The only people who could have profited were the money-lenders and the providers of luxuries – the least useful members of society.

Had it been merely a question of Henry's personal extravagance, no very serious blame need be attached to him. The really disastrous side of his spending was that of his wars, from which there never came any solid gain, and, as a concomitant of his wars, the financing of his allies. These, believing in his inexhaustible treasury, or taking advantage of him, came forward with open hands and promises they rarely carried out.

It may be true, as Dr. Brewer asserts, that Wolsey, when he came into power, contrived greatly to reduce public expenditures

---

though it was increasing in numbers and in wealth. In using the 1 to 25 ratio I do so with no assurance that it is correct, but merely by way of offering it as a general guide. I cannot see how it could be less; it may well be considerably more.

by a strict scrutiny of accounts, for though Wolsey lived on a scale of magnificence almost equal to that of the King, he was the kind of man who got full value out of every shilling paid out, unlike the squandering Henry. But even the figures Brewer produces to substantiate his contention show clearly that, during the war years, the King spent sometimes four and sometimes nine times as much as was regarded as normal, and that the "normality" of Henry VIII was double (if that is the way of putting it) that of his father. The most that can be said is that Wolsey, by careful management, got the public expenditures down to something less than £80,000 a year (or about £2,000,000 in modern values), whereas there had been an outlay in 1513 of £700,000, or £17,500,000 in modern values. If even this figure seems small, it must be remembered that the charges against the royal exchequer were few. There was no standing army, and for the navy only a handful of "King's ships" were maintained (and they not fully manned except in time of war); nor was there any police force—the local constabulary (such as it was) being supported by the parish; and the costs of education and the keeping up of the roads and dykes and sea-walls and bridges were usually looked after by monastic or similar bodies. Moreover, the better paid of the officials got no salary from the Crown but were rewarded (when they were ecclesiastics, as was usually the case) with livings at the charge of Church endowments, or (in the case of laymen) with a portion of the estates of those lying under attainder or convicted of treason. The King, in short, could live in sufficient splendour and keep up the few really essential services for about £50,000 a year. As the Crown lands brought in twice that amount a year, the King merely had to show a reasonable amount of business sense, and to avoid getting into war, to keep far away from debt. Henry VII had managed it; there was no reason on earth why Henry VIII should not have done the same.

It was, however, never part of Wolsey's program to attempt any curtailment of the King's personal extravagances. Had he done so, he was well aware that he would have instantly fallen out of Henry's good graces. Therefore he rather encouraged the King to spend freely, as this justified his own luxurious scale of living, though this was provided by the Church. Moreover Wolsey, even had he wished to do so — which he did not — could not have turned Henry aside from his continental adventures. These accorded with Wolsey's foreign policy and were inspired as much by his secret ambitions as by those Henry more openly proclaimed. It would be hard to say which man led and which man followed. Perhaps the best way of putting it is that Wolsey advised the King to do what he knew the King wanted to do; it was also what Wolsey wanted the King to do.

Sixty years before this the English had lost all their possessions in France, with the exception of the bridge-head of Calais. Since that time, in the desperate mood that follows frustration, England had plunged into a series of bloody and treacherous civil wars. These had ended only with the Tudor usurpation. But Henry VII — apart from an unlucky adventure that warned him against meddling in continental affairs — had bent all his energies to consolidating his rule in England. But now that the dynasty seemed to be firmly established, Henry VIII and, it must be confessed, the majority of unthinking people were all for renewing the old pretensions to France. Scotland had proved unconquerable; Ireland was precariously held by a district round Dublin; Wales did pretty much as it pleased. Yet Henry and Wolsey, leaving these problems on one side as scarcely worth consideration, decided that the time had come to restore England to its place as a continental power.

A wiser policy would have been that of trying to weld the British Isles into a single political whole. From time to time this was, in fact, attempted, though without any success, except in the case of Wales, and then late in the reign. The same amount of effort and a quarter of the money spent in a useless attempt to reduce France — from which in the end not a single foot of ground was won — could have ended the Scottish annoyance and pacified Ireland. Then there would have been a group of Catholic nations directly ruled by the King of England or under his suzerainty, a kind of empire of the West, so strong as to fear no aggressor, and yet at one with the soul of Europe. Instead, English arrogance and vanity, as shown by the King and the more warlike nobles and the kind of people with whom any kind of a war is popular (but especially a war with the traditional enemy France) dragged the country into futile and wasteful adventures.

Not for all of this can Wolsey be justly blamed. He did encourage Henry, but his advice, during the first years of the reign, was far from being decisive in the Council. The time was indeed to come when he would end all discussion with a heavy blow of his fist on the table; but that time was not yet. For the moment he was not doing much more than flow with the tide, and with that tide also flowed the Parliament that met on February 4, 1511.

Henry's real motive in seeking war was of course that of asserting those claims to the French Crown which, though not for some time pressed, had never been formally abandoned. The motive as given out by Henry was that Louis XII had committed outrages against the Holy See and had become virtually a schismatic. This was therefore to be represented as a holy war, just as holy a war as that in which the wily Ferdinand, aided by the great Isabella, had ejected the Moors from their last stronghold of Cordova. It was the King of Aragon who was the contriver of the plan of campaign, and in it he thoroughly hoodwinked his too-trusting young son-in-law.

Ferdinand was too well informed a man and too experienced a soldier not to be aware that France could not be conquered by England, or even by England and Spain in coalition. His aims, which were concealed from Henry, were more moderate; to achieve those aims the English could be used, but they were to get nothing. He realized, what Henry did not, that the military power of England was despicable as compared with that of some other countries. In England there was, to begin with, no trained army, but only a royal bodyguard, at this time of about fifty men. Its forces had to be levied under a feudal system already obsolescent. In France, on the other hand, there were professional armies available, with mercenaries ready to be hired. Of these the most redoubtable were the Swiss, always willing to serve the highest bidder, men whose trade was war, who spent their whole lives either fighting or making their weapons ready for the next fight. But the German lance-knights were almost equally formidable, and Spain, as the result of her long series of wars — pressing the Moors slowly backwards — had produced an infantry that was soon to be regarded as beyond compare. Against these the English could employ archers — the best archers in Europe — but using a weapon that was now all but out of date. A Cressy or Agincourt was no longer within the range of possibilities.

In their civil wars they had fought valorously, but in the outmoded mediaeval style. So little were they aware of the changes that had occurred in the military art, that, still putting all their trust in their bowmen, archery was encouraged as a sport by laws passed against the popular football or even against the use of the cross-bow. They had next to no artillery, and their tactics and formation disregarded the existence of artillery on the side of their enemies. They were capable of putting on a very brave show, and of dying bravely; they were not capable of winning battles against the new armies. Their one advantage was that they enjoyed a prestige on account of their ancient victories which made them more feared than they should have been; it was all completely out of proportion with their real power. And by holding Calais they could at any time land an army in France.

The use of Calais was not permitted to them now; it did not suit Ferdinand's purposes. All he wanted was an English army to guard his flank in Biscay while he annexed Navarre. Henry was promised Guienne; and he fell into the trap.

The expedition was put under the command of the Marquis of Dorset, son of Wolsey's first patron, while the organization of supplies was entrusted to the royal Almoner, Thomas Wolsey.

That Wolsey, a cleric with no knowledge whatever of war, should have been given this post indicates very clearly the confidence that Henry had in his ability to do anything. But though the transportation of 10,000 men to San Sebastian – and their provisioning – was a feat far surpassing that of a mere crossing of the Channel, Wolsey neglected one little point of great importance: he failed to provide the army with an adequate supply of beer. The result was that the Englishmen, nearly all of them archers of course, sweltered under the July sun, never getting any chance to do any fighting, while the Duke of Alva with 17,000 men poured through the passes of the Pyrenees into Navarre. The idle English, having nothing else to do, took to swilling down bucketfuls of strong Spanish wine in the torrid heat, with the result that all of them got dysentery and 2000 of them died. When they asked their commander when they were to advance to the attack, he could only answer that he was awaiting orders and reinforcements, in particular the cannon and cavalry that failed (like the beer) to arrive. In an angry mood they raided a village or two, not always discriminating between those of their allies and their enemies, and some of them were hanged for indulging in these little unauthorized pleasures. By the end of that dreadful summer, which seemed to them to have consisted of nothing except filth and lice, they demanded to be taken home. It was in vain that Dorset sent a desperate message to Henry asking that he send a herald to deliver his personal orders; the men had had more than enough: they were so mulish in their insubordination that they would have killed their officers had they resisted further. There was nothing for Dorset to do except yield to their mood.

Henry was furious and talked loudly of decimating the bedraggled army that returned, though it had already lost one fifth of its men by disease. It was to this that his martial ambitions had come – the most shameful campaign in English history.

He was brought to realize that what had happened was not so much the fault of his men as of his tricky father-in-law. Ferdinand, to cover up his perfidy, wrote complaining that the English had deserted at the very moment when he was about to deliver Guienne to them. He suggested that Henry make a truce with France; as for Guienne, Ferdinand would conquer it for him if Henry would pay for 10,000 German lance-knights. The disillusioned Henry had just sufficient sense not to send him the money he asked for.

Fortunately the blame could be laid upon Ferdinand, otherwise Wolsey might have been made the scapegoat for the fiasco. As it was, Wolsey's unpopularity started at this point, for the army and the mass of the English people held the Almoner responsible. They knew nothing about the devious ways of politicians; all that they understood was that Englishmen had been allowed to die like flies – just for lack of a little beer. Even with the King and his Council Wolsey had to rehabilitate himself. And this he did by advising an attack in force at a more vulnerable quarter. Henry should himself lead an army into France through Calais. Then the prestige of English valour, now covered with ridicule, would be retrieved.

Such a decision, though unsound, was perhaps hardly avoidable. Yet if the Scots, the French allies, had not attacked before, this was due to the presence of Henry in England and the fact that only a relatively small body of men had left the country. The next time, however, while he was absent – and with him his main army – the Scots would be sure to take advantage of their opportunity. That risk had to be accepted; as a precaution against it Henry left behind the Earl of Surrey, whom he admitted to be, after himself, the best English commander. Appointing Katherine as his regent, he sailed for France.

There were still voices in England that counselled peace. John Colet, the Dean of St. Paul's, who had already got himself into hot water with the clergy for a sermon preached before Convocation, in which he reproved their shortcomings, was now equally blunt when preaching on Good Friday, 1513, before the King. In this sermon he had spoken so strongly in favour of peace that the King felt his words might prove a discouragement to his soldiers. It was, however, characteristic of Henry — at least at this time of his life — that he was willing to permit a good deal of plain speaking, especially if it could afterwards be tactfully explained away. This explanation Colet had at hand when the King sent for him: he had not denounced war but only unjust war. Henry was perfectly satisfied, for if that was the case, of course what Colet had said did not apply to him. So he dismissed the Dean with a friendly paw on his shoulder, and said to those who had gathered expecting something very different, "Let every man have his own doctor; this is my doctor."

Could any war be holier than this? On April 5, 1513, the new Pope, Leo X, through his envoy signed a treaty which obliged him, along with the Emperor and Margaret, the Regent of the Netherlands, and Ferdinand and Henry to attack France. Accordingly, on the 10th of the same month an English army, guarded by the royal navy, which had recently been augmented with thirteen new ships, sailed for Brest. There they were beaten off but returned to invade through Calais, with a force which some contemporaries estimated as 50,000 men. It was actually not above 30,000, but was bolstered by a force of nearly 15,000 German mercenaries.

Such an army had never crossed the Channel. Its main defect was that it was encumbered with many people taken along only for pomp and display, including over a hundred singers and musicians for the King's entertainment. Some of the English nobles were similarly weighted down by showy non-belligerents. It is small wonder that the invaders did not get very far into France.

Henry's pious conduct on this campaign was applauded even if his military prowess was not a great deal in evidence. He did, as might be expected of him, the ostentatious things, such as riding about in full panoply, alternating this with competing with his archers and inspecting the camp at night. He allowed no pillage and hanged some of the Germans who had burned a church at Ardres. And he felt extremely exalted when the Emperor Max himself turned up in camp to serve under him as a private soldier, at the fantastic pay of a hundred crowns a day for his personal services.*

On August 12th was fought the one battle of the war, known as that of the Spurs. It consisted in hardly more than manoeuvering between the English and Burgundian cavalry, on the one side, and that of the French on the other, and the French were under orders not to fight, because there was no sense in their wasting men in a campaign which they knew would accomplish nothing. There were, however, some notable French knights who were cut off and captured, among them the Duc de Longueville and the celebrated Chevalier Bayard. Ten days later Thérouanne was taken and, at the insistence of the Emperor, razed to the ground, and in September Tournai fell, Wolsey being rewarded with its bishopric, only to find its revenues difficult to collect in face of a French claimant to that see. All this took place in the debatable land close to the sea between France and Flanders. Though Louis XII had sustained no great injury, Henry could claim victories of a sort, and the prestige of English arms had been redeemed.

Meanwhile Henry's brother-in-law, James IV of Scotland, did just what was expected of him and invaded England, proceeding to lay siege to Norham Castle. Katherine, as Henry's regent, acted with the courage and decision that were to be looked for in her mother's daughter. She raised an army, placed it under the command of the Earl of Surrey, and set herself to repel the Scots. If contemporary accounts are to be believed this army was the most perfect model of Christian arms that has ever existed. There were no women camp followers; there was not even any swearing; and most of the men said the rosary every day.

---

* This equals £500 a day in modern values.

A brilliant and daring operation cut the Scots' line of communication at Flodden, and James, declining in his pride to take advantage of the favourable position he still held, came down from his heights against the English. At the end of the day James lay dead, surrounded by the bodies of an archbishop, two bishops, an abbot, and twenty-six peers, not to count the fifty knights and the 12,000 men who fell. The English suffered losses of about an eighth of that number.

It has sometimes been said that Katherine tactlessly boasted of her victory when reporting it to Henry, drawing a galling comparison between their respective performances. There are those who have seen in this the beginning of the trouble between Henry and his Queen. It was not so; though the forthright Katherine was not noted for her tact, whatever light jest she permitted herself gave no offense. Apparently quite seriously she wrote to tell Henry that she attributed his victory at Thérouanne to his piety. The Pope evidently thought so too, for he rewarded Henry by sending him the cap and sword. It was an honor that Henry considered insufficient; he claimed to have been promised, by the dead Julius II, that the title of Most Christian King, hitherto borne by the French monarchs, would be taken away from Louis XII, who had forfeited it, and bestowed on himself.

Peace with France was signed on July 10 of the following year, and as by this time Louis had patched up his quarrel with the Pope and had lost his wife, the chance came to Henry, who was now more than ever disillusioned with Ferdinand, to attempt a new tack of diplomacy. It was that of an alliance with France which would leave Ferdinand out in the cold. This was to be cemented in the firmest possible way by the marriage of Henry's sister Mary to Louis XII.

The marriage was suggested by the Pope. He counted upon binding Louis all the more firmly to the Holy See, to which he was now reconciled, in this way. In the negotiations that went on the Duc de Longueville, who was whiling away an easy captivity at Henry's court by hunting with him and winning large sums of money from him at tennis, was more useful than the formally accredited ambassador. It was in vain that the eighteen-year-old girl, beautiful, high-spirited, and self-willed, protested against a marriage to a man who was not only thirty-four years older than herself but prematurely old and sickly. The best she could extract from her brother was a promise that the next time she married she should be allowed to choose her husband herself.

The chance to do so came sooner than anybody expected, so soon that the French marriage, which had been expected to last at least long enough to establish friendship between the two nations, even if it failed to result in a child who would eventually rule France, proved to be of no diplomatic use at all. Henry had even cherished the fantastic hope that Louis, his new brother-in-law (until now his enemy), would undertake to help him to obtain at least a portion of Castile, as belonging to Katherine, in return for which he would help Louis eject Ferdinand from the recently filched Navarre. Henry's main notion was to revenge himself upon his double-dealing father-in-law by doing some double-dealing on his own account. To the Venetian ambassador he confided his confidence in his own perfect rectitude. "I do not see," he said, "any faith in the world save in me only, and therefore God, who knows this, prospers my affairs."

Mary had been betrothed to Charles of Ghent, Henry's nephew and the future emperor, at this time a boy of fourteen, a year short of what was then considered a marriageable age. If Charles was thrown over in favour of Louis, Henry may have thought that, after his resentment had been satisfied, there might still be time, as the decrepit Louis was not likely to last very long, to patch up the Charles-and-Mary engagement again, whatever promises had been given. In this way he would have both satisfied his anger against Ferdinand and have gained solid political profit.

The marriage was performed by proxy in London, the Duc de Longueville taking the part of Louis. But when the French King received his bride, marriage proved too much for him. He gallantly did his best, and he submitted for eight weeks to the rounds of festivities demanded by his vivacious young bride. Then on January 1, 1515, he died, and the kingdom of France passed to his nephew, the long-legged, long-nosed Duc d'Angoulême, now Francis I.

The Princess Mary had been escorted to the French Court by Charles Brandon, the chief of her brother's boon companions. That his father had been Henry Tudor's standard-bearer at Bosworth and had been killed in that battle gave him his start, but he owed far more to having the same kind of brawny good nature that was Henry VIII's, though without a tenth of Henry's brains. But his brains must have been considered sufficient for the purpose, and his lack of political scruples obtained a condonation for his lack of personal morals. Only Wolsey had advanced so rapidly, and in Wolsey's case there were good reasons for the advancement, whereas nobody has ever been able to account satisfactorily for Charles Brandon's getting on as he did. At the beginning of the reign he was no more than an esquire. Then a knighthood had been conferred and, in 1513, a peerage, with a dukedom the following year. So hard is this to explain on any other grounds that it probably is true that he was created Duke of Suffolk to make him eligible for the hand of the twice-married Margaret of Savoy at the time Henry was seeking to strengthen his alliance with the Hapsburgs. But though the twice-married lady was attracted by the man (as what woman was not?) prudence in the end prevailed – prudence, or, as she said, an ample enough experience of the married state. Brandon himself had been married twice already and one of these wives was still living, with the marriage annulled.*

* Brewer's amusing description of Brandon (*Letters and Papers of the Reign of Henry VIII*, Vol. XI, p. xxxiv) is that he twice committed bigamy and was three times divorced, beginning by marrying his aunt and ending by marrying his daughter-in-law. Like most amusing remarks it is a bit exaggerated. What happened with regard to his last wife, the daughter of Lady Willoughby, who had been Maria de Salinas, one of Katherine's

That occasion arose when he was sent by Henry to fetch back from France his sister, Louis' young widow. Mary, who already had a *tendresse* for Brandon, lost no time in coming to the point: she told Brandon that he must marry her, and at once. King Francis, himself already a famous lady-killer, made some amorous advances on his own account, and though these were not rejected with quite the horrified indignation imagined by Brewer, as soon as Francis saw what the situation was, he decided that his failure as a lover (in this instance) might be compensated for by his success as a politician. By promoting the match between Mary and Brandon he would at least destroy her value in the game of diplomacy.

It has been suggested that Wolsey was in the know from the outset, and even that Brandon's dukedom was conferred with Mary rather than Margaret of Savoy in mind. But though Polydore Vergil says this, it does not fit the facts; when Brandon was made a duke it was supposed that Mary would be, at least for a few years, queen of France. The contrary supposition – that Wolsey had deliberately thrown Brandon in Mary's way, in the expectation that she would marry him and by doing so ruin him, is equally far-fetched. Wolsey had no reason to ruin Brandon, a man not at all dangerous to him. Nor could he, or Henry, as Lingard believes, have supposed that Brandon, though he was not the brightest of men, would have been so foolish as to permit himself this entanglement.

The young couple soon realized their grave predicament and dared not return to England until they had received the King's pardon for marrying without his consent. Mary wrote explaining to her brother that she had not "carnally, and of any sensual appetite" married her lover. She took the blame on her own shoulders by saying: "I put my Lord of Suffolk in choice whether he would accomplish the marriage within four days, or else that he should never have enjoyed me; whereby I well know that I

Spanish attendants, was that she was engaged to Brandon's son, but when he found himself free at the death of Mary Tudor, he married the girl himself.

constrained him to break such promises he made your Grace." To Wolsey Suffolk wrote saying that Mary was already with child and begged him to stand their friend.

The pardon was in the end effected by Wolsey, though on very stiff terms. He wrote to Suffolk to tell him, "Ye and the Queen [Mary] bind yourselves by obligation to pay yearly to the King during the Queen's life £4,000 of her dower." The remaining third they might keep. It was an ultimatum: "Whereat if ye deeply consider what danger ye be in and shall be in, having the King's displeasure, I doubt not both the Queen and you will not stick, but with all effectual diligence endeavor yourselves to recover the King's favour."

The terms had to be accepted. Because of his sudden promotion to a dukedom, without any claims whatever to one, Suffolk was aware that he had incurred the animosity of the English nobility. He was glad to escape with his head. As a private (and therefore a questionable) marriage had been performed, the position was regularized. Suffolk later also regularized his divorce, one of those cynical arrangements not too difficult to the rich and powerful of the time, and he and his Mary, still officially a dowager queen, returned to England, where they were married again in the presence of the King and the Court on May 13, 1515. Suffolk could indeed thank the Cardinal for his good offices, but as might be expected of such a man, hated Wolsey all the more heartily in consequence.

Wolsey's rise had been meteoric. In the year following that in which he doubtfully obtained the bishopric of Tournai he was created Bishop of Lincoln. Immediately and with the most amazing effrontery he suggested that the Pope appoint him *legate a latere* for England. And when Cardinal Bainbridge, the Archbishop of York, died the same year, Wolsey succeeded him, thereby becoming more eligible both for the cardinal's hat and the position of legate.* Though the legateship was refused at

---

* Bainbridge was serving in Rome as Henry's ambassador to the Holy See. His death was so "opportune" that charges of poison were made, probably without any foundation. Though one of his chaplains is said to

this time, the military successes of Francis I in Italy so frightened the Pope that the red hat was conferred as a means of buying English support. At the same time Wolsey replaced Warham as chancellor, and proceeded at once to such a concentration of power as had never been known in any country.

What the young Cardinal – he was only just turned forty – was aiming at was nothing less than the Papacy when Leo X should die. It did not matter much that Leo showed no disposition to do this just then; Wolsey could afford to wait, meanwhile cultivating both Francis and the Emperor for the powerful interest they could exercise in the next conclave.

The plenitude of Wolsey's power in Church and State did not come at once. Such matters took time and had to be handled carefully, and it would have been rash for him to have shown his hand too soon. But there is no doubt that he, with Henry's hearty backing, had a well-thought-out scheme. He was to be pope and Henry was to succeed Maximilian as emperor. Between them they were to dominate Europe.

Such a scheme was, of course, entirely fantastic. Wolsey may have had some chance of the triple tiara; Henry had absolutely none of the imperial crown. In his case not much more was involved than a puerile jealousy of Francis I, who was also going to be a candidate for the Empire.

It is amusing to see how Henry's vanity manifested itself. On May Day Pasqualigo, the Venetian Ambassador, had gone by invitation to have breakfast with the King at Greenwich. The weather was so fine that the meal was laid in the garden. Henry arrived dressed in green from his cap to his shoes and began to talk in French.

"Talk with me a while," he said. "The King of France, is he as tall as I am?"

The answer was that there was not much difference.

"Is he as stout?" Henry demanded.

---

have confessed to this, there is nothing to indicate Wolsey's complicity. The most that can be said is that he undoubtedly benefited from Bainbridge's death.

That could be answered more definitely; Francis was lean.

"What sort of legs has he?"

"Spare."

At this Henry opened his doublet and putting his hand on his massive muscles said: "Look here: I also have a good calf to my leg."

Pasqualigo was very much amused, much more amused than Henry was when word came in September that Francis, at the head of a French army of over 100,000 men, had crossed the Alps at a place at which they were supposed to be impassable and had defeated the invincible Swiss mercenaries at Marignano.

Henry, of course, believed that he had been betrayed. In April a treaty had been signed between England and France, and Henry interpreted this as a pledge that Francis would seek nothing in Italy. Treaty or not, Henry boasted that he could in a few days land an army of 60,000 in France. He told Bishop de Mesa, the Spanish Ambassador, to tell his master, "The French will not attack Milan without my leave." But the French had dared to do precisely that and had proved to be anything but what the English had called them after the Battle of the Spurs, hares in armour. To make matters worse, Francis had shown great personal valor in the field and had added to his offence by sending a small French army into Scotland under the Duke of Albany, by way of warning that the Scots would invade England the moment the English invaded France.

Henry did have, however, a real grievance, had he felt it politic to show his displeasure at this time. His sister Margaret, who as an Englishwoman had never been popular in Scotland, had married as her second husband the Earl of Angus, a man whom she later divorced and referred to as "Anguish." To the Scots themselves he was now Anguish, so they felt themselves justified in placing the protectorate of the kingdom in the hands of Albany until Margaret's son by James IV should be of an age to rule. She fled to England for protection.

Henry was almost stirred to carry out his threats against France. But he contented himself with large talk. In October he took the Venetian envoys to see the launching of the pride of the royal navy, the huge *Henry Grace de Dieu.* Then the King dressed himself as a sailor, though in cloth of gold, and had a whistle as loud as a trumpet which he kept blowing like a small boy. But in the upshot not even Scotland was attacked, for the campaigns of 1512 and 1513 had proved too costly. Already the famous treasury left by Henry VII was almost exhausted, and the taxes voted by Parliament in 1514 were bringing in only half what was expected. It was a warning that the country was not to be pushed into another foolish war. All that Henry could do for the moment was to play off the hated and distrusted kings of France and Spain against each other.

To effect this he had at command a master of foreign affairs in Wolsey — the greatest of all English statesmen, in the eyes of Brewer and Creighton, and really so if mere virtuosity in deceit is the test of statesmanship. The only justification for the policy decided upon was that France and Spain and the Papacy (as a temporal power) were all playing much the same game. In this the Pope had some excuse, for to maintain the precariously held papal states, he was obliged to stand in the middle of the see-saw and throw his weight now on one side and now on the other. The circumstances which obliged him to do this were not of his making.

Henry and Wolsey had no such excuse. No true English interests were served in promoting that balance of power which was a papal rather than an English invention. All that was accomplished was that England obtained a kind of nuisance value in European politics and that at every point one was conscious of Henry and the English Cardinal pulling strings. In this they could represent themselves as being the champions of the Holy See (and perhaps thought of themselves as such); actually the two men were primarily concerned with their selfish personal ambitions.

Their performance was relieved by moments of high comedy.

When Wolsey's red hat arrived in England in November, 1515, he staged a show that surpassed even the King's coronation. To make it perfect the Pope gave a plenary indulgence to everybody who should be present at the Cardinal's investiture.

A bishop and an earl were sent to meet the hat at Blackheath. In London the Lord Mayor and the city corporation turned out on horseback, with the city guilds on foot, to escort it to Westminster Abbey. The Archbishops of Canterbury, Armagh, and Dublin, and eight abbots assisted at the Mass, which was sung by Warham, and at which a bishop chanted the Epistle and another bishop the Gospel. Then the hat was solemnly laid on the high altar, while Wolsey was escorted to his Palace of York by eighteen peers of the realm. However legitimate may have been the design to impress people, it need only be said that other English bishops had been made cardinals – Morton and Bainbridge within everybody's memory – without finding it necessary to celebrate the occasion with ceremonies that would have come rather close to being idolatrous had they not been so absurd.

Not till the following Sunday was the hat at last put on. Then Colet preached a sermon – on humility, of all things! – and when Warham, as Primate, at last placed the hat on Wolsey's head the abbey was filled with a triumphant *Te Deum,* after which the new Cardinal was escorted out of the abbey between the dukes of Norfolk and Suffolk. It was noticed that whereas Warham hitherto, by virtue of his position as archbishop of Canterbury, had had a silver cross carried before him, now he had none. Instead Wolsey had two crosses, one as cardinal and the other as archbishop. He was acting as though he were already legate, though even had he been that, one would have supposed that Warham would still have been entitled to his cross. From that day until his fall, fifteen years later, Wolsey was supreme.

A few months later – on May 18, 1516 – Mary, the only viable child of Henry and Katherine, was born. Henry was understandably disappointed that the child was a girl, but he consoled himself with the thought expressed to the Venetian Ambassador, "The Queen and I are both young; and if it is a girl this time, by God's grace boys will follow."

That none did follow was incomprehensible to Henry, the pious King daily at Mass, the most orthodox of men, the staunch friend of the Papacy. The Pope could reward him, and did reward him, giving almost everything that was asked for, though often only under pressure which contained a veiled threat. But why did not God reward him by sending him a son to inherit the throne? Henry could not understand it, though for some years he could still continue to hope.

He had brought himself to believe that he was being blessed by God in every particular except this one. While it is not easy to see upon what Henry founded his belief, unless he attached an exaggerated importance to his victories of 1513, he certainly had it. The kingdom, it is true, remained undisturbed by rebellions or serious plots, with such occasional riots as there were being ferociously suppressed; but Henry, after intruding himself into continental politics, felt that he was surrounded by treacherous enemies whose machinations he had foiled only by the aid of divine Providence. His gratitude towards God would have been admirable had it not been linked with a feeling that God should be grateful to him. He came darkly to wonder why he was not rewarded according to his deserts.

That the Cardinal lived in a splendour all but equal to his own, and far surpassing that of any of the nobles, did not make Henry jealous. For this was a man directly dependent upon himself; therefore his glory only added to the glory of his King. When Wolsey gave his palace at Hampton Court to Henry, this, though it was in part a device for avoiding taxation (for Wolsey continued to live there), was a graceful way of acknowledging that everything he possessed was really the King's. Nor did Henry mind when it was reported that Wolsey, who had begun by saying, "The King will do such and such a thing," changed to "the King and I," and finally to "I will do it." It was no more than a recognition of the fact that Wolsey did transact all official business, a convenient arrangement. Wolsey was under no illusion: he knew that he could be destroyed in an instant; but he could not imagine that Henry would ever wish to destroy him. Where else could so loyal and efficient a public servant be found? In his confidence in this Wolsey felt completely secure.

So secure did he feel that time after time he browbeat the Pope, wringing concession after concession from the Papacy, either on the plea that England had rendered it great services or hinting that England's support would be continued only at the price of further favours. Some of these requests, or demands, made by Wolsey came ostensibly from the King himself, and always with the King's knowledge and approval. It would, for instance, have been unseemly for Wolsey directly to ask the Pope to create him a cardinal, though he saw to it that his agents in Rome asked for (or suggested) the red hat, as though on their own responsibility.

In the same way the pressure on the Pope was often indirectly applied. Thus Convocation, when asked by the Pope in 1515 to make a contribution towards the crusade he was trying to organize against the Turks, petitioned to be excused on the ground that the English clergy had already had to pay such heavy taxes for the French war, which they alleged to have been undertaken at the instance of Julius II, that they were unable to bear a new burden. Convocation even ventured to point out that by one of the decrees of the Council of Constance, "The Pope could impose no tribute on the Church, but in case of necessity, and by a general council." All of which, however politely phrased, has all the ear-marks of the Wolseian insolence and must be supposed to have been prompted by Wolsey.

The most extraordinary instance of Wolsey's insolence was the way he obtained the legateship that had been asked, and refused, at intervals since 1515. In the spring of 1518 Leo thought that the time had come when he might renew his project of the crusade. With this in mind he proposed sending legates to the various European countries, Campeggio being selected for

England. The Pope was informed that it was not customary to permit the exercise there of legatine authority on the part of any foreign cardinal. The King, however, would waive this objection, providing that Wolsey was associated with Campeggio.

Rather than have his project fall to the ground, Leo made this concession, but when Campeggio arrived at Calais, he was told that he could proceed no further until another little matter was settled. The Cardinal Hadrian de Castello was one of several foreigners who held English sees, at least to the extent of enjoying the title and some part of the revenues, as a reward for service to the English Crown. It was in Cardinal Bainbridge's time that Hadrian had been useful and had been given the bishopric of Bath. But Wolsey looked upon Hadrian as an enemy and had been calling for his deprivation. Now the Pope was coolly told that Hadrian had to be deprived before Campeggio could be admitted into England. Again Leo yielded and Wolsey assumed the administration and the revenues of Bath, but without going near the place.

When this had been done Campeggio was given a magnificent reception. A Knight of the Garter was sent to conduct him to England, and all the way from Deal to London the Legate was feted and flattered by the bishops and the nobility. At Blackheath he was formally received in a tent of cloth of gold by the Duke of Norfolk and several peers and bishops, Ruthall of Durham making a long, florid Latin oration.

The cavalcade consisted of 4000 horsemen, a procession that extended two full miles. In London the streets were lined with friars and monks and members of the secular clergy, dressed in copes, chanting hymns; and as the Legate passed along sprinkling them with holy water, he could hardly be seen for the clouds of incense. At London Bridge he was met by two more bishops, who gave him the relics of the saints to kiss, while the guns of the Tower boomed a welcome. At Cheapside he had to listen to another Latin oration — one probably worth hearing, as it was delivered by England's most famous scholar, Sir Thomas More.

After a third oration in St. Paul's Campeggio gave the papal blessing to the congregation and was conducted to his lodgings at Bath House, where Wolsey received him. This was a really delicate touch, for Bath House was the London palace of the deprived Cardinal Hadrian.

Wolsey, the associate Legate, defrayed the entire expenses of the occasion, which surpassed even the adoration of the hat three years earlier, out of the revenues of Bath. Only the King failed to grace the day with his presence; he was afraid to go to London that summer because of the sweating sickness. To escape it he was flitting from one to another of his country seats. The less fearful Wolsey – having too much at stake in the city just then – contented himself by carrying in his hand a pomander, "a very fair orange . . . wherein was vinegar and other confections against the pestilent airs."

Wolsey not only snatched his legateship out of the hands of the Pope but made this an opportunity for carrying through what, if it had only worked, would have been of vast benefit to all Europe. The essence of the Pope's plan was to effect peace in Christendom so as to unite it against the Turks who, under Selim the Grim, were already threatening Rhodes. Wolsey went the Pope one better; he would draw up a pact which would make perpetual the peace that had prevailed during the past two years. And this should be done in London so that Wolsey himself should have the credit. A kind of League of Nations was to be established, which Christendom had always been theoretically, but this time with the component parts bound together by firm treaties. It was to be virtually the re-establishment of Christendom.

The conception was in the best vein of modern statesmanship: all treaties that were at variance with the pact signed in London on October 2, 1518, were by that very act to be made void; all disputes that hereafter arose were to be submitted to arbitration; there were even to be sanctions against any breaker of the peace in which all the other members of the Union were to join. Instead of quarrelling among themselves, all were to form a coalition against the Turks.

In the case of England everybody thought it most disinterested; for England, being on the fringe of Europe, was in far less danger from Islam than any other Christian country. Henry was loud in his professions of the crusader spirit and for a moment saw himself in the role of Richard the Lion Heart instead of that of Henry V. He even made a vow that if God would give him a son he would personally lead an army against the infidel.

Wolsey and Henry could not forbear at this very moment from something that looked like the kind of diplomatic thimble-rigging that had already caused so much suspicion. Three days after the Treaty of London was signed, the Princess Mary, a baby of two, was betrothed to the Dauphin, another child. Wolsey placed a large diamond ring on her tiny finger, and Tunstall, the Bishop of London, preached a sermon admonishing her as to the honorableness of matrimony.

International goodwill all round did not last very long; indeed, it had from the start to contend with too much international suspicion – a league made with one hand while the other hand made a marriage at variance with it. So when the following year the Emperor Maximilian died and his grandson Charles of Ghent was elected to succeed him, it meant that the Hapsburg possessions were now united to the kingdoms of Spain and the two Sicilies. It was the beginning of a new and more bitter rivalry with France. In it England was to revert to the policy of playing one power off against another.

CHAPTER FOUR

Problems and Prejudices

EARLY sixteenth-century England was of all countries probably the one least plagued by heresy. There were, it is true, people to be found who retained this or that fragment of the Wycliffite hodge-podge of doctrine, or who had invented some novelty of their own. But such people had no organization, and if they met at all, it was not so much for religious exercises as for the venting of their grievances. These meetings were of course very secret, for though there was little attempt to hunt out heretics – simply because they were not taken seriously – the statute *De Comburendo Haereticorum* could still be applied in a notorious case. There were not a great many burnings under Henry VII, and there appear to have been none under Henry VIII during the early years of his reign.

Yet if actually heretics were so few as to be virtually non-existent, there was an immense amount of irritation with the clergy, particularly the secular clergy, as these had charge of the ecclesiastical organization that existed side by side with the organization of civil government. And the secular authorities were growing more and more impatient with the insistence on certain clerical privileges. For example, it resented the sanctuary system, whereby felons and even traitors could often escape punishment. Still more it resented the claim that all ecclesiastics, including those in minor orders, should be subject only to ecclesiastical courts for their misdeeds.

There was not much popular disapproval of sanctuaries or the pleading of benefit of clergy; rather the contrary. A man who had a son in minor orders was of course glad to see him escape the gallows on this technicality, and he might himself escape the gallows for a felony by hiding in a sanctuary until the storm had blown over. What caused great irritation was that the clergy controlled so many matters affecting the people's daily life. All wills had to be probated by the ecclesiastical courts, and these exacted fees that were considered exorbitant. And what came up more often than wills, and so was all the greater an irritant, were the mortuary dues payable at burial. To have a priest at the time of death and grief demanding, with a hard face and a harder heart, that he get the best thing owned by the deceased, bore heavily on the poor and angered even the well-to-do. At last in 1514 a kind of test case was forced in the matter by Richard Hunne, a merchant-tailor of London. When his infant child died and the parish priest demanded the child's bearing sheet as a mortuary, Hunne retaliated by bringing an action against the priest in the secular courts on a charge of Praemunire.

That Hunne should have resisted this demand – one that strikes the modern reader as callous – arouses our sympathy. What should be remembered, however, was that Hunne was known to be a contentious person and was suspected of heresy, as was later proved against him. Moreover, he had no justification in attempting to cloud the issue by using Praemunire, the law that forbade the exercise of papal or other foreign authority in England. It had nothing to do with the case. In any event the law was merely permissive; papal authority was in one way or other constantly being exercised in England. All that Praemunire attempted to do was to prevent the abuse of such authority in contravention of parliamentary statute. The diocesan authorities retaliated by arresting Hunne and sending him to the ecclesiastical prison known as the Lollards' Tower to await trial for heresy.

It should be noted that Hunne's house had been searched by the diocesan officers, who found there a number of heretical books and who also obtained information that the man was in the habit of attending a secret gathering of heretics. They were therefore in the position of being able to burn him unless he made a public recantation and "bore his faggot."

When one morning, shortly before his trial, Hunne was found hanging dead in his cell, the ecclesiastical authorities said he had committed suicide in apprehension of his fate. The mass of Londoners, on the other hand, who knew nothing about his heresy but who were indignant about the bearing sheet taken as a mortuary, believed that he had been murdered. Dr. Horsey, the Chancellor of the London diocese, along with the sumner of the bishop's court and the bell-ringer of the Lollards' Tower, were arrested. One of these men brought forward as an alibi the fact that he had spent the night of Hunne's death in a house of prostitution, but another made some kind of a confession. But it is hard, to say the least, to see why Dr. Horsey should go to the trouble of murdering a prisoner he was sure he could convict.

It is not necessary, at this late date, to try to solve the Hunne mystery. I merely remark that the consensus of opinion among modern historians is that Hunne was a suicide. What matters here is that he was turned into a kind of hero by people who had long suffered clerical exactions, and that the public mind was so inflamed that the Bishop of London, Richard Fitzjames, appealed to the King on the ground that it was impossible that those accused of the murder should be given a fair trial. Were they as innocent as Abel, he said, any London jury would still find them guilty. Henry therefore stopped the proceedings and appointed a commission to sit at Baynard's Castle to enquire into the circumstances of the case.

The Hunne affair may look to us like a tempest in a teapot. It was, however, very important as a sudden revelation of widespread animosity, in London at least, against the priests. Nor were matters made any better when Hunne was given a post-mortem trial for heresy and, upon conviction, his body burned. This was set down to clerical malice and only served as a further irritant.

All this had no bearing whatever on doctrine, which nobody thought of questioning, however much it may have tended to induce a mood in which heresy, when it appeared, would find ready acceptance. Least of all did it have any bearing upon the question of papal authority. However little enthusiasm there may have been for this, it was taken for granted. It was not the Pope who was hated but the local clergy who were suffering as a body on account of the more grasping men among them. In short, there was a lively anti-clericalism but not a trace, so far, of anti-Catholicism.

This anti-clericalism, however, was a dangerous thing, for though it may be possible to be what is called anti-clerical without having any opposition to religion as such, attacks upon the priesthood invariably lead in the end to an attack on the religion of which the priest is a minister. Let the priest be too keen on his profit and people will inevitably come to regard the mysteries he serves (and in which he may sincerely believe) as hardly more than a means of extracting money to pay for the luxuries of hypocrites. And a dozen good men will be indiscriminately blamed for the faults of an unworthy member among them.

The criticism of the clergy was to a considerable extent justified, though, as always, it was much too sweeping. Not only was there a good deal of clerical greed and clerical arrogance, there was often a perfunctory discharge of clerical duties and conduct not very becoming to clergymen. Yet it should be noted that we hear very little at this time of what is now covered, too loosely, by the word "immorality." There was a certain amount of clerical concubinage, though this was usually a more respectable thing than might appear. The term "uncanonical marriage" indicates a settled relationship, though of course an irregular one and as such to be deplored. But even this was rarely known except in far-away places, such as Wales, where authority of no kind could be strictly enforced. A few ecclesiastical dignitaries — men like Wolsey, who were secular functionaries rather than pastors — also had uncanonical wives. It was not general.

That this is so is amply proved by the silence of the earliest books against the clergy — those written by Simon Fish and Christopher St. German. These pass over such matters and lay their stress elsewhere. And though John Colet, the Dean of St. Paul's, when preaching before Convocation in February, 1512, minced his words so little that an attempt was made to punish this most orthodox of men for the accusation he had brought against the clerical body of "carnal concupiscence," his meaning, when taken in its context, is not what might be supposed. What he said was: "Hath not this vice so grown and waxen in the Church . . . that there is nothing looked for more diligently in this most busy time of the most part of priests than doth delight and please the senses? They give themselves to feasts and banqueting; they spend themselves on vain babbling; they give themselves in sports and plays; they apply themselves to hunting and hawking; they drown themselves in the delights of the world."

The same sort of thing was condemned by Convocation early in Henry VII's reign, but unbecoming as it may be, it is hardly to be called "carnal concupiscence." As the sixteenth century was somewhat given to the use of exaggerated language, we would probably be safe in making some deductions from Colet's charges. He was himself an excellent example of the best type of English priest, a scholar, devout, zealous. This friend of Thomas More's, who was also More's confessor, used his private fortune, inherited from his father, a former lord mayor of London, to establish and endow St. Paul's School, a model of education.* But he seems to have been a bit censorious.

Colet's friend Thomas More also bears his testimony as to the condition of the clergy. While admitting that there were a few

*I cannot refrain here from saying that Colet's guiding principle was that a Christian should live in exquisite equipoise between fear and hope, not leaning even slightly to either side, one of which might lead to presumption, the other to despair. We have a drawing of him made by Holbein showing a noble and intellectual face. History might have taken a very different course had the reform of the English Church been entrusted to men of his sort rather than to Wolsey.

priests who are "naught," he declares that the spirituality of England compared favorably with that of any other country. The trouble, he thinks – and he adds that he knows some bishops who agree with him – is that too many men were being ordained. "The time was when few men durst presume to take upon themselves the high office of priest. . . . Now runneth every rascal and offereth himself for able." This was a hang-over from the Black Death when there was such a shortage of priests that men below the canonical age and with slender qualifications were ordained in a hurry for want of better. Now, so More went on, there were too many priests for the benefices available. Therefore many of them had to make what kind of a living they could by trying to get a "trental" – that is a series of thirty Masses for the souls in purgatory – or obtain a chantry and teach a country school, or act as bailiffs or secretaries or tutors in some nobleman's house. It is little wonder that men employed in this way, or employed irregularly, and not being where they were under the eyes of the ordinaries, should sometimes have been the cause of disedification.

It is, however, obvious that, when there was an excess of priests, not many of them could have got very fat. Of the incumbents of benefices the majority had low incomes. But what the public saw and resented were the richly endowed beneficiaries, of whom there were not a great many in proportion to the whole of the clerical livings. The Church was therefore regarded as inordinately wealthy, and every ecclesiastical due, however justifiable, was coming to be fiercely resented.

The situation with regard to the monasteries was rather different. The monks were upon the whole popular, and the friars more popular still, as being men who went among the people and who did not possess much. Some of the abbots kept great state and, by virtue of their manorial holdings, sat in the House of Lords, with the rank of peers. As landlords they were, for the most part, more easy going than the squires, and under the Benedictine Rule (which most English monasteries followed) they had a positive obligation of hospitality. They supported crowds of pensioners, and they constituted the main — in fact, the only — source of poor relief of the times.

Along with the esprit de corps holding together the whole clerical body — of which there was perhaps a little too much — there could also be noticed some jealousy and friction between the regulars and the seculars. For this reason Thomas More, when replying to St. German's anonymously published *Division Between the Spirituality and the Temporality*, suspected the author to be a disgruntled monk. As religious, it may be that some of the monks may have been inclined to give themselves airs; as religious they were debarred from most of the pickings enjoyed by those seculars who had official positions; but as religious they also escaped most of the criticism directed against the clergy, because they were not as a rule connected with the ecclesiastical courts whose exactions were so obnoxious.

Yet if criticism to a great extent passed them by, they were, as subsequent events were to show, far more vulnerable than the secular clergy. Except for the orders of friars, which made up so many compact groups closely linked with their brethren abroad, each abbey lived in isolation, being autonomous and, in effect, almost a distinct religious order. The number of "exempt" houses — those free from the jurisdiction of the ordinaries — was large. Adding it all up, the monks may be described as being of the clergy and yet apart, men who lived on their own estates asking nothing of the people. Their weakness was that their wealth (real or imaginary) was to prove too great a temptation to the King, and that they could be dealt with piecemeal.

Such was the general religious situation: the Catholic Faith unquestioned, the ecclesiastical organization functioning by the side of the secular government (but being increasingly resented), piety of a somewhat formal kind relieved by the sort of jolly piety exemplified by Chaucer's pilgrims, but with real religion at a rather low ebb — sincere enough but taken casually and, except in individual instances, not a burning fire in the soul.

It so happens that regarding much of this we have in Thomas More's voluminous writings a very full and frank account. More also records, in the raciest fashion, as a man who was present, what happened at the enquiry at Baynard's Castle into the Hunne affair. His integrity is something that nobody has ever questioned, and he had at his command a power of description and a faculty for dialogue such as were without parallels in his day. After reading what he has to say about the matter, one cannot fail to see how ridiculous was the belief in London that Hunne had been murdered.

A witness presented himself at Baynard's Castle who held this belief. He claimed to have "another insight in such things than other men have." He was asked how this could be, and he said that he knew more about them than even a professional hangman and could tell merely from looking at the body whether the man had hanged himself or had been hanged by somebody else. How many bodies had he seen, he was asked: a hundred? No, he had not seen fully a hundred. Had he seen four-score and ten? He pondered the question as though in doubt before answering, No. The Commissioners, getting impatient, dropped their figures: had he seen twenty? This time he had no hesitation: No, not twenty. They brought him down to fifteen and ten and at last to three. Now he said, "And more too." It turned out that he had once seen an old Irishman named Crook Shank hanging in a barn. One of the Commissioners – possibly More himself – commented that "because he was not yet cunning enough in the craft of hanging, it was a pity that he had no more experience thereof by one more!"

Another witness had heard a priest say that it was because Hunne had brought an action for Praemunire that he had been accused of heresy. The priest, when he had been sent for, said he had said something a little different: that had Hunne not been accused of heresy he would not have brought a suit of Praemunire. The witness, supposing that he had been fully corroborated, exclaimed, "Lo, my Lords, I am glad you find me a true man!" They mystified him by remarking that the order of words seemingly made no difference to him, that a mill horse and a horse mill were the same thing, or drink ere ye go and go ere ye drink. He thought they were offering him a drink!

Still another witness knew a man who knew who had killed Hunne. That man was summoned, and it turned out that he himself did not know but that he knew somebody who did. But this third man turned out to be a woman – a gipsy palmist who could tell such things merely by looking at one's hand. Even had they wanted to question her, she was not available, as she had gone abroad.

An examination of this sort demonstrated how baseless were popular suppositions regarding Hunne's death. This unfortunately did not alter the fact that such suppositions had hardened into conviction. It should have been a warning to the English clergy that their hold over the English people was slipping, and that the more they tried to tighten their hold – in the sense of insisting on the privileges and so-called rights of their order – the greater would be the eventual disaster. That warning was not heeded: there was a greater insistence than ever upon such things, to the neglect of what was really essential. It was all the worse because the stiffest insistence commonly came from those to whom religion seemed to mean little more than the profit and position of the clerical body.

Coincident with the Hunne affair was an uproar of a very different kind, that caused by the arguments of Dr. Henry Standish regarding clerical privileges. He was the Guardian of the Grey Friars in London and a man of rigid orthodoxy, so much so that, like Edward Lee, the future archbishop of York, he attacked Erasmus. He maintained in Convocation in 1512 and again early in 1515 – backed in this by John Veysey, Bishop of Exeter, another very orthodox man – that clerics in minor orders could be summoned before a secular court without any contravention of the law of God. He dismissed the often quoted text from the Psalms, "Touch not mine anointed," as beside the point, and gave it as his opinion that no reasonable interpretation of the Bible could be made to cover the immunity of clerics from the civil law.

The question had been under discussion for some time. During the reign of Henry VII Parliament had ordained that convicted clerics should be branded in the hand, and in 1512 under Henry VIII another law was passed depriving felons in minor orders of benefit of clergy, but not affecting those above the subdiaconate. It was, however, to be in force only until the next Parliament met, so that when the members assembled in January, 1515, the issue was raised again.

So angry was Convocation with Dr. Standish that it would have proceeded against him had the case not been carried to the King, who heard it in person, assisted by his judges. Their decision was startling: it was that Convocation by taking action against Standish had made itself liable to the penalties of Praemunire. Though this appears rather far-fetched, and indicates that Praemunire was being stretched beyond the purpose of the statute, at least common sense should have warned the clergy that the pleading of privileges that were out of date had become positively dangerous.

Praemunire was brandished merely as a threat. Nevertheless the decision caused such consternation that Wolsey, not yet a cardinal, kneeling before the King interceded for Convocation and expressed its opinion (and his own) that the conventing of clerics before secular courts seemed to be a matter that touched the liberties of the Church. On his going on to suggest that the question be referred to Rome, Henry answered curtly, "We think Dr. Standish has sufficiently replied to you in all points." It was clear that the King was going to protect him, and in fact three years later he nominated him for the bishopric of St. Asaph.

Even after Henry's answer the clergy were not satisfied. Fox, as their spokesman, said hotly, "Sir, I warrant you Dr. Standish will not abide by his opinion but at his peril." And Archbishop Warham made a pointed reference to St. Thomas of Canterbury, the great Becket, who in former days had suffered martyrdom in this quarrel. But the Chief Justice, Sir John Fineaux, pointed out that if a clerk committed murder or felony the ecclesiastical courts had no authority for imposing the punishment that the law, and common justice, decreed. Tempers were high and in the end Henry summed up with words that seemed sweeping then but gained a deeper and darker significance from later events. He said: "We are, by the sufferance of God, King of England, and the Kings of England in time past never had any superior but God. Know, therefore, that we will maintain the rights of the Crown in this matter like our progenitors; and as to your decrees, we are satisfied that you of the spirituality act expressly against the words of several of them, as has been shown you by some of our spiritual Council. You interpret your decrees at your pleasure; but as for me, I will never consent to your desire, any more than my progenitors have done."

Henry would not recede from this position, but the case was compromised to this extent: the clergy's protest stood but was of no practical effect, nor did they dare to press the action they threatened against Dr. Standish. On the other hand the King removed Dr. Horsey, who had been indicted by the grand jury for Hunne's murder, from prosecution. He was allowed to plead not guilty and was discharged at a private hearing at the Court of the King's Bench. This did not affect the principle under dispute. Instead the King had asserted a claim that prepared the way for the far more extensive claims he was to assert later. The clergy had staked their case on a minor, and perhaps a false, premise, and the King, by being so quick to recognize and seize his advantage found himself stronger, as against the spirituality, than any of his predecessors. He had successfully maintained that the King of England had no superior but God. It did not mean that he had rejected the Pope's authority – this it had not yet occurred to him to do; but it did mean that he intended to keep the clergy of England in what he considered their place.

Two years later Henry had an opportunity of demonstrating his power in another way. There was in London a large community of foreign merchants and workers in luxury goods. These men had grown rich, and though they were not in serious competition with English artisans, who were not very adept in the specialized trades followed by these Germans and Flemings and Italians and Spaniards, the artisans felt in some obscure fashion that they were being injured by the foreigners' presence. In 1516 there had nearly been trouble, and popular resentment came to a head the following spring. Dr. Standish had been asked to preach against the foreigners but had wisely refused. A Dr. Beale, however, consented, and in his sermon declared that "as birds would defend their nest, so ought Englishmen to cherish and defend themselves and to hurt and grieve aliens for the common weal."

Sermons in those days were the usual means of announcing news or of promoting opinions. And Dr. Beale's sermon was enough. On May Day – a day that came to be known as Evil May Day – the London prentices, having a holiday, staged a riot. They may not have intended to do much serious harm, and no lives were lost, but the Blanchechapleton district of the city, where most of the foreigners lived, was attacked and some of their furniture and goods destroyed. Thomas More, the Undersheriff of London, went out to meet the mob that was roaring down Cheapside with the cry of "Prentices and clubs!" and had almost persuaded them to go home when a sergeant-at-arms who was standing beside him got hit with a stone. In a rage this man, one named Downes, started to lay about him, and the crowd which, until then, had been fairly good humoured, retaliated by throwing bricks and wrecking some more houses. A force of armed men was now sent against them, and forty prentices were taken and hanged by the Earl of Surrey, the son of the victor of Flodden and later Duke of Norfolk himself. Thirteen of these wretches were strung up on a single gallows. Surrey was repeatedly to show himself good at butcher's work.

Four hundred other men, and eleven women, were rounded up, and these were brought before the King in Westminster Hall, dressed only in their shirts and with halters round their necks. That they were to be spared had probably already been decided upon, for the Lord Mayor and the Aldermen of London, with the eloquent More as their spokesman, had asked for mercy. But pardon was not pronounced until Queen Katherine, and the King's sister, the dowager Queen Margaret of Scotland (who happened to be in England just then), and the dowager Queen of France, Henry's other sister, now Suffolk's duchess, went down on their knees begging for the lives of these people. So they were let off with a scolding administered by Cardinal Wolsey in the royal presence. Upon this they all threw up their halters to the roof and cheered, and a number of other men who had crowded in with them and who feared arrest if the case were pressed, hurriedly stripped to their shirts, and put round their own necks the halters with which they had come provided, so as to partake in the pardon.

All the executions had been carried out under martial law, not for treason but on the ground that an old statute (which everybody had forgotten) had been violated, one that gave safe conduct to these foreigners. Henry always wished to act with some show of legality. This was an excellent chance for him to let these rioters – who had nothing further from their thoughts than doing him any harm – know how rebels might expect to be treated. He had been badly scared, and his ferocity was the index to his fear.

What terrified Henry even more was the sweating sickness which, arriving in England with the army that fought under his father at Bosworth, recurred a number of other times, usually in summer. It was a strange disease, marked by a profuse sweat, which struck without warning and carried off its victims in a few hours. If they could live the first twenty-four hours they recovered, but there seemed to be no remedy against it and it was noticed to be specially dangerous to full-blooded people. Henry knew that he was just the sort of man to be stricken, and so flitted from one place to another in summertime, seeking an uncontaminated air.

Sir William Osler has said that the sweating sickness was a filth disease and that it is still to be encountered where unsanitary conditions prevail. The modern Englishman has become almost fanatical on the subject of fresh air. Not so the people of Tudor times. Erasmus in one of his letters showed himself wiser than most doctors when he attributed this pestilence to the fact that most of the windows in England were kept shut tight in rooms strewn with rushes which were usually allowed to stay until they were rotten and had gathered unspeakable foulness below.

In one season forty thousand people were attacked in London, though the majority pulled through. The Duke of Norfolk was attacked, as was Wolsey, several times; and among those who died were Sir William Compton, one of Henry's circle of special friends, and his Latin secretary Ammonius. Later Anne Boleyn and her father nearly succumbed. No wonder Henry was frightened. If he escaped the disease this was probably not so much due to the electuaries his doctors (and he himself) devised* but to his habit of spending much of his time in the open air. Those living in London, with its narrow streets and its utterly inadequate system of sewage disposal, were peculiarly vulnerable. One must conclude that nobody would have escaped had not the Englishmen of that day managed, through centuries of unsanitary living, to establish an immunity in themselves.

The country parts of England meanwhile were going through a quiet agricultural revolution of vast importance. Thorold Rogers has said: "The fifteenth century and the early years of the sixteenth were the Golden Age of the English husbandman, the artisan, and the laborer."** That Golden Age was about to end and the change began with the peasantry. Professor Tawney remarks, "Cobbett and those who follow Cobbett in representing the economic evils of the sixteenth century as the fruit of the religious changes, err in linking as parent and child movements which were rather brother and sister." One might go further

---

*Brewer gives several of these ineffective prescriptions in an appendix to his second volume.

***History of Agriculture and Prices*, Vol. IV, p. 23.

and point out that the economic changes antedated those in religion, however much the religious changes were afterwards to affect economic life. What was occurring, and had begun as early as the reign of Henry VII, was the practice of enclosing lands, hitherto cultivated in long, narrow, hedgeless strips. Small owners, and large owners too, commonly had these strips widely separated; in such cases they were finding it to their advantage to group their holdings by sale or exchange with other holders. And when such parcels of land were enclosed by hedges – often as an afterthought – it was found that their value went up. All that was so far involved, and it was all to the good, was a more economical and profitable method of farming. It was not in this that the revolution lies.

The revolution came about when the larger owners, who had hitherto put their lands to the plow, began to enclose large tracts for the raising of sheep for the sake of the wool that brought such high prices abroad. On one pretext or another their tenants were turned out with no means of employment immediately to be discovered. For of course for every ten men who had been needed for agriculture proper, one sufficed to look after the sheep. Though it is likely enough that not more than 5 per cent of all the land was affected, that was enough to create widespread hardship for the laborers, however much it profited the few rich owners.

More noted in his *Utopia* that this was the cause of the immense increase of vagabondage, which was treated as a crime, and the petty theft and brigandage punishable by death. It has been estimated that an average of two thousand people a year suffered on the gallows during Henry VIII's reign, and though this number may be exaggerated, a large proportion of the "criminals" were those who had been obliged to take to some unlawful expedient to keep alive after their employment was gone. It was mainly due to that land hunger which had seized society and which might have been beneficial had it been controlled. Here we may find the first roll of the movement which was eventually to place the monastic holdings in the hands of a new and rapacious class of men. The enclosures – or rather the sheep-raising made possible on so wide a scale by the enclosures – did not cause the Reformation, but once the Reformation had started, the land-grabbing which had begun with the enclosures made the Reformation a vested interest.

To do Henry and his government justice, they were not unmindful of the dangers of this agrarian revolution. Wolsey was specially active in his efforts to arrest the process, with the result that he grew unpopular with the landowners for doing as much as he did, and unpopular with the peasantry for failing to do more. The truth is that, whatever laws were passed, there was usually some means for defeating their object. Hugh Latimer in one of his sermons mentions the device of putting a single furrow across a wide field, thus making it "arable land," and then continuing to graze sheep there. The kind-hearted Thomas More, witnessing what was going on, described it as sheep eating men.

More mentions that some of the abbots were among the worst offenders in this matter. Though the holders of monastic estates were more likely, if only because of their natural conservatism, than secular owners of rural property to continue in the old ways and leave their tenantry undisturbed, monks were not always more averse than other men from easy gains, especially when, as was often the case, their estates were encumbered with debts.

In doing this the monks were unconsciously preparing for the spoliation they were soon to suffer, for they helped to open a little further the dam that had hitherto held back excessive greed. That is a far more important consideration than the precise amount of land affected by the enclosures. As to the distress that was brought about, we have in the *Utopia* an unforgettable page. There More wrote in pity and indignation: "One covetous and insatiable and very plague of his native country may compass about and enclose many thousands of acres of ground within one pale or hedge, the husbandmen be thrust out of their own, or else by covin or fraud, or by violent oppression they be put besides it, or by wrongs and injuries they be so wearied, that they be compelled to sell all; by one means therefore or other, either by hook or crook they must needs depart away, poor silly wretched souls, men, women, husbands, wives, fatherless children, widows, woeful mothers, with their young babes, and the whole household small in numbers, as husbandry requireth many hands. Away they trudge, I say, out of their known and accustomed places, finding no place to rest in." So angry was More over their plight that – mild as he was in private life, so mild that his son-in-law Roper, who lived with him for sixteen years, said he had never seen him in a "fume" – he characterized government as a conspiracy of the rich against the poor.

The *Utopia* was a book written in Latin for scholars. It at once excited a wide interest throughout Europe, and later in its innumerable translations has had a prodigious effect upon social thought. It is almost alone among works of its class as nourishing the heart as well as the mind – the revolutionist's *vade mecum*. Yet it was actually a protest of conservatism against the new politics and the new economics. Properly understood (as it seldom is) it may be regarded as a kind of prophecy of the *Rerum Novarum* of Leo XIII and the *Quadragesimo Anno* of Pius XI. Incidentally, it explains better than anything else the secret springs of the Reformation, doing so only a year before the breaking of the storm.

It was in More's house that More's dearest friend Erasmus wrote the *Praise of Folly*, a book dedicated to More. It was largely because of the support that More was able to obtain for Erasmus that his edition of the New Testament was produced, though the book was eventually published at Basle by Froben. The work was eagerly snatched up and used by the reformers against the Church, much to the annoyance of Erasmus, who vigorously repudiated the suggestion that it was he who had laid the egg which Luther hatched. His words regarding the Scriptures – "I long that the husbandman should sing portions of them to himself as he follows the plough, that the weaver should sing portions of them to the tune of his shuttle, that the traveller should beguile with their stories the tedium of his journey" — were to be closely rephrased by Tyndale. It must never be forgotten that the effort to make the Bible better known was initiated by Catholics. Only by accident was the publication delayed of the great polyglot version of the Scriptures made in Spain under the direction of Cardinal Ximines; otherwise it would have been out before the work of Erasmus. In other words, the Counter-reformation started before what is called the Reformation. The true terms of course should be the Catholic Reformation and the Protestant Revolt.*

Many of the things that Erasmus wrote in the days preceding the advent of Luther, though in general intended to effect reform by means of satire, were thrown out irresponsibly and merely in order to be amusing. Erasmus himself made a disclaimer later in his *Spongia* by writing: "What is said over a glass of wine ought not to be remembered and written down as a serious statement of belief." And Gasquet has commented: "Erasmus, like many of his contemporaries, was perhaps often injudicious in the manner in which he advocated reforms. But when the matter is sifted to the bottom, it will commonly be found that his ideas are just." Erasmus himself declared, when faced with the inescapable issue, "Christ I know, Luther I know not," and wrote to the Pope, "I have never, even in jest, defended [Luther's] paradoxes. . . . In all that I have written I have not deviated one hair's breadth from the teaching of the Church."

This was Sir Thomas More's view too, when attempts were to claim Erasmus for the side of the Reformation. Then he wrote: "Had I found in Erasmus, my darling, the shrewd intent and purpose which I find in Tyndale, Erasmus, my darling, should be no more my darling. But I find in Erasmus, my darling, that he detesteth and abhorreth the errors and heresies that Tyndale plainly teacheth and abideth by, and therefore Erasmus, my

* Lord Acton, however, disagrees. *Lectures on Modern History,* p. 121.

darling, shall be my darling still." What More did admit, however, was that as men were drawing harm even from the Scriptures (because they were misreading them), he would be against the translation of the *Moria* into English and would even help to burn it, harmless though he still thought it to be, along with some of his own early works, "rather than folk should (through their own fault) take any harm of them, seeing that I see them likely in these days so to do."

This then was the intellectual climate of England – a King orthodox and, in a formal fashion, devout; a people sound at heart but not very clear in the head, taking their faith for granted but usually practicing it in a perfunctory style; a clergy rather negligent in their pastoral duties and too insistent upon the privileges of their order, and arousing by too close attention to their personal profit a great deal of criticism; a hierarchy too richly rewarded, often non-resident, having their episcopal functions performed by suffragans. But quiet reforms were already being initiated which would have been of immense benefit had they been carried out. They were mainly along the unspectacular line of trying to raise the standard of education.

To this cause all the humanists in England were devoted. Linacre, Grocyn, Vives the Spaniard, More and Colet and Colet's High-Master at St. Paul's School, William Lily, were educational reformers and aimed at an improvement in the standard of the clergy. John Fisher had long been labouring at Cambridge, and Wolsey, with however too much concern for his own glory, was thinking of doing great things for Oxford. Even Henry approved and encouraged, though he did little enough in any active way.

CHAPTER FIVE

The Years of Glory

WHEN Gustiniani, the Venetian Ambassador, reported that people found it better to approach Wolsey than Henry, "lest he should resent the precedence conceded to the King," there was a misjudgment of the situation. Wolsey was after 1518, if not before, both Vice-Pope and Vice-King in England, but he held, and knew that he held, his unprecedented authority only by Henry's favour. He also knew that, though he could bully the Pope, wringing unheard of concessions from the Holy See almost at the point of a gun, he could not bully the King, though he counted upon being able to manage him. His ecclesiastical honors and power had been obtained only because the King had actively backed him and felt that the glory of his minister reflected glory on himself. Finally, Wolsey knew that he could retain what he had on the sole condition that he continued to prove his usefulness. As to that he had no doubts whatever: vain as he was, he did not in the least overestimate his abilities. He was a man who could never be replaced.

Nevertheless, there might arise, as he was aware, a political situation that would prove dangerous to himself. Should his foreign policy meet with disaster, his many enemies among the nobility would be sure to clamour for his removal. That danger he felt he could disregard, so negligible did he consider his opponents and so sure was he of being able to manipulate affairs successfully. In this, his judgment was sound. What he never saw was that the ecclesiastical, as well as the political.

situation held dangers. Least of all did he see—how could he possibly see?—that the King's infatuation for a commonplace but determined young woman was going to wreck everything that his great Minister had so skilfully built up.

That this was possible was due to the weakness of the English Church, which Wolsey fondly believed he had greatly strengthened but which he had actually made very vulnerable by concentrating all its authority in his own hands. He was able to do this only because of a weakness that had been increasing for some time. The bishops were, for the most part, secular functionaries rather than pastors of their flocks. It cost the Crown nothing to reward an ambassador or a minister of state for his services by giving him a rich benefice. Though there was some advantage in the system, in that those appointed to bishoprics were, as a rule, able men, this hardly offset the disadvantage of the inevitable neglect of their dioceses. Not until these men were out of favour at court, or infirm and old, did they retire to their charges, thinking it advisable to set their spiritual accounts in order before meeting their God.

The bishops working under this system sought to soothe their consciences with the reflection that, by accepting secular posts, they were increasing the power and prestige of the Church. The idea was fallacious: they were weakening the Church by making it increasingly dependent on the Crown. Few would be other than subservient when all their hopes of promotion rested in the King. Moreover, the part they played in politics increased the jealousy of the nobility and of the new class of lay bureaucrats. For them there could be no reward commensurate with what bishops and other holders of the wealthier benefices received.

Cardinal Wolsey had accentuated this weakness since he became papal legate in 1518, and in 1524 legate for life, with constantly widening powers over the Church and, as lord chancellor, a domination such as nobody before him had ever had over the state. The separate powers were, in his case, fused into one, each heightened and enlarged and intensified. They seemed to be of a strength never so much as imagined until then. Nothing, however, could be less strong, for as this concentration was permitted by the King, and depended on the King, it could be taken away by the King, who would then have an instrument which he could not have forged himself, but which he could use as he wished.

Wolsey was never satisfied; right up to the time of his fall he was demanding, and usually receiving, fresh extensions of his legatine authority from the Pope. These concessions were reluctantly granted, for a legate who was the subject of the king in whose dominions he served was obviously (and especially when he was also that king's chief minister) more closely bound to the king than he was to the pope. Yet because of the need the Papacy had of secular support at that moment, it thought no price too high to pay for the backing of England in its difficulties. This amounted, as Professor Pollard remarks, "to papal abdication and led straight to a disruption of the catholic government of the church." To quote Pollard again: "The papal legate had cowed the English clergy before they submitted to Henry VIII."* What the Pope supposed would happen, and reluctantly accepted, was that a man like Wolsey would try to take advantage of him; what was of course not foreseen was something infinitely more serious, the loss of England to Catholic unity.

The most tragic factor in the situation was that Wolsey firmly believed that, in the exercise of his legacy (as it was called), he was serving the best interests of the Church – indeed, that he alone was able to serve those interests to the fullest degree. He probably did have it within his capacity, had he addressed himself to the problem with a spiritually illumined insight, to have effected the kind of reform in England that would have saved England, and, by saving her, have saved Europe. Such an insight he completely lacked; though he wished to be a reformer of education and of the monasteries and of diocesan administration, he was so jealous of his authority that he would allow

---

* *Wolsey,* pp. 185 and 364. By permission of Longmans Greene & Co., publishers.

nobody else — among them men much better qualified than himself to achieve reform — to have any share in what he proposed to do. Even Warham, the Archbishop of Canterbury, when he proposed to effect some reforms in his own province, was peremptorily forbidden to proceed further and was threatened with the penalties of Praemunire. Wolsey was counting upon succeeding to Canterbury as soon as the ageing Warham died. Similarly he prevented all appeals to Rome on the part of the other ordinaries under the same threat of Praemunire. He was determined to enjoy alone all the credit that was obtainable.

At the same time he hampered the usual processes of ecclesiastical administration. Episcopal visitations were forbidden, unless they were conducted by bishops acting as his agents, in which case the Legate pocketed most of the fees, exacting them to the last penny, whereas customarily they were in large part remitted. There was not an archdeacon in England who did not have to pay Wolsey a handsome sum for permission to exercise his office.

It is no wonder that this aroused fierce resentment. When Warham ventured to sign himself in a letter to Wolsey as his "brother," he was instantly given to understand that he was not a brother, even though he happened to be the Primate, but the Legate's subject. And when the Benedictines were ordered to reform themselves, they were a good deal less than co-operative with a man known to have kept a mistress by whom he had had a son and daughter.

Further resentment was created by Wolsey's insatiable pluralism. We have seen how he contrived to oust Cardinal Hadrian from the see of Bath in 1518, taking its administration (and its revenues) himself. This he resigned only in 1524 to assume the temporalities of the much richer see of Durham, held by him until Tunstall was about to be translated there from London. And Durham was surrendered only because Fox died in 1528, enabling Wolsey to become Bishop of Winchester as well as Archbishop of York.

Nor is this all. He obtained the abbey of St. Alban's *in commendam,* appropriating its revenues and allowing only what he thought fit for the monks. Though he did not succeed in getting his son, who passed under the name of Thomas Winter, the bishopric of Durham, he did load that amiable but not very effectual youth with at least a dozen rich benefices, keeping over £2,000 derived from them in his own hands and paying his son about a tenth of that amount. Pluralism was fairly general in England, but nobody had ever practised it on so stupendous a scale as this reformer of the Church. One might have thought that a good place to begin reform was at this point.

There is no need to stress his relations with Miss Larke. That connection did not last very long, and eventually Wolsey found her a husband, more or less forcing the man to take on his discarded mistress and paying the lady a substantial dowry. Wolsey's most conspicuous faults did not lie in this direction. At any rate in his later years, when he was Legate, as Cavendish his gentleman usher records, he was strict in his formal piety, never neglecting to say his office, whatever the pressure of business might be, or prayers at the end of meals. He presumably considered this fitting in one who embodied in England the Pope's authority, and to that extent gave good example, despite the scandal of his pluralism and non-residence. Incidentally, but very badly, he further weakened the Church's power of resistance in the House of Lords by holding several dioceses in his own hands, or by conferring them upon foreigners, who lived abroad, for some service rendered to him or to the Crown. The result was that in the Parliament of 1529, in which twenty-one bishops should have sat, there were only fifteen.

The administration of Wolsey, efficient though it was in many respects, was not only detested by the bishops upon whom the Legate's heavy hand fell but — because of the character of its efficiency — brought about a further detestation of the whole clerical body. By doing away with the old easy-going methods and insisting upon a strict rendering of what he felt to be his dues, the Cardinal obliged those who found themselves mulcted to recover some part of what they had lost by mulcting others.

There was more than a little truth in Tyndale's bitter gibe: "The parson sheareth, the vicar shareth, the parish priest polleth, the friar scrapeth, and the pardoner pareth; we lack but a butcher to pull off the skin." All the way down the line did Wolsey's exactions go, while at the same time the reforming Legate was giving his clergy an example of absenteeism and neglect of duty which many were quick to copy.

Among the most unpopular of Wolsey's plans for reform was one which, properly carried out, would have resulted in much good. This was his idea of Cardinal's College at Oxford, which was to be the largest, the most magnificent, and the most richly endowed institution of the kind in the world, and which was to be fed by a kind of preparatory college at Ipswich, the place of his birth. Unfortunately, like so many schemes which profess to be for the greater glory of God, this bore the initiator's glory too much in mind. Yet even with that deduction, one might still give Wolsey praise had he not laid himself open to serious criticism on other grounds.

To be able to carry out his plans Wolsey obtained from the Pope permission to suppress a certain number of monasteries – about thirty – in which the monks were fewer than their endowments warranted, to transfer the religious to other establishments, and to use the balance of their revenues for his own admirable purposes. Such a suppression of religious houses, though it was on a larger scale than anything attempted before, had some precedents. During the fourteenth century a number of alien priories had been dealt with in this way, while war was going on, because they were houses dependent on abbeys in enemy country, to which abbeys the priories made some financial contribution.

This, however, was not the only instance of monastic suppression. John Fisher, who had been chancellor of Cambridge University since 1504, inspired Henry VII's mother, the Lady Margaret, with the idea of building two new colleges there – Christ's and St. John's – which early in the new reign he was able to complete. Part of their endowments was derived from two run-down convents and a hospital that had ceased to serve any particularly useful purpose. And as others had done the same before Fisher, there were precedents for what Wolsey did.

There was also considerable justification for it, at least in theory. The argument Wolsey used with the Pope was that there were a good many monasteries in England in which the number of monks or nuns had dwindled to five or six. So small a group were not able to chant the office with sufficient solemnity. The good of religion for this and other reasons would be served by putting these little handfuls of religious elsewhere, and, after duly providing for their maintenance, diverting the rest of the income of their houses more advantageously.

The building of his colleges was only one part of Wolsey's program, though the only part that he did much about. Another part was the erection of some new badly needed dioceses. It was a sound enough argument that by adjustment and amalgamation and more economical and efficient management of the property possessed by some of the religious orders they would lose nothing and that the Church in England would, as a whole, gain a great deal.

The methods Wolsey employed were, however, open to very serious objections. He used as his chief agent a John Allen, a man later to be as hated in Ireland (where as archbishop he was assassinated) for his overbearing ways as he was feared by the monks he so roughly handled in England. And Allen had as his chief coadjutor, his practical man of business, the adventurer Thomas Cromwell, who now began to discover how weak the English clergy were.

Cromwell discovered in his dealings with the monks a new and profitable field for his money-lending activities. And he grew adept at picking up little bribes and gifts as he went along, though, as he was dealing with Wolsey (who was given to a strict examination of accounts) he had to be careful not to go too far. Even so there were many complaints about him at this time, some of which reached the ears of the King.

In these proceedings it was Wolsey himself who was the

greatest extortioner. It was common enough for him to threaten a house with dissolution to obtain a large donation for his colleges. For instance, pressure was put on the Abbot of Peterborough to resign — or make a contribution of 2000 marks. William Finch, the cellarer of St. Bartholomew's, Smithfield, offered "£300 to your college at Oxford for your favour towards his preferment." Another man offered 500 marks if the Cardinal would appoint him under-treasurer of his college. But perhaps the most amazing instance of venality was a request that came from the Earl of Northumberland that he be allowed (quite illegally of course) to imprison a man against whom he had a grievance. What he would do in return was to give the handsome service books that had belonged to his father, £200 in cash, and a benefice worth £100 a year.

The abuses were so flagrant that in the end Wolsey drew a reprimand from the King. Though it is true that, in the particular occasion that caused this, Wolsey happened to be in the right, the rebuke, if taken as covering a long series of offences, was eminently just. It came in 1528 when the election of a new abbess of Wilton was promitted to him — that is, he was allowed to appoint directly, when he often gave to the highest bidder. This time he chose the Prioress, Isabel Jordan, in preference to Anne Boleyn's nominee, Eleanor Carey, the sister of the man who had married her sister Mary, who had been the King's mistress. As Miss Carey had been of anything but exemplary morals, the Cardinal thought this was asking too much and so persisted in his own choice, while pretending that he did not know it was contrary to the King's wishes.

Henry in writing about it used his best more-in-sorrow-than-in-anger manner, in which he could be really superb. He accepted Wolsey's explanations but passed on to remark about the Oxford college: "There is great murmuring of it, throughout all the realm, both good and bad. They say that not all is ill gotten that is bestowed upon the college, but that the college is the cloak for covering all mischiefs. . . . One thing more I perceive by your own letter . . . and that is, that you have received money from the exempts for having their old visitors. Surely this can hardly be with a good conscience. For, and they were good, why should you take money? And if they were ill, it were a sinful act. Howbeit your legacy might therein, peradventure, *apud homines* be a cloak, but not *apud Deum*. Wherefore you, thus monished by him who so entirely loveth you, I doubt not, will desist, not only from this (if your conscience will bear it) but from all other things which should tangle the same; and in so doing, we will sing, *Te laudant angeli atque archangeli, Te laudat omnis spiritus*. And thus I make an end of this, though rude, yet loving letter, desiring you as benevolently to take it, as I do mean it, for I ensure you (and I pray you think it so) that there remaineth at this hour no spark of displeasure towards you in my heart. And thus fare you well, and be no more perplexed. Written with the hand of your loving sovereign and friend, HENRY R."

It must be remembered that all through this period Henry was not only very orthodox and very devout but also very papal. A few little moral lapses occurred, but these were fewer than in the case of most kings. In 1518 he had taken up with Elizabeth Blount, the daughter of Sir James Blount and a cousin of Lord Mountjoy's, and he had a son by her. A little later he had an affair with Anne Boleyn's sister Mary. He considered himself, however, and may be considered by us, a very moral man for one in his position.

He was also a pious man, a firm supporter of the Papacy, not only as a secular power but as a spiritual force. It is true that it made him feel very grand to have in England in Wolsey a permanent Vice-Pope, whom he could always keep under his own thumb. It is also true that in coming forward as the champion of the Church he expected a reward, as he expected one for everything else he did for the Holy See. But there can be no question of Henry's attachment to the Catholic and papal cause.

This he signalized at the end of 1521 with the publication of his *Defence of the Seven Sacraments*, written in reply to Luther's

Babylonian Captivity of the Church. It won for Henry the title he had long regarded as his due. Julius had promised to transfer to him the title of Most Christian King, after Louis XII had forfeited it by setting up the schismatic synod of Pisa, but on the understanding that Henry should do something to justify the grant. Then Julius died and the new pope, Leo X, said he knew nothing about the arrangement. What Henry now received was something more personal, more clearly indicative of special service: he was to be known hereafter as the Defender of the Faith.

The title was well deserved. Though the *Assertio Septem Sacramentorum* is a good enough piece of theology, and also of Latinity, it is said to have raised some question as to whether the King could have been its real author. As to that it is perhaps sufficient to say that the theological learning displayed is not of so profound a sort as to have been beyond Henry's powers. The book is able, but rather commonplace, citing the kind of authors who could be found in any of the compendiums that were in vogue. Though it is likely enough that Henry asked Bishop Fisher to check his arguments for possible errors, and may have got somebody to polish up his Latin a bit, there is no reason to doubt the King's authorship.

We might suspect that Sir Thomas More, who was at this time very intimate with Henry, had a hand in the work, were it not for More's explicit statement later that he was no more than "the sorter out and placer of the principal matters contained therein." This has usually been taken to mean that More compiled the index, but as almost anybody could have made the very brief index it contains, I surmise that More did a little rearranging of a confused manuscript.

What is more to the point is that More (again according to his own statement) advised the King not to take quite so high a line in defense of the Pope's authority. "I must put your Highness in remembrance of one thing," he said, "and that is this. The Pope, as your Grace knoweth, is a prince as you are, and in league with other Christian princes. It may hereafter so fall out that your Grace and he may vary upon some points of the league, whereupon war may grow between you both. I think it best, therefore, that the place be amended and his authority more slenderly touched." More was of course thinking of the Pope's temporal power. This power was at the same instant too much and too little: too little to make the Papacy independent of the great powers, and too much not to lead those powers to regard the Papacy as something upon which they should exert political and military pressure. At this time More had not reached his final conclusion regarding the Pope's spiritual authority.

To the objection the King's emphatic reply was, "Nay, that shall not be; we are so beholden to the see of Rome that we cannot do too much honor to it."

He gave More some reasons for this. One was a "secret" or confidential reason which More never revealed, and which may have been an admission that he hoped for some such title from the Pope as the one he obtained.* He said further: "Whatever impediment be to the contrary, we will set forth that authority to the uttermost. For we have received from that see our crown imperial." More admitted afterwards that he had not heard this before and did not seem to know what the King meant. One may conjecture that Henry was referring to the bull issued by Innocent VIII in 1486 giving the most ample recognition possible of the usurping Henry VII's right to the throne. It was a document extremely useful at a time when the Tudor hold on the English throne was still very insecure.

What was involved in Henry's controversy with Luther was not the protest made in 1517 against the way indulgences were being disposed of; for it may be admitted that the cheap-jack methods of Tetzel — not to mention the "rake-off" obtained by the young Hohenzollern Archbishop of Mainz** — had some of

*It may, however, have had something to do with the dispensation Henry had received to marry Katherine. At that time the last thing he wished was any diminution of the Pope's authority.

**He also held the sees of Magdeburg and Halberstadt and was consecrated long before the canonical age, obtaining his appointment largely the worst features of a "racket." For this reason, though the purpose of the indulgence was good (the building of St. Peter's) and though the indulgence was not paid for but given to those who contributed to this pious project, Cardinal Ximines denounced it and it was not allowed to be preached in some of the French dioceses. Henry prescinded from all this and dealt with the position Luther took up later in questioning the sacramental system of the Church. It was, in short, a controversy over fundamentals; and in this Henry showed himself completely orthodox.

He was also far more strongly "papal" than the majority of people at this time. It must be remembered that the prestige of the Holy See had been badly damaged both by the Avignon captivity and the Great Schism. Though those wounds had been healed (not without some danger of a new schism or even something like a new Avignon occurring) yet a commonly prevailing view of the Pope's authority was that it was historically necessary rather than of divine institution. The nature and extent of this authority was not to be defined until more than three hundred years later.

It is worth noting what Henry actually wrote on this point. He pointed out that Luther admitted that he had formerly acknowledged the supremacy was given "by human consent and for the public good." Henry said he would not so wrong the Bishop of Rome as even to argue the point, for "[Luther] cannot deny that all the Faithful honor and acknowledge the Roman See for their Mother and supreme." On another page he wrote: "[Luther] may easily find that since the conversion of the world, all Churches in the Christian world have been obedient to the See of Rome." Though there was no "Thou art Peter" argument, what the King wrote was considered strong enough for Thomas More to give him an unheeded warning. One sentence in this chapter is specially worth remembering: "What a great member

---

through the tactful use of large sums of money borrowed from the Fugger bankers. His share in the proceeds of the indulgence went to repay the Fuggers.

of the Devil is he, who endeavors to tear the Christian members of Christ from their head!"

On the subject of Holy Orders Henry makes the point, ordinary enough but sound: "His denying Orders to be a sacrament is as it were a fountain to all the rest, which, being once stopped up, the other small springs must become dry of themselves." On Matrimony, however, Henry writes with a feeling eloquence: "Who does not tremble when he considers how he should deal with his wife, for not only is he bound to love her, but so to live with her that he may return her to God pure and without stain, when God Who gave, shall demand His own again?"

The chapter on marriage is, in fact, one of the longest and best in the book. It opens: "Marriage, the first of all sacraments, celebrated by the first of mankind, and honored with our Saviour's first miracle, being for so long time had in a religious veneration for its very name of a sacrament, is now at last . . . denied by Luther to be any sacrament at all." Henry on the other hand puts forward the Catholic teaching: "You see how the blessed Apostle [Paul] teacheth everywhere, that the marriage of man and wife is a sacrament, which represents the conjunction of Christ with His Church: for he teacheth that God consecrated matrimony, that it might be the mystery of Christ joined with His Church." He says later: "If God is rightly called in Scripture a Bridegroom, and the soul of man the Bride, there is certainly something betwixt God and the soul, of which what consists in marriage between man and woman is the image." And leaving mysticism for another consideration, hardly less valuable, he asks: "What should the conjugal act itself be but concupiscence, if God had not made it the remedy thereof."

The *Defence of the Seven Sacraments,* even if not a very wonderful performance in itself, must at least be regarded as wonderful as coming from a king. Henry was disposed to be inordinately vain of his book and even to credit it with having saved the Faith in Europe – that is, until changed circumstances made his *Defence* embarrassing to him. It served, however, to get him the special title he wanted from the Holy See.

It would be unfair to suppose that the obtaining of this title was Henry's sole motive in writing, but at least it was one of his motives. He was sincere when he said, "Would to God that my ability were equal to my good will; but I cannot but think myself obliged to defend my Mother, the Spouse of Christ." All the same he took care that his theological treatise should be drawn to the attention of the Pope.

He chose as his emissary John Clerk, Dean of Windsor and one of Wolsey's chaplains, who was rewarded for this service in 1523 with the bishopric of Bath. Moreover Clerk presented the volume, richly bound in cloth-of-gold, to Leo in full consistory, making an eloquent discourse that was much admired. Still greater was the admiration professed by the Pope and the cardinals for the book itself. They were overwhelmed not only by its learning but its Latinity, and the dedication was considered very beautiful:

> *Anglorum rex Henricus, Leo Decimo, mittit*
> *Hoc opus, et fidei testem et amicitiae*

As Leo was short-sighted and might overlook the verses, Clerk read them aloud, keeping to himself the fact (if he knew it) that these were among a series of distichs Wolsey had composed for the King, among which he could choose what he preferred. The Pope took the book out of Clerk's hands and, holding that page close to his eyes, read the lines three times himself, commending them mightily. He said gracefully in reply, echoing the *O Felix Culpa*, "We all but welcome Luther's crime since it is the occasion of your noble championship." His letter to Henry, dated November 4, 1521, was marked on the back, "To Our Most Christian Son in Christ, Henry of England, Illustrious Defender of the Faith." This was probably intended to convey that the title conferred was to be regarded as the equivalent of that of Most Christian King which Henry had expected to be taken from Louis XII and given to himself. The King was so pleased that he could afford to laugh when his fool chortled, upon the news reaching England, "O good Harry, let thou and I defend one another, and let the Faith look after itself!"

As Defender of the Faith Henry was not particularly active, if the defence be measured by activity against heresy. Perhaps Henry considered that he had done enough by writing his book. Or it may be that, like Cardinal Wolsey, he could not imagine heresy getting any lodgement in England. There were actually not many heretics to prosecute and most of these were of the cautious donnish type who took good care not to publish their views. A little group at Cambridge met secretly at the White Horse Inn, which came to be known as "Little Germany," but Cranmer, the worst of the English heretics, does not seem to have attended their sessions. Their leader, Dr. Robert Barnes, the Prior of the Augustinians (Luther's own order), preached a sermon on Christmas Eve, 1525, denouncing the observance of special occasions, such as Christmas, and for this he had to abjure before the Vice-Chancellor and then before Wolsey as Legate. At this little ceremony at St. Paul's he was accompanied by three of the German merchants of the steel-yard. William Roper, Thomas More's son-in-law, was similarly affected for a while, but was let off with a friendly warning from Wolsey and, after More's arguments had failed, was converted by More's prayers. The truth is that Wolsey was disposed to be a bit lax in these matters, either because he was too busy with other things or because he did not take heresy in England very seriously. As the Legate took this view of the matter, the King did not feel it necessary to indulge in the burnings by which he sought to prove his orthodoxy during the later years of his reign.

If Tyndale could have been caught – and efforts were made to induce the Emperor to hand him over – he would no doubt have suffered at the stake; but this was because Tyndale was too notorious an offender to be ignored. As hands could not be laid on him, Tunstall, the Bishop of London, bought up a whole edition at Antwerp of his translation of the New Testament and burned that instead.

This calls for a few words of explanation. Wycliffe's was far from being, as is too often supposed, the first translation of the Scriptures into English. As to this we have many testimonies, including that of Sir Thomas More, who declared: "I myself have seen and can show you Bibles, fair and old, written in English, which have been known and seen by the bishop of the diocese, and left in the hands of laymen and women, whom he knew to be good Catholic people and who used the books with devotion and soberness." The prohibition of unauthorized versions of the Scriptures in the vernacular by the Constitutions of Arundel in 1408,* was made with the Wycliffite translation in mind. These constitutions presupposed the eventual appearance of a translation that could be officially accepted by the hierarchy. But there was as yet no printed edition of the Scriptures in English, and though many bishops thought this was needed, they had not yet found anyone whom they considered competent for the task. Tyndale had offered himself to Tunstall but was regarded with suspicion (as the event proved, with good cause), so he did his work abroad, financed by an English patron.

What Tyndale produced was something based on Luther's translation, having heretical notes and translating many key words in a definitely heretical sense. Thus "Church" was turned into "congregation," "penance" into "repentance," and "priest" (except in the sense of heathen priests) into "elder." The implication was clear: it was a denial that a visible Church existed, for the word "congregation" could apply to an assembly of Jews or Mohammedans. Holy Orders were rejected with the reduction of priests to elders, and the seven sacraments were cut down to two — baptism and the Eucharist, and the Eucharist itself emptied of its main significance.

Never was there any objection in Catholic England, or anywhere else, to an accurate translation of the Scriptures, though it was held that discrimination should be shown in their use. In short, nobody could be subjected to any charge regarding the

*Before that the Synod of Oxford (1281) prohibited heretical versions, which would indicate that such had already appeared.

Bible, still less to any punishment, unless heresy was involved. On this and all other points of doctrine Henry was – and prided himself on being – the most orthodox of men. He imagined that the matter had been adequately dealt with by the burning of Tyndale's version, organized by Tunstall and presided over by Wolsey while John Fisher preached. After that no heretic would dare to show his face in England – not while the Defender of the Faith sat on the English throne.

These years – 1518 to 1527 – were of great glory both for the King and the Cardinal, though each received a disappointment. Henry's was one that he could not have taken very much to heart; it was that he was not elected Emperor.

Wily old Ferdinand of Aragon had died in 1516, with his grandson Charles inheriting his kingdoms.* And a couple of years later the Emperor Maximilian, Charles's other grandfather, died, leaving him by far the strongest contestant for the imperial title. Max was a strange, disreputable, down-at-heel but rather engaging figure who, right at the end, when he suddenly succumbed from exposure in hunting the chamois, had been dreaming of leading a crusade down the Danube against the Turks, going on from there to free the holy places, of then resigning the empire and of becoming pope, with canonization to top it all off. He wrote to his daughter, "You won't be able to get out of it; after my death you will be obliged to adore me!" How much the fantastic old man believed in these dreams of his, and to what extent he was trying to be amusing, it would be hard to say.

There was nothing fantastic about his grandson. Dull, conscientious, and industrious – but also a Hapsburg – no other candidate for election had any real chance against him. Henry entered his name mainly because Francis I also did so, but when he saw what was going to happen, he gave out that, as against Francis, Charles was his choice. On June 28, 1518, the question was settled that had never been in any serious doubt.

*As his mother, poor insane Joan, lived until 1555, she was technically co-ruler with him in Castille.

The solemn blue-eyed youth of twenty who was the new emperor, unprepossessing in appearance and showing for the first time (but to a degree never again equalled) the famous Hapsburg jaw, was far outclassed in natural gifts by Henry and Francis, yet was more than able to hold his own against them because of his tenacity. The extent of his possessions was greater than anything known since Charlemagne and included the Germanies (at least nominally), Spain, the Low Countries, the two Sicilies, as well as the fabulously wealthy Mexico and Peru. Yet he never seemed to have enough money for his needs and his territories were too scattered to permit that concentrated effort against his enemies – in particular Francis – which he expected would give him the hegemony of Europe. He had to be continually moving from one country to another to keep all under control, and his problems in Germany were accentuated by the adhesion (mainly for political reasons) of the German princes to the Lutheran religion.

Wolsey's disappointment was far more bitter. When Leo X died in 1521 Richard Pace, Dean of St. Paul's, was sent to Rome by the Cardinal, plentifully supplied with money for bribes, and supported by the promise that Charles would back him in the election for the new pope. Henry let the Emperor know that he was anxious beyond words "that your Majesty should concur" in Wolsey's ambitions, and Wolsey made the monstrous proposition through the Bishop of Badajoz that Charles should march the troops he already had in Italy against Rome, so as to intimidate the conclave. He would undertake to send 100,000 ducats for the expenses of this military demonstration. The advantages of his own election were indicated: there would be no adherent of the French party, and the English Cardinal's chief care, when he became pope, "would be to place the imperial crown on Charles, to exalt his own king, and to make an expedition first against the French and then against the infidels." In spite of these really handsome offers, Charles distrusted Wolsey, and his old tutor was elected as Adrian VI on January 9, 1522. In one scrutiny Wolsey received seven votes and in another nine.

Henry was as disappointed as the Cardinal himself, for with Wolsey as pope, he felt that he might be in a better position to dominate Europe than even as emperor. When a new chance occurred in 1523, Adrian having had a very short pontificate, again the methods of bribery and intimidation were attempted. This time Charles, who knew that Wolsey suspected him of not having kept his word, wrote Wolsey a letter that contained a copy of the instructions to the imperial agent in Rome. Charles also took the precaution of seeing that the bearer of these instructions should be detained in Barcelona so that he would arrive at Rome too late. Though Charles could not hope that his duplicity would not eventually come to light, and embitter Wolsey against him, that was preferable to seeing the English Cardinal as Pope. He had no confidence whatever in Wolsey's willingness to serve Spanish interests, for though he might do this as against France, the main lines of his policy would be directed to the aggrandizement of England.

In the election of 1523 Wolsey did not receive a single vote. The election of a foreigner two years previously had been unpopular in Rome, and Adrian VI (admirable man though he was) was heartily disliked. There would have been an uproar had a foreigner been chosen again. After a long conclave Giulio de' Medici, the bastard cousin of Leo X, was elected, taking the name of Clement VII.

His reign was one of the most unlucky in the history of the Papacy. The new Medici Pope was tall, graceful, good looking (in spite of a slight squint), and as yet without his heroic beard. But in spite of his excellent mind and pure morals he was lacking in courage or the power of reaching a decision about anything. While it would be unjust to say that he thought of nothing except the advantage of his family, he thought of this too much, and put an excessive reliance on a skill in manoeuvering that got very small results. For England his reign was disastrous, and, because of England, for the world.

The political intrigues of Henry and Wolsey went on, becoming, if possible, more devious than ever. In June, 1520, the long-planned meeting of the Kings of England and France took place at the Field of Cloth of Gold.* As it had been so often postponed, each king had vowed not to shave until they met – a delicate compliment! – and each king fancied himself so much with a beard as to retain it ever afterwards. As Henry's, though sparse, came out a ruddy gold, it was considered very handsome.

He was still without his grotesque corpulence or the cruel look that a self-indulgent life gave him. Giustiniani in one of his dispatches describes him as being a tall young athlete and continues: "He is very accomplished; a good musician; composes well; a fine jouster; speaks good French, Latin and Spanish; is very religious; hears three Masses daily when he hunts, and sometimes five on other days. He hears the Office every day in the Queen's chamber; that is to say, Vespers and Compline. He is very fond of hunting, and never takes his diversion without tiring eight or ten horses, which he causes to be stationed beforehand along the line of the country he means to take; and when one is tired he mounts another, and before they get home they are all exhausted. He is extremely fond of tennis, at which game it is the prettiest thing in the world to see him play, his fair skin glowing through a shirt of the finest texture." Though he was, as Falieri records, as bald as Julius Caesar, a fact that he could conceal (except when he was in Church) by wearing a hat, in outward appearance he was otherwise not very different from the youth who had ascended the throne. In interior disposition, however, he was becoming, under all his expansive bonhomie, secretive and suspicious; and in politics his unhappy experience with his father-in-law had infected him with a cynicism, which he overlaid – now and for the rest of his life – with a magnificent capacity for cant. His egotism had grown; he was still immature.

*This is commonly, but incorrectly, called the Field of the Cloth of Gold. Cloth of Gold was the name of a material, with as definite a meaning as silk or velvet. It was often used for awnings on specially sumptuous occasions. Because it had never been used on so lavish a scale before its name was given to this meeting.

There was so much distrust on both sides that when the two Kings first came in sight of each other, each surrounded by glittering cavaliers, neither group was quite certain that some treachery was not meditated. The slightest untoward incident, had it occurred at that moment, would have turned a friendly meeting into a battle. Francis a day or two later tried to dissipate all suspicion by riding over, unattended and unarmed, one morning before his brother of England was out of bed, and by acting as his valet, warming his shirt before the fire for him. But Henry only attributed this pretty courtesy to some deep dark cunning. Nor was he really convinced of Francis' sincerity in spite of all that was done to make the party a success. The most delicate and rare food was spread on plates of gold in vain; the richest wines outpoured. The best musicians of France and Italy played their entrancing airs; the most beautiful ladies in the kingdom danced; the most luscious flattery was laid on thick. Henry remained suspicious.

Katherine the Queen did her best to make amends. When she and Queen Claude were at Mass and the pax was presented, each tried to yield precedence to the other, until they gave it up, laughed, and kissed one another instead of the pax. Henry distributed valuable presents among the French courtiers and took care to lose large sums of money at dice to the more important among them. But throughout the festivities he never really thawed, at least not towards Francis.

What was at the bottom of all this was his vanity. He showed off his horsemanship, but it was no better than that of Francis. And when one day the two Kings had a wrestling match, the long-legged Francis threw Henry, much to his anger and humiliation. It served to increase the jealousy that had gnawn him since Francis' great victory of Marignano. There the French King had proved his personal valour, whereas Henry had never exposed himself in the campaign of 1513, such as it was. All that he could boast was skill in the tilting-yard, and Francis was his equal even there.

Henry had the best of reasons for distrusting Francis: Henry was getting ready to double-cross him, and the English King's famous conscience had to find some means of justifying itself. Only a few days before the Cloth of Gold there had been a meeting with the Emperor, as though by chance — when Charles came to England to see his aunt, Queen Katherine, whom he had never met until then. Such an unprecedented event as a visit from the Emperor was considered very significant, and though nobody knows what was discussed in private, it did not require much penetration to surmise that this boded no good for Francis. Then immediately after the Cloth of Gold — on July 5th — there was another meeting, this time on imperial territory at Gravelines. Rumours reached Francis that Henry was proposing to cement an alliance between England and the Empire by a marriage between Charles and his little daughter Mary — and this though Mary had been betrothed two years previously to his own small son, the Dauphin. Joint action by England and Spain against Francis would in fact probably have taken place had not the Emperor at that moment been obliged to hurry back to Spain to quell an insurrection there.

Francis, for his part, might have seized so excellent an opportunity for crossing the Alps and invading Italy to assert his claim to Milan — perhaps even to gobble up the kingdom of Naples — and at the very least to enforce the Pope to comply with his will, had it not been for one awkward fact. The Treaty of London, signed in 1518, was still in force, under which perpetual peace had been pledged. Francis remembered that under this treaty England would be obliged to give aid against any aggressor who broke the peace. While he could not be sure that Henry would live up to his promises, it was obviously not safe to give so good a justification for the invasion of France. It would be much better to wait until he was himself attacked by Charles; then perhaps Henry would honour his word and help to resist the attacker. It was already evident that Wolsey's grandiose plan of a League of Nations was not going to last very long.

During the year following the meetings between Henry and

Francis and Henry and Charles no war took place, but in England there occurred something which, at the time, seemed even more startling than a war would have been. It was another proof of the suspiciousness that was spreading in Henry's character.

Among the nobles who had attended him at the Cloth of Gold was Edward Stafford, Duke of Buckingham, Constable of England. He had grown up with the children of Henry VII after his father had suffered execution under Richard III. He had therefore every reason to be attached to the Tudor dynasty, though he was not a man of such intellectual force as to wish to take much part in politics, and perhaps regarded its routine demands as beneath the dignity of a person so illustrious as himself. For he was of royal blood, of much better family than the upstart Tudors. Of this he was very conscious, though his position was so secure (as he imagined) that he did not feel any ambition.

There is the well-known story, related by Polydore Vergil, of his having deliberately poured water on the Cardinal's shoes when obliged to perform the distasteful office of holding the silver ewer for him while the Cardinal washed his hands. This was undoubtedly rather an indication of the animosity between the two men than its origin. Wolsey, knowing that the only possible reaction against him would be one on the part of the aristocracy, and that of the English aristocracy the Duke was the leading figure, decided on his destruction.

It was not very difficult to arouse the King's suspicions. He was reminded of the pretenders to the throne during his father's reign, and of the Earl of Warwick – poor boy! – who was no pretender but who suffered death because he was the son of the Duke of Clarence, brother to Edward IV and Richard III.* The Beaufort line of the Plantagenets descended through John of Gaunt, whose bastard children by Katherine Swynford, though given legitimization by statute, were excluded from the line of succession. Yet if that line had any claim at all, Buckingham's

*Buckingham's mother and Edward IV's wife were sisters, so the Duke was Henry's second cousin. He was also connected by marriage with the Plantagenet Poles and the Duke of Norfolk.

claim was almost as good as Henry's. And Henry was getting nervous about a possible challenge to Mary's right – as she was only a girl – after his death. He was persuaded that Buckingham should be removed.

Enquiries were made and it was learned that the Duke (possibly very idly) had speculated as to what might come about if anything happened to the King. It turned out that he had done even worse: he had consulted a Carthusian monk named Nicholas Hopkins, who had a great reputation for holiness and was credited with prophetic powers. From him there had come the somewhat enigmatic word that he "should have all."

Less than that was enough in those days for a charge of high treason. Buckingham received on April 8th a message that the King would like to see him in London, so he set out at once from his vast estate at Thornbury in Gloucestershire, quite unsuspectingly, supposing only that the King wished his advice or to show him some courtesy. He rode along the Thames valley with his attendants, still suspecting nothing until he perceived that he was being followed at a distance by some knights and that groups of the royal yeomen were on the road.

Upon arriving in London he went to see Wolsey but was told that the Cardinal was ill. At London Bridge he was arrested and taken to the Tower. On May 13, 1521, he was tried before his peers in Westminster Hall, the tribunal being presided over by the Duke of Norfolk, a relative, who was in tears as he passed sentence.

In anger and pride Buckingham told his judges that he would not sue for mercy – which in any event he would not have received – and eight days later his head was struck off. He died because he had too much royal blood in his veins and because Cardinal Wolsey wished to serve notice of what his enemies might expect.

The English aristocracy stood, as a group, for an anti-French policy. Wolsey, on the other hand, was still thinking of the possible advantages of a French alliance, not to mention his private grudge against the Emperor. But in the shifts and turns of diplomacy it was the anti-French policy that now prevailed. In 1522 the Emperor visited England again, where he was greeted on the road to London with a Latin oration delivered by Sir Thomas More whose politics (in so far as he concerned himself in such matters) was imperialist. It was while Charles was in England that Clarencieux Herald was dispatched to France to hurl formal defiance against its King.

In the August of that year the Earl of Surrey, soon to succeed his father as Duke of Norfolk, led an expedition into France. It was a moment when the Turks were about to take Rhodes and had already invaded Hungary – a moment of imminent peril to Christendom. But that was disregarded. In fact the stock argument was that France, as the disturber of Europe, must be dealt with first, that Francis was the Great Turk. It was this attitude that made the disaster of Mohacz possible. But England, at the fringe of things, did not believe itself threatened, except by the French. Henry felt little responsibility for the general good, or much power to imagine a good except in matters that closely touched himself. Though he had two or three years previously made a vow to go personally on crusade if a son were born to him, that no son had come made him feel that God had cheated him.

Surrey was by no means so good a soldier as his father; he did nothing except ravage the Boulonnois and Artois. As the French refused battle, knowing very well that the English would soon have over-extended lines, all that Surrey accomplished was a cruelty after his own heart. He burned every village and farm and church and barn and cornfield in his path, and then reported: "The Boulonnois is so burnt and pillaged that the French have good reason to be angry. . . . When we have burnt Dorlance, Corby, Ancre, Bray, which I think will be in about three weeks, I cannot see how we can do much more." His smug complacency reveals that nothing was intended except destruction. By October the pointless campaign was over. As the Scots, under the Duke of Albany, were threatening the northern border, they were by then a more serious threat than any on the other side of the Channel.

The danger from the Scots passed. Albany returned to France, and when Parliament met at Blackfriars in April, 1523, under their new speaker, Sir Thomas More, the project of the French war was revived. Wolsey was making a demand for the unprecedented subsidy of £800,000, and as the House objected that it was impossible to collect so large an amount, Wolsey proposed going there in person to overawe the members. There was some discussion as to how he should be received, until More suggested with that quiet humour of his: "Masters, forasmuch as my Lord Cardinal lately, ye wot well, laid to our charge the lightness of our tongues for things uttered out of the House"—Wolsey had complained that the then secret business of Parliament was being discussed in every alehouse—"it shall not be in my mind amiss with all his pomp to receive him, with his maces, his pillars, his pole-axes, his crosses, his hat, and his Great Seal too; to the intent that, if he find the like fault with us hereafter, we may be the bolder from ourselves to lay the blame on those his Grace bringeth with him."

Wolsey arrived and from this and that member demanded his opinion; all kept what the Cardinal called "a marvellous obstinate silence." When More himself was finally appealed to he answered that "it was neither expedient nor agreeable with the ancient liberties of the House" to be forced to reply. The Cardinal, who had declared that he would "rather have his tongue plucked from his head with a pair of pincers than to move the King to any less sum," went off in a rage.

Thomas Cromwell, who was a member of this Parliament, made (or at least wrote, for it is uncertain whether it was ever delivered) a remarkable speech.* It becomes all the more remarkable when we remember that Cromwell was already in Wolsey's service. One is left with the feeling that he was put up to say what Wolsey dared not say himself.

*It is given in full in Merriman's *Cromwell,* Vol. I, pp. 30–44. A condensation of it is in *Letters and Papers,* Vol. III, Part 2, pp. 1246–1249.

This speech was a masterly performance. Cromwell urged that in view of the uncertainty of the succession it would be foolish to risk the King's life in battle. (As though that were likely!) While the war might harm France, it would harm England still more by exhausting the treasury. No advance far into the country would be safe unless strongholds were held along the lines of communication, and what would be the permanent value of "such ungracious dogholes"? But even if France could be conquered, could it be held? "Who that intended France to win," he quoted, "With Scotland let him begin." It was foolish to think of subduing France, which was separated from England by the sea, while Scotland was suffered to remain under a different polity. There was yet another proverb, "In Scotland there is nothing to win but strokes." Very effectively Cromwell poured buckets of ice-cold water over the whole project.

Cromwell was by no means alone in these opinions. Warham, for instance, who had always been a peace man, told Wolsey again quite plainly that, even if Henry could conquer France, England would only be impoverished because the cost of holding it would be even greater than that of the war itself. After all the outlay of money, he reminded Wolsey, the King "hath not one foot of land more in France than his noble father had, who lacked no riches or wisdom to win the kingdom of France, if he had thought it expedient." These wise counsels were disregarded: Henry was aflame with his absurd ambition, and the aristocracy was, by tradition, anti-French and the merchant-class imperialist because of their business connections.

Parliament in the end compromised with the King to the extent of agreeing to the French war, which indeed it could not prevent, except by refusing any subsidy. This it dared not do, but Wolsey was forced to accept a good deal less than what he had demanded in the name of the King. Even that proved very difficult to collect, though the sum was spread over several years. Here and there riots, close to being insurrections, occurred. The leader of one in East Anglia, when captured, explained, "Poverty is our captain, for he and his cousin Necessity have brought us to this doing." It was the truth. The limit of taxation had been reached.

The plan of campaign was that the English force – this time under Suffolk – was to effect a conjunction with the Burgundians and then turn upon Boulogne. This was, however, a plan so advantageous to Henry and so little to the advantage of Charles, that the Emperor soon lost interest. So again nothing was accomplished except the destruction of the farms and crops of a number of French peasants. The army came home covered with the glory of useless pillage. Not a foot of French soil had been won.

During this same late summer Pope Adrian VI died, and the possibility of Wolsey's obtaining the triple tiara after his failure eighteen months before deflected the attention of the Cardinal and the King from a war that was not going well. But once again popedom eluded Wolsey, and his last chance was lost with the election of Clement VII. To make Henry's discomfiture worse, he could see that the Emperor had profited; England by engaging France in war had enabled Charles to recover Milan and Genoa and Tournai. All that Charles had done in return was to double-cross Wolsey a second time in his efforts to be elected pope.*

Henry was still reluctant to abandon the imperial alliance, as he hoped that it might yet lead to his obtaining what he wanted in France. He believed that the campaigns of 1522 and 1523 had failed only because Charles had not done his part – so during 1524 a different kind of campaign was devised. The Duc de Bourbon, who in 1523 had turned traitor against Francis, was to invade Provençe from Italy, financed to the extent of 100,000 crowns in gold from the English treasury. Then Henry would invade France in person, providing he was supplied with 4000

*It should be pointed out, however, that though Wolsey might have been elected pope in 1521, had Charles given the support he had promised, not even the Emperor's strongest efforts could have given him, in 1523, more than the votes of the imperialist cardinals. Wolsey found it difficult to accept this unpalatable truth; he simply felt that he had been betrayed.

imperial troops. To the Pope all this was represented as an alliance of Henry and Charles against Lutheranism; it would also forestall all danger of a second Avignon captivity, which might occur if France became too powerful.

Bourbon did invade Provençe at the end of 1524, and Francis saw his chance of invading Italy, where he laid siege to Pavia. But now Marignano was reversed. While the French were investing Pavia, they found themselves invested, and a brilliant movement effected under cover of the night caught Francis on the morning of November 24, 1525, with his magnificent cannon pointing the wrong way. He was utterly crushed, all his guns and he himself being captured. Taken to Spain, he was obliged to take a humiliating oath to Charles (which he privately announced he did not intend to be bound by) and had to give his two sons into the Emperor's keeping as hostages.

When Henry received the news of Pavia, he at once fell on his knees, sobbing with joy. "My God," he exclaimed, "I thank Thee!" To the messenger he said, "My friend, you are like the angel Gabriel announcing the birth of Jesus Christ!" Now he thought he would be able to complete the ruin of Francis.

"Not an hour is to be lost!" cried Wolsey. An embassy was sent at once to the Emperor, proposing that France be partitioned between them, Henry taking the throne and Charles Burgundy. There was no question of Henry's seeking to redress the balance of power by coming to the aid of the French. This never was Henry's (or Wolsey's) policy, except in the sense of backing the Papacy in its efforts to prevent either France or the Empire becoming dominant in Europe.

The Emperor was cool to these proposals. He had no wish to establish Henry in France. Moreover, he had no money available for the kind of war that would be necessary; even the pay of his army in Italy was in arrears. Germany was aflame with the Peasants' Revolt, and he knew that nothing more was to be expected in the way of an English subsidy. England could not raise the money she herself needed for the conquest of France, and even had this been possible, Henry was brought to see that this would be a hopeless task if he attempted it single-handed. He had therefore to content himself with the reflection that his daughter Mary was still betrothed to the Emperor and that their son would inherit not only Charles's personal vast possessions but would no doubt eventually succeed to the imperial crown as well. Eventually, too, Scotland would be subjugated, all Ireland brought under English domination. Intoxicated by such a dream it no longer seemed to him a matter of much importance that Wolsey had not become pope. The Emperor of the World — his grandson — would nominate to the Papacy, and future conclaves would have hardly more importance than the elections of cathedral chapters in England.

It was a glorious and grandiose vision. Unfortunately Charles, who was greatly pressed for ready money and knew he could not extract it from Henry, was preparing to ditch Mary. On June 25, 1525, he wrote to the Archduke Ferdinand: "I see no way except for me to marry Isabella of Portugal, with whom the King offers a million ducats, but I shall not take any step without the consent of the King of England, as I have sent him word. I wish for no war this year, but to attend to my marriage." What could Henry do but give a scornful consent? But it was the end, not only of his dreams regarding his grandson, but of all his ambitions in France.

Henry was now all the more uneasy about the succession in England. Mary's right to the throne, if she were not married to a powerful husband, might be contested. But if she married an Englishman, the nobility would be jealous of her choice. He began to wonder whether he had not made a bad mistake in throwing over the Dauphin in favor of Charles, though that might result in England's becoming hardly more than an appendage to France. He had been brought to believe that the only possible husband for her was the Emperor, and now the Emperor had coolly asked to be released from the obligation. In consenting Henry informed his nephew (who had also been his prospective son-in-law) that all treaties between them must be considered abrogated. In this way he soothed his indignation but was of course left out in the cold.

As an insurance against possible eventualities, Henry brought forward the bastard son he had by Bessie Blount and began to groom him as his successor. Since 1519 he had known that Katherine was not likely to bear another child, and he came to know this positively about this date. An illegitimate son might be safer to rely on than a legitimate daughter.

The pleasant little six-year-old boy was led on June 15, 1525,* into the long gallery of Bridewell Palace, where, with the King sitting on a dais, and the Cardinal beside him, surrounded by the lords, spiritual and temporal, Henry Fitzroy was made a Knight of the Garter, the patent of which fell to Sir Thomas More to read aloud. Upon him were also conferred titles that were very significant, as they had been formerly held either by Henry VII or Prince Arthur. He was created Duke of Richmond and Somerset, Lord High Admiral, and Warden of the Marches. There was even some talk a little later of making him King of Ireland, though Henry was officially only "Lord" of that country. To maintain such dignities large grants of land were conferred, and to prepare him for the position he might occupy the eminent scholars, Richard Croke and John Palsgrave, were appointed his tutors. Katherine was, of course, very angry at the public parade made of her husband's bastard and knew that it might end in the deprivation of Mary's right to succeed her father.

Henry, however, was, as usual, wavering in mind. He had made no final decision but was merely preparing for eventualities. It was far from certain whether Parliament would allow him to bequeath the crown, and he was a little afraid to test the point. Still less was it certain what the country would do after his death, whatever it might be that Parliament had reluctantly done. Therefore, while indicating Richmond's availability, Henry gave nine-year-old Mary Ludlow Castle, the official

*Though the letter from Charles about Isabella of Portugal was written after this date, it was in April that a special envoy had been sent to Henry to break off, as gracefully as possible, the match with Mary. What happened to Richmond was a direct consequence.

residence of the Prince of Wales, and made her Princess of Wales in her own right, something that had never happened before and has never happened since. Probably all that Henry intended was to provide a male heir in case a queen proved to be unacceptable. And there was always the possibility that the project of a French marriage for Mary could be revived.

The bewildering shifts and stratagems of policy have been sometimes described as the beginning of the English devotion to the doctrine of the balance of power. That the name for this was not invented until the eighteenth century would not, of course, rule out the prior existence of the thing itself. But the key to the whole matter is that English policy was pro-papal. When the Pope made an alliance against a preponderant Empire, England joined it; when the Pope considered France to be threatening him, he made an alliance against France, and again Henry joined. It was a policy of no advantage to England and damaging to the spiritual authority of the Papacy, by making it take on too many of the characteristics of a mere secular monarchy. Yet the popes of this time can hardly be blamed for the situation, though they may be blamed for attaching too much importance to political considerations. Theirs was a legacy inherited from the past, when the Papacy was engaged in a life and death struggle with the Empire. Carried over into the sixteenth century it was unfortunate for all concerned.

Wolsey played his part in this with consummate skill and lack of scruple. Sometimes it would seem that in foreign affairs he had no other object than that of displaying his virtuosity, for such results as were obtained were dazzling rather than substantial. There is this much to be said for him, however; he did succeed in putting England on the map of Europe again. Nothing ever happened without the Cardinal of York pulling some of the strings. Though English armies did nothing, and could do nothing, except ravage a few square miles of France or Scotland, and no foreign marriage project was ever carried through, England remained a danger, always able to invade France through the gateway of Calais and always able, by holding the narrow seas, to prevent any trade with the Low Countries or the Baltic, while herself remaining impregnable. That everything attempted by Wolsey ended in smoke was forgotten because, the instant one project failed, he was bringing pressure at some new point. From having been regarded as a small island on the fringe of things, where barbarous nobles were constantly at war with one another, and (since 1485) as a kingdom precariously held by a usurper, England had now definitely become a European power again. The English people might groan under their taxes, but there was a lustre round the throne. The only criticism that can be made of Henry's diplomacy is the criticism that Mr. Mattingly makes: "He had learned all its lessons, except the important one – that he did not have to play it." He won indeed a kind of glory, but the national safety did not call for it, and the national prosperity was impaired.

Wolsey's personal grandeur surpassed anything previously known. Giustiniani estimated his income as being 42,000 ducats, or what would be about £200,000 in modern money. His successor estimated it – by that time Wolsey's income had increased – as nearly four times that amount. And though these estimates may be exaggerated, they did not take into account what the Cardinal received in the form of foreign pensions or the other odds and ends he was adept in extracting. His household, Cavendish tells us, consisted of over eight hundred men, his gentlemen clothed in a livery of the best crimson velvet, with chains of gold round their necks, his yeomen and lower officers in scarlet "guarded with black velvet one hand beneath." His silver crosses – one for his legateship and the other for his archbishopric – were carried before him, wherever he rode or walked, by two of the tallest priests in England. His yeomen of the guard were similarly chosen for their great height. With them were his mounted pillar-bearers, and his attendant footmen each carried a pole-axe in his hand. Nine or ten peers were in constant duty with him, each of whom had two or three men to serve him, except the Earl of Derby, who had five. When Wolsey and the King of France met, it was as equals; the Cardinal did not dismount and remained with head covered, as though he were himself a king. That he was in effect – Deputy-King and, for England, Deputy-Pope as well.

His ability and industry were prodigious and yet were less than his vanity. Plain homespun Sir Thomas More, who succeeded him as lord chancellor, was amused by some aspects of the great man and had some good-natured stories to tell of him when, waiting in the Tower for death, he wrote his *Dialogue of Comfort.* That he does not actually name Wolsey, any more than he names his own wife, the redoubtable Dame Alice, in his tales about her, in no way conceals whom he is writing about.

Once, it seems, Wolsey showed a treaty to somebody who had served on several embassies (and so might be supposed to know something about such matters), asking him to give his candid opinion of it. He wanted nothing less than that, he said. When this man ventured mildly to criticize one of its clauses, he got roundly called a fool – and of course never again told the Cardinal what he really thought. This ambassador may have been More himself; certainly Wolsey called More a fool in the council chamber for objecting to one of the proposals he was accustomed to have accepted without question. More good-humoredly quipped, "It is a good thing, your Grace, that the King has only one fool on his Council."

Another of these anecdotes was ostensibly of an ecclesiastical dignitary in Germany who had made a speech, and afterwards at dinner expected everybody to praise it. As nobody spoke, he insisted that everyone give his opinion, and they would start with the man placed lowest on the board. Each had some tidbit of flattery to offer more luscious than the man who had spoken previously, and as the famous doctor who sat at the Cardinal's right heard what was being said, and wondered how he could possibly outdo it, he positively sweated in his anxiety. Yet he did find a way – the old fox! – to surpass all the others: when his turn came at last, he heaved a deep sigh, rolled his eyes to the ceiling, and, completely overcome, heaved out an "Oh!" The speech, More admitted, was in truth a very good one, but he said that half the praise it received would have more than sufficed.

This vanity not only betrayed the fact that Wolsey was at bottom a vulgarian, it also indicated a serious moral weakness. He was not a bad man, whatever were his faults. But he had no definite principles and founded his astonishing career on nothing but the royal favor. A lion when dealing with difficulties, so long as Henry was behind him, he gave way instantly when confronted by the royal will.

Even some of his good qualities were tainted, or a taint was discovered in them. Thus Lord Herbert believes that Wolsey was impartial in his administration of justice only because he loved nobody, just as he fell from office because nobody loved him. This, however, was not entirely fair: Wolsey bore heavily on the rich and powerful, as he wished to depress all rivalry. But he did what he could for the unprotected, and he was kind to his servants and those in distress. As Lord Chancellor he took no bribes, but as Legate he wrung out the last farthing of his dues, and he ruthlessly extorted money for his colleges. Infinitely rapacious, he was not corrupt. Nor was he cruel.

He believed that he was serving the Church's best interests, though of them he took a narrow view, and they were never separated from his own ambitions. His projected ecclesiastical reforms were excellent, but he never had time left over from politics to carry them out. He was sincere also in upholding the liberties of the Church, and he did not foresee that the concentration of all authority in the English Church into his own hands would result in the transference of that authority to the King. This nevertheless was the sole lasting achievement of this incredibly efficient and short-sighted man.

The moment of his decline began when it seemed to everybody that he had reached the very summit of his glory. This was during the French embassy to England in 1527, and his own embassy to France later in the same year. In the first of these he was to confirm a new French alliance by the marriage of the Princess Mary either to the Dauphin or to Francis himself. For he and Henry had been obliged to fall back on this after Charles had failed them. In the second he sought to make the alliance still firmer by marrying Henry to the French King's sister-in-law, the daughter of the dead Louis. He knew that a divorce from Katherine was projected; he had no idea as to whom Henry had in mind for his second wife. He was to find it true what the King said to Cavendish: "Three may keep counsel if two are away, and if I thought my cap knew my counsel I would throw it in the fire." In this matter the King had not confided in the Cardinal.

Cavendish vividly, if rather lusciously, describes these occasions. Gabriel Grammont, the Bishop of Tarbes, arrived in England, and Wolsey sang the High Mass at St. Paul's Cathedral, administering Holy Communion – dividing the Host between the King and the Bishop as the representative of Francis. It was the most binding of oaths, one that would guarantee perpetual peace between the two countries. Francis had sent Henry the highest order of France, the St. Michael, and Henry sent Francis the Garter. Francis undertook to pay Henry a pension of 50,000 crowns in gold and a yearly consignment of salt worth another 15,000 crowns. Yet the arrangement was so unpopular in England that Henry had to explain to the Bishop of Tarbes that Mary was as yet – she was eleven – too young to be sent to France. Wolsey was already thought, for a moment, about to fall.

For the French ambassadors Wolsey gave a banquet that eclipsed all previous splendours. It was in Hampton Court in the presence chamber, where the walls were lined with arras, over which there were hung at intervals large disks of gold the better to reflect the light of the silver candelabra. Trumpets blew guests to supper, but the Cardinal did not come; he waited until they had eaten their first course, so as to make a dramatic entry. Then he came in all booted and spurred, still in his riding clothes: "He called for his chair and sat him down in the midst of the high table, and was there as merry and pleasant as ever I saw him in my life."

The second course, now brought on, consisted of jellied dishes, all different, shaped like castles or birds or men fighting with swords or using cross-bows, dancing ladies, and knights on horseback. Cavendish specially noted a chessboard, complete with the pieces, and thought "the Frenchmen never saw the like." The cup went about so freely that "many of these Frenchmen were led to their beds." Even those who managed to remain sober at supper probably did not remain sober in their rooms, in each of which was "a great silver pot with plenty of wine and sufficient of everything."

Equally splendid was the Cardinal's state when he went that summer to France. He rode over London Bridge with his servants and tall guards all clad in orange-tawny coats, with a retinue of gentlemen in velvet with chains of gold round their necks. He himself rode his mule "very sumptuously, like a cardinal" in crimson velvet and with gilt spurs. When on one of the feasts of St. Thomas of Canterbury – then kept on July 7 – he arrived at Canterbury, he piously visited the Saint's shrine. And a special verse was at his command put into the litany sung in the cathedral, "*Sancta Maria, ora pro Papa nostro Clemente.*" Cavendish saw him kneeling on his silk cushion "weeping very tenderly." Well he might weep. News had come of the sack of Rome and of the Pope's standing siege in Castel Sant' Angelo. Two days previously, when Wolsey visited John Fisher at Rochester, he had assured the Bishop that there was no substance in the gossip about the King's divorce. All that Henry wanted to do was to have his conscience set at rest about his marriage to the Queen.

It would be tedious to follow Cavendish through his pages of description of the magnificence of the Cardinal's reception by Francis – the feasting and the jousting and the dancing and the hunting of the boar. These were things that the amazed eye of the perfect gentleman usher never tired of beholding. He also noted his master's undiminished power of work. One day he rose at four in the morning to write dispatches to England, his chaplain in attendance, vested for Mass, waiting for the Cardinal to finish. It was not until four in the afternoon that Wolsey had completed his letters, and all that time he had not stopped for an instant, even for a morsel of food.

What Cavendish knew nothing about were the negotiations that went on in private. Nor probably was he aware that, while at Compiégne, Wolsey acted as though he were the Pope's vicar-general by conferring, over Cardinal Salviati's protest, the insignia of the cardinalitial office upon one only so far designate, the Frenchman Du Prat. Yet these two men joined with Wolsey in writing to the Pope asking that, during his captivity, he delegate his authority to the Cardinal of York. It seems that Wolsey was prepared to start a temporary Avignon all over again could he have found sufficient encouragement from Francis and the four cardinals with him. There was even some talk of England and France turning themselves into a patriarchate, to be presided over by Wolsey as Archbishop of Rouen. Plans of this sort remained possibilities until, on December 6, Clement escaped to Orvieto.

On his return to England the Cardinal got the shock of his life. He had lied to Fisher, as he knew very well that Henry was going to seek a divorce from Katherine; his first act, had Clement appointed him vicar-general, would have been to pronounce this divorce. Katherine had distrusted and disliked him since he had gained his ascendancy over her husband's mind, and Wolsey felt dislike, mixed with some contempt, for her. It would have perfectly suited his policy to have her marriage declared null and void, for then a French marriage could have been arranged for Henry. He did not doubt that Katherine would yield to necessity, or that the Pope could be managed.

What Wolsey did not know until he got back to England was whom Henry had in mind as Katherine's successor. He hurried at once to Richmond and his messenger asked the King, who had Anne Boleyn at his side, where he wished to see the Cardinal.

Anne answered for Henry: "Where should the Cardinal come except where the King is?" A whole roomful of people heard the strident remark and noted that Henry accepted Anne Boleyn's orders. It was in the presence of this young woman, who as Wolsey knew had cause to be a bitter enemy, that he had to give his first account of his embassy to France.

CHAPTER SIX

The King's Conscience

NOBODY is likely to think it cynical to point out that by 1527, when Katherine was past her forty-first year — and a bit dumpy and dowdy — it was hardly surprising that a husband such as hers should have lost all interest in a wife five and a half years older than himself. Nor is it surprising that Henry found in Anne Boleyn — as he had previously found in her sister and before that in Bessie Blount — somebody more to his taste. For though it is hard to understand the hold that Anne Boleyn — referred to by Wolsey as the Crow of the Night — had over him, at least she had relative youth and much sprightliness, and Henry was by no means the only man who thought her fascinating. So much do these things have to be allowed for that it may appear to be gratuitously paradoxical to credit Henry with any conscience in the matter of his divorce.

A conscience, however, he really did have, even if one must add that, being an egotist — perhaps the most monstrous that the world has ever seen — he could convince himself that everything he wished to do must be right. The famous text in Leviticus over which he stumbled might have been explained to his satisfaction had it not been that he had suffered the penalty of that text: "They shall be childless," for his daughter Mary did not count, in his estimation, being of no dynastic value. Here he was, a man who had taken God into partnership, and God had rewarded him, except in the most important thing of all: God had given him no son. It must be the punishment for some great sin. And what great sin had he ever committed except that of marrying his brother's widow?

It was no doubt extraordinary, as Brewer remarks, "How the King's scruples of conscience coincided with his inclinations," but this does not alter the fact that, lie as Henry might, or cruel as he might be in the attainment of his ends, he was perfectly sure that he was not merely justified in seeking a divorce but in conscience bound to seek it. Never, on this point, did he have the slightest misgiving.

Henry was not, as is commonly supposed, a very sensual man. I am inclined to agree with Froude that he was rather frigid by nature. What Thomas More wrote in his *Richard III* of Edward IV scarcely applies to Edward's grandson, who took after him so strongly in appearance: "He was of youth greatly given to fleshly wantonness, from which health of body in great prosperity and fortune, without a special grace, hardly refraineth." Henry's youth, on the contrary, was well-nigh blameless. There was progressive degeneration in his later years, but this was probably due not so much to sensuality as to middle-aged vanity. In 1527 when he took up with Anne Boleyn, he was, it is true, only thirty-six, but he was older than his years, and when he died at fifty-six he was thought of as extremely old. As kings went at that time, Henry was a very moral man, almost a model husband. If he had any mistresses prior to 1527, except the two that have been mentioned, we have no positive information regarding them.*

Furthermore, it should be remembered to Henry's credit that he might have taken his divorce and remarriage into his own hands, getting Wolsey to pronounce the decree and presenting the Pope with an accomplished fact, counting upon Rome's accepting the situation. Clement VII in his embarrassment over the matter several times said petulantly that he wished this were done, so that he could escape responsibility. This was

---

*The Duke of Richmond was his only acknowledged bastard. Though the Elizabethan adventurers, Sir John Perrot and Sir Thomas Stukeley were reputed to be his sons, it is very questionable whether they were so.

precisely what Henry would not do; he was a loyal son of the Church and meant to do everything in regular form, as in the case of a king, the decision should be made by the Pope and not by a local ecclesiastical court. It was not merely a divorce that he wanted, but a divorce beyond all question, a divorce that came from the Holy See.

It need not be said, it is to be hoped, that when the word "divorce" was used, nobody thought of divorce in the modern sense. It was simply to be a declaration of nullity, such as was frequently enough given in those days* and is still obtainable when a reputed marriage can be proved null for any one of a number of good reasons.

Henry had brought himself to believe that a remarriage, with the possibility of a son, was necessary for the security of the succession. But while stressing this as something that gave added weight to his plea, he understood that, standing alone, it could not be decisive. It was a principle, however, more or less recognized, that, where dynastic interests were involved, some stretching of the point might be permissible.

Though the King changed his mode of approach several times, and started with the argument that there were technical defects in the dispensation given in 1503 for his marriage to Katherine, he did this only because he was advised that this would prove the surest and most expeditious method. From the beginning of the divorce proceedings he was convinced that his marriage with Katherine was contrary to the law of God and therefore beyond the jurisdiction of the Pope.

Henry must be admitted to have had at least an arguable case. There was no definitive ruling as to whether he *could* marry his sister-in-law, supposing that her previous marriage had been more than nominal. There were what might have been considered precedents for this – for two of Katherine's sisters had been married in succession to the same man, King Manoel of Portugal.

*The Church's doctrine about marriage was abstractly the same as now. But it was, unavoidably under the circumstances, less efficiently applied. Law courts, under pressure from the powerfully placed, were sometimes too indulgent.

These cases, however, were not quite parallel to his: the texts in Leviticus (18:16 and 20:21) applied only to a man marrying his brother's widow, that is if they applied at all, for John Fisher of Rochester and Clerk, the Bishop of Bath (among others), held that the application was only to a living brother's wife. If against Leviticus there could be cited Deuteronomy 25:5–9, in which a positive duty seems to be laid upon a man to marry his childless sister-in-law. Henry could argue that this was merely permissive and a regulation peculiar to the ancient Jews: as such he held it to be irrelevant. The Church had not decided on the matter; many theologians agreed with him; Henry, whatever his motives, with perfect propriety raised the question.

Henry was also persuaded that, even if there were any doubt about the case, he should be given the benefit of that doubt. What had Louis XII, who had obtained a divorce, ever done for the Church? He had set up the schismatic Council of Pisa and had been excommunicated. What had Henry's sister Margaret, who had obtained a divorce from a second husband, ever done for the Church? Or Charles Brandon, his brother-in-law? Henry was the Defender of the Faith; he had written a book against Luther; he had consistently befriended the Papacy in its difficulties. He no doubt attached too great an importance to what Brewer has called "his occasional acts of parsimonious liberality," but this was because he took too seriously the flattering phrases in which he was thanked. Thus Campeggio had written on February 7 of the year in which the divorce proceedings began, "The cardinals are unanimous in declaring that Henry was God's blessing to them." Similarly he had heard so often that his wonderful book against Luther had saved the Faith, that he came to believe it. Now it was the Pope's turn to do something for him.

There can be no doubt that the question of the succession worried him, especially after 1525 when Mary's betrothal to the Emperor fell through. This was the reason for his bringing the Duke of Richmond forward in that year as a possible successor. It was, however, he knew, an unsatisfactory solution. Would the country accept a bastard as king? Might it not happen that both Richmond and Mary would be rejected in favor of Courtenay or Montague, the head of the Pole family? Both were of royal blood; either might be preferred to Mary. New civil wars might result. Henry had reason to be anxious.

Even had he been sure that Mary would be accepted as queen, it made Henry nervous to see the Tudor succession hang on that single life. For though his sister Margaret (or rather her son, James V of Scotland) was next in line after Mary, it was not likely that this fifteen-year-old boy (as he was in 1527) would be permitted to ascend the English throne. Nor did Henry relish that prospect, unless Mary should marry James and be queen of England in her own right. The dynastic problem must be admitted to have been a thorny one.

Henry was not such a fool as to fail to realize that, by divorcing Katherine and taking another wife, he might endanger the succession. Mary would be automatically bastardized; on the other hand, he could not be sure that a new wife would bear him a son, or even a daughter. If he did not think of this himself, Reginald Pole, his cousin, told him so rather bluntly. To all such arguments the King merely smiled and said, "You do not know my secrets." It really came back to this: the only reason – so Henry believed – why he had not had a son who lived was that he had incurred the penalty attached to the prohibition in Leviticus. Let him break this incestuous marriage of his and God would promptly reward his high-minded obedience to the divine law by sending him a son. Henry therefore did not think that he was taking any risk at all; he was in the position of a man betting on a certainty. Though Mr. Fisher, the author of the best history of Henry's reign, makes the devastatingly gentle comment, "Into the sanctuary of the royal conscience it would be profane to enter," we can at least see far enough into its murky recesses to be convinced that Henry was convinced of his perfect rectitude. It is impossible to gaze except with awe at such self-righteousness.

Who put the idea of the divorce into Henry's mind has

been a matter of much dispute. Katherine herself believed that it was Wolsey. So did Mendoza the Spanish ambassador and Charles V, though they may have been merely accepting Katherine's opinion. The Emperor set it down to revenge for his not having set Wolsey in the chair of Peter. That Wolsey publicly contradicted this belief (receiving as public a confirmation from the King) is hardly enough to rule the supposition out. Neither man had any superstitious veneration for the truth, and at that time (1529) Wolsey was sitting with Campeggio on the legatine commission appointed by the Pope to try the case. As one of the judges he naturally wished to be cleared of the appalling impropriety of deciding a cause which he had initiated.

Cavendish tends strongly to confirm this by recording the Cardinal as saying angrily to Anne Boleyn's father, "You and others of the Council have put fancies into the head of the King, whereby you trouble all the realm, but at the end you will get but small thanks both of God and the world." This, however, may have been merely an attempt to throw the blame on somebody else when unforeseen difficulties were being encountered. Wolsey had believed that he could secure the divorce easily enough for Henry, and had hoped to use it to bring about a French marriage for him. Since then Wolsey had entered into a kind of alliance with Anne. Nevertheless it is very unlikely that he suggested the divorce, however much he afterwards did to effect it. What would seem most probable is that the Boleyn group — which included not only Anne's father but her clever, scheming brother and her cousins, Sir Francis Bryan (the rake pleasantly known as the "Vicar of Hell") and Sir Thomas Wyatt the poet, and her uncle the Duke of Norfolk — planned the whole thing once they saw it might be possible, and stage-directed Anne, though they could not have accomplished their purpose had not Anne been a woman of extraordinary coolness and pertinacity.

Other names appear in this connection — those of Longland, Bishop of Lincoln and Henry's confessor, and Grammont, the Bishop of Tarbes, who came to England early in 1527. Longland may indeed have been so pestered by Henry with his scruples that he wearily conceded that there might be something in them. And the Bishop of Tarbes may have raised some doubts as to Mary's legitimacy when he was in England to arrange for her betrothal to the Dauphin. But though Henry talked a good deal later about Tarbes' having made the first suggestion, we know this to be a lie because there had been some talk of a divorce prior to 1527.

Professor Pollard has sought to show that the question went back as early as 1514. If so it removes any justification that may be found in Henry's anxiety over the succession, for children were born after that date (though of these only Mary was viable), and Katherine was in fact pregnant again that very year. One of Pollard's "proofs" is a letter written in August, 1514, by a Venetian Banker in Rome.* Gossip coming from so far away is obviously likely to be even less reliable than gossip nearer at home (though that is not to be depended upon either); there is no record of the matter being mentioned in England – even by way of reported rumour – at that time.

There is, however, evidence of a stronger character produced by Pollard, including a document discovered recently in the Vatican archives which at first sight seems decisive. It is dated 1514 but it is only an index reference to a letter that has not been found "to be written by the Pope to Henry, King of England, about the pretended nullity of his marriage." Professor Mattingly plausibly suggests** that this is an error of date due to the pasting of a loose slip of paper into a ledger under the wrong year, which should be 1534, when Clement's brief was issued. He points out that Katherine's pregnancy of 1514 rules out the possibility of Henry's wishing to divorce her at that of all moments. It is unthinkable that he would not at least have waited to see whether the expected child would prove to be the son for whom he was longing.

What seems to me very likely is that, though Henry's slow

*This letter is to be found in the *Venetian Calendar,* where it appears as document No. 479 in Vol. II.

***Catherine of Aragon,* pp. 451–453.

secretive mind may have begun to turn over the possibility of a divorce as early as 1525, after he had ceased to live with Katherine as her husband (probably from a disinclination rationalized later as a scruple) he kept his counsel to himself for a long while. When at last he did begin to talk, very cautiously at first, about what he was thinking of, he would have found many people to come forward with the kind of arguments he was looking for. I am inclined to believe that the idea originated, however vaguely, with the King himself.

It was Anne who finally hurried him into action.

Before she did so, she had other little adventures which should be noted. She had been brought up at the French court as a young girl and had returned to England in 1521 or 1522. There her cousin, Sir Thomas Wyatt, though he was a married man, made love to her, but prudently withdrew when he saw the King's interest in her, announcing this in a sonnet in which he said he saw written in diamonds round Anne's neck, "Caesar's I am."

A more serious affair, probably coming before the one with Wyatt, was that with young Sir Henry Percy, the heir to the earldom of Northumberland. Anne would undoubtedly have married him had the marriage not been prevented. Percy was one of the gentlemen attached to Wolsey's household and Wolsey earned Anne's undying enmity by forcibly breaking off the match. He not only publicly berated Percy, and Anne herself, he also sent for the old Earl and made him threaten his son with disinheritance unless he behaved himself.

Cavendish, who witnessed these pretty scenes, jumped to the conclusion that the Percy marriage was forbidden because Henry already had an eye on Anne for himself. The truth would rather seem to be that Anne was intended at that time for a marriage with Sir Piers Butler, the claimant to the earldom of Ormonde, to which Anne Boleyn's father was also laying claim. The King, wishing to do something for Boleyn, whose daughter Mary was at this time his mistress, hit upon the ingenious expedient of marrying Anne to Butler. She was herself partly of Norman-Irish extraction. At all events Sir Henry Percy was so thoroughly scared that he not only dropped Anne but sought to allay all further suspicion by marrying (very unhappily) the daughter of the Earl of Shrewsbury. Yet before this he had sent Anne a message through a friend, "Bid her remember her promise, which none can loose but God only."

Sir Thomas Boleyn was made Viscount Rochford in 1525, as a suitable reward for having been so complaisant about his daughter Mary, though Mr. Belloc takes the date of the viscountancy – May 18 – as that of the start of the Henry-Anne affair.* It would seem much more likely that Henry did not start pursuing Anne until 1526 and that Boleyn's reward with regard to her was the earldom of Wiltshire he received in 1529. He was a sly, dapper little man, whose chief characteristic was an inordinate love of money. He was well-to-do to begin with, as his grandfather had made a fortune as a mercer in London and had served as lord mayor. His mother was a daughter of the Earl of Ormonde and he was a good enough catch to be able to marry a sister of the still unrestored Duke of Norfolk. The Howards had lost most of their wealth by attainder, so the rich Mr. Boleyn was, under the circumstances, acceptable. He was looked upon as a parvenu and was tolerated because the age was that of many other "new" men, whose main occupation was that of feathering their own nests.

The morals of the Boleyns may be gaged from the fact that they were willing for two of their daughters to become, in succession, the King's mistresses. But they had learned something from Mary's case. She had been discarded by Henry without having very much done for her, as was true also of Bessie Blount. This time, as the Boleyns probably caught very early some hint of a possible divorce, they aimed higher. Now the favoured Boleyn should have all or would give nothing.

In 1526 the King rode in the lists under a new motto, far more

History of England, Vol. IV, p. 65.

ambiguous than "The Loyal Heart." It was "Declare I dare not." At this time he expected Anne to be as accommodating as her sister had been. But coached by her family, and fortified by her remarkable will power, she fought Henry off, not because of any moral scruples, but because she clearly saw that only in this way could she fulfill her whole ambition. She did not realize of course in 1526 that she would have nearly seven years to wait; otherwise the prospect of this might have so daunted her that she would have yielded sooner. At that time she was at least twenty-four, and therefore already, according to the standards of the time, regarded as an old maid. But then neither did Henry have any notion of how long his divorce would take; neither did Wolsey. As it was, all through the wearing time of waiting, Anne gave the King no satisfaction and had none herself, except the perverse pleasure of seeing this ageing and egotistic man brought more and more under her imperious domination. One is tempted to admire the skill with which she played him, and the iron resolution she displayed.

Most of that time she was imagined to be the King's mistress. Katherine thought her such, Wolsey thought her such, the Pope thought her such – at least during the initial stages of the affair when they were counting upon the glutting of Henry's appetite to release him from her hold. And for a certainty he would have been quickly released had Anne been so weak as to yield to his written and (we must suppose) spoken importunities. Though the actual date of her surrender cannot be definitely placed, this at least may be said: had it come any time between the institution of the divorce proceedings and the time when Cranmer was to be appointed Archbishop of Canterbury Henry would have quickly turned from all idea of marrying her, though he might still have proceeded with his divorce. For much as he wanted the particular person, Anne Boleyn, he also wanted a son. Even in January, 1533, he would not, I think, have married her – whatever his oaths might have been – had she not been pregnant. She first had to prove to him that she was capable of bearing his child; otherwise she would have been ditched at the last minute. She dared not risk giving this proof until marriage was actually within her grasp.

The first move for a divorce was a collusive suit, a disgraceful beginning. Nothing was said about Anne of course; for that matter, hardly anybody imagined in the beginning that it could be this woman whom the King intended to marry. Warham, the Archbishop of Canterbury, and Wolsey, the Archbishop of York and Papal Legate, were privately to summon Henry before them to answer a charge of living in incest. The case was to go "against" him, and he was to "submit" to the decision of the court. Wolsey could be counted upon to do whatever Henry wanted, and Warham was not expected to raise any opposition. He had been dubious about the legality of the marriage before it occurred, so he could now with a good grace declare it null and void – after the counsel appointed for the two sides had conducted their sham battle. Accordingly on May 17, 1527, Henry was summoned "to answer for eighteen years sinful cohabitation with Katherine." It was all preconcerted. But after two sittings, on the 20th and 31st of the month, the plan was abandoned. Katherine had learned from Iñigo de Mendoza, the Spanish ambassador, of what was afoot; it was dangerous to proceed further.

There was another reason for stopping. Just at this time the imperial army under the Duc de Bourbon, having their pay long in arrears, dragged their officers to the sack of Rome. This occurred on May 6; news of it reached England while Warham's and Wolsey's court was sitting. The Pope, who was now bottled up in Castel Sant' Angelo, could not possibly give any confirmation of the court's sentence.

Henry now had to explain to Katherine. He told her what Wolsey had already written to Lee and Ghinucci, his agents in Rome, that nothing was intended except a resolution of his scruples, but he managed to combine this with an expression of his conviction that he was living in sin. She was asked to associate herself with him in seeking a decision. Katherine saw through him and declared with a conviction at least equal to his own that she was his wife. He left her in tears having accomplished nothing.

Fisher innocently swallowed this explanation, which he received from Wolsey's own lips in June, and would in fact have expostulated with the Queen for being so blind to her own interests as not to consent to this harmless enquiry being made. Wolsey had some difficulty in persuading him not to go at once to Katherine with his fatherly rebuke. That would not have done because Fisher had no doubt as to the validity of her marriage and, by expressing this opinion, would have only strengthened her opposition. Leaving Katherine to be dealt with later, Wolsey went on to France, having in mind the scheme for getting himself commissioned to act for the Pope during his captivity. That scheme also failed.

Henry meanwhile, being fertile in expedients, had thought of another plan. He sent William Knight, his secretary, afterwards Bishop of Bath, to the Pope asking for two things. He did not ask outright for a divorce, as he knew that that would require a court hearing. But in the confident presumption that a divorce would be eventually obtained, he asked for a dispensation, in most ample terms, freeing him and the lady he might marry from any impediments. So far as Anne was concerned there was the possible impediment of a precontract with Percy. More important as a barrier were Henry's previous relations with Anne's sister. Affinity therefore had to be dispensed. Moreover, in case the divorce turned out to be more difficult to obtain than he expected, Henry asked for a dispensation for bigamy. Fortunately Wolsey met Knight at Compiégne and told him that not even the King's services to the Holy See quite warranted permission to take a second wife.*

The absurdity of the proceedings, the huge blunder that had been committed, showed Henry that only the Cardinal was competent to carry this business through, and so was of advantage

*It seems astounding that this request should have been even thought of. But Henry was aware of Old Testament polygamy and believed that, at least in such an exceptional case as his, it might be permitted to Christians. Later, in desperation, as we shall see, he did sound the Holy See about this.

to Wolsey. Anne, who hated him because of the Percy affair, had tried to act behind his back. She was brought to see that she must reach an understanding with the Cardinal and leave matters in his hands; after she was queen, she could take her revenge. Friedmann remarks that Henry's new instructions to Knight read "more like the composition of a schoolboy found out by the master against whom he plots, than like the letter of an absolute king." Now only the dispensation was to be asked for. It was readily given and was comprehensive, but it only meant that Henry might marry again when he was free to marry again.*

The masterly Wolsey now took charge. Clement having escaped to Orvieto on December 6, Stephen Gardiner and Edward Fox, the King's Almoner, followed him there, finding him installed in three small rooms where the ceilings were falling and the Pope's furniture, "bed and all," was not worth twenty nobles. There they sat with Clement, several times into the small hours, arguing the case, with Gardiner roughly browbeating the Pope and the Pope always parrying with unperturbed good

*Froude in a long appendix to the last of his volumes on Henry VIII says that of course it would be true that the King showed "amazing effrontery" and "a hardy insolence without parallel in history" for asking for a dispensation which was intended to remove an impediment similar to the one he was simultaneously declaring could not be dispensed by the Pope. At the same time he argues that Henry had never had any relations with Mary Boleyn. These, however, have been proved to the satisfaction of all historians. (See Gairdner's article, "Mary and Anne Boleyn," in the *English Historical Review,* Vol. VIII, pp. 53–60.) What has to be rejected is the belief of the Elizabethan historians, Harpsfield and Sanders, that Henry also had relations with Anne's mother, and that Anne may even have been his daughter. Though the date of Anne's birth is not quite certain — ranging from 1500 to 1507, with 1502 or 1503 as most probable — she was at least old enough to rule the more hideous supposition out. It would be unfair, however, to take advantage of the way Froude twice stuck his chin out here. The effrontery and insolence were less than might appear, for though the case of Henry and Mary Boleyn was "similar" to that of Henry and Katherine, they were at least sufficiently different to justify the King in his own mind. He was staking his case on the prohibition in Leviticus. But that applied only to a brother's widow. This being the law of God, so he maintained, could not be dispensed; whereas the other impediment was only part of canon law — like the prohibition of the marriage of cousins. Therefore it could, according to his argument, be dispensed. The decision finally reached by the Holy See was that both fell under canon law and were equally dispensable.

humour and skill. He protested that he was no canon lawyer himself and so would need advice. And when Gardiner told him that the Pope had all knowledge locked up in his breast, Clement waved a deprecating hand and answered that, in that event, he must have lost the key.

The instructions sent these English agents were that they should inform the Pope that he was probably labouring under a misapprehension and thought that the King had initiated his cause, not so much "from fear of his succession, but out of a vain affection or undue love to a gentlewoman of not such excellent qualities as she is here esteemed." They were to set the Holy Father right on these points. "The King's desire is founded upon justice, and does not spring from any grudge or displeasure to the Queen, whom the King honors and loves. . . . But as this matrimony is contrary to God's law, the King's conscience is grievously offended." But as for the "said gentlewoman," whose existence now had to be acknowledged, "the purity of her life, her constant virginity, her maidenly and womanly pudicity, her soberness, chasteness, meekness, humility, wisdom, descent right noble through high and regal blood" – she did, as a matter of fact, have a few drops of that from her Howard mother – "educated in all good and laudable qualities and manners, apparent aptness to procreation of children, with her other infinite good qualities" – these, in short, were the grounds on which the King's desire was founded.

To make things easy for the Pope he was not asked to make a declaration – which would have been embarrassing to him – that his predecessor, Julius II, had erred in giving a dispensation contrary to the law of God, though Henry never concealed that such was his conviction. Instead Clement was to declare the dispensation of Julius II invalid merely on the grounds of its technical defects. For good measure, Wolsey discovered another argument: even supposing that the marriage between Arthur and Katherine had never been consummated, it had taken place "in the face of the Church"; therefore there was the impediment of "public honesty." This argument, however, was not pressed long. Instead no less than five technical defects in the bull of dispensation were indicated, any one of which would invalidate it. Henry, it was said, had not been aware of the dispensation at the time it was given, in 1503; there had been misrepresentation, for the bull had been issued for the ostensible reason of preserving peace between England and Spain, but they *were* at peace at the time; people mentioned in the bull – Katherine's mother and Henry's father – were dead before the marriage took place; and finally Henry had, at the age of fourteen, made a disavowal of his betrothal and had thereby renounced the privileges of the dispensation. All the points were mere quibbles but it was hoped that they would serve, as such quibbles often do in law, to get the bull of Julius declared defective by Clement.

Wolsey, through his agents, asked and obtained a legatine commission to act in England to enquire into the matter. But the points for discussion were selected, and what was arranged for was, in effect, a prejudged decision. No appeal was to be admitted, on the points of law indicated in advance; as for the facts, there could be no appeal, for only those beyond dispute were to be considered.

Such was at least the general tenor of the decretal bull, though as it was of a secret character and was to be destroyed after being read to the King, we do not know the precise terms in which it was drawn. It is, however, reasonably safe to suppose that it followed the general lines of what the Pope was asked to sign, of which we have several but no sure drafts.* The supposition must be that Clement was ashamed of what he was doing and that he was trying to safeguard himself by some ambiguity that would render the commission of little if any force.

The Pope had shown great weakness, and was tacking desperately in the hope of escaping from a difficult situation instead of facing the issue squarely. It was not only with regard to Henry's matrimonial affairs that he was hesitant and shifty, for that was the cast of his mind. His excuse here was that he was

*See Thurston in *English Historical Review*, Vol. XIX (1904), pp. 340, 342.

confronted with a complex case and a political tangle that would have taxed the resources of the strongest of popes. That Clement was at the moment almost at the mercy of the Emperor, Katherine's nephew, must be given its due weight; any pope would have been obliged to step warily just then. Charles could not be alienated in the very midst of his efforts to deal with the Lutherans in Germany; on the other hand Henry's loyalty had to be held. Not until the imperial pressure was momentarily relieved in April, 1528, did Clement feel able to do anything at all. To help relieve this pressure Henry sent Clarencieux Herald, accompanied by the French Herald Toisson d'Or, to Charles at Burgos earlier that year with a declaration of war. That did not bother the Emperor unduly, as he knew this to be mainly a matter of form, designed to make Henry appear as the champion of the Papacy. He knew that England had no serious intention of prosecuting war against him. It was Lautrec's victories in Italy that made Clement feel a little safer as against Charles.

Throughout all the sad business, in so far as there was any favouritism it was for the benefit of the English King. The Papacy was not only indebted to him – not so deeply as Henry imagined, but still indebted; it wished, very cautiously to be sure, to give encouragement to any power capable of checking the imperial preponderance. Yet along with these political considerations, Clement must be credited with a determination that justice should not be violated. The blame that attaches to him is for seeking to accomplish this end by diplomacy and delay.

The Roman curia was notorious for taking its time about everything; this was an occasion when procrastination was deliberate. If the case could be dragged out long enough, the situation might change: Henry might die, Anne might die; Katherine might die; the mathematical chances were good that one of the principals would disappear. But there was another strong possibility: Anne might become Henry's mistress, if she was not that already. Clement might hope, from what he knew of men, and especially from what he had been told of Henry's character, that, once Anne had yielded to the King he would be much less eager to marry her. With a realism almost cynical, Clement balanced the probabilities and possibilities. He would play for time.

He did not neglect to explore other avenues of escape. If the King was troubled in conscience about the dispensation given by Julius, he would give another dispensation to cover the matter and set the King's scruples at rest. That was of course the last thing Henry wanted, so it was refused. Nor was Clement's hint taken that the ecclesiastical authorities in England deal with the case and so relieve him of responsibility. Henry was going to be content with nothing less than a divorce that came from Rome. With a sigh, regretting what he was doing and regretting it still more afterwards, the Pope signed the decretal bull on April 13.

He did even more than that for Henry; he provided him with the legates he wished. Wolsey naturally would sit on it as papal legate for England, though had the Pope known of the collusive suit of the previous May, he would have been obliged to rule out the Cardinal of York as invalidated. As the English had asked that Campeggio be associated with Wolsey, Campeggio was appointed. He was amply qualified as a distinguished canon lawyer — he had been a professor at Bologna, but the death of his wife in 1509, after having borne him five children, opened for him a career in the Church. His qualifications, however, to be an impartial judge were somewhat impaired by the fact that he had held, nominally, the English bishoprics of Hereford and Salisbury. It would be difficult for him to do anything that might jeopardize his revenues.

Clement weighed these considerations and, with them, another; Campeggio might be under obligations to Henry, but he was an honest man and he could be trusted to carry out his instructions. Moreover, by appointing him the Pope saw another opportunity for delay — not a great delay but enough to be useful, for every week gained was something. Campeggio suffered so badly from gout that he would be obliged to travel very slowly without being unduly suspected of having a diplomatic illness. Therefore, though he left Rome in June, he did not reach

Lyons before August 22, Paris in September, and London in October. Wolsey in his impatience offered five hundred crowns for his travelling expenses and all the horses, mules, and money that were needed in France. Campeggio, to keep his hands free, and not to be rushed, insisted on paying his own way. And when after his arrival he was offered the immensely wealthy bishopric of Durham, he declined that obvious bribe. If he permitted the son who accompanied him to accept an English knighthood, that could be looked upon as being no more than a courtesy which it would be discourteous to refuse.

Meanwhile, at Epiphany, the Pope was taken ill while saying Mass, and on February 6 the false report reached England that he was actually dead. Wolsey at once set the wheels in operation, greased with plentiful bribes, for his own election. Only six key votes needed to be bought, so it was calculated, for Wolsey to win. But in the event of Wolsey losing again for the third time, it was under consideration in England to put in operation the plan that had been discussed in the summer of 1527 and set the Cardinal of York up, supported by England and France, as an antipope. Even to that extreme was Henry ready to go to obtain his divorce. That schism would have been less disastrous than the one that actually occurred.

Clement, however, recovered, and Campeggio carried out his instructions. He was not to open the hearings of the legatine court at once but first see whether it was not possible to reconcile the King and Queen. This looked rather hopeful. Anne was not there, as Henry had packed her off to Hever Castle so that she should not be in evidence. Moreover, as there was that summer of 1528 a new and unusually severe outbreak of the sweating sickness, Henry, as usual in terror of his life, was at Mass every morning, often receiving Holy Communion with Katherine and joining in the other pious practices of the Franciscan tertiary. He could not, in spite of this, forbear writing more of his greasily ardent letters to his absent inamorata. She must not be allowed to feel that she was in any danger of being thrown over.

Campeggio had another ingenious suggestion. If the King was troubled about the succession and feared that Mary would not be accepted as queen, perhaps she could marry her half-brother. He believed a dispensation would be obtainable, under the circumstances, for that.* The Duke of Richmond as an illegitimate son might not be acceptable, standing alone; but as Mary's husband his position would be much stronger, and so would hers, when she was married to her father's son. There was one weakness – apart from its feasibility in law – in the plan: it was that, though Mary was now almost of a marriageable age, Richmond was only nine. But of course the real objection was that Henry was determined to have a divorce and marry Anne Boleyn.

As soon as it was evident that a reconciliation between the King and Queen was going to be impossible, Henry's conscience being as adamant as ever, Campeggio proceeded to the second of his instructions – to persuade Katherine to enter a convent, a device that had facilitated Louis XII's divorce from Jeanne de Valois. Katherine need not even become a nun, strictly speaking. All she would have to do was to live in a convent, keeping up her royal state, and retaining her dowry and the charge of her daughter. It was what was termed "lax religion." She was to put herself in the hands of the legatine court and not contest or appeal against its decision. Terms would be made easy and honourable for her.

Honourable? Katherine did not consider the terms honourable at all. Truth must be served. She told Campeggio that she had come as intact a virgin from Arthur's bed as from her mother's womb. As a man he believed her, as a lawyer he doubted whether her assertion would stand in a court of law. His personal opinion was that the question as to whether her marriage to Arthur had been consummated or not was really irrelevant to the issue, and

*This suggestion seems astounding, but it must be remembered that, though Campeggio in his desperation entertained it, the idea did not originate with him but with Wolsey. On this point Father Thurston's article in the *American Catholic Quarterly Review,* Vol. XXIX (1904), pp. 301–302, might be consulted.

that even had it been consummated, the Pope had the power to dispense. But he knew that there were canonists and theologians who held otherwise, and he could not take it upon himself to deliver a definitive ruling on the point. Indeed, under the terms of his commission he was forbidden to make such a ruling. It was something that the Pope would himself not undertake to do until after thorough consultation with the cardinals.

There was another difficulty, another cause for delay, though this was not of Campeggio's making. He had been strictly ordered to read the decretal bull to Wolsey and the King, but on no account to let it pass out of his own hands; after this had been done, he was to burn it. Now, as that document empowered either of the legates, if they were unable to act together, to give a decision on the points of law, Henry very much wished to get hold of it. Had this been permitted, of course Campeggio would never have got it back. But as Henry had somehow to get possession of the bull, which was useless to him unless its contents were made public, he sent off agents to the Pope begging him to permit this. Clement's answer was to send further instructions to Campeggio to destroy the bull at once. Campeggio did so.

A fresh complication had arisen. Katherine had received from the Emperor a copy of a brief supplementing the original dispensation; it had been sent at the request of Ferdinand to comfort Isabella on her death-bed. She had been worried that the first document had twice used the word *forsan* (peradventure) when referring to the consummation of Katherine's marriage to Arthur. And though she had been solemnly assured by Doña Elvira Manuel that this consummation had never occurred, Katherine's parents knew how tricky Henry VII was; therefore to protect themselves and Katherine against a possible claim that, as she had been truly married, her dowry would revert to the King of England as his son's heir, they asked the new Pope, Leo X, to protect her with an amplification of the first dispensation, He did this with a declaration that the dispensation had been given "on other good and definite grounds" (which were carefully left unspecified). And the word *forsan* was now significantly omitted. Had this not been done there was no telling but that Henry VII would not have stuck to that portion of Katherine's dowry already paid, broken the betrothal contract with Prince Henry, and sent Katherine home. As we know that the fourteen-year-old boy was made secretly to repudiate his engagement, the precautions of Ferdinand and Isabella were well advised.

The discovery of this document by Dr. Puebla's son among his father's papers came like a bombshell. Henry took the line that it was impermissible as evidence unless the original could be produced and refused the offer of a notarially attested copy, such as would have ordinarily been accepted in any court of law. When Charles refused to let him have the original he asserted that this must be because it was a forgery that would not bear examination. His "conscience," he said, told him that it must be a forgery!

There was some irregularity in the dating of this second brief, though this has been accounted for on the ground that it was antedated in order to make it accord with the first dispensation. Nor is there much weight in the argument that it was produced too opportunely for credence, for that would apply to any document produced only when it was needed. Dr. Puebla must be presumed to have shown the brief to Henry VII and then retained it in his own safe-keeping. It is enough to say here that the document has been found in the Vienna state archives, and while some historians are still inclined to question its authenticity, it has been examined by Friedmann who reports, "It has been inspected by several other persons well versed in paleography, and from none of them have I heard any expression of doubt as to its authenticity."* Moreover the terms of the brief correspond to the terms that Ferdinand instructed his ambassador at Rome, Rojas, to ask for.

Henry was of course very anxious to get the original of this brief in his possession. But it is worth noting that, doubting very much whether it would be sent, and realizing that it might be

*_Anne Boleyn_, Vol. II, p. 327.

argued that its existence invalidated the decretal commission, whose powers were limited to the examination of a few carefully selected points, he sent Sir Francis Bryan and Peter Vannes to Rome to sound the Holy See about that project for bigamy which, at Wolsey's advice, he had discarded the previous year. It was not until two days after the departure of these envoys that he dispatched Drs. Knight and William Benet to Rome asking for an amplification of the powers of the commission, under which it would be able to declare the brief a forgery. All of which, it must be remembered, happened before the legatine court had opened its deliberations, and indicates the confusion into which Henry had been thrown.

The Legates, of course, could not make any pronouncement without having seen the brief and heard arguments from both sides as to its authenticity, so Henry persuaded the counsel who had been appointed for Katherine's defence to write to Spain asking that the brief be produced, urging that it was necessary for the Queen's defence. Whatever their doubts may have been as to the use that would be made of the document, were it received, they did not dare venture to express them. Fortunately Henry overshot the mark by making Katherine write as well.

Katherine was no fool. Though she wrote the letter dictated to her, she contrived to send a secret message to the Emperor, warning him not to take her letter at its face value. This message was very difficult to smuggle out, so closely was she watched to prevent any private communications. But Mendoza, the Spanish ambassador, managed to get into her apartments in disguise and a messenger named Francisco Felipez was dispatched to Spain. When he got as far as Abbeville he was caught by Wolsey's spies and his head and arm were broken. Luckily he did not have a scrap of paper upon him, but as he was unable to continue his journey to Spain in his condition, the only thing he could do was to return to London and report what had happened.

What Katherine was allowed to do was to send one of her chaplains, a man named Thomas Abell, to Spain with a letter to the Emperor asking in general terms for help. Nothing was said in the letter about the brief, but a monitory message was entrusted to the Spaniard who was to accompany the English priest as guide and interpreter. Nothing, except the harmless letter, was given to Abell of whom, as he was an Englishman, Katherine was a little suspicious. This was why Henry permitted him to go.

His selection was lucky for Katherine. On the way to Spain he learned from his companion what the message was that the Queen was sending and determined to appoint himself her emissary. Once in Spain he gave the strongest warnings against the production of the brief; this, had it ever reached England, would have either been destroyed or falsified in some way. Abell was a clever man and, what is better, a brave man. He remained Katherine's steadfast champion, later writing in her defence and, after six years' imprisonment in the Tower, was hanged in 1540 at Smithfield.

As Henry did not get the brief, he wrote to the Pope demanding that he declare it a forgery. But this of course Clement could not do; nobody could do that except after full examination of the matter. The most that Charles would undertake to do was to show the Pope the brief in person; he would not allow the document to pass out of his own hands, and he was unable to visit Rome just then. In England therefore the case had to proceed without the brief. Its authenticity had to be left, for legal purposes, an open question. But though it would have completely cut the ground under Henry's case as to the technical invalidity of the dispensation issued by Julius II, it was not a factor in the decision in Katherine's favour reached in 1534 in Rome. The original dispensation was then pronounced quite sufficient as it stood.

Little of the evidence presented at the legatine court was really relevant. If it could have been shown that the dispensation of 1503 was technically defective, an annulment could have been pronounced on those grounds. Yet, as a reliance on mere legal tricks would have created a scandal in a case of such notoriety, Henry's witnesses mainly tried to prove that Katherine's marriage with Arthur had been consummated. It had no bearing upon the argument that the dispensation was technically invalid, but it did prepare the ground for the new argument upon which Henry was already preparing to fall back – that the Pope could not dispense at all for a marriage – a real marriage – of a woman to her brother-in-law.

It must be admitted that ordinary presumption must be in favour of the consummation of the marriage, even the marriage of a boy of fifteen to a girl of seventeen. The fact that Arthur was not very robust may lessen the probabilities slightly, but that he died so soon after marriage was used to support the suggestion that being married was too much for his adolescent constitution. Against this there could only be Katherine's steady denial of consummation, and while nobody who has studied her character is likely to doubt her word, her legal case (if it depended solely on this) was not very strong. Henry's meanness* was that of availing himself of such a presumption and of allowing witnesses to give evidence tending to support it.

What most of these witnesses had to relate was what everybody already knew, and their evidence was given in rather general terms. Among those who took the stand were the dowager Duchess of Norfolk, Sir William Thomas, Sir Anthony Poins, Lord Darcy, Lord Mountjoy, and Sir Henry Guildford. They testified to what nobody denied, that Arthur and Katherine had been duly (and of course publicly) bedded.

There was, however, testimony of a somewhat different sort.** The Earl of Shrewsbury "believed that the Prince had known

*Gairdner in his *English Church in the Sixteenth Century* (p. 93), says that Henry *knew* that she was a virgin when he married her. I cannot see upon what he bases this. Henry, indeed, never actually denied the truth of what Katherine said, but it seems to me probable — almost to the point of certainty — that he did not himself know the fact of the matter. At all events he did not know, when he married his fifth wife, Katherine Howard, in 1540, that she was *not* a virgin, though by that time he was "experienced." How could the callow boy of 1509 have been better informed?

**The evidence may be found in *Letters and Papers*, Vol. IV, part 3, but was previously given by Lord Herbert.

his lady carnally." His reason for this belief was that he himself had been competent for this when he was married at eighteen. The Marquis of Dorset deposed that the Prince had been of "a good sanguine complexion, and able, as he supposed, for that purpose." The Marquis also said that he had heard one Maurice St. John relate how, the morning after the wedding, the Prince had called for drink and had confided, "I have been in Spain this night." The Duke of Suffolk said that he also had heard St. John tell that story. He added that St. John had also told him that the Prince had begun to decline after his marriage.*

This tale, repeated at second hand by several witnesses, was the main item of evidence. The Duke of Norfolk had heard it, and he believed that a boy of fifteen was capable of consummating marriage, as he himself had been capable at that age. Sir Arthur Willoughby, however, improved on St. John (now dead and so unable to appear as a witness) by deposing that the Prince had said to him, "Willoughby, give me a cup of ale, for this night I have been in the midst of Spain." Prince Arthur had also said, "Masters, it is good pastime to have a wife." We must believe that Arthur did say something like this, though what importance should be attached to the boyish boast is another matter.

Archbishop Warham testified that he had questioned the validity of the King's marriage, before it occurred, in conversation with Bishop Fox of Winchester and Henry VII; but after the dispensation had been given he did not question it any more, until the King's conscience began to trouble him. The aged Nicholas West, Bishop of Ely – he, like Warham, was among the counsel who had been appointed to defend the Queen – said he could depose nothing concerning the *carnalis copula,* but that he doubted it, because the Queen denied it. This was virtually all the evidence, except that taken, as a matter of form, regarding the dates of Arthur's birth and death and the method of dating bulls – this last intended to cast doubts on the authen-

*Such was indeed the fact, though whether it had anything to do with his marriage, as cause with effect, is another matter.

ticity of the supplementary brief. And a statement by Bishop Fox, who had died in October, 1528, was read, telling of the King's repudiation of his betrothal contract when he was fourteen. It was not much to have elicited from thirty-seven witnesses (actually about thirty, as some of them appeared more than once), but it amounted to this: as Arthur was of an age when he could have consummated his marriage, he must be presumed to have done so. The only bit of direct "proof" is what Arthur is supposed to have said, and one is left wondering whether he had really done more than make a humorous answer to the kind of ribald jest which young bridegrooms (and also brides) were rarely spared in that not over-delicate society.

Katherine heard none of this evidence, as she refused to recognize the authority of the court and withdrew before any of the witnesses were summoned. But she did something so dramatic and moving as to outweigh everything else. As this was not presented as formal testimony it could not be accepted by the court, though it is entirely convincing at the bar of history.

The court opened on May 31, 1529, but only to appoint counsel and to summon the two sovereigns to appear on June 18. It was on that day that Katherine, who had already got an appeal through to Rome, protested against the partiality of the tribunal. It was on the 21st that the court reconvened to pronounce on her protest.

When the crier called, "Henry, King of England," he answered, "Here," from his raised seat. But when the crier called, "Katherine, Queen of England," instead of answering, she rose and went to where the King sat and, kneeling before him, said in her broken English: "Sir, I beseech you to do me justice and right, and take some pity upon me, for I am a poor woman and a stranger, born out of your dominions, having here no indifferent counsel and less assurance of friendship. Alas! Sir, how have I offended you? . . . I take God to be my witness I have been to you a true and loyal wife, ever conformable to your will and pleasure. Never did I gainsay your mind, but always submitted myself in all things wherein you had any delight, whether it were little or much, without grudging or any sign of discontent. I have loved for your sake all men whom you have loved, whether I had cause or not, were they friends or foes. I have been your wife this twenty years, by whom you have had many children, and I put it to your conscience if there be any cause that you can allege either of dishonesty or of any other matter lawfully to put me from you, I am willing to depart with shame and rebuke; but if there be none, then I pray you let me have justice at your hands." Then she came to the issue she knew would be made the central one: "And when ye had me first, I take God to be my judge, I was a true maid, without touch of man. And whether this be true or not, I put to your conscience."

Henry did not answer the kneeling woman. At last she rose and, making him a low curtsey, walked on the arm of her attendant, Mr. Griffith, towards the door.

At this the King ordered the crier to summon her again.

The clear voice rang out, "Katherine, Queen of England, come into the court!"

Griffith whispered to her, "Lo, you are called again."

She only returned, in a voice all could hear, "Go on. It is no fit court for me, therefore I will not tarry."

It was then that Henry spoke: "I will in her absence declare unto you all: She hath been to me a true, obedient wife, and as comfortable as I could wish or desire." It was the least he could say, and after he had finished, Wolsey took the opportunity to ask: "I humbly beseech your Highness to declare unto this audience whether I have been the first and chief mover of this matter or not, for I am suspected of all men."

"My Lord Cardinal," Henry answered, "you have rather advised me to the contrary than been the mover of the same."* He went on to attribute his uneasiness of conscience to what the Bishop of Tarbes had said, and also to the counsel of his

*That was true at least to this extent: when Wolsey discovered that the King meant to divorce Katherine in order to marry Anne Boleyn, he begged him, on his knees for a couple of hours, to give up the project.

confessor, the Bishop of Lincoln, saying that the Bishop had advised him to consult the other bishops. But as for Katherine, "I have not had any displeasure in the person or age of the Queen, with whom I would be well contented (if our marriage stand by the law of God) as with any woman alive." He reiterated that he would accept the judgement of the court "to which, God willing, I will be well contented to submit myself and obey the same."

All this, though magnificently said, for the King was a most impressive speaker, was full of palpable insincerities. Henry had submitted himself to that court, whose judges he had handpicked, only because he took it for granted that its decision must be in his favour. He could afford to praise the virtues of the Queen, which were undeniable, as he knew that they would have no bearing on the issue. But so anxious was he to cut the best possible figure that on the previous November 8 he had made a speech in Bridewell Palace — that too a magnificent one — in which he explained his position to his people, about whose good opinion he was still sensitive. He was thinking of the succession, he told them, and the likelihood of civil wars after his death; so he had asked the Holy See to judge whether or not he was living in wicked incest. This was his sole motive, he protested, "before God and on the word of a prince." That at least was the version given by Hall. Du Bellay, the French ambassador, adds that there were some remarks to the effect that if any man spoke of the marriage other than he ought, he would soon learn who was master, "and his head should fly, though it were the highest in the kingdom."

Henry knew Katherine to be not only popular but beloved, so he would say nothing against her. At Bridewell he had said: "As touching the Queen, if it may be adjudged by the law of God that she is my lawful wife, there was never anything more pleasant and acceptable to me in my life . . . so that if I were to marry again, if the marriage might be good, I would surely choose her above all other women." But there was the nub of the matter: his mind was clamped close. As Campeggio reported when writing to Rome, an angel out of heaven would be unable to convince Henry that his marriage to Katherine was valid.

There were many theologians who would have agreed with Henry on his interpretation of Leviticus. Many, if not most, of the English bishops did, though in some instances their sincerity may be suspect. One of the bishops, however, the most learned and venerated of them all, was very positive on the other side. This was John Fisher of Rochester. When on June 28 a document was produced in court by Warham upholding the King's position, and Fisher discovered that his name was among the subscribers, as though signed by him and under his seal, he at once rose to protest.

"No, sir," he said to Warham's face, "not so, under correction; for you have not my hand and seal."

Henry took the paper and, turning to Fisher, asked, "No? Is not that your hand and seal?"

"No, forsooth," answered Fisher.

"How say you to that?" the King asked Warham.

"Sir, it is his hand," the Archbishop told him.

Then Fisher said that the Archbishop had indeed asked for his signature but had been refused it, adding, "My hand and seal shall never be set to such a document, God willing."

It was an awkward moment for Warham, who was being publicly accused of forgery. He said lamely, "You say the truth. Such words you used, but you were fully resolved at the last that *I* should subscribe your name and put your seal, and you would allow the same."

It is impossible to imagine that John Fisher would stoop to such an evasion. He retorted coldly, "All which, under correction, my lord, is untrue."

He had given the Primate of England the lie direct. The best that can be said for Warham is that, before death came for him, he too found the courage to stand firm.

Fisher went even further. He handed in a "book," or as we should say, a longish statement of his position in writing. In presenting it he told the court that he had forborne until then to express his opinion, and that if he did so now it was not to be unfaithful to the King, or neglectful of the duty he owed the truth. It was also to avoid the damnation of his soul. He concluded with, "As John the Baptist in olden times regarded it as impossible to die more gloriously than in a cause of matrimony (and it was not then as holy as it has now become, by the shedding of Christ's blood) he could not encourage himself more ardently, more effectually, or face any extreme peril with greater confidence than by taking the Baptist as his example."

Henry said nothing in public to Fisher, but he was very angry and wrote a bitter and sarcastic reply to his old tutor, complaining, justly enough, that it would have been better to have made his protest to him privately. He made another effective point — that Fisher, "as a religious and obedient prelate [should] acquiesce in the sentence of his Holiness who had sent judges here, admitting the necessity of the case, rather than thus accuse the Pope of levity, as if the cause which he had remitted here for decision was so clear." But Fisher of course had no intention of trying to take the decision out of the hands of the court. He had all the more right to give his opinion in full after the trick that Warham had attempted to play. We still have the copy of Henry's statement that was sent to Fisher, with the Bishop's marginal comments. He probably knew that he had signed his own death warrant.

Meanwhile Katherine, who was as sure of the justice of her cause as Henry was of his, went her usual serene and smiling way. This was a good deal to the annoyance of the King, who thought her conscience should be at least perplexed and she downcast. At the same time he was glad to have her continue little wifely services for him, such as seeing to the laundering and the mending of his linen, though this was greatly to the irritation of Anne Boleyn, who was afraid that, out of mere comfortable habit, Henry might take the Queen back.

He had, however, no intention of doing so. Even during the

sessions of the court there were attempts made by Wolsey and Campeggio, sometimes separately and sometimes together, to persuade her to be more reasonable. Every possible argument was used, from promises to threats. If she lost her case – and they let her see that they considered this inevitable – she would be disgraced. On the other hand, if she would give up the contest, she would rank as the King's sister, and could bring up Mary. As they saw that she was troubled about Mary's being disinherited, they undertook to guarantee that the Princess' right to the succession should be safeguarded. Because of the good faith of her parents at the time of their marriage she would escape bastardization, whereas bastardization could not be escaped if the law had to run its course. That Katherine should have had such pressure put on her by the men who were judges of her case would seem to be most improper, though perhaps it may be partially justified by the fact that the court hearings were very informal, with apparently anybody free to make personal statements or explanations at any time.

It was a few days after the reading of John Fisher's "book" that Henry sent for Wolsey to go to him at Bridewell. When the Cardinal left the palace with the Bishop of Carlisle in his barge and was mopping that heavy red-jowled face of his, he responded to Carlisle's remark that it was a hot day with, "Yea, if you had been as well chafed as I have been within this hour, you would say it was *very* hot." He had just spent an hour listening to Henry rant.

To recover his composure Wolsey went straight to bed. Two hours later the Earl of Wiltshire – Anne Boleyn's father had recently been given that higher title and her brother had become Viscount Rochford – arrived at York Palace. He bore orders from the King that the two Cardinals were to go at once to see the Queen. It was at this interview, as described by Cavendish, that Wolsey bitterly charged Wiltshire with having "put fancies into the head of the King."

Wolsey got up and dressed and, having picked up Campeggio, went to try once more what they could do with Katherine.

She was sitting in her reception room with some of her ladies-in-waiting, skeining silk, perfectly composed, as though nothing were happening, and smiling as always. Even when she saw her enemy Wolsey, she rose smiling and came forward to greet the Cardinals, a skein of red silk round her neck.

Wolsey said, "If it please your Grace to go to your privy chamber, we will show you the cause of our coming."

At this her face grew a little hard. "My lords," she returned, "if you have anything to say to me, say it before all these folk, for I fear nothing that you can say to me or against me; but I am willing all the world should both see and hear it." She preferred to have witnesses, lest Wolsey should afterwards give a distorted account of the interview.

The Cardinal of York began to speak to her in Latin.

She cut him short with, "Nay, good my lord, speak to me in English, though I do understand Latin."

They explained that they had come from the King to "know her mind" and also "to declare to you secretly our counsels and opinions."

She replied that she thanked them for their goodwill but she could hardly make answer without deliberation and advice, "For I need counsel in this case which concerns me so nearly, and friends I have none. Also, my lords, I am a poor woman of too weak capacity to answer such noble persons of wisdom as you are in so weighty a matter."

This was said for the benefit of the other people in the room. She knew that she had many friends in England; indeed that, except for the Boleyn circle and the court sycophants, nearly everybody was her partisan. There was no need for her to talk about her "weak capacity"; she had not only played the best of possible cards in relying upon an absolute honesty as her best defence, she had made the best of legal moves in refusing to appear before the legatine court and in appealing directly to the Pope.

She now took the two Cardinals by the hand into her private sitting-room and shut the door, so though Cavendish could hear her loud emphatic voice, he could not distinguish what was said. It is easy enough to guess what this was. It could have been nothing but a last-minute appeal to her to enter a convent and drop the contest. In offering this Henry must have thought he was being generous. He was now sure what the verdict of the judges would be, and he expected a decision within a few days. He wished to spare Katherine the humiliation that would follow; he was giving her a last chance to retire gracefully.

Campeggio had several times done his best to induce the Queen to consent to the compromise, and, while he admired her constancy and believed her to be telling the truth, he also considered her unreasonably obstinate. "I assure you," he wrote to Salviati, "that from her conversation I have always thought her to be a prudent lady, and now more than ever. But as she can, without much prejudice to herself, avoid such great perils and difficulties, her obstinacy in refusing this advice does not please me." Such a compromise was what the Pope himself wished; it would have got him out of a most embarrassing position. On one side the Emperor was pressing, on the other side Henry. And Henry was already hinting at schism. As Campeggio wrote to Cardinal Salviati on October 26, 1528: "[Wolsey] often impresses upon me that, if this divorce be not granted, the authority of the Holy See in the kingdom will be at an end." Though this may have been another instance of Wolseian bluff, Campeggio realized that Clement would probably lose Henry's political support of the Papacy. Wolsey was sincere to this extent: he had counted upon the granting of the divorce attaching Henry all the more firmly to the Holy See. He therefore thought that, in threatening the Pope, he was working in the Pope's best interest. All the difficulties would have been solved had Katherine only been accommodating.

The decretal bull which Campeggio had brought with him to England, and had been ordered to destroy — as it was not meant to be of any effect — ostensibly provided for a prearranged verdict in Henry's favor. Therefore Clement must be admitted to have acted trickily. The later instructions sent to Campeggio also looked like a trick. Though what he was told to do may have been technically "correct," it was also open to criticism as sharp practice. When the court convened on July 23, 1529, expecting sentence, Campeggio rose and announced that, as it formed part of the Roman consistory, it must follow the Roman rules. The vacation had now begun; the court would not meet again until October 1. Actually the Pope had, on July 13, revoked the case to Rome.

All this was disingenuous, to say the least. Clement had no intention that the court should meet again in England. Though Campeggio did in fact stay on in England until October, as it was possible that Clement might change his mind again and allow the hearings to continue there, neither Campeggio nor anybody else could have had any real hope of this. Henry was left feeling that, at the very moment when victory was within his grasp, it had been snatched away.

Wolsey had been hurrying on the proceedings of the court to prevent what his agents at Rome had warned him was about to happen. They had therefore been instructed to play for delay, to hold off the advocation a few weeks longer. But now Campeggio followed his announcement by saying that he could not give judgement until he had consulted the Pope further. He added that he had not come for any favour or reward, or in fear of any person alive. The defendant's appeal would have to be heard. "I am an old man," he concluded, "both weak and sickly, and look every hour for death; what shall it avail me to put my soul in danger of God's displeasure, to my utter damnation, for the favour of any prince in this world?" He at least had acted with what was, upon the whole, considerable dignity, in view of the position in which he had been placed.

No sooner was the court dissolved than Suffolk, prompted by Henry, stood up and roared in anger, "By the Mass, now I see that the old-said saw is true, that there was never legate nor cardinal that did good in England!"

Wolsey was of an irascible temper, but he controlled himself and said quietly: "Sir, of all men within this realm, ye have least cause to dispraise cardinals; for if I, poor cardinal, had not been, you should have had at this present no head upon your shoulders. You best know what friendship I have shown you. I never did reveal it to any person until now, either to my own praise or your dishonour." It was he, of course, who had saved Suffolk from Henry's wrath at the time of his unauthorized marriage to Henry's sister. Dismayed though he was by the turn of events, he could not but say, for the benefit of all there, "Consider that we be but commissioners for a time, and cannot, ne may not, by virtue of our commission proceed to judgement, without the knowledge and consent of our authority of him obtained, which is the Pope."

Both Legates had been from the start in a difficult situation. Campeggio had written to Cardinal Salviati: "When I shall know positively that the King is in the wrong, I shall be found ready to give sentence against him fearlessly, even were I to suffer death that moment; and of this do not doubt." But he continued, "I understand that the desire of His Holiness is that we should not go on to pronounce judgement, and that I keep on procrastinating as long as I can." As procrastination was no longer possible, he ended the hearings.

Wolsey's situation was much worse than that of Campeggio. He was committed to the obtaining of the divorce and had assured the King that it would be obtained if his advice were followed. But everything had gone wrong, and as early as June 24, just after the trial had commenced, he had lamented: "The Pope has refused all the concessions which, relying on him, I had promised the King . . . and that will be my ruin." It is true that, in giving the secret decretal bull, the Pope had given a promise that he did not intend to keep. Afterwards Clement was to say that it was only a conditional promise, depending upon Katherine's willingness to co-operate. As she had refused all compromise but instead had made an appeal to Rome, he could not refuse to hear that appeal. Had he done so, the whole system of papal justice would have been discredited. Even so, he emerged from the sad business with little credit to himself.

CHAPTER SEVEN

Eclipse of the Cardinal

THE story of King Henry's divorce must be interrupted at this point by that of the fall of Cardinal Wolsey. This was directly due to the Cardinal's failure over the divorce, and for a while – so long as Wolsey lived – nothing further of importance was done about the divorce. The collapse of that grandiose power seemed for the moment to be the event that overshadowed everything else.

Nothing happened to Wolsey until Cardinal Campeggio's departure, perhaps out of fear that Campeggio himself might be involved, for though he held an English bishopric, he was not one of Henry's subjects and he also enjoyed diplomatic immunity. Moreover, something was going to be done which could not be done except when Campeggio was in the very act of leaving. It was something that gave Wolsey a faint chance of survival.

That Wolsey was out of favour was, however, instantly clear, though he continued to hold his position as lord chancellor and to act as papal legate. Signs of what was impending appeared when Anne Boleyn's father proceeded to collect the revenues of the see of Durham, which the King had assigned to him some little while before but which Wiltshire dared not try to collect until August. During the same month Rowland Phillips, the Vicar of Croydon, a man who had been so stirred by the publication of More's *Utopia* that he wished to be appointed bishop there to bring the Utopians into the Church, wrote to Wolsey: "I have been with the Abbot of Wigmore and showed him your gracious mind, that he should have forty marks pension; which of late he would have taken gladly, but now, as he trusts to a great change, and especially to the extinction of your authority, he refuses the offer." In face of things like these the Cardinal could only brace himself to meet impending fate.

It was not long in coming.

In the middle of September Wolsey went with Campeggio, who was about to take farewell of the King, to Grafton in Northamptonshire. There, from the reception he met with, he got an inkling, if he had not had it before, of what he might expect.

Out of courtesy to the foreign Cardinal both men were received by Henry's officers with the usual ceremony, after which Wolsey, having shown Campeggio to his room, was about to go to his own when he was told that none had been prepared for him. The situation was for the moment saved by Sir Henry Norris, the Groom of the Stole, who offered Wolsey the use of his own room while another was being made ready.

When the two Cardinals were conducted into the King's presence he was sufficiently affable, but there were many who had crowded in with them in order to watch the King's face. There had been bets that he would refuse to speak to Wolsey, and this would have been to many a welcome sight. Instead Henry bent down to the kneeling figure in scarlet silk and drew him up with both hands, almost as friendly as in the old days. He even took Wolsey apart to a window recess and talked with him alone.

Then he said to Wolsey: "Go to your dinner, and take my Lord Cardinal to keep you company, and after dinner I will speak further with you." Henry that day was dining privately with Anne Boleyn in her room.

At dinner the two Cardinals sat with some members of the Council, and Wolsey happened to remark that it would be a good thing if the King sent his non-resident bishops and chaplains home to look after their charges. At once the Duke of Norfolk seized upon that chance word and growled, "Yea, marry, and so it were meet for you to do also."

Wolsey answered in a more humble tone than he was wont to use, "I would be very well contented therewith if it were the King's pleasure, and with his Grace's leave to go to my cure at Winchester."

Norfolk said icily: "Nay, to your benefice of York, where your greatest honor and charge is."

The conversation passed to other topics, but Wolsey knew from this that the Council did not want him near the King. He was to go as far away as possible, to the York he had never visited, though he had been appointed its archbishop fifteen years ago.

Cavendish heard afterwards that Anne, dining with Henry that day, showed herself distinctly annoyed that he had received Wolsey as he had. She went so far as to tell him, "There is never a nobleman but if he had done half so much as he hath done, were well worthy to lose his head." The King returned with mild amusement, "I perceive you are none of my Lord Cardinal's friends."

She had, however, worked upon Henry successfully. For though after dinner he again talked privately with Wolsey until it was dark – so that the Cardinal's enemies were afraid he had triumphed over Mistress Anne – he found when it was time to go to bed that he was not going to be lodged in the King's house and so was obliged to go by torchlight to a Mr. Empston's house near by, a very humiliating thing.

He clung to one hope; the King had told him at parting that he would like to see him again in the morning. But when morning came and he went to Grafton, it was only to be informed that the King had already left. He had said good-bye to Campeggio but he pointedly omitted this courtesy to Wolsey.

There was nothing for it but for the Cardinals to leave after an uncomfortable dinner.

From that day Wolsey was waiting for the blow to fall. He still had, however – though this was something he did not know – one very slim chance. It was that when Campeggio's baggage was searched at Dover, as happened prior to his sailing, the Pope's decretal bull would be found. If it was there Wolsey might have recovered his position; he would have been needed to pronounce the divorce under the terms he knew to be in that document. Either commissioner was empowered to do this, if they could not act together.

This search was an outrageous act. It was done under the pretence that Campeggio was suspected of carrying out of the kingdom most of Wolsey's portable property – his best jewels at least – so that the English Cardinal would have something to fall back on later. Even had Campeggio not been privileged as the Pope's Legate, the customs officials had no right to search the baggage of a man who was leaving England, but only of one entering. That, however, is what they did, turning over every article of clothing, looking into linings and into shoes, to find what would have been to Henry the most precious thing in the world. They did not find it; Campeggio had long since destroyed it.*

The Italian Cardinal at once protested to the King. He had in reply a letter from Henry in which he notes that the Cardinal considers what had been done "disrespect shown to the pontifical dignity, and the violation of your legatine authority." Henry dismisses the incident as a "trifling offence," and tells Campeggio that his legateship automatically expired when he terminated the court proceedings. "I wonder," he added, darkly threatening Praemunire, "that you are so ignorant of the laws of this country, seeing you are a bishop here, and bound to respect my royal dignity, as not to be afraid to use the title of legate when it has become defunct." After getting that letter, dated October 22, Campeggio was glad to be allowed to sail on the 26th.

Couriers had three weeks before hastened to London with the

*Froude says that "according to tradition" Campeggio had with him those letters of Henry's to Anne Boleyn that found their way to Rome. The "tradition" is merely a gratuitous supposition and one demonstrably false. However those letters got to Rome, it was not in Campeggio's baggage. Every scrap of writing it contained was examined. The letters would have been instantly confiscated had they been there.

news that the Bull could not be found. So swiftly did events move that it would seem that the charges against Wolsey had already been formally drawn up to permit them to be used instantly. On October 9 a writ of Praemunire was presented.

The Dukes of Norfolk and Suffolk were sent to Wolsey to demand that he surrender the Great Seal of the chancellorship. The Cardinal was well aware that it was no use to refuse, yet refuse he did, despite the high words of the Dukes, because they had brought no written authorization from the King. On October 16 they were back with this, and then Wolsey did what was required.

There seems to have been some debate as to who should succeed him. If the chancellorship was offered to Warham, who had held it from 1504 to 1515, this was only as a matter of form. It was well known that the Archbishop would plead his age and infirmities. Everybody knew that this time a layman would be chosen. This had happened two or three times during the middle ages, but since then it had become a settled thing that the chancellor should be an ecclesiastic. This was never to happen again except under Mary Tudor, when Stephen Gardiner and then Nicholas Heath held the office.

Sir Thomas More was the man finally selected – to everybody's approval, even Wolsey's – though More was most reluctant to accept. He may have hoped that the King, who was now despondent after seeing that the difficulties of obtaining a divorce were going to be much greater than he had anticipated, would abandon the whole idea. It seems that at this time Henry was in just such a mood. But to safeguard his own integrity More took office only on his own conditions; so he reminded the King of the words used at the time when, in 1518, he had given up a lucrative legal practice to enter the royal service. Henry had told him then that he must be willing to look to God first, and after God to him. It was, More said, "The most virtuous lesson that prince ever taught his servant" – as though he needed Henry to teach it to him! He stipulated that he was not to be asked to take any part in what was called the "King's Great

Matter." He had already told Henry what his views were regarding that.

Sir Thomas More had been, and still was, a close personal friend of the King's. Henry had enjoyed his witty conversation so much that More found, that if he was ever to have the company of his beloved children and his wife, he would have to be less sparkling. He contrived this very cleverly, by degrees, lest Henry should see through the device of dullness. Yet even then the King would not leave him alone but would drop in uninvited at Chelsea to take pot-luck. When Roper, having seen how his father-in-law and the burly Henry walked in the garden after dinner, with Henry's massive arm round More's neck, congratulated him, he only got the wry jest, "Howbeit, son Roper, I may tell thee that I have no cause to be proud thereof, for if my head could win him a castle in France, it should not fail to go."

As Lord Chancellor, More made an attack on Wolsey in the House of Lords which, if reported correctly by Hall, sounds rather ungenerous. But he was speaking as the mouthpiece of the government when he said: "As you see that amongst a great flock of sheep some be rotten and faulty, which the good shepherd sendeth from the good sheep, so that great wether that is of late fallen (as you know), so craftily, so scabbedly, yea and so untruly juggled with the King, that all men must needs guess that he thought in himself that he had no wit to perceive it." More ended by saying that the Cardinal would receive only a "gentle correction, which small punishment the King will not to be an example to other offenders."

Wolsey did escape the expected charge of high treason, much to the disappointment of the Londoners who had crowded the river banks and had gone out in barges and boats to get a better view of the hated Cardinal on his way to the Tower. A howl of rage went up when they saw that his barge was heading up and not down the river.

He came very near to attainder. This was defeated in the House of Commons largely through a speech made by Thomas

Cromwell. It was almost certainly delivered at the King's instigation, for Henry remained in two minds about Wolsey. The Cardinal's enemies were in mortal dread that he would be recalled, and Henry was torn between anger over Wolsey's failure to effect the divorce and wonder whether anybody else could serve his purpose so well.

In the House of Lords on December 1 a bill of forty-four charges was brought against him, signed by the leading peers, with the name of Sir Thomas More, by virtue of his office of Chancellor, at the head of the list. The charges contained much that was trivial and one thing that was absurd: "That the Cardinal, knowing himself to have the foul and contagious disease of the great pox, broken out upon him in divers places of his body, came daily to your Grace, rowning in your ear, and blowing upon your most noble Grace with his perilous and infective breath." It was only God's mercy, the accusation went on, that the King had been spared—from this rather strange way of contracting syphilis!

More to the point, excepting the charges under Praemunire, were those relating to Wolsey's ecclesiastical extortions. Stress was laid upon his methods of getting money for his colleges, and one of the items said that he had made "untrue surmise to the Pope's Holiness against the clergy of your realm, which was, that the regular persons of the said clergy had given themselves in *reprobrum sensum* . . . which slander to the Church of England shall for ever remain in the register at Rome against the clergy of your realm." As a number of the signatories to this bill were later to associate themselves with even worse slanders against the monks than any that Wolsey had made in his pose of reformer of the Church, it might be as well to bear this official protest in mind.* It assuredly greatly offsets many of the accusa-

*It may be said of course that here Wolsey, as legate, proved in advance the charges made by the visitors of the monasteries and convents in 1535–1536. But the point is that Wolsey was known to have grossly exaggerated conditions to the Pope in order to suppress some monasteries with whose revenues he intended to endow himself. The Wolseian methods were used—though on a much larger scale—a few years later, when the King suppressed all the monasteries in order to endow himself.

tions that were subsequently brought against the monasteries when it suited the book of the Defender of the Faith to despoil them.

The article about Praemunire (No. XXVIII) deserves some further comment. The charge was brought more moderately in this bill of December 1, 1529, than some Catholic (and even some non-Catholic) historians have sometimes led us to suppose. As a preliminary to further discussion I quote the words actually used: "When the said Lord Cardinal did first sue unto your Grace to have your assent to be legate *de latere,* he promised and solemnly protested before your Majesty, and before the Lords both spiritual and temporal, that he would nothing do or attempt by virtue of his legacy, that should be contrary to your gracious prerogatives or regality, or to the damage or jurisdiction of any ordinary, and that by his legacy no man should be hurt or offended; and upon that condition, and no other, he was admitted by your Grace to be legate within this your realm, which condition he hath broken, as is well known to all your subjects. And when that he made this promise, he was busy in his suit to Rome, to visit all the clergy of England, both exempt and unexempt."

This casts a rather different light upon the matter than, for example, Mr. Belloc's representation of it. He writes that Professor Pollard says that "Wolsey was not prosecuted for having been Legate, but only for having done legatine acts," and then proceeds to pour scorn upon the distinction.* What Pollard actually wrote, however, was that "it was not for being a legate that Wolsey was condemned, but for what he did as a legate."** Wolsey had, strictly speaking, no right to act as legate after the

---

*A *History of England,* Vol. IV, in a footnote on pages 92–93. I might indicate here my opinion that while Mr. Belloc often exhibits a brilliant insight, he is often very misleading. For all his contemptuous talk about "official historians," I confess that I find them, if he means such men as Brewer and Gairdner and Fisher and even Pollard (with all his prejudices), a good deal more trustworthy than Mr. Belloc himself.

** *Wolsey,* p. 246. By permission of Longmans Greene & Co.

death of Leo X in 1522 until he had been confirmed in authority by the new Pope. This confirmation was not given until 1524, yet during the interval Wolsey continued to act as though his commission remained in force. Though that perhaps may be excused on the ground that a renewal of the legateship could be presumed, there can be no doubt that Wolsey, as Belloc himself points out, exercised his legacy unjustly and (as article XXVIII of the bill of charges says) in contravention of the reasonable limits the King had indicated. Although Henry undoubtedly came to connive at the way Wolsey abused and exceeded his authority, the only time he seems actually to have reproved Wolsey (as we have seen, very gently and without any threat) was when Anne Boleyn spurred him on to do so because the Cardinal had refused to appoint her loose-living sister-in-law to be Abbess of Wilton.

For the King to make Wolsey liable to the penalties of Praemunire – not for being Legate but for the way he had performed his functions – was sufficiently legal, though it was not at all just. It was legal if for no other reason than that, under the constitutional fiction, the King, however deeply he may have been himself implicated in the Legate's indefensible proceedings, can do no wrong. It was even possible to charge the whole country – clergy and laity alike – with sharing Wolsey's guilt, because of their acquiescence in his legatine procedure, this though they detested Wolsey and his methods. The only person it was not possible to touch under the law was the King himself.

So fantastic a conflict between reality and legalism has rarely existed. But it was legality that counted in Henry's mind; therefore he used the law for all that it was worth. And as the legatine office had been accepted only under the royal permission, it was also legal for the King to deprive Wolsey of his authority. Regarding this the Pope made no protest. Clement had suffered under the hands of the bullying Cardinal, and may well have been secretly glad that he had fallen. Nor was there even any protest from the Holy See when, after Wolsey was condemned in the court of the King's Bench to perpetual imprisonment (which, however, he did not have to suffer) and to forfeiture of all his goods, Henry stretched this so far as to seize York House, which was not Wolsey's personal property but that of the archbishopric of York. It seemed that Henry was asserting a claim that all ecclesiastical property was, in the last resort, vested in the Crown. For he also proceeded to appropriate the house at Tittenhanger, which belonged not to Wolsey but to the Abbey of St. Alban's which he held *in commendam.* Nevertheless the Pope passed these matters over in silence, so anxious was he not to say anything that might lead to further conflict between the King of England and the Holy See.

Wolsey personally directed the laying out in York House of all the rich hangings and furniture it contained, described by Cavendish as silk in all colours, satins, damask, taffeta, grogram, scarlets, and a thousand pieces of fine holland, in addition to "such abundance of plate of all sorts as was almost incredible." As Henry was entitled to this, according to the law, Wolsey said to Sir William Gasgoigne, when he came to take possession, "I would all the world should know that I have nothing but it is of right from him, and of him I have received all that I have. It is therefore convenient and reason that I tender the same to him again." He knew that to those who completely acknowledged the fault they were supposed to have committed, the King would sometimes be rather generous.

He nevertheless protested when York House itself was demanded a day or two later. To Sir William Shelley, who arrived to take its surrender, Wolsey submitted but could not forbear remarking that the judges had done wrong to tell the King that this was lawful. Even were it lawful, the Cardinal went on, "Yet it is not conscience [justice]; for law without conscience is not good to be administered by a King or his Council nor by any of his ministers. Now I ask you, Master Shelley, have I a power or may I with conscience give away what is not mine for me and my successors? If this be conscience, I pray you show me your opinion."

Shelley admitted that there was no great justice in it, "but having regard to the King's great power, it may the better stand with conscience, who is sufficient to recompense the Church of York with double value."

That answer evaded the issue. As Wolsey pointed out, it was "only a bare and simple seizure of another's right; if every bishop should do so, then might every prelate give away the patrimony of the Church." Whether or not the King gave anything back was beside the point; he had no right to take it, though he should afterwards restore double. Wolsey asked the Judge to remind the King that "there is both heaven and hell." It was a daring remark. As for himself, he said he absolved his own conscience on the ground that he was yielding to force.

Had Wolsey been of sufficient moral stature, he might at that moment have struck such a blow in defence of the Church as to have saved it. But that, he realized, would have cost him his life, and he was no hero. To have been a different kind of man then he would have to have been a different sort of man all his life. He had exercised his legatine authority in such a way that all the English bishops hated him; it was in fear of them that he surrendered to the King, or such was Du Bellay's estimate of the situation. With his fall the English hierarchy regained their freedom. And though some among them may have perceived that a new principle was being introduced that would prove the gravest of dangers to the Church, their immediate profit was so great that they rejoiced to see the Cardinal removed, even at the price of an unwarrantable exercise of royal power. It was something that explains a good deal in what followed during the next years. Wolsey had not only fabricated the machinery with which the King was to rule the Church, he had also created an atmosphere in which the King's authority would seem less oppressive than that exercised by the Legate.

The Cardinal made his submission and, on February 12 was pardoned, being restored two days later to his archbishopric. He had already been allowed to retire to a house at Esher belonging to his bishopric of Winchester.

On his way there he was met, upon disembarking at Putney, by Sir Henry Norris, who gave him a ring the King had sent him as a private assurance of his friendship. Wolsey was so moved by this, as he took it as a sign of his eventual restoration to complete favour, that he at once dismounted from his mule and knelt in the mud on both knees to receive it. To show his reverence further he pulled off his scarlet velvet cap in such haste as to break the strings that tied it under his chin. Norris was so astonished that he knelt down too.

Wolsey in return sent the King some presents. One was a piece of the true cross, which hung in a locket round his neck; the other was his clown, a man named Williams but generally known as Patch. "This poor fool," he said, "I trust that his Highness will accept, for surely for a nobleman's pleasure, he is worth a thousand pounds." It speaks volumes for Wolsey's kindness towards his servants that poor Patch was unwilling to leave him, even to enter the King's service, and that he went only because he was forcibly taken away by six yeomen of the King's guard.

A servant of a different sort accompanied Wolsey to Esher. This was Thomas Cromwell, a man whom he had employed in suppressing monasteries. He quite bluntly asked the Cardinal at dinner at Halloween whether a reward was not to be given to those who had served him so faithfully.

"Alas, Tom," the answer came, "you know I have nothing to give you." And when Cromwell reminded him that his chaplains had been preferred to benefices – some worth as much as five hundred or even a thousand pounds a year – "and we, your poor servants, take more pains in one day's service than all your idle chaplains have done in a year," Wolsey, instead of pointing out, as he might have done, that Cromwell had managed to feather his nest in other ways, sent for all the attendants and, with tears streaming down his face, told them that he was sorry he had not done more for them in the days of his prosperity. Now, he concluded, "I have nothing left me but the clothes on my back."

Probably none of them really believed that. At any rate

Wolsey's enemies on the Council believed, and made Henry believe, that the Cardinal had vast sums of money hidden somewhere. This may have been one reason why they did not proceed to extremes against him; they were hoping to extract information as to where his secret treasures had been concealed. It was for this reason, too, that Wolsey was allowed to stay as long as he did at Esher, where an eye could be kept on him, instead of their hurrying him to York, as had first been intended.

So far from there being hidden treasures, Wolsey was in such hard straits that Henry, without letting his Council know what he was doing, sent the Cardinal four cartloads of furniture, of which the house at Esher was sorely in need. When this favour became known — and what it indicated of Wolsey's poverty — it had the effect of making his enemies press for his being ordered north to his archdiocese. While the King remained in a double mind with regard to his fallen minister, they feared for their own position and safety should he return to power.

For the moment there was no need for fear. Wolsey was so broken that he fell seriously ill. The hardest blow for him to bear was not the loss of the chancellorship, or even the legateship; it was the ruin of his project for building the great Cardinal's College at Oxford. This preyed upon him to such an extent that he began to languish away. When Henry heard of it he sent Dr. Butts, his own physician, to see him, and when Butts reported that Wolsey would be dead in three or four days "if he receive no comfort from you shortly," the King replied, "Marry, God forbid that he should die, for I would not have him die for twenty thousand pounds."

To cheer Wolsey up the King sent him another ring, and turning to Anne Boleyn said, "Good sweetheart, as you love me, send the Cardinal a token." As she dared not refuse, she handed him the tablet of gold that hung at her waist as her gift. Such a pledge coming from his bitterest enemy would be solace.

Dr. Butts returned to Esher at once, accompanied this time by three other royal physicians, Drs. Cromer, Wotton, and Clement. The last named was a former secretary of Sir Thomas More's, and tutor in his household, who, after teaching Greek at Oxford, was now in medical practice in London, married to More's adopted daughter, the learned Margaret Giggs. These famous doctors "set him again upon his feet, and got him a good stomach to his meat" – all in four days. Nor would they accept any fee from Wolsey, telling him that everything was at the charge of the King.

Meanwhile Cromwell – familiarly "Tom" to Wolsey – had taken his advancement into his own hands, as nothing more was to be got out of the Cardinal. On All Saints' Day Cavendish saw a most unusual sight when, going into the great hall, he found Cromwell standing at a window reading the Little Office of Our Lady. As he prayed tears were streaming down his face. Cavendish asked, "Why, Mr. Cromwell, what meaneth this dole? Is our Lord in any danger that ye lament for him?" Cromwell answered with a cynic's honesty, "Nay, it is for my own unhappy adventure. For I am like to lose all that I have laboured for all the days of my life. But this much I will say to you, that I will this afternoon, when my Lord hath dined, ride to London to the Court, where I will either make or mar, or ever I come again."

Just what was said by Cromwell when he got to the Court we do not know. He could hardly have produced at that first interview a complete policy for Henry to follow, though he may have hinted at things he would be able to effect. Especially he may have indicated means of terrifying the clergy into submission, for his dealings with them had given him a contemptuous opinion of their powers of resistance. He may even have suggested, in a general way, that he would be able to make Henry the richest and therefore the most powerful king in the world. Nor is it impossible that he proved his value by presenting Henry with a document purloined from Wolsey, "the King's license, under his hand and Broad Seal," as Cavendish puts it, for the exercising of his legatine powers.*

*If such a document was stolen, Cromwell, as Wolsey's scrivener, was

Cromwell's ability was already well known, and the immediate use made of this ability was that the bill of attainder against Wolsey was thrown out of the House of Commons mainly through Cromwell's instrumentality. We may suppose, when we remember the other favours Henry showed the hated Cardinal, that Cromwell was acting as the King's agent. It was not in his nature to risk anything. He continued to act as the go-between of Wolsey and the government, helping Wolsey, it is true, but writing to him in a tone that scarcely veiled his disdain. He was, nevertheless, careful not to burn any bridges; if Wolsey should ever regain his former position, Cromwell wished to be able to say that he had served him even through the time of his disgrace.

Wolsey, upon recovering his health, was allowed to go to his house at Richmond. From there, to demonstrate that he was now a changed man, he moved for a time into the lodge built by Dean Colet in the grounds of the Charterhouse at Sheen near by. There every afternoon he sat in retreat with one of the Carthusian monks, "who converted him to despise the vainglory of this world," and, still more remarkable, got him to accept and occasionally wear (if Cavendish is to be believed) a hair-shirt. It may be uncharitable to surmise that this conversion was only skin-deep, but one cannot help feeling that, had any chance occurred for regaining power, Wolsey's repentance would have been as easily discarded as his hair-shirt. There is not the slightest sign that he felt that he had anything to regret in the way

---

in the best position for abstracting it. Therefore the finger of suspicion points at him. But would such a theft have been necessary? Everybody knew that Wolsey was appointed legate, and had obtained ever increasing powers, because this was what the King wanted. Wolsey was never charged with having been legate without the King's permission but with having exceeded his authority. The likely supposition is that he had a bundle of letters from Henry consenting to this or that specific act, and that such letters might have been used to justify almost any of his legatine acts. The production of such letters would of course have been most embarrassing to the King. This, however, can only be guess-work; Cavendish, as gentleman usher, was not in a position to know what was the nature of Wolsey's correspondence. We must believe that Wolsey made a complaint that the "King's license" was no longer in his possession; in talking as he did, Wolsey very probably greatly exaggerated that document's importance.

he had accumulated benefices to which he never gave any service, or in his pride or ambition, or in his arbitrary rule of the Church in England which had, because of him, been made so vulnerable.

Nor were Wolsey's enemies convinced by his conversion. When Cromwell came to tell him that the Duke of Norfolk had said he had better go home to his benefice, Wolsey returned, "Well then, Thomas, we will go to Winchester." But Winchester was too near London. A day or two later he got another message from Norfolk: "Tell him if he go not away, I shall tear him with my teeth!"* Rather than that should happen Wolsey prepared for the journey to the York he had not so far seen. To provide for his expenses Cavendish says that Henry sent him £10,000 and a kind message saying that he had been assigned a pension of a thousand marks a year from the diocese of Winchester. That was certainly not bad provision.

During these last months of his life the Cardinal showed a changed demeanour. Cromwell, hearing of it, wrote to him piously, "I do reckon your Grace right happy that ye be now at liberty to serve God, and to learn to experiment how ye shall banish and exile the vain desires of this unstable world. . . . Wherefore, in mine opinion, your Grace being as ye are, I suppose ye would not be as ye were to win a hundred times as much as ever ye were possessed of." Cromwell must have grinned over his pen when writing that. Wolsey was doing no more than make a virtue of necessity, yet it must be noted to his credit that he went in procession on Palm Sunday with the monks of Peterborough, and on Maundy Thursday, April 14, he

*This Duke of Norfolk had succeeded his father, the victor of Flodden, in 1524. He had done savage butcher's work after Evil May Day, and was to distinguish himself in the same style but on a much larger scale in 1537. His one great feat of arms was the ravaging of France in 1523, when he was still Earl of Surrey. There was always the possibility of an aristocratic reaction headed by him, and so far as this ever happened, it was happening now, when he was leading the enemies of Wolsey. When Cromwell fell in 1540 he was looked upon as the titular chief of the Catholic party. He had, however, no religion, except that the conservatism of his class preferred that religious changes should not be carried too far.

washed the feet of fifty-nine poor men, one for every year of his own age. To each he gave a present of twelve pence, material for shirts, a pair of new shoes, and a cask of red herrings. On Easter Sunday he sang pontifical High Mass and bestowed his blessing with an indulgence on the congregation.

Nor did his piety end there. At Scroby, which was in his diocese, he stayed until Michaelmas, doing many deeds of charity, and nearly every Sunday — always when the weather was fine — went to one of the churches near by to say Mass and to have one of his chaplains preach. This belated attention to pastoral duties was common enough among bishops who had been state functionaries, and in old age wished to do something to straighten their accounts with their Maker. Wolsey showed himself exemplary in such practices. Cavendish was able to declare, "The common people held my Lord in great estimation for his purity and liberality, and also for his familiar manners and good behaviour amongst them, and by means thereof he gained much love of all the people in the northern parts of England." It would have been well had he paid some attention a little earlier to these matters.

His enthronement in York minster was set for November 7; meanwhile he stayed at Cawood Castle, seven miles away. His chapter had come to tell him that it was customary for their archbishop not to enter his cathedral before the day of his installation. To that custom Wolsey said he would adhere, but when he was told that it was also customary for the archbishop to walk to the minster from St. James's chapel upon carpets, he answered, "Although perhaps our predecessors have gone upon cloth, yet we intend to go on foot without any such pomp or glory." Humility of this sort was most edifying, especially as it came from the hitherto arrogant Cardinal Wolsey.

Away in London his enemies on the Council were much less impressed. They had succeeded in working upon Agostini, Wolsey's Italian physician, and from him they heard that the Cardinal had been in communication with Rome and the French court. It was something which, if true, might be susceptible of a treasonable interpretation. What had really alarmed them was that Wolsey had recently attempted to get in touch with Henry. At all costs he had to be prevented from regaining the royal favour. An imputation of treason, even if it were insufficient to bring about his conviction, might serve to put him permanently under a cloud.

The upshot was that on November 4, just three days before the date set for the Cardinal's installation as Archbishop of York, the Earl of Northumberland, the same Percy whose match with Anne Boleyn Wolsey had broken off, entered the castle to arrest him for high treason. So much was Percy still in awe of his former master that he stammered out the words in a very faint voice. And Wolsey, scornful of so poor a human specimen, refused to yield to him, though he consented to accept Northumberland's associate, Sir Walter Walsh, as his captor.

There was no hurry to get him to London. Norfolk feared that it might lead to a meeting with the King or, if not that, to a defence that might be damaging to the Cardinal's enemies. Wolsey was known to be in failing health; they preferred that he should die before reaching the Tower. He was accordingly taken to the house of the Earl of Shrewsbury, of course under technical arrest, and there he was treated as an honoured guest.

Wolsey remained there until Sir William Kingston, the Constable of the Tower, arrived with a guard consisting of men who were mostly the Cardinal's former retainers. From them he received great respect, and Kingston, a handsome bearded giant of a man, assured him that the King had as much goodwill as he had ever had and did not doubt that he would completely clear himself. To which Wolsey answered sadly, "Do not try to bring me into a fool's paradise, for I know what is provided for me."

The Cardinal got no further than Leicester Abbey. He was by that time so ill that he had to be carried in. He at once told the Abbot that he had come to lay his bones there. To Kingston he said, "Let me advise you, if you be one of the Privy Council, as by your wisdom you are fit, take heed what you put into the King's head, for you can never get it out again." Yet whenever he had occasion to mention the King's name, he showed extravagant reverence, kneeling up in bed, ill though he was, and bowing his head. It was in one of these conversations with Kingston that he used the famous words Shakespeare made him speak to Cromwell (who of course was not present): "If I had served my God as diligently as I have done the King, He would not have given me over in my grey hairs."

Through Kingston Wolsey sent a message to Henry that "In God's name he have a vigilant eye to suppress the hellish Lutherans, that they increase not through his great negligence." It was good advice, yet if heresy had made any headway in England, this was largely because of the Cardinal's own negligence. Even at that hour Wolsey probably had no conception as to what was to come. Nobody could imagine that as yet.

He died on November 29, at eight in the morning, just as he had foretold. They laid his body to rest in the abbey, close to where Richard III was lying. People spoke of that nave afterwards as the "tyrants' grave."

When the news got to London there was unabashed rejoicing. His enemies were glad that his convenient death had spared them the risk of putting him on public trial. They signalized their joy by staging a farce that showed the Cardinal's descent to hell. Wolsey had, however, confessed his sins and had made a good death.

If Henry mourned his passing, he manifested no special signs of grief. He did, it is true, tell the kneeling Cavendish, whom he received "in his nightgown of velvet furred with sables," that he would give twenty thousand pounds had the Cardinal lived. Nevertheless the questioning was all about a sum of fifteen hundred pounds that Wolsey had had. As Cavendish was able to put him on the track of this money, he was paid his wages for the nine months they were in arrears – his salary was £10 a year – and in addition a reward of twenty pounds.

If Wolsey had not left the King much wealth, Henry was his heir in a much wider sense. How to suppress monasteries was one item in this bequest; how to enrich himself was another; but by far the most valuable item of all was that concentration of power in both Church and state effected by the Cardinal. Henry was now able to take this into his own hands and to proceed to any end he might have in view.

CHAPTER EIGHT

Completion of the Schism

It must always be borne in mind that, during the years immediately following the sudden termination of the divorce hearings in England, the issues involved had nothing of the clarity with which we can see them. No logical coherence was apparent, nor was there any definite doctrinal division between the disputants. Although the Boleyn group came to be associated with the "advanced" party in religion, this was only vaguely so, and for hardly any other reason that they needed some sort of a platform on which to stand. But it was quite possible for a strong Catholic – even in the sense of a strong papalist – to hope for and work for the obtaining of the royal divorce. Such a man might be as bitter a foe of the Cardinal as Anne Boleyn herself, and for better cause. On the other hand, the vast majority of Katherine's partisans understood nothing, and cared less, about the relations between the Crown and the Papacy. They comprised virtually all the common people of England, and they were actuated mainly by warm human sympathy for the badly treated woman they had come to love.

Only later and by degrees did the real question become plain, if it ever became plain at this time to any except a few very intelligent men. Of those who supported the Papacy in its quarrel with the King, most thought of the Pope's primacy as something that had arisen rather because of historical necessity than as something divinely ordained. The changes that occurred were so gradual as hardly to be noticed. Henry told Chapuys, the Imperial Ambassador, that he was carefully observing public sentiment, so as to discover how far he might safely go and at what point he had to stop. He took no step forward until he had consolidated his position behind him. By the time he was ready to take the last step and to sever England from the Roman obedience, his supremacy over the Church had already been asserted in such a way that to all save the exceptionally clear-sighted, it seemed natural and desirable. All of which was possible only because the issues involved were clouded from the people, and even, until right at the end, from the King himself.

It must be doubtful as to whether Cromwell had a fully worked out program. He was an opportunist, fertile in expedients, who operated on a day-to-day basis. We know that the project of fining the whole body of the clergy for implication under Praemunire, for having accepted Wolsey as legate, if not actually suggested by him, was known to him at an early date. His assurance to Wolsey "The prelates shall not appear [in the] Praemunire. There is another way devised"* is the first indication that the plan decided upon was that of extracting money by subjecting them to fear. It was a form of blackmail, such as Cromwell the money-lender had often practised and was often to practise again. The plea was that there might be a war on account of Katherine, and that, in any event, huge expenditures had already been necessary in connection with the divorce; it was only just that the clergy – though they already paid double in taxes because of not bearing arms – should contribute. That they showed themselves so abject in face of these threats was an invitation to Henry to take advantage of the situation and make further demands.

It was, however, necessary to make the country believe that everything being done originated with the King; only on that condition could it be made acceptable. The personal adulation Henry received, the fantastic reverence accorded his office, the bowings and scrapings at the mere mention of his sacred name –

*It is in a letter of his dated October 21, 1530, in *Letters and Papers,* Vol. IV, p. 3019.

these are hardly conceivable by the modern mind. Though Henry found it prudent to proceed slowly, he was free to proceed in any direction he wished, sure that whatever he did would be, if not always approved, at least never actively resisted. Unpopular as the divorce was, the blame for it could be laid at the door of the Cardinal. And when later other scapegoats were found – chief among them Cromwell and Cranmer – Henry himself was never blamed. Instead commiseration was extended to him for having been led astray by bad advisers.

For some time Cromwell was kept very much in the background. Henry made use of him in various ways, especially in Parliament, but he was not appointed to the Council until 1531, nor, until that year, was anything done that suggested how drastic coming changes were to be. The severance of England from the unity of Christendom happened only because Henry saw there was no other way by which he could divorce his wife and marry Anne. It was not a thing carefully planned but was brought about by the pressure of events, many of them quite unforeseen.

Foxe the martyrologist was to try to turn Cromwell into a Protestant hero – "this pillar set up in the Church of Christ" – but actually the man was indifferent to religion, and certainly had no hatred of Catholic doctrine, though of course Catholic discipline might interfere with his policies. His distinction was that of introducing the maxims of Machiavelli into English public life and giving them an application never known anywhere before. Only political considerations weighed with him. He was not cruel; he was merely without mercy: personal feeling never entered into anything he did. Professor Merriman says simply and truly that Cromwell can be best described by the phrase, "a strict attention to business."

He was of lowly origin, his father having kept a public house at Putney with a blacksmith's forge on the side. Early in life, having got into some sort of a scrape in England, he had to go abroad. There he worked for a while as a clerk (under the assumed name of Smith) at Antwerp, and later in the banking house of the Frescobaldi in Italy. By about 1513 he was back in England, where he took up the study of law, combining it with money-lending and wool-dressing. Yet he found time somehow to be a collector of Wolsey's revenues in 1514 and afterwards his agent for the suppression of monasteries. There was always something mysterious and shady about him, though it should be added that there was no stain on his private life and that the indications are that he was regular in the external practices of religion.

We know exactly what he looked like from the Holbein painting of him now in the Frick Collection. But verbal accounts tell us also that he was short and stocky, that he waddled a little when he walked, and that people, on first acquaintance, took him to be patient and plodding but rather stupid. In his heavy pasty face there were set little pig-like eyes. With these he had a way of giving sidelong glances. His lips hardly moved when he spoke, yet he could be very witty and amusing. Then his eyes lit up and his features became animated. Chapuys, though he set him down as a consummate scoundrel, enjoyed his society. Without trusting him a particle, he found Cromwell to be the kind of practical realist with whom it was possible to do business. People less intelligent than Chapuys usually hated and despised him.

Before any of Cromwell's suggestions were adopted other expedients were tried. They indicate that Henry was bewildered and that he had probably begun to regret the lack of Wolsey's skilful services. To have sent Lord Wiltshire, Anne Boleyn's father, on a mission to the Emperor in January, 1530, reveals an ineptitude of which the Cardinal would never have been guilty. No ambassador less acceptable to Charles can be imagined, and when Wiltshire had the effrontery to offer the Emperor 300,000 crowns of his aunt's dowry, he was coldly told that she was not for sale. All that eventuated was that at Bologna a summons was served upon Boleyn, as Henry's representative, for the King to appear in person or to send a proctor for the hearing of the divorce case in the Roman courts. Yet on March 27 the Bishop of Tarbes, now Francis' ambassador at Rome, wrote to assure his master: "The Pope had told him more than three times in secret that he would be glad if the marriage between Henry and Anne were made already, either by dispensation of the English Legate, or otherwise, provided it was not by his authority and in diminution of his powers of dispensation and limitation of divine law."

It was not that kind of a divorce that Henry wanted. The Pope had to pronounce – though of course in his favour. In an attempt to make the Pope pronounce, the English nobility signed a petition to him in June, 1530.* As threats were in this petition, it brought a rebuke, though a good-natured one, from Clement, who wrote: "We pardon your transport of impatience, exhorting you, with a fatherly affection, to keep your temper: and we hope that your prudence and piety will prevail upon you to make no resolutions but what are wise. But if a patient be ungovernable, and will embrace no advice but what is destructive, the physician ought not to be blamed." He reiterated that he could not decide on so important a matter without further time for consideration.

Katherine's view was simple, perhaps too simple. She held then, she was always to hold, that the Pope should speak out and end the discussion. Nor can one feel otherwise than that she may have been quite right. Certainly a decision of this sort should not have been rushed, but overhasty judgement is one thing and deliberate dilatoriness something else again. Clement went on playing for time, mainly in order to avoid offending Henry, though also with side-glances at Charles. And the Pope's failure to protect Katherine, as Chapuys pointed out, was damaging the prestige of the Holy See in England.** There were those who, having come to feel that as the Pope had betrayed his

*One of the signatories was Wolsey; but the man who now took precedence over all others in England by virtue of his office, Sir Thomas More, did not sign.

***Spanish State Papers*, Vol. IV, part i, pp. 366–367; Vol. IV, part ii, pp. 70–71.

own cause, they were absolved from continuing the struggle.

This feeling, however, was as yet not definite, for matters were still in a confused condition. Henry himself, except for clinging obstinately to his resolve to obtain a divorce, was confused. Not many months after the dissolution of the court at Blackfriars, he and Katherine had had a fierce quarrel, and he had gone off to Anne Boleyn, licking his wounds and looking for sympathy. He got none. She broke in upon his story to tell him that he was a fool to argue with Katherine, as he was invariably worsted. She was afraid that the Queen would in the end succeed in winning Henry back, or at least succeed in detaching him from herself.

It was about this time that Anne came to make an alliance both with Cromwell, the new manager of affairs, and with a man hitherto unheard of, but whom chance now brought upon the scene. This was Thomas Cranmer, an obscure Cambridge don about forty years old, who, until then, expected to live and die in his obscurity and, since he was without ambition, asked for nothing better.

His was a strange character. He was the younger son of a good family, and for that reason alone had decided that he must make his way — at least to the extent of making his living — in the Church. Yet urgent as that necessity was, it had not prevented his marrying a barmaid at Cambridge, upon which he had to resign his fellowship and give up all thought of the priesthood. Only the early death of the barmaid bride, Brown Joan, enabled him to retrieve himself. In all other respects a model of circumspection, a certain weakness with regard to women was again to show itself in him, almost to his total ruin. Nobody at this time suspected the mild and inoffensive clerical don of heretical tendencies.

An accidental meeting with Gardiner and Edward Fox at Waltham Abbey and a suggestion Cranmer had to offer, catapulted him into eventual fame. Yet his suggestion had been made by at least two men in 1527 — Wakefield the Hebrew scholar and a monk of Syon — but at a time when it was considered inopportune, as another course of action had been decided upon. But now Cranmer said that he thought the opinions of the universities of Europe should be obtained on the divorce and then presented to the Pope as the judgement of what might be called a "scattered council." It was taken for granted that, in general, these opinions would be in Henry's favour, for there were ways of making sure of that; it was also taken for granted that Clement VII, so far from raising any objections, would be glad of this device for relieving him of an embarrassment.

The views of the faculties of theology and canon law undoubtedly would have weighed with the Pope had they been freely obtained. This, however, was notoriously impossible. The universities in the imperial territories were not approached; these would be likely to declare for Katherine. But Oxford and Cambridge could be counted upon, and for good measure those of France and northern Italy, where Francis could exercise his influence.

English gold proved an irresistible argument. For though, to be fair, the probability must be admitted that many of the scholars consulted would have declared a marriage between a brother-in-law and a sister-in-law to be contrary to the law of God, even had no rewards been held out, we do happen to know that there was a heavy outlay in bribes, and it would seem to be a fairly safe inference that bribes were offered only in case of necessity. At Padua, for example, Richard Croke offered £500 to the canonists and even raised his price, but in vain. He then turned to the faculty of theology and obtained a favorable opinion from some of its members, which was represented to be a majority decision. Bologna, Ferrara, and Pavia gave decisions of the same sort, obtained by the same methods. The Italian, Ghinucci, who was titular Bishop of Worcester and who had long acted as an English agent in Italy, was very useful in these little transactions. In France not much money had to be spent, as Francis could virtually dictate what he wanted. And though Jewish rabbis could not be considered as part of the scattered council, they were not overlooked. As Hebrew scholars their opinions were worth obtaining, especially as they could be bought cheap – twenty-four crowns being considered enough in their case.

In England Henry disdained to bribe. His subjects would of course be only too glad to give their opinion – the right opinion – for nothing. They turned out to be unaccountably reluctant to do their duty. The King, according to Strype, sent six of his "best learned men" to Oxford and Cambridge to debate the proposition, "Whether it were lawful for one brother to marry his brother's wife, being known of his brother?" But though the question was framed in such a way as to assume the consummation of the Katherine-Arthur marriage as a proved fact, the universities were at first unanimous that, with the Pope's dispensation, such a marriage was lawful. Eventually at Cambridge, after two divisions had failed to give Henry the vote, a select committee had to be appointed to do what was required, and for them the proposition had to be modified. Similarly at Oxford opposition was not overcome until after the planing down of the proposition and threats of the King's extreme displeasure. Then it passed by a very small margin. When the Vice-Chancellor went to register the decision he was stoned by the angry women of Oxford.

Clement VII again showed weakness. On May 31, 1530, he prohibited all ecclesiastical judges and lawyers from taking part in the discussion under pain of excommunication. Then on August 4 he issued a new brief making this prohibition apply only to those who voted to win favour or money, which of course made it meaningless in practice. Not until January, 1531, was an absolute prohibition of such discussion issued, and by that time Henry had obtained enough in the way of theological and canonical opinions to justify himself. If it be objected that this was obscurantism on the Pope's part, most reasonable persons will think that even obscurantism is to be preferred to corruption. But of course the decision was one that had to be reserved to the Holy See.

Cranmer had been sent to serve in a minor capacity in the

entourage of Wiltshire. He won favorable opinions in Rome, for he was gentle and of amiable manners and adept at concealing his real views. Clement appointed him Penitentiary for England. Later he went on to Germany to try and persuade the Lutheran divines of the justice of Henry's cause. Their views on matrimony were notoriously lax, and they refused to admit it as a sacrament. At the same time they felt a grudge against Henry and they had some common sense. They refused to support the King, even though his plea was based on the only authority they would recognize, that of the Scriptures.

Cranmer had his own private adventures among the Lutherans. He was a kindly man and, as one would infer from his affair with Brown Joan the barmaid, susceptible to women. At any rate while staying with Andrew Osiander, one of the new brethren, at Nuremberg, he so far forgot himself as to marry Osiander's niece. Though he was under a vow of celibacy, he may be presumed to have considered himself dispensed by the "Gospel" he had secretly embraced. At all events this marriage proves that he was devoid of ambition; he neither expected nor wished the archbishopric that was soon to be thrust upon him. In it his marriage was an acute embarrassment and an ever-present danger.

Henry had from time to time threatened the Pope. He now proceeded to show that his threats were not idle. And yet, as was his way, he wished to avoid extreme measures. In December, 1530, he took up Cromwell's suggestion that the whole body of the English clergy could be made liable to the penalties of Praemunire.

It goes without saying that no group could have been less guilty. They had always resented Wolsey's methods of exercising his legateship. Indeed, what happened in 1531 resulted in a riot of the London clergy. They broke into the chapter-house of the time-serving Stokesley, who had succeeded Tunstall, shouting, "My Lord, twenty nobles a year is but a bare living for a priest, now victuals and everything is so dear, and poverty constraineth us to say nay. Besides, we never offended in Praemunire, for we meddled never with the Cardinal's faculties. Let the bishops and the abbots who have offended pay."

What brought this about was that when the Convocation of Canterbury met, early in 1531, they were informed that they were expected to pay a contribution to the King much larger than usual if they were to escape Praemunire. They supposed that this was merely a device for extorting money out of them and voted £40,000. When that was rejected as insufficient they voted £100,000. They still did not realize how helpless the fall of Wolsey had left the Church and how his misdeeds were to be used against them. They soon found out. Henry refused to pardon them, even on the payment of this enormous grant, unless they acknowledged him to be supreme head of the Church.

This did not mean that the King was, at that moment, claiming what he afterwards was to claim, but it was more than enough to arouse protests. The Baron del Burgo, the Pope's nuncio in England, though a layman, went to Convocation and begged the clergy to stand firm. They were so frightened that they almost forcibly ejected him. As the Baron was not a strong character he left, merely hoping that they would uphold the rights of the Church.

They managed to effect a compromise. Lord Rochford, Anne Boleyn's brother, was sent to them to say that if they preferred the formula, "The Supreme Head After God" to "Protector and Supreme Head of the English Church and Clergy," this would be acceptable. Convocation considered it still worse. In the end Warham suggested an alternative formula: "We recognize his Majesty as the Singular Protector, and only Supreme Lord, and so far as the law of Christ allows, even Supreme Head." Dead silence greeted him, and when he said, "Silence gives consent," a voice was heard, "Then are we all silent!"

In this way, and with this qualification, the proposal passed the Convocation of Canterbury. In the Convocation of York, presided over by Tunstall (as no archbishop had yet been appointed), it also passed, but only after Henry had explained that it was not intended to extend beyond temporalities. It nevertheless marked the beginning of the surrender of the English Church. The qualification might, for the time being, soothe consciences; but the King had carried his point. He had fined the clergy for a crime they had not committed; he had discovered that they could be terrified. The rest might wait; what that was would depend upon what the Pope did in the matter of the royal divorce.

One pauses now for a moment upon a curious interlude. In March, 1531, an attempt was made to poison John Fisher. Poison had been put into some broth, of which he happened not to drink, but of which several in his household died. Fisher's cook, upon being arrested, said that he had been given some powder but did not know that it was poison. Nor would he reveal who had given him the powder.

Henry, very much alarmed – for a king was no more immune against poison than a bishop – drove a special bill through Parliament, with retrospective action, making poisoning an offence punishable by boiling in oil, and mentioning the cook's name, Richard Rouse. If under the examination of torture he implicated anybody else, nothing was officially divulged. In popular estimation this served to confirm the suspicions that the real culprits were the hated Anne Boleyn and her brother.

Be this as it may, Henry's own horror at the crime was clearly unfeigned. Moreover, he still had a high respect for Fisher's learning and sanctity, and had no reason to suppose that he would not eventually be able to win him over. Finally, he was frightened, as usual, on his own account. If it was possible to poison the Bishop of Rochester's broth it might be possible to poison the King's meat or drink. Rouse accordingly died in the extremity of pain, hanging on a chain and dipped in and out of a cauldron of oil as an exemplary warning.

It was rumoured in Parliament that the penalties of Praemunire would be extended to the whole nation. At once the

Commons took alarm and there were pointed words. "The King," one member said to the approval of all present, "had burdened and oppressed his kingdom with more imposts and exactions than any three or four of his predecessors and should consider that his strength lay in the affections of his people." All of which meant that, though they did not object to the clergy being fined, they were not going to fine themselves. Henry took the hint and did not press the issue further. This concession having been made, he asked that the opinions of the universities be read to the House and that the members do their best to publish these throughout the country.

In the House of Lords the same matter was brought up, Sir Thomas More as Chancellor being obliged to act as the mouthpiece of the King, and to declare that his Grace was moved in the matter of the divorce only by his conscience and not, as was reported, "out of love for some lady." Upon this Longland, Bishop of Lincoln, and Stokesley of London "took it on their conscience," according to Roper, "that the marriage of the King and Queen was more than illegal." Two other bishops gave a different opinion and the Chancellor was appealed to for his real view. More answered merely that he had many times given it to the King and would say no more. It was, however, clear, even had the fact not been well known, that he disapproved. The Duke of Norfolk had to rise and tell the House that the report of the universities had been brought to them for their information, not for their action. With that the question was dropped.

Mr. Brewer, the first editor of the enormous collection of state papers of Henry VIII's reign, remarks that "Parliament was nothing better than a court to register the King's decrees, and assume a responsibility for acts, the unpopularity of which he did not wish to take upon himself." Similarly the seventeenth-century Lord Herbert, the first of Henry's biographers, remarks: "I cannot but observe of him, that if where he did ill, he made or found many accomplices; where he did well, he had almost the glory alone." But though Parliament could usually be brought to do what the King wanted, even Henry could not drive it too far. A virtual deal was made between it and the King: as regards the Church, it would do as was required, but as regards taxation it expected to have its views respected by the Crown. Henry drove Parliament hard but knew when it was politic to stop.

The situation was all the more remarkable in face of the fact that the Parliament elected in 1529 was packed. This packing has sometimes been denied on the ground that we have too little documentation as to the individual elections. Yet it was looked upon as ordinary procedure that a member be sent to the Commons because he was nominated by a privy councillor. Sir Thomas More, speaking out at last in his trial in 1535, refers to this as a notorious and uncontested fact. "What kind of Parliament God knows!" he said before his judges in crowded Westminster Hall.

John Fisher declared in the House of Lords that in the Commons the cry was all, "Down with the Church!" For this he was delated to Henry by the Speaker, Audley, and had to explain his words away. Nevertheless Fisher was right, although many of the new laws were, in themselves, desirable. The probate fees of the ecclesiastical courts were reduced; pluralities were forbidden, but without disturbing the existing pluralists; non-residence was also prohibited. As the Church had failed to deal with these crying abuses, there was much to be said for parliamentary action. The clergy could have put their own house in order, and should have done so. They were inviting disaster by insisting that these questions were their own concern, and then showing the weakest kind of obstinacy by doing nothing.

If the King and his Council could pack the House of Commons by nominating the candidates for election, it was still more easy to pack the Lords. The King could always create new peers. If he did not do so on a large scale in a body where the spiritual peers outnumbered the lay lords, this was only because outright packing was not necessary when subservience was found and when only a few bishops and abbots attended. Moreover it was always possible to fall back upon the device of pointedly "excusing" the attendance of anyone likely to cause too much trouble.

Even with all these advantages the King met with some opposition. The Annates Bill, passed in January, 1532, stopped the payment to Rome of a newly appointed bishop's first year's revenue. The act was driven through with considerable difficulty, and only after the King went down to the House of Commons to make the members vote the right way beneath his eye. Even then its operation was suspended for a year. Yet Norfolk shamelessly told the Nuncio, del Burgo, that the King had accepted it merely to satisfy the Commons. More shamelessly still, Henry wrote to his agent in Rome, "You shall instill into their ears how incessant have been our efforts to resist the importunity of our people for passing this statute; and so secretly has the whole transaction been managed that no foreign prince should know of it or take occasion thereby to get a similar edict in his own country." It was a broad hint that Henry might try and get Francis to act in the same way. Meanwhile Norfolk let the Nuncio know that the King could permanently suspend the Annates Act, and that he would do so, if only his Holiness were amenable.

One must admire the way in which Henry, aided by that adroit manipulator of Parliament, Cromwell, obtained what he wanted. On May 15, 1532, what is rightly known as the Submission of the Clergy occurred. With that done, Parliament was prorogued and Sir Thomas More, pleading ill health, was permitted to retire into private life.

The enactments of Parliament were skilfully led up to. Early in January, 1532, the device was used of having a delegation from the House of Commons make, as though spontaneously, such representations against the clergy as the King wished. When the bishops drew up a point-by-point reply, the King sent for Audley (who was again accompanied by a deputation from the Commons) and said: "We think their answer will smally please you, for it seemeth to us very slender. You be a great sort of wise men. I doubt not but you will look circumspectly on the matter and we will be indifferent between you."

How indifferent Henry was is shown by his insisting on May 10 that Convocation renounce all its powers to make ecclesiastical regulations and give these over to a committee of thirty-two, half lay and half clerical, but all appointed by the Crown. As a directive to Parliament he said a day or two later: "Well-beloved subjects, we thought the clergy of our realm had been our subjects wholly; but now we have well perceived that they be but half our subjects, yea and scarce our subjects. For all the prelates at their consecration make an oath to the Pope clean contrary to the oath they make to us, so they seem to be his subjects and not ours." Convocation tried to save its face by explaining that in accepting what was demanded, the transference of its authority to the King was to him personally, not to his office, because of the confidence the clergy had in his "excellent wisdom, princely goodness, and fervent zeal to the promotion of God's honour and of the Christian religion." The fulsome flattery was without effect; nothing was reserved; instead the clergy had made an abject surrender and this was eventually given statutory force.

The clergy had behaved with anything but dignity. But that Sir Thomas More was able to resign without at that time creating any breach between himself and the King shows that some degree of independence was still possible. It was possible also in the Commons, as when a member named Temse introduced that April a motion that the King take the Queen back again. Ten months previously Henry, not having the courage to face Katherine, had crept out of Windsor Castle at daybreak, while the Queen was still asleep. He was never to see her again. But as Mr. Temse had spoken his mind so boldly, Henry sent for the Speaker, Audley, and told him that "he marvelled any among them should meddle in business that could not be determined there. As for this particular, that it concerned his soul so much, that he many times wished the marriage had been good, but since the doctors of the universities had declared it unlawful, he could do no less than abstain from her company. Which therefore he wished them to take as the true reason, without imputing it to any wanton appetite; since, being in the one and fortieth year of his age, it might be justly presumed such motions were not so quick in him."

Such effrontery is really stupendous. One would think that his scruples of conscience arose from the opinions of the universities, whereas we know that Henry's attempts for a divorce were made long before the universities were consulted at all, and that then the learned men – in so far as they supported him – were often bribed or bludgeoned into doing so. Henry had recently received a letter from the Pope, dated January 5, 1532, in which Clement asked (but did not order) him to take back the Queen. Though this letter contained many compliments upon the royal virtue and piety, the Pope put his finger upon the point by saying: "What can be more unnatural to you, or less agreeable to your integrity, on the one hand, both by your letter and ambassadors, to implore our assistance in determining your cause, and on the other, by your actions to judge and decide it yourself?"

Henry, as the Pope knew, had decided to take the matter into his own hands. Though the Pope had not decided against him, the King had come to despair of any decision satisfactory to himself being taken in Rome and so approached Warham in the matter. He would have much preferred getting his divorce pronounced by the Pope, but the Archbishop of Canterbury would have to do it. In 1527 or 1528 (and even at some moments later), Clement would have been relieved by such action, but as the case had been thrust on him by Henry, and as Katherine had lodged an appeal, a Canterbrigian solution of the problem was no longer admissible.

Nor had Henry any right to complain of unconscionable delay. As a matter of fact, he had been instructing his agents to play for time, as he was by now aware that the decision would go against him. It was Katherine who had urged prompt action; in not giving it, Clement was guilty of favouritism to Henry, though of course he continued to hope that delay, if it could be stretched out long enough, would settle everything.

Warham might have acted at one time. He could no longer do

so, as Henry, by his appeals to every kind of tribunal that could be bought or intimidated, had obliged the Pope to prohibit any action except what he might take. Warham, while hitherto compliant, had now been pushed to a point beyond which he would not move; he was going to respect the Pope's order. It was useless for Cromwell to charge him under Praemunire and to talk of hanging him on the highest of gallows; Warham was too near death not to be afraid of One more powerful than the King. In his palace at Lambeth he prepared a speech to deliver in the House of Lords, asking for the repeal of all the statutes that had been passed against the Church. "I intend nothing against the King's highness," he dictated to his secretary, "but I intend to do only that I am bound to do by the laws of God and Holy Church and by mine order, and by mine own oath made at the time of my profession. . . . It were indeed as good to have no spirituality as to have it at the prince's pleasure."

That speech was never delivered. Nor was any action taken against Warham. The eighty-two-year-old Archbishop was known to be near death; it would be best to wait until he had departed from this life. The King still wished to keep on good terms with the Pope. He had not broken with the Holy See, and he had every intention of avoiding this except at the moment chosen by himself.

On August 24, 1532, died William Warham, Archbishop of Canterbury. The road was now clear.

Just eight days later Anne Boleyn was created Marquis of Pembroke.* A significant point was that the patent did not, as was customary, secure the succession to her legitimate heirs, for the words "lawfully begotten" were omitted, so that an illegitimate child might succeed her in the title and estates with which she was now endowed.

Henry had, of course, taken a hundred solemn oaths that he would marry her as soon as he had obtained his divorce, and

*She was not, of course, addressed except as Lady Pembroke. But the patent was for a marquisate, to indicate that she possessed it in her own right and that her son could inherit the title.

this divorce at last seemed within reach. But if anything should happen at the last moment to prevent it, Anne would at least have her title and lands — secured also to her heir. In becoming the King's mistress now she had at least obtained far better terms than those given to Elizabeth Blount or her own sister Mary.

Many people regarded this marquisate as payment in full, in which they were vastly mistaken. Anne could now confidently count upon being queen; the marquisate was no more than a part payment of the full price she had demanded for her surrender. She had held out for six years against Henry's importunities, and though she had risked the cooling of his ardour, she had in fact contrived to increase it. She felt she could hold him until the divorce, now obtainable because of Warham's death. To refuse her lover at that moment might seem like lack of trust and was sure to be resented. Added to the store of resentment that already existed, it might mean the loss of everything. In surrendering she had to risk something; she did not risk much.

She knew her Henry and, knowing him, did not trust him too far. Therefore the marquisate. And one may suspect that a murky idea was at the back of Henry's secretive mind: if he married her, could he be sure she would bear a child? He would test that point first. Anne had several times goaded him into action by crying that her youth was going, for at thirty, as she was in 1532, she was almost double what was then considered the marriageable age for women. She might already be too old — too old to bear a child. She knew that she would have to yield without any further argument; and it would be very much to her advantage to become pregnant in short order.

Henry, on the other hand, could not afford to wait long after he had ascertained Anne's capacity to bear; otherwise she might present him with a child outside of marriage, one of no more dynastic use to him than was his son the Duke of Richmond. The divorce from Katherine had to be obtained at once. A message was sent off to Cranmer: he was to come home, he was to be archbishop of Canterbury.

Cranmer was very much embarrassed when he got the surprising news. Though he had no objection to the breach with the Papacy which he saw to be now almost inevitable – for he said afterwards that he had been praying for this for years – he realized that there might be all kinds of complications and difficulties, and these he disliked even more than most men. Besides, he had married in Germany; what on earth was he to do with Mrs. Cranmer? He therefore took his time about returning, though he did not have Campeggio's excuse and was a notably good horseman. This appointment was something he did not wish; he accepted it only because he had to.

Nobody had ever thought of him as a bishop, much less as the primate. He had had no official position in the ecclesiastical organization, so far. He had served, without special distinction, on embassies since 1530, but he was really only a kind of chaplain to the Boleyns, in which capacity he had given a certain amount of instruction to the ill-educated Anne, by way of preparing her for her future position. He was still essentially the gentle-mannered, inoffensive clerical don of Cambridge. The obvious choice for Warham's successor was Gardiner. Gardiner, however, would not do. Though he had served Henry well, he was not without some spirit of independence. Only Cranmer could be counted upon to do exactly as he was told.

His very usefulness as a tool, however, made the situation delicate. It would be at once guessed at Rome why Henry was making this very strange nomination for the see of Canterbury. The Pope might conceivably respond by launching an excommunication of both Cranmer and the King. Yet what Henry meant to do was, at the same instant, to inveigle the Holy See into issuing the necessary bulls for Cranmer's consecration, and to make Parliament pass an act forbidding all appeals to Rome, thus of course cutting off Katherine from redress. Henry managed the astonishing trick by taking del Burgo, the Papal Nuncio, with him everywhere, so as to lead him to inform the Pope of the friendly goodwill the much maligned Henry had for his Holiness. At the same time the appearance of the Nuncio at the King's side was intended to create the impression in England that nothing was further from Henry's thoughts than any breach with the Papacy. The act forbidding appeals to Rome, as it was meeting stiff resistance in Parliament, was eased through by assurances whispered to the members that the Emperor was now willing to accept the Boleyn marriage and that the Pope was about to change – that he had changed – his position.

Pending Cranmer's arrival Henry wished to take Anne with him to France, a visit that occurred at Boulogne the month following her marquisate. But as she could not very well be openly presented as his future wife, she could go only as his mistress. As such Francis – a notorious philanderer himself – was perfectly willing to receive her, but he was not willing that his wife should do so, especially as she was the Emperor's sister and Katherine's niece. He therefore pleaded that she was expecting a child and tried to persuade his sister, Marguerite of Navarre, to be his official hostess. But the authoress of the *Heptameron* refused to meet Henry's mistress – his whore was what she called her – so the Duchess of Vendôme was proposed instead. As she was a lady notorious for her gallantries, Henry, feeling very aggrieved, decided that Anne had better remain at Calais and that he go to Boulogne alone. Anne was mollified only when Henry sent Katherine a written order to surrender her jewels. These Anne wore.

Through Francis overtures were made, even at this last minute, to the Pope and the Emperor asking for a court to decide on Henry's matrimonial status on neutral territory, Cambrai being suggested. This had been talked of before, but nothing had come of it because one or other of the parties had always objected. This time the Emperor consented, counting on the case being dragged out another year, which might be more than long enough to make Henry tired of Anne. The Pope also was weighing the suggestion favorably, perhaps for the same reasons that operated with the Emperor. And such a court would take off Clement's shoulders what he always wished to avoid, responsibility for the decision.

Henry's talk about Cambrai was probably merely a way of

throwing dust in the eyes of the Pope. It succeeded so well that, though Chapuys was very emphatic in the warnings he sent that Cranmer was nominated archbishop only in order to pronounce the divorce, Rome was brought to believe that nothing would be done in a hurry. At all events, this was the hope of the Curia; it seemed better to treat that hope as something substantial than, by the refusal of Cranmer's bulls, to provoke an explosion. For his part Henry, until the bulls had been safely received, would do nothing against the Pope. He even paid Cranmer's expenses – always heavy on such occasions – so as not to allow them to be an obstacle.

To obtain these bulls Cranmer had to promise to take an oath of loyalty to the Holy See; therefore he took it. But the curious kind of conscience he had obliged him to disavow on March 26, before a select group of four in the chapter-house of St. Stephen's, Westminster, any intention of being bound by his oath. Pollard is probably alone among historians in defending this action, saying that it was due, rather than to bad faith, to "an excess of scruple on Cranmer's part." On March 30 the perjured man was consecrated archbishop of Canterbury.*

Meanwhile Henry and Anne had been married, not waiting for the King's divorce from Katherine. The ceremony was performed secretly on January 25, not even Cranmer being told until later. It was a little irregular for Henry to marry a second wife while still bound to the first, and such irregularities he disliked; but in this case he did not have any choice. A form of marriage had to be gone through at once, as Anne was with child; the marriage could be validated later. The priest who officiated is generally supposed to have been Rowland Lee, afterwards Bishop of Litchfield. Chapuys, however, said that it was George Browne, the Prior of the London Augustinians. Cranmer was debarred from officiating, as it was he who was, as Primate, to give the divorce from Katherine and, after that, to pronounce the slightly bigamous marriage to Anne "good."

*Even had Chapuys' advice been followed and a specially stringent oath demanded, the result would have been the same.

It should be noted that Convocation prepared for this by voting as the King desired. Two questions were presented: the theologians were asked whether the Pope was empowered to dispense a man from marrying his deceased brother's wife after her first marriage had been consummated; the canon lawyers were asked whether the evidence presented in the legatine court of 1529 proved the consummation of the marriage between Arthur and Katherine. The vote was overwhelmingly in Henry's favour, though there were some notable exceptions. Gardiner was one of these. He had been rewarded for his services with the extremely wealthy diocese of Winchester, but, like many other advocates of the divorce, he cooled off after he had obtained his fee. Edward Lee was another dissenting voice, when the Convocation of York voted, on the same points and with the same result, a few weeks later. He had been rewarded by being appointed Wolsey's successor. It is somewhat to the credit of these men that they asserted some scrap of independence, though in the days to come they were most careful not to go so far as to arouse the King's resentment. He never minded a little opposition, so long as it did not prevent his gaining his point. And what Convocation gave was only moral support, not a judicial decision.

This motion passed the Convocation of Canterbury on the day of Cranmer's perjury, March 26. The King at the opening of Parliament the month before, though he was already married to Anne, seated the Papal Nuncio beside him by way of publicly proclaiming his loyalty to the Holy See. Chapuys was puzzled and wrote: "Many think there is some secret intelligence between the King and the Pope." This, of course, was just what Henry wanted to be thought, and del Burgo's timidity played into his hands; he had in his possession a signed order from the Pope ordering Henry to separate from Anne, but he had taken advantage of the clause saying that he was to wait for an appropriate occasion for presenting it, not to present it at all. When Chapuys reproached him for this, he shrugged the matter off by saying that he was a poor man and had his living to make.

He did, however, remind the King of his book against Luther, and got the reply that further study had changed his mind. The King paused weightily and added that still further study might make him revert to his original position. It was a last-minute effort to avoid the breach with Rome. If only the Pope would do as he was told, he would find no more obedient son than Henry.

Henry by now had no hope of getting what he wanted from Rome. All that he was trying for was to keep the Pope from excommunicating him until after he had accomplished his own purposes. So on April 11 the King obtained from Cranmer a letter, written in most abject terms, asking that he be permitted to do the very thing for which he had been appointed archbishop. As this letter was not considered grovelling enough, Henry sent it back with his own emendations, changing "upon my knees" to "prostrate at the feet of your Majesty." He also added a passage in which Cranmer is made to call Christ as his witness that he wished to try the case truly and impartially. When this second letter arrived, the King gave his gracious permission to Cranmer to divorce him, at the same time admonishing him not to be guided by any human consideration but "to make an end according to the will and pleasure of Almighty God, in our said great cause of matrimony." All this though Cranmer by now knew that the King had married Anne Boleyn two and a half months before!

Cranmer established his court on May 8 at Dunstable. That little town was chosen as being far enough away from London to assure the necessary secrecy; in London its proceedings could hardly have been concealed, and would probably have caused a riot, if not a rebellion. But there was the further advantage that Katherine was living at Ampthill near by; nobody should say that she had not been able to attend. She was therefore summoned to appear — three times in all, though there was nothing that Cranmer dreaded so much as her appearance. Writing on May 17 to Cromwell he said that he hoped "the noble lady Katherine would not change her mind, as that would cause delay." To make sure that she should have no effective counsel, Fisher was put under arrest.

They need not have been so afraid. Chapuys had advised Katherine that, as she had an appeal pending in Rome, it would be improper for her to recognize Cranmer's court. The verdict was predetermined; all that she could have done was to have made some complications and gained a little time. Chapuys tried to make the Papal Nuncio serve on Cranmer a brief that had arrived from Rome forbidding the proceedings, but this del Burgo was too frightened to do; nor would it have done any good. Taking everything into consideration, Katherine was behaving not merely correctly but wisely. She was left free to refuse to recognize any decision from Dunstable. On May 23, 1533 – the very earliest day permitted by the rules of procedure – the decision was reached: Henry's marriage to Katherine was null and void.

There were still a few loose ends for Cranmer to tie up. To this he attended with the utmost dispatch. Only five days after the sentence at Dunstable he pronounced at Lambeth another sentence – one declaring the marriage of Henry and Anne valid. The public had not been told until then that any marriage had taken place, nor (for all too obvious reasons) was any announcement made as to its date.

To make up for the hole-and-corner secrecy, Henry wished, now that Anne was to be produced as queen, to have everything done as publicly as possible. She was to be crowned, though the crowning of a queen-consort is never necessary and was, in this instance, rather absurd. But as Katherine had been crowned (with Henry) Anne insisted on being crowned in her turn, though it had to be alone.

The King was well aware that Anne was personally unpopular and that the vast majority of his subjects heartily disapproved of the divorce. The previous August, just before the conferring of her marquisate, the Venetian Ambassador reported that she had been waylaid by a mob of seven thousand women and men disguised as women, when supping at a villa on the river, and had barely escaped being torn in pieces. And when on Easter Sunday, 1533, Dr. George Browne (the man Chapuys said married her to the King) publicly prayed for her at St. Paul's, the entire congregation rose and left the Cathedral. Henry had to send word to the Lord Mayor that, if anything of the sort happened again, there would be severe punishment.

These demonstrations were not confined to the common people. On one of Queen Katherine's last appearances in public Anne's aunt, the Duchess of Norfolk, and her sister-in-law, Lady Rochford (who was on bad terms with her husband), had cheered her. And the King's sister, the Duchess of Suffolk, had made no effort to conceal her dislike of one to whom, from this time on, Chapuys used to refer in his official dispatches as the Concubine and whom her subjects were apt to style Nan Boleyn the Whore. Her coronation, arranged for June 1, three days after the announcement had been made of Henry's marriage to her, was to be the King's defiant answer.

It was not very easy to conceal her condition even with a loose and voluminous dress. Nevertheless she wore white satin, as though she were a virgin bride, and her long hair was left unbound, another token of virginity. It greatly impressed the susceptible Cranmer that her hair was so long that she was able to sit on it in her litter. It was he who was to crown her, his patroness. The crowds, however, were sullen. She might have secured a little momentary popularity had she distributed among the people the purses of gold she received on her journey from the state apartments in the Tower to the Abbey; these, however, she kept.

There were some conspicuous absentees from the coronation ceremony. The Duchess of Norfolk was one. The Earl of Shrewsbury was another. Still another was Sir Thomas More. His friends Bishops Gardiner, Tunstall, and Clerk had sent him twenty pounds for a new robe as a means of compelling his attendance, but he stayed quietly at home at Chelsea. When he met the

Bishops shortly afterwards he told them a story about a Roman emperor who made a law that a certain offence that was punishable by death would not apply to one who was a virgin. But the very first culprit turned out to be a virgin, whereupon the clever suggestion was made, "Let her first be deflowered, and then after she may be devoured." More went on to say that though these friends of his had, so far, kept themselves pure virgins, they should take heed that they keep their virginity still. He foresaw that because they had attended the coronation, they might be called upon to speak and write in favour of the King's new marriage: "And when they have deflowered you, then they will not fail to devour you. Now my Lords, it lieth not within my power that they may devour me; but God being my good Lord, I will provide that they shall never deflower me." He was well aware that Anne felt that he had insulted her and would seek her revenge.

Anne's tenacity had triumphed. After her marriage, but before it had been announced, at a time when she knew herself to be already pregnant, she could not forbear throwing out hints of this. She began telling people, who supposed that she was still only the King's mistress, that unless she found herself with child by Easter she would make a pilgrimage to the shrine of Our Lady of Walsingham. Before that, on February 23, Chapuys wrote to Nicholas Granvelle, the imperial Chancellor, that she had spoken, in the presence of Sir Thomas Wyatt, of her longing for apples. She added, "Do you know what the King says? He says it means that I am with child. But I tell him no. No, it couldn't be, no!" Then after having spilled her great news in this way, she broke into one of her shrill peals of laughter, much to Wyatt's embarrassment. She could not speak more openly until it had been publicly announced that the King had been divorced from Katherine.

After the coronation she paraded her motherhood. She was sure that she was going to bear a son, and so was Henry. This time God would reward him for having renounced his incestuous marriage. "God," he said, "who knows my righteous heart, always prospers my affairs." But to make further sure the King consulted professional astrologers, "wise women," and did not disdain even the predictions of beggars who claimed the gift of second sight. All these were careful to promise him a son, and from one of them he accepted the advice that a certain magical jewel and the skin of a snake, if laid upon the thighs, would ensure a speedy delivery. What the large, comfortable Dr. Butts thought of this prescription, or how it commended itself to the brilliant Dr. Clement, is not recorded. Henry thought there would, in any event, be no harm in following necromancy as well as science.

He was so confident of a son that he drew up in advance a proclamation that announced the birth of a prince. It may still be seen with the addition of an "s" — there was no room for two extra letters — in Henry's own handwriting. This he had to squeeze in when he was disappointed, for on September 7, 1533, Elizabeth was born.

There were bonfires in the streets. But Henry knew that the rejoicing was really because the detested Anne had not produced a male heir and that, in popular estimation, the bastardized Mary was still the rightful successor to the throne. He also knew that a boy would have dissipated much of the opposition to his marriage among the people. Now Anne — or was it God? — had failed him.

He gave Anne the benefit of the doubt. She had, after all, proved her capacity to bear a viable child. A year almost to the day after he had at long last won her as his mistress, and hardly more than six months after marriage, she had given him a child. This was much better than Katherine had been able to do. Not until seven years after marriage was Mary born.

Something of Henry's old passion for Anne momentarily revived, though he had already been casting roving glances on other ladies. When Anne had complained, he had brutally told her that she must learn to close her eyes to these things, "as her betters had done." But now some movement of tenderness stirred in him. He took into his arms the body of the weeping woman and told her, "I would rather beg from door to door than forsake you!"

For Elizabeth's christening, at which Cranmer was godfather, and the Duchess of Norfolk and the Marchioness of Dorset – who took the place of Henry's sister Mary, recently dead – were godmothers, the King demanded Mary's christening robe of her mother. This Katherine refused; she was not going to have her daughter's robe worn by the child whom Chapuys used to call in his dispatches, "the little bastard." Reports came to Henry from Hilsey, the Provincial of the Dominicans who had been commissioned to visit all the orders of friars, that many of the brothers were circulating the unseemly joke that the warm water used at Elizabeth's baptism was not nearly hot enough for her.* As a result preachers were ordered to keep silent for a year, though long before that time was up, they received a new order – to preach against the Pope.

Chapuys as early as September 25 sounded Cromwell. The two men were friends after a fashion, having some artistic and scholarly interests in common. And Chapuys understood that Cromwell was a practical man and a realist. On that day they were out hawking together, and nobody else was within earshot, he asked him whether he would not work with him against Anne. Cromwell listened willingly enough but shook his head. He answered that the time for that had not yet come. The Queen might yet bear a son.

---

*This did not spring altogether from sympathy for Mary and opposition to the new-born child. But everybody shuddered at the thought of Elizabeth's becoming queen with Anne and Rochford as regents.

CHAPTER NINE

The First Martyrs

EVEN after his marriage to Anne and the birth of Elizabeth Henry did not give up all hope of eventual reconciliation with Rome. Clement had not, after all, given any decision regarding Katherine. And though Henry had made himself liable to grave censure for acting as he had done, there was still a possibility, he thought, that the Pope might prefer to overlook this and even pronounce in his favor rather than have a schism. So while Henry was instructing his agents in Rome to play for time, Katherine was writing to Clement in the opposite strain, sometimes not very respectfully, hotly demanding a decision. Indeed, when at last in consistory on March 24, 1534, a decision was reached – with nineteen cardinals pronouncing Katherine's marriage valid and only three advising further delay – the Pope was rather disturbed. He had not, according to Lingard, expected this result, though he acceded to the opinion of so large a majority. He was still ready to meet Henry more than half-way.*

In reaching its decision the consistory concluded that the dispensation issued by Julius II was amply sufficient. It was sufficient even had Arthur's marriage to Katherine been consummated. Therefore, while the Roman court reviewed the evidence

---

*This was in large part because Clement was himself so weak, but it was also because of his failure to understand Henry's fantastic egotism. Chapuys had written to the Emperor on April 16, 1533, that the King had said to some other person: "You have heard the Ambassador hint at excommunication. It is not I that am excommunicated but the Emperor, who has kept me so long in mortal sin. That is an excommunication that the Pope cannot take off."

given at Blackfriars in the summer of 1529, it did not consider the part that related to the consummation of the marriage relevant. Nor for that matter was the supplementary brief brought under consideration. The marriage stood on the bull of Julius II.

This decision came after every conceivable thing had been tried. Henry had gone so far, a year after Campeggio's departure from England, as to revive the request he had made in 1527 and again in 1528 for permission to commit bigamy. Gregory da Casale wrote to the King on September 18, 1530, that the Pope had suggested this himself. It is, however, made clear by another letter dated October 27, that it was only a "great divine" who had suggested this as a possible solution and that the Pope had said, "No." As the point is still sometimes grossly misrepresented, it is worth a moment's attention here. What Dr. Benet reported was: "I asked Clement VII if he were certain that such a dispensation was admissible, and he answered that it was not; but he added that a distinguished theologian had told him that in his opinion the Pope might in this case dispense in order to avert a greater evil; he intended, however, to go into the matter more fully with his council. And indeed the Pope has just now informed me that his council (known as the Consistory of Cardinals) had declared to him plainly that such a dispensation was not possible."*

A few months before the ruling by Rome, as the Pope and Francis I were to meet at Marseilles to arrange for the marriage of the Duke of Orleans and Catherine de' Medici, the Pope's niece, Francis offered his services as a go-between, for he wanted England as an ally but not as an ally in schism. Unfortunately Bonner, an able but very rough-spoken man, was sent to gild the diplomatic lily, and this he did by pushing his way into the

*This letter is quoted from Pastor's *History of the Popes* (English translation published by Routledge and Kegan Paul Ltd., London), Vol. X, p. 276. An extended footnote says that the distinguished theologian was probably Cardinal Cajetan, who held the opinion that polygamy was not against the law of nature, though of course he did not regard it as permissible. By permission of B. Herder Book Co., St. Louis.

Pope's presence and announcing that an appeal would be taken against him to a general council. This little incident, which happened on November 7, 1533, made Francis furious and he told Gardiner, "As fast as I study to win the Pope, ye study to lose him. Ye require a general council and that the Emperor desireth, and I go about to bring the Pope from the Emperor and ye drive him to him. Can my brother call a council alone?" The position taken up was not merely insulting but absurd.

Francis tried to undo the damage by sending Du Bellay to London to persuade Henry, if possible, to withdraw his appeal to the council and resume his negotiations with the Papal court. But Henry was not to be budged. Du Bellay carried to Rome an ultimatum that had no chance of acceptance: before Easter, 1534, the marriage to Katherine should be pronounced null and void and the marriage to Anne should be recognized. The answer of Rome was given shortly before Easter, on March 24. It went, as we have seen, against Henry.

In anticipation of this the King pushed through Parliament, when it assembled early in the new year, the Act of Supremacy. And as Henry's excommunication was likely, and with it an interdict laid upon the whole country, it was made an offense punishable by law for any priest to obey it by refusing the sacraments. With that England was at last in schism.

During the years of strain between the English King and the Papacy, and afterwards too, Henry was careful to demonstrate how very orthodox he was. He might quarrel with the Pope but nobody was going to take him for a Lutheran. Wolsey had been rather lax in the suppression of heresy and had been succeeded as Chancellor by the most conscientious but also the kindest of men. Sir Thomas More was in duty bound to apprehend heretics, and during the three years of his administration a handful of heretics were condemned, though more were charmed out of their errors by one who, in any event, was not empowered, under the law, to sit in judgement upon them.

After the breach with Rome, or while it was seen to be all but inevitable, Henry from time to time insisted upon the execution of the laws against heresy, and among those who suffered in 1533 was a young priest named John Frith, a man with whom More had had some controversy and whose heresy had been proclaimed for all to hear. His case was remarkable because, though the man responsible for his condemnation was his ordinary, Stokesley the Bishop of London, on the commission that examined Frith were Anne Boleyn's father and Cranmer. We may pass over Wiltshire's connection with the matter, as he does not seem to have had any distinct religious sentiments. What is instructive to note is the part that Cranmer played. He made a written statement, which still remains, as to how he had personally questioned Frith and had tried to persuade him that there is "a very corporal presence of Christ within the Sacrament of the Altar." It was the thing that Cranmer also denied, but as yet only in his heart. Largely on the strength of Cranmer's report – though of course there was also Frith's published controversial writing – the condemned man was burned at Smithfield.

Such burnings occurred during the rest of the reign and, though done with one eye on the rest of Europe, indicated a sincere desire to keep England orthodox. But after 1534 the King, without quite forgetting heresy, was mainly concerned to enforce the law of treason against those who refused to take the oath recognizing him as Head of the Church. From then until 1540 – the period of Cromwell's dominance – was a reign of terror.

The story we come to is sad, but far more glorious than sad, in so far as it concerns the handful of men brave and intelligent enough to face the Prince's wrath, which, so Norfolk (and even Warham) used to go about saying was death. It is the story of defeated idealists – that is, if idealism is ever really defeated.

The case of one of these idealists – one of the few among them who escaped martyrdom – is instructive. It is that of Reginald Pole, the King's cousin and as such in the line of royal descent. He might have married Mary when she came to the throne, for though he was by that time a cardinal, the Pope could have dispensed him. And before that he would himself for a certainty have been elected Pope (in 1549) had he chosen to lift a finger in his own cause. He was too much of an idealist even to do that.

He and the King were genuinely fond of each other. Henry had paid for Reginald's education at Oxford and Padua and Paris and had given him, though he was not yet in orders, the deanery of Exeter. When he returned to England soon after Wolsey's fall, Henry, still very fond of him and recognizing his moral and intellectual distinction, offered him the archbishopric of York. Pole refused it, as he knew that he was expected to give an opinion on the divorce that was favourable to the King.

Even so Henry insisted on getting Pole's opinion, undertaking to feel no resentment, whatever it might be. What he wanted was Pole's honest view. So this was set out in a fashion which, Pole hoped, would please the King and yet not be too far removed from what he really thought. But he knew in his heart that the statement prepared had stretched things too far, so when he met Henry at York House by appointment, he suddenly saw that he must say nothing but what he felt to be the absolute truth. As he spoke, the royal brows darkened, and the blood flushed the massive royal face. For an instant indeed Henry's hand went to his dagger but, controlling himself, he walked out of the room. Pole was allowed to leave England, to which he did not return until Mary's accession.

Pole was the reverse of a politician. On a previous visit to England he had had a conversation with a man who was nothing but a politician – Thomas Cromwell. He tells of Cromwell's offering to lend him a book, saying, "If you must needs have books, you should at least read those who allow more to experience than to speculation." He went on, "I have here one of a very acute modern, who does not, like Plato, publish his own dreams. He has laid down maxims and observations, of which daily experience confirmeth the truth." The book Cromwell wanted to lend Pole was Machiavelli's *The Prince.**

---

*This has been questioned on the ground that *The Prince,* though written in 1514, was not published until 1532. What must be remembered is that in those days books often circulated in manuscript before being

If Reginald Pole escaped at this time, and subsequently eluded all the efforts that were made to have him assassinated or kidnapped, there were also a few others who managed to escape during the early days of the schism. Of these the most notable was William Peto, who in Mary's reign was made Legate, replacing Pole, much to the Queen's annoyance, popular resentment, and his own embarrassment. What he should be remembered for is not his cardinalate and legateship but for having dared to reprove Henry to his face.

He was the Provincial of the Franciscan Observants, Katherine's favourite order, and at one time Henry's too. Preaching before the King at Greenwich in May, 1533, he took as his text, "Even where the dogs licked the blood of Naboth, even there shall the dogs lick thy blood, O King." To make matters worse, and to tighten the linking of Henry with Ahab, he went on to inveigh against the "false prophets" around the King and added, "I am that Micheas whom thou wilt hate, because I must tell thee truly that this marriage is unlawful." He even ventured to say, "take good heed lest, being seduced, you find Ahab's punishment, which was to have his blood licked up by the dogs." Never could there have been a plainer and bolder admonition.

Henry was very angry but did nothing except arrange for a Dr. Curwin to answer when Peto was absent the following Sunday. When Curwin did so, taunting Peto with having "fled for fear and shame as being unable to answer my arguments," a friar named Elstow called from the rood-loft, "Good sir, you know that Father Peto has gone to Canterbury, and not for fear of you. He will return tomorrow. In the meanwhile I am here and will lay down my life to prove that all those things are true that he hath taught out of the holy Scripture." When Elstow

printed. Cromwell seems to have returned to England in 1513, but one cannot always follow his movements, except that it would appear likely that he made several visits to Italy between that date and his immersement in politics. Even apart from that, he retained Italian connections, and there were many Italians in London. He was to show himself so complete a master of the Machiavellian doctrine that it is impossible to imagine what other book he could have offered to Pole for his instruction.

had finished, another of the Observants vehemently accused Curwin of preaching as he did in hope of preferment. This reward he got all right, for he was made Dean of Hereford and eventually Archbishop of Dublin.* As for Peto and Elstow and the other friar they suffered nothing worse than a wigging from the King, and were permitted to go into exile. But this of course was before the question of the royal supremacy had reached its climax. The rest of the Observants were not then so fortunate, for about two hundred of them were cast into prison, without trial, and there many of them died. One of their number (about whom we shall hear more later) was to have the unique distinction of being executed as both heretic and traitor.

Elizabeth Barton, "the Holy Maid of Kent," can hardly be classed as a martyr; she was rather a victim. But she certainly suffered in the Catholic cause and was used as a means of trapping those whom Henry wished to destroy. As her story is closely connected with that of Fisher and More – though they would have eventually been put to death even had she never lived – it must be briefly related here.

She had been a servant girl in Aldington in Kent (which Erasmus held as a benefice, though he gave no service there) and had been cured – she said miraculously – of epileptic fits. Perhaps she had not been cured so completely as she imagined, for there is reason to think that she remained at least highly hysterical. But after she had become a Benedictine nun at Canterbury she achieved wide fame as a visionary. All kinds of people consulted her – a fact that was to be used in terrifying some of the powerfully placed among them into submission.

Absolutely fearless herself, she visited the King and also Wolsey, though apparently she did not have much to say to either. Later, however, she gave out that, if Henry married

*It is rather remarkable how many of the men who made themselves useful to the Crown during this period got this diocese. It was not then regarded as one of the greater ecclesiastical plums. Strong royal partisans were sent there presumably to curb the papalism of the Irish. Curwin proclaimed himself a Protestant upon Elizabeth's accession.

Anne, he would not live for seven months. That prophecy was proved to be false, and as Elizabeth told somebody else that she had seen in vision the precise spot in hell that was to be occupied by Henry, one cannot but recognize a mind somewhat unhinged. We should, however, get a false picture of her if we thought of her as doing nothing but deliver startling divinations. As a rule she did not do more than speak of spiritual matters, in many instances to excellent effect.

Many people were impressed by her sanctity, though the number that sought her out because of curiosity or as a soothsayer was doubtless much greater. Fisher was one of her admirers, but More was not. From the beginning he was very sceptical and, when at last he was persuaded to meet her, he warned her not to touch upon anything relating to politics, reminding her that it was on account of a chance word spoken by a monk that the Duke of Buckingham had lost his head in 1521. His warning went unheeded and, as the government was looking for a means of terrorizing the disaffected, Elizabeth Barton was arrested. It was expected that she would implicate others more prominent than herself; Cromwell even thought at one time that, through her, he could catch Queen Katherine in the toils.

Her trapping was left to Cranmer. He sent for her and, using his silkiest tones, began to question her. She was taken in by his sympathetic manner and laid aside what little reserve she ever practised. His Dean of Arches, Dr. Richard Gwent (afterwards Archdeacon of London), who was present at the interview, wrote to Cromwell: "He does yet but dally with her, as if he did believe every word, and as soon as he has got all he can out of her she shall be sent to you."

She soon found herself in the Tower, along with some of her advisers, among them a couple of Franciscans and a couple of Benedictines. But she was treated with ostensible respect, almost as though she were of noble blood, subjected to no torture, merely questioned. So transparent a soul needed nothing more. As so little incriminating evidence was secured, she and her friends were made to stand on a platform in November outside

St. Paul's while she read a confession that she was an imposter. There it was supposed the matter would end. She had been discredited, and even More wrote to Cromwell congratulating him upon having brought such manifest hypocrisy to light. She could have been laughed at and let go.

Rather, that could have happened except for one thing: her guilt had to be regarded as grave if it were to be used to implicate others. Nothing except the most trivial contacts could be established between Elizabeth and the Countess of Salisbury and the Marchioness of Exeter (who had been aimed at), but she could be (and was) used to give weight to the bill of attainder being prepared against John Fisher and Thomas More. When Fisher and More refused to submit to Henry's demands, even in face of that threat – then, but not till then, were the poor young woman and her friends sent to Tyburn.*

In a bill charging misprision of treason, introduced early in 1534, the names of More and Fisher were included. Fisher, who had been guilty at least to the extent of neglecting sufficiently to safeguard himself, managed to compound for a £300 fine. More's name, however, had to be dropped because he was able to prove that, so far from ever encouraging the Nun of Kent, he had warned her against mixing in politics. Even so Henry was for going to the House of Lords in person to force the attainder through. When he was told that the Lords meant to hear the former Chancellor in his own defence and that the King might receive a bad rebuff from Parliament, Henry remained obdurate until Cromwell and Audley whispered to him that he would be well advised to go no further; they would undertake to find some "meeter matter" before long.

This meeter matter came when, in March, the Act of Succession was passed, securing the succession of the throne to Anne Boleyn's children. Its preamble asserted that the King's previous marriage had been against the law of God and therefore by

*The dates should be noted; More and Fisher refused the Oath of Supremacy on April 13; Elizabeth Barton was executed on April 21, 1534.

implication denied the Pope's right to pass on the question. It was demanded that everybody should take an oath in accordance with this statute.

Parliament had, however, prescribed no form of oath to be taken, and it is quite likely that the oath would not have been so stringent as it was had it not happened that, at this very moment, Clement and his consistory had decided that Katherine's marriage was valid and that Anne's was not. Henry's angry answer to the Pope was to demand from his subjects not merely loyalty to the new line of succession but also an oath that accepted the preamble.

At Lambeth Palace, where as a boy more than forty years before he had been a page in the household of Cardinal Morton, Thomas More was received with courtesy by the commissioners, who had demanded his attendance. All of them wished him well, even Cromwell, who protested that he would rather his own son should lose his head than that More should refuse the oath. The other men were Sir Thomas Audley, More's successor, handsome, urbane, and empty; the mediocrity William Benson who had been made Abbot of Westminster as the price of his adhesion; and Cranmer of the doe's eyes and the rabbit's face. They pleaded with him to do as the King wanted, and when he refused they suggested that he go into the garden and consider the matter again. There, or in the corridors of the palace, he saw a number of men he knew — all priests, for he was the only layman summoned that day — among them Rowland Phillips, the Bishop of Utopia, and Hugh Latimer in such jovial spirits that he put his arm round the necks of several men there. Of this More afterwards wrote to his daughter Margaret: "If they had been women I would have weened that he was wanton."

More remained resolute. He was willing to take the oath as recognizing the right of Anne's children — she had only Elizabeth — to the succession, as the determination of this was within the competence of Parliament. But he was not willing to swear to the preamble, as that repudiated the Pope's authority.

Cranmer, a kindly man (though we have seen his tricky handling of Elizabeth Barton), made a characteristic suggestion privately to Cromwell. Let More and Fisher swear to what they felt they could accept; then it could be given out that there had been no reservations. This was passed on to the King while More was kept for four days in the custody of the Abbot of Westminster. When Henry decided that no reservations would be permitted, More was sent to the Tower.

There he remained for fifteen months, with Fisher and Dr. Wilson, one of the King's chaplains (who later yielded), as fellow prisoners. He was allowed to have a servant and books and, at first, to write as much as he pleased. Under such circumstances he produced his wise and gay-hearted *Dialogue of Comfort* and some of the most charming and tender letters ever penned. Dame Alice went to visit him and expressed, in her raciest language, her astonishment that so intelligent a man was willing to be shut up in a cell with rats and mice when, by speaking a few words, he could return to his home in Chelsea, with its beautiful garden and his books "and me, your wife." When he tried to explain she impatiently cut him short with "Tilly-vally! Tilly-vally, man! Will this gear never be left?" She could not understand his obstinacy when all the most learned men in England, Fisher excepted, had taken the oath. More's daughter Margaret understood better and told him as a good joke what their former fool, Henry Patenson, had said: "Why, what aileth him that he will not swear? Wherefore should he stick to swear? I have sworn to the oath myself!" She and More's son and his three sons-in-law – all three members of Parliament – had taken the oath, but in a less rigorous form. Because of their well-known disapproval of the divorce More and Fisher had been selected for an unequivocal submission.

They were in the Tower only under a charge of misprision of treason. Though this was sufficiently serious, as it meant the confiscation of all their possessions, more than that could not be charged as yet. To make more possible, a new act of Parliament went through that November making it high treason in any way to deny the King his supremacy. There was a great deal of "sticking" at this, and it passed only after Parliament had insisted on twice inserting the qualifying word "maliciously." More was to contend at his trial that this word had exactly the same effect as the word "forcible' 'in a charge of forcible entry, but he knew perfectly well that the lawyers would get round it. His only hope was in keeping absolute silence on the matter.

It did not save him, or Fisher, who followed the same tactics. A test case was made of three Carthusian priors — John Houghton, Robert Lawrence, and Augustine Webster. They, along with the Bridgettine monk Richard Reynolds and the secular priest John Hale, in vain pleaded that there was no malice in the refusal of the oath. Reynolds told his judges that in England the vast majority believed even as they, the accused, did, "although outwardly, partly from fear, partly from hope, they professed" otherwise. Pressed to say who were these secret supporters, he answered simply, "All good men." When the jury would not convict, Cromwell went to them and threatened them with death unless they brought in the right verdict.

On May 5 More was standing at the window of his cell with Margaret when he saw them being bound to hurdles to be dragged to Tyburn. "Lo! dost thou not see, Meg," he said, "that these blessed Fathers be now as cheerfully going to their deaths as bridegrooms to their marriage?" He envied them. He had come close, very close, when he was a young man to joining the Carthusians and had lived at the London Charterhouse for four years while he was studying law.

Other Carthusians were to follow before long, among them Sebastian Newdigate, a former friend of the King's in the days when he was a courtier and a famous rider in the tilting-yard. These were subjected to abominable tortures, chained in such a way that they could not lie down or help themselves at all. Margaret Giggs, whom Sir Thomas More had brought up in his household and who was now married to Dr. Clement, made her way to them disguised to feed them and to take away their ordure. Dying thirty-five years later in exile at Mechlin for the Faith, on the anniversary of More's execution, she saw standing by her bed, not (as one might have expected) the man whom, when she was a child she used to provoke by some small naughtiness to enjoy his gentle reproof, but the Carthusians she had befriended. She called her husband, More's former secretary, and told him that she could no longer stay; the holy Fathers had come to take her with them.

The story of the Carthusians has been told with moving simplicity and tenderness by one of their number, Maurice Chauncey, who submitted to the King and who regretted ever afterwards the loss of his martyr's palm. But for that matter, even John Houghton, after a previous short incarceration in the Tower, had allowed himself to be persuaded by Bishop Stokesley and Archbishop Lee that the question of the succession (that was how they represented it) was not one in which he should lay down his life. It was only with the passage of the new act at the end of 1534 that he saw that he would have to renew his refusal, for now there was an explicit affirmation that the King was Supreme Head of the Church.

Houghton assembled his community and said that his heart was heavy, "especially for you, my younger friends." There they were living in their innocence; how would it go with them when, as he foresaw, they would have to "mingle with the Gentiles"? How could he save those whom God had entrusted to his charge?

They all burst into tears and said with one voice, "Let us die together in our integrity."

The Prior, a little man of delicate face and features, shook his head gravely. He told them, "Me and the elder brethren they will kill; and they will dismiss you who are young into a world not for you. If, therefore, it depends on me alone – if my oath will suffice for the house – I will throw myself for your sakes on the mercy of God. I will make myself anathema." He was prepared to take the new oath to save the other monks.

Nevertheless Houghton advised them to prepare for death,

"that the Lord when He knocketh might find us ready." And the next day in chapter he rose from his place and, going to the eldest of the brethren, kneeling down asked forgiveness for "any offence which in heart, word or deed he might have committed against him." And so to all the brethren, imploring from each, down to the youngest novice, his pardon.

"The third day after," wrote Chauncey, "was the Mass of the Holy Ghost, and God made known His presence amongst us. For when the Host was lifted up, there came, as it were, a whisper of air, which breathed upon our faces as we knelt. Some perceived it with the bodily senses; all felt it as it thrilled into their hearts. And there followed a sweet, soft sound of music. . . . Our hearts rejoiced as we perceived that God was with us indeed."

Thus they prepared themselves. And when Robert Lawrence, the Prior of Beauvale, and Augustine Webster of Axholme arrived to consult with Houghton on a concerted course of action, they decided to anticipate the arrival of the royal commissioners by themselves going to Cromwell. He answered by putting them under arrest.

Theirs was the most austere of orders, and almost the only order that has never needed any reform. It is unique in that the Carthusians will never permit the introduction of the cause of canonization of any of their members.* One would imagine that to follow such a rule as theirs is possible only to saints. These were men who had spoken no word against the royal marriage and divorce. All such things belonged to the world they had left; they asked no more than to be permitted the silence and seclusion of the cloister. But the King had followed them there with his insistent demands. And when (like the outspoken Observant friars in this) they stood firm, they were struck down. So far from their holiness saving them, that was all the more reason for extracting from them an unqualified adhesion to the royal will. As though to emphasize this, they were executed in

*The Carthusians whose story is told here are, however, beatified as among the English martyrs.

their habits. Those standing round the scaffold noticed that the Fathers, as they witnessed what was being done to the sufferer under the disembowelling knife, which was a few minutes later to work upon them, did not so much as pale at the sight. To each was offered a pardon at the last moment if he would but submit.

The execution of the Carthusians was merely a preliminary to the trial of More and Fisher. As neither man would express any opinion, neither could be convicted. Various tricks were tried: each man was told that the other had taken the oath, so as to break him down. When that failed, Richard Rich, the Solicitor General, told Fisher that the King had requested his opinion, as a bishop, for the guidance of his conscience. As a bishop Fisher could not refuse this, and the government seized upon it as the evidence it needed. Let us hope that Henry was not implicated in this despicable plot and that Rich was acting on his own responsibility. John Fisher was accordingly convicted and probably only because he was too frail to endure being dragged to Tyburn was given the merciful block on June 22.

When he was awakened too early on the morning of his execution, he said he would like to sleep another hour or two. He asked his servant for a clean shirt, saying, "Dost thou not mark that this is our wedding-day, and that it behoveth us, therefore, to use more cleanliness for solemnity of the marriage?" And, as the morning was chilly, he wore a fur tippet, explaining that God meant him to take care of his health to the last. At the scaffold he asked the witnesses to pray that he would not falter at the instant of death's stroke in any point of the Catholic faith. As he stood there, tall, gaunt, and aged, "a very image of death, death in a man's shape and using a man's voice," the sun suddenly shone out and there seemed to be a halo round his head.

Sir Thomas More from start to finish had never said a word about the question at issue. But he was brought to trial in Westminster Hall, where he had often presided as judge, and accused of having been in collusive correspondence with Fisher during their imprisonment. More did not deny that letters had passed between them but said that they had been on indifferent matters. The prosecution was not in the position of being able to affirm the contrary, as the bearer of the letters, who had been asked to keep them to prove their innocence, had burned them, lest he should get into trouble. It was, however, inferred that there must have been some collusion.

The main evidence against More was presented by the prosecuting counsel, Rich, who contrary to all legal procedure left the bar and went into the witness box. As though such an outrage were not enough, Rich doctored a conversation he had had with More in such a way as to make the evidence perjury.* For this he received such a public castigation as has never been heard from a prisoner accused of any kind of an offence. Before the row of his judges, presided over by Audley, and including most of the judiciary of England, More told them that it was a notorious fact, known to all of them, that Rich was a liar and a man of infamous life. He asked them was it a likely thing that he would make confidences to such a man, when he would not do so to "the King's Highness himself, or any of his honourable Council."

Not until he had received sentence of death did he speak his mind. Then in words that were to ring all over Europe, he affirmed that the government of the Church belonged only to St. Peter and his successors, and that it was given them by Christ himself. It was impossible for one part of Christendom to make a law in contradiction to that universally accepted principle. He quoted Magna Carta to them, reminding them that

---

*What happened, as recorded by Roper, was this: Rich had asked More if, in the event of Parliament making him (Rich) king, More would accept him as such. More said he would. Rich then went on: Supposing Parliament made him Pope, what then? More distinguished: Parliament, he said, could deal with temporal affairs; but he would ask Rich a question: if Parliament made a law that God was not God, would that change the fact? Rich embellished this conversation by making More add: "No more could Parliament make the King Supreme Head of the Church." It was of course what More *believed*, but he had been most careful not to say anything of the kind.

the King at his coronation, and they themselves on taking office, had sworn to uphold the liberties of the Church. "No more might this realm of England," he said, "refuse obedience to the See of Rome than might the child refuse obedience to his own natural father."

They heard him out to the end. And when he had finished he saluted them – all of them men he knew and some of them his personal friends, saying that he hoped that, though they had been his judges, "we may yet hereafter in heaven merrily all meet together, to our everlasting salvation."

On his way back to the Tower, Margaret Roper met her father and, unmindful of the fact that she was about to bear a child, thrust through the guards to embrace him, returning a second time for a last kiss. Sir William Kingston, the Constable of the Tower, like the other beholders was in tears.

The day before his execution on July 6, More wrote Margaret a final letter, sending her at the same time the hair-shirt he had worn since youth and the laundering of which had been her special care. He had no further use for it. On the morning itself he dressed in a new gown a rich friend had sent him – he himself was of course quite destitute now – but took it off when Sir Edmund Walsingham, the Lieutenant, told him that it would be claimed by the headsman as his perquisite. More followed Walsingham's advice, but as the executioner was going to do him such a signal service, he sent him a gold piece instead.

On his way to the block More was met by a Winchester man who had formerly consulted him about his temptations to despair. This man pressed out of the crowd to tell him that his temptations were as strong as ever. More promised to pray for him, and never again did the temptations return.

At the scaffold he jested with Walsingham, asking his help up the rickety structure, "and for my coming down let me shift for myself." As the King had asked that he make only a short speech from the scaffold, More was very brief. The speech was much to the point and contained an allusion that Henry would understand, one to the King's admonition when he first entered the royal service. He asked the prayers of the bystanders and promised them his prayers elsewhere. He begged them to pray for the King, that God would give him good counsel. "I die," he concluded, "the King's good servant but God's first." His signed pardon, as in the case of the Carthusians and Fisher, was there – if only he would say, in effect, that he was the King's good servant first.

As the headsman was nervous More admonished him to make a clean stroke for the saving of his professional reputation. He blindfolded himself and, after he had put his head on the block, made his last joke. The long beard he had grown in prison was in the way; he would like to pull it aside. "At least that has committed no treason."

Henry received the news while he was playing at dice with Anne. He turned on her angrily and accused her of having brought about "that man's death." After which he went into a room alone. He had admired More and had probably loved him more than he had ever loved any other man. But he had brought himself to believe that, by standing out against him, More had shown malice. Towards his friends Henry was always specially vindictive, for the opposition of those whom he had favoured or to whom he had shown affection was an outrage. He could not admit that anybody had a right to follow his conscience except himself.

A thrill of horror ran through Europe. Pole was to write to Henry, "You have killed of all Englishmen the best." The new Pope, imagining that Henry would take it as a compliment, had nominated Fisher to the cardinalate, only to have Henry roar, "Yea, is he yet so lusty? Well, let the Pope send him a hat when he will. He shall wear it on his shoulders, for head he shall have none to set it on." When the Consistory heard of what had happened, the cardinals were agreed that the most severe punishment should be imposed. A bull was accordingly prepared which deposed Henry, absolved his subjects from their allegiance, and placed England under an interdict. But there was no way, at the moment, of having it executed. Francis feared that the ruin of Henry, who was still in alliance with him, would aggrandize the Emperor; *that* he could not permit, disapprove though he did of Henry's actions. The publication of the bull was therefore postponed. The truth is that the time had come when such fulminations had ceased to be effective. Nothing was done because nothing could be done.

Henry, knowing himself secure, marked his contempt for Rome and the Church by applauding a farce produced at court in which he was depicted cutting off the heads of his clergy. It was produced on July 23, and Henry, who had come in from the country to Greenwich to witness so delightful a spectacle, enjoyed it so much that he suggested to Queen Anne that the play be performed again on the eve of St. Peter. It was a jest in the very worst possible taste, but was of course taken by the sycophants round him as the very acme of wit. By way of demonstrating his orthodoxy he had ordered the burning of thirteen bewildered Anabaptists who had just landed from Holland.

The King's orthodoxy was politic. The country was in an exasperated mood, deeply shocked. That summer it rained so incessantly that most of the crops were ruined. At any time the resultant distress would have caused murmuring, but now people said that it was because of the executions, and these they blamed on Anne. Henry himself continued to escape most of the criticism; he was King and he could do no wrong.

The first and greatest martyr, in one sense, was Katherine of Aragon, with her daughter Mary playing a part hardly less noble. But of course they did not actually suffer death; they were merely prepared to suffer it. And if Mary eventually made an ostensible submission, this was not until after her mother had died and after Chapuys advised the taking of the oath as a thing inescapable. Even then she did not yield at once — not until Anne Boleyn was dead and Jane Seymour was in her place.

It was very largely for Mary's sake that Katherine had taken the line she did. It is possible that, had it not been for Mary,

Katherine would have accepted the compromise offered to her over and over again during 1528 and 1529. She did not need to be told that in this way she could prevent England from drifting into schism, for even at that time schism was threatened. Though it may not have been an error of judgement to believe that Henry would yield if only the Pope would plainly declare himself, Katherine persisted in this belief long after events had proceeded too far to make Henry yield before anything except a successful rebellion or an invasion.

All such speculations are idle; even had Mary never existed, it is likely enough that Katherine's sense of honour would have forbidden her to accept any compromise. What we know is that to the commissioners who went to her after the Dunstable divorce, and tried to browbeat her into acknowledging the King's new marriage, she had but one answer: she was Henry's lawful wife. When they read a long document to her, she asked to read it to herself the next day. Then she took a pen and with vigorous strokes, which scratched the paper (on which they may still be seen), she struck out every reference to herself as the "Princess Dowager" — that is, Arthur's widow. When her servants were forbidden to address her by any other title, she said in that event she would dismiss those who failed to call her Queen.

They offered her honour and ample provision; she was not to be bought. Though she haughtily demanded that she be sent to the Tower — knowing very well that Henry would not venture that — she was sent instead to a succession of houses in remote country parts, but always to a house that was unhealthy, perhaps in the hope that she would die. She was so afraid of poison that she would eat only the food prepared in her own room by her own maids.

In 1533 Cromwell attempted to implicate her in the so-called conspiracy of the Nun of Kent, as he confessed to Chapuys, but he also admitted that nothing could be found against her. As a matter of fact Chapuys was in contact with a number of English nobles, who said that they were prepared to rise in her defence, but she would not hear of such a thing, so, for want of her adhesion, a focus was lacking. He had lined up Lord Hussey and Lord Darcy, Lord Abergavenny and the Earl of Shrewsbury, the Marquis of Exeter, eventually even the Earl of Northumberland and Sir William Kingston, who as Constable of the Tower would have been invaluable at the start of any coup; and Wales or Cornwall had already been selected as the place for a landing, should the Emperor come to his aunt's assistance. But even if Chapuys was not over-optimistic, Katherine was always a stumbling-block. Her loyalty was logical and inflexible: she owed obedience in all lawful matters to Henry both as her king and as her husband. He must have had at least some inkling as to what was afoot, but he knew of Katherine's generosity and took advantage of it. He was secure so long as Katherine felt as she did, and she was not a woman to change her mind. While she lived she would not be a danger, merely an embarrassment.

At first she was under the charge of Lord Mountjoy at Ampthill, later she had less friendly jailers. She was able, however, to keep a kind of small court, surrounded mostly by Spanish attendants – about ten ladies-in-waiting, a doctor and an apothecary, and Jorge de Ateca, the titular Bishop of Llandaff, her confessor, with Thomas Abell for chaplain, the brave Englishman who had prevented the Emperor from surrendering the brief in 1529 into Henry's hands.*

To Buckden, in Hertfordshire in the Fen country, she was sent before 1533 was out, being cheered all the way as their rightful queen by such people as saw her. There the Duke of Suffolk visited her to try and get her to admit the validity of the Dunstable divorce. She answered passionately that to do so would be against her own honour and that of her husband. When Suffolk got angry, she went into her room and shut the door, refusing to open it. The Duke was afraid to break it down, for word had got out that force was being threatened against the beloved Queen. Men were gathering and Suffolk could see that he was in for trouble. In the end he retired, having accomplished

*The number of ladies-in-waiting, of course, steadily diminished; so also with the servants; and Abell was taken into custody in 1534.

nothing, but taking Father Abell with him for an incarceration in the Tower that was to end, six years later, on the gallows.

Katherine was moved to Kimbolton, which was to be her last home, a gloomy, strongly fortified house surrounded by a moat, where she could be held in stricter custody. There was always the possibility that, though she would make no move against the King, others might rescue her by force. On the point of her departure she wrote to her daughter urging her to be faithful to God and advising: "sometimes for your recreation use your virginals or lute, if you have any." She sent her two books in Latin, a life of Christ and the Letters of St. Jerome. Above all she urged that Mary keep her heart with a chaste mind, and her body free from all ill and wanton company. "I dare make sure," Katherine went on, "that you shall see a very good end, and better than you can desire. I would, good daughter, that you did know with how good a heart I do write this letter unto you. I never did one with a better, for I perceive very well that God loveth you." As for what she is suffering, "I set not a rush by it. We never come to the kingdom of heaven but by troubles." She signed herself, "Your loving mother, KATHERINE THE QUEEN."

She continued to believe that Henry was good at heart and had acted as he had done only because he had fallen into the hands of bad advisers. So she went on praying for him and for England and hoping for better days. It was not for her to play the part of divine Providence by means of a rebellion, any more than it had been for her to save England by speaking words that she knew to be untrue. The future she would leave in the hands of God. Her own case did not worry her in the least; what she did worry about was that Henry was in danger of losing his soul and of being the cause of damnation to others. She was made of the metal of the martyrs. Chapuys, writing in 1555, said that she was "the most virtuous woman I have ever known, and the highest hearted, but too quick to trust that others were like herself, and too slow to do a little ill that much good might come of it." There can be little doubt that, had she been willing to compromise in the matter of the divorce, the Reformation would not have occurred in England, at any rate not in Henry's time. Her dogged obstinacy was the despair of the practical men like Chapuys and Campeggio and Clement. And so it is still to anyone who realizes how simple a matter it would have been for her to have prevented an enormous disaster. It is almost impossible for commonplace common sense to regard her with sufficient patience. This is possible only to those who believe that the end cannot ever be made to justify the means, and who also believe that it can be only illusory good that is obtainable by any other principle. Like Katherine herself, we have to leave such matters in the hands of God.

Eustache Chapuys had been chosen as imperial ambassador largely because he was not a Spaniard but a Savoyard; as such it was supposed that he would be likely to be free from the too ardent partisanship one of Katherine's own countrymen would have felt. Actually no one could have been more devoted to her cause. Charles the Emperor perhaps did what honour required for his aunt, but he certainly did not go beyond that. He never was going to allow himself to be too gravely inconvenienced by her, and he came to look upon her as a nuisance, hampering him in playing off England against France. Not so Chapuys: Katherine was the first concern in his diplomacy; to her he was, in her letters, her *especial amigo,* a form of address reserved for him alone.

He was, after the divorce, rarely permitted to see her, out of fear that he might be able to persuade her to consent to a rising. There was much justification for this, for it was well known to Cromwell and the King that the ambassador was constantly intriguing, even though they could not put their finger on anything definite. Eventually he was not allowed to have any communication with her at all.

It was not that he was bluntly refused; it was merely that his requests that he be allowed to visit Kimbolton were always on one pretext or another put off, so that in the end he had to stage a demonstration that was as clever as it was amusing. Giving out that he was going on a pilgrimage to Our Lady of Walsingham, he said that he hoped to make a call on the Lady Katherine at the same time. He did everything in the most public fashion, taking not only his own entourage but the Spanish merchants in London on parade through the city. And he engaged the noisiest of bands so that everybody should look at them.

A messenger was sent after him telling him that he was not to visit Katherine. He smiled sardonically at having drawn Henry's fire. But he went on his way until he was five miles from Kimbolton, and there Chapuys stopped. But he let some of his young men go on to have a look at Kimbolton Castle from the outside; there could be no harm in that. At the edge of the moat they sang Spanish songs and engaged in badinage – or what was taken to be such – with Katherine's Spanish maids on the castle walls. To cover the matter up further, the Spanish fool they had brought with them performed on the bank of the moat and, perhaps deliberately, fell into the water. At this there was more laughter and more jests – under cover of which some information was conveyed across the moat. By these means Chapuys established channels for future communication. So far from trying to keep things a secret, he returned to London another way. He wanted as many people as possible to know that he had tried to see the Queen and had been prevented from doing so.

There was, however, not much that he could do to help, as Katherine was resolute in her refusal to give her name to any rebellion. It should be remembered that when Henry's subjects had been released from their allegiance, one might have argued, if one wished to be pedantically legal, that Mary had succeeded to her father's throne. But of course Chapuys was most careful not to make any such assertion, as it would have resulted in the prompt attainder of both Mary and Katherine, a move which was, in fact, under consideration. Instead he advised Katherine and Mary that, though they should not take the oath recognizing Henry's supremacy over the Church unless it was to save their lives, if it came to that point they should swear. Katherine would have taken it under no circumstances, but Mary eventually did. Yet ready as Katherine was for martyrdom, she had no wish to be murdered, so she followed Chapuys' advice to keep all doors and windows fast at night, and guarded herself more carefully than ever against poison. It was not so much Henry that she feared as Anne and Anne's brother and Cromwell. She remained serene, though the smiles of happier days had gone. As for her troubles, she was almost glad to endure them, in so far as they merely affected herself. They were a kind of expiation for Warwick's murder and for all the harm she felt she had done England.

No rebellion occurred in England during her lifetime, or after her death, except one that was not really a rebellion at all, though it was punished as such. But in Ireland there was one.

The early Tudor Irish policy was wiser than that of Elizabeth in that it sought the adhesion of the Irish chieftains by giving them English titles. Even so, there was little law and order—in the English sense—beyond the Pale. In the hope that an Irishman would be more acceptable as Lord Deputy, the head of the Geraldines, Gerald Fitzgerald, the Earl of Kildare, was appointed in 1513. Though he was removed at the Ormonde instance in 1520 he was reappointed in 1524. Again removed in 1526, he was appointed Deputy for the third time in 1533. But he was finally arrested for high treason and imprisoned in the Tower where he died the following year.

His son, popularly known as "Silken Thomas" because of the fringe he wore on his helmet, succeeded him in the title and was made Deputy Governor. But the changes in religion were too much for him. He had part in the assassination of Dr. Allen, the Archbishop of Dublin, formerly one of Wolsey's agents in the first suppression of the monasteries. The new Earl was more Irish in sympathy than his father had been, as the older man had been brought up in England. Now Silken Thomas proclaimed himself the Pope's adherent and sought an alliance with the Butlers, promising their head, the Earl of Ormonde, half

Ireland as his reward. Butler, however, due to the usual factional jealousies, refused, and Silken Thomas in the end surrendered to Sir Leonard Grey, his uncle, after an undertaking that his life should be spared.

The dashing young man, braver than he was wise, was taken to London with his five uncles (who had been captured in the usual way by treachery), but none of them were immediately executed. Though it would not have troubled Henry's famous conscience to have put to death a man who had surrendered upon terms, it was not as yet politic to do this, as it would have discouraged other surrenders that were hoped for. Not until the finishing touches had been given to the suppression of this Irish rising were Silken Thomas and his uncles dealt with. Then on February 3, 1537, they were executed, not given the block, which was almost the right of the nobility, but hanged at Tyburn.

Before they died Katherine herself was dead. She had held off rebellion against her husband. In the fall before her death there was a most propitious moment, as Charles had just ended triumphantly his campaign against the Moors in Tunis; he had always pleaded that it was this that tied his hands regarding England. But though Katherine would not change her position about rebellion, she was now willing to ask for stronger pressure to be put upon Henry. On October 15, 1535, she wrote to Pope Paul III saying: "The lukewarm will fall away if they find none to help them, and the greater part will stray away like sheep without a shepherd. I write frankly to your Holiness, as one who can feel with me and my daughter for the martyrdom of these good men, whom, it comforts me to hope, we may follow in their sufferings though we cannot imitate their lives." The point was that Paul must now issue his Bull of excommunication against Henry. Charles had put difficulties in the way of its execution, though Katherine had written to her nephew the previous year, "Beg his Holiness to act as he ought for the tranquility of Christendom. All other considerations, even the lives of myself and my daughter ought to be put aside." It had always been her contention, especially as against the dilatory and over-cautious Clement VII, that a decisive word, promptly spoken, would have prevented all the ills that had overtaken England. But this time, as before, the Emperor raised difficulties; the political complications were too great, his political profit too uncertain.

Nothing was done. Paul III was not so weak as his predecessor, but he was too amiable and too sanguine. He had heard reports that Anne Boleyn was tottering to her fall. Then things would right themselves. He held his hand waiting for further developments. He held his hand too long.

CHAPTER TEN

Sweet Taste of Gold

WRITING in reply to Simon Fish in 1529 Sir Thomas More said that he knew only seven members of the nobility who were in favour of seizing Church property, and of these seven three were dead. But that he could say even as much as that shows that there was already talk about the matter, and many, even in those days, may have had greedy longings that they found it prudent to keep hidden. Be this as it may, Chapuys reported in January, 1534, before the schism had actually occurred – though not before it was planned – that the King intended to seize the Church's manorial holdings, keeping part for himself and distributing the rest among the gentry to gain their support. This plan, in fact, seems to have been more drastic than the one later carried out, as it would have appropriated even the revenues of the bishoprics, putting the bishops themselves upon salaries. If it was abandoned, it was mainly because it would have at once alienated the hierarchy, upon whom the King was counting for backing in the religious changes he was about to introduce. But also it did not seem sufficiently attractive, at this stage, to the nobility. They could not be sure that they would get enough out of the spoils to compensate them for the loss they would incur as highly paid stewards – as many were – for the wealthy bishoprics. Moreover, the spoliation, as first suggested, was of so bare-faced a kind that it could not be justified and therefore might cause a rebellion. It was decided that it would be better to wait until things had settled down, and then to proceed cautiously and by stages.

An indication, however, of what might happen occurred in 1534 when the houses of the Franciscan Observants were taken from them and given to the Augustinians, an order whose loyalty to the King was assured by George Browne, their Prior in London. The Franciscans were reasoned with first. When they pointed to their rule, they were told that this was made for Italy, where it was of course natural that the friars should obey the Pope. When that argument failed to move them, the friars were told that the chapter they were quoting was a later interpolation. In any event not even the Pope or St. Francis "could take away one jot of the obedience they owed the King by God's laws." As the Observants did not agree they were sent by the cartload to jail.

Yet the very fact that their property was given to another order shows that there was, at that moment, no intention on the part of the King to take over what belonged to the Observants, whatever the implication might be that a right was claimed to dispossess according to the royal will, without even an act of Parliament. And when later the outright suppression began, it would seem that no general attack on monasticism was contemplated. It could be argued, as in the case of what Wolsey had done in the line of suppression, that the good of the monastic system as a whole was aimed at, and that the lopping off of a few dead branches would invigorate the tree. Just as Wolsey could talk of how he could endow his colleges in this way, and so raise the intellectual standards of the clergy, so Henry could talk of the benefits he was going to confer. New bishoprics would be founded; new chairs at the universities would be established; there would be new schools; and, best of all in the public estimation, the burden of taxation would be eased. The immediate need, though, was to find money to pay for the royal divorce and to prepare for the war that might yet result from the divorce. Henry had used that argument in 1531, when he fined the whole clerical body for their guilt under Praemunire; now that the money had slipped through his fingers he did not hesitate to use the same argument again.

Nevertheless, he was probably not altogether insincere in his protestations about monastic reform. Nobody could deny that reform was necessary. He could use the Wolseian plea: many monasteries were in a state of decline; their buildings and lands had been allowed to run down; their communities had diminished in numbers, in some instances there were too few monks or nuns left in a house for the fitting performance of the divine office. If such religious were transferred to more flourishing houses, with a due provision made for their maintenance, there would still be a surplus left. The King could use this for public purposes without anybody being injured. Such would be the conclusion of this argument.

England was among the most monastic of countries. It owed its faith to the preaching of monks, and within a very short time after its conversion it had seen the emergence of many mellow scholars, of whom the Venerable Bede is one of the best examples. Since that time fervour had lessened, the enforcement of the rule had been relaxed – something that all too easily could happen in Benedictine houses, as every abbey is autonomous – and here and there disorders no doubt existed. Probably a good many monks had become slack, and even a few nuns (though it is well known that women are usually more conscientious than men); there is hardly any evidence that the situation was worse than that.

Surprising as it may seem, there were about four times as many monks in England as there were nuns. It might be possible to infer that, because the religious houses of men were, taken as a whole, relatively rich and those of women relatively poor, the cloister was more attractive to men than to women. Probably far too many people were entering religious orders in the expectation of having a care-free and comfortable life rather than because they had any real vocation.

An index to the decline in the religious spirit may be discovered in the fact that only eight monasteries and convents had been founded between the years 1399 to 1509. This, however, should not be pressed too far; there was no need for new foundations, and there was less land to give away than in previous ages.* But a sufficiency of manorial holdings was a prime requisite as an endowment, and because of the land hunger that had seized society, and which was manifesting itself in the enclosure movement, the monasteries were suffering, as they were to suffer still more.

I can find no evidence for Mr. Belloc's assertion that a complete scheme of spoliation existed from the outset in Cromwell's mind, or that he believed it was necessary completely to uproot monasticism and to distribute the looted property in order to make the reconciliation of England with the Holy See forever impossible. It is true that that was the result, but it need not have been the result. There came a moment in 1536 when Cromwell considered that the thing had gone far enough. Unfortunately by that time Henry was more and more urgently in need of money and had found how easy it was to obtain it from this source. Sir Thomas More, shortly after his resignation from the chancellorship, had said to Cromwell, "If you will follow my poor advice, you shall in your counsel-giving unto his Grace ever tell him what he ought to do, but never what he is able to do. For if a lion knew his strength, hard were it for any man to rule him." It was true: having started Henry on his course, Cromwell was unable to stop him. The man who had begun as a reformer was, because of his own greed and (perhaps even more) because of the greed of others, to end as a brigand.

At the outset Henry had imagined that it would be possible to appropriate everything (or nearly everything) to the Crown. Had he been able to do this, he would have made the English monarchy unassailable as against any combination of nobles — that is, if it had been within the power of such a wasteful man to hold on to his wealth. But he soon learned that the spoliation would receive the sanction of Parliament and the support of the aristocracy only on condition that the loot was shared. Then

*This did not apply, except to a very slight extent, to the orders of friars, as these lived poorly and on small gifts from day to day.

Cromwell — who was himself caught in this trap — had to reconcile Henry to such sharing with the reflection that it was, upon the whole, very much to his advantage. The more people implicated, the better. It was a principle that Henry acceded to all the more readily because it was the one that he steadily followed in all his unjust acts. These were never done on his sole responsibility, which meant that he did nothing until he had wrung approval from his Council and the Peers and the Commons. To obtain this approval threats were sometimes used, but Henry preferred the making of a deal or the offering of a bribe; in this instance the most enormous bribe in history was offered.

This much, however, must be admitted: the success of the Reformation in England is not altogether to be explained by greed. That would be far too simple an explanation. Nobody can doubt that greed was a large factor in the matter, and had it not operated the Reformation would probably have failed. But cynicism is not enough of a force to accomplish anything. What was behind Henry's assertion of Supremacy was the belief, held with varying degrees of sincerity no doubt but still widely held, that the King should be paramount in the Church as well as the state. And there was a wide-spread discontent with the existing ecclesiastical system. One ought to be able to find religious enthusiasm as well, but the odd fact is that it seems to have been conspicuously absent, far more lacking in what may be roughly (and in this connection, not very accurately) called the anti-Catholic side than in that handful of men who, being intelligent enough to see what was involved and brave enough to resist the King, suffered martyrdom for their convictions. What was accomplished was served most of all by the general religious indifference.

The idea of monastic expropriation was not altogether new. In 1410 in Henry IV's reign Sir John Oldcastle, better known as Lord Cobham, had introduced a Parliamentary bill along these lines. It had been estimated then that it would be possible to take enough of the surplus wealth of the Church to endow 15 new earls, 1500 knights, 6200 squires, and to leave the King an extra £20,000 for himself. Forty thousand clerics were to be allowed under this fantastic scheme a stipend of seven marks a year, which bare living this notorious Lollard considered quite sufficient.

A somewhat similar scheme was offered in 1528 in Simon Fish's *Supplication of Beggars,* though, as the title indicates, Fish argued that the wealth of the Church should be distributed among the poor or used for public purposes. He wrote primarily against the friars, who had little land but, so he calculated, an annual income of £436,333.6.8. He arrived at these figures by saying that there were 52,000 parishes in England, each with an average of ten households, every one of which might be presumed to contribute a penny every quarter to the five orders. In reply to Fish with his *Supplication of Souls* Thomas More had no difficulty in showing that such calculations were preposterous. But Fish had not levelled his argument only against the friars; he had also estimated that the Church possessed nearly one third of the wealth of the country and then, warming to his subject, half the wealth. Why, he asked, should the clergy who were to the laity in the ratio of one to four hundred be so richly endowed?

As a matter of fact the entire valuation of Church property, as made by Henry's commissioners themselves a little later, came to a yearly rental of only £320,280.10.0, or a quarter or perhaps no more than a fifth of all manorial holdings, and of this a little more than half was in the possession of the religious orders. While this may show that the ecclesiastical body was, taken as a whole, disproportionately wealthy, the vast majority of priests were sufficiently poor. Many had no livings at all and eked out their livelihood by all sorts of odd jobs, not always of a strictly clerical character; many others who did have benefices were no more than adequately remunerated. The real scandal was that the fatter benefices were often held by men who had been given several of them and did no more than pocket the revenues and pay a vicar a small salary.

That many of the abbeys were richly endowed is of course

perfectly true. But even their wealth in many cases was less than it appeared to be, because of various drains upon their resources. The Crown had a way of ordering them to pay pensions which should have properly been its own charge. And usually the founders had made contracts in perpetuity not only for prayers but for the relief of necessitous relatives. There were a vast number of such corrodies, as they were called, and many of the religious houses also had guests whom they had accepted under something like an annuity system, such annuitants (as is commonly the case) having a longevity that made the contract disadvantageous to the religious. While, according to paper calculations, such monasteries were wealthy, the obligations they had contracted, the debts with which almost all of them were burdened, put them in a tangle of financial difficulties. This was one of the reasons why the monasteries put up such little resistance against Henry; it was not worth fighting to preserve an existence which was already so hard. The argument was also advanced that the Crown ought to take over estates suffering from economic mismanagement.

The first step was the appointment of Cromwell as the King's Vicar-General, something Henry was empowered to do without a new statute, as Parliament had already made him Head of the Church. But now Cromwell, as his Vicar, took precedence over all the bishops, as in Parliament he was ranked above every noble in the land. Though neither he nor the King claimed the right to preach or administer the sacraments, Cranmer came to suggest that this was within the King's competence, even that the King could not merely appoint but ordain bishops. The bishops were at all events uncertain enough regarding their status under the new regime as to take out licenses (given at Cromwell's discretion) for the exercise of their episcopal functions. Moreover, as the King's Vicar, Cromwell abrogated all rights of visitation, reserving these to himself. In this matter, as in others, he found Wolsey's methods a highly serviceable model. Cromwell started to work with a visitation of the religious houses in the summer of 1535. There had always been a certain number of exempt monasteries, free from the visitations of the ordinaries and subject only to the Pope. Now that Henry was Pope in England, these of course at once fell within Cromwell's jurisdiction. Though his ostensible purpose was to enquire into the state of discipline, great uneasiness was aroused by the fact that the first thing the visitators always did was to make an inventory of the valuables as well as to assess the monastic estate.

Cromwell was well qualified for this kind of investigation, as it was what he had done when he was in Wolsey's service. At that time, too, he had discovered how feeble was the resistance likely to be put up. The man whom Foxe praised as the "Hammer of Monks" did not hate monks; he merely despised them. He had long since learned how ready they would be in their weakness to pay bribes, to buy momentary relief at almost any price. Equipped in this way, he and his agents set to work.

Anything like thoroughness in the investigations was impossible in view of the speed with which they were made. But all that Cromwell and his men wanted was to gather enough scandal for immediate use. General reports often had to suffice, but the most useful method was to find some dissatisfied member of the community who would bring charges against the others, or the superior. It need hardly be said that a man of that sort usually had his grudge because he was himself in disgrace. But armed with his complaints, the visitators would try to break down some of the other religious by the use of alternate threats and promises. It is to be noted that those willing to co-operate in this way obtained a reward, a promotion, or a pension; those who would not co-operate, whether as a group or individually, were harshly treated. There was, as may be seen from the recommendations made as to which houses were to be spared, little or no relation between good discipline and the mercy sometimes accorded. Several of the houses that were given the worst character were allowed, for the time being, to continue. On the other hand, though the nuns at Catesby — to take a specific instance — were acknowledged in the official reports to be in perfect order under a "pure, wise, discreet and very religious woman as prioress," they were ruthlessly suppressed.

In a later chapter something will be said about the way Cromwell and his agents extorted bribes from the monasteries; the opportunities for that sort of thing were already present (as they had been under Wolsey), but venality on the grand scale came a year or two later. What needs to be touched on at this point is the justification that was offered for doing what was actually done. To offer as the sole ground for suppression the fact that a community was small and poor was hardly enough; it was necessary also to show that these small and poor communities were also corrupt. The purpose of the preliminary visitations during the summer of 1535 was to provide such proofs.

Edmund Burke once said, "I rather suspect that vices are feigned or exaggerated when profit is looked for in the punishment. An enemy is a bad witness, a robber is worse." But though, on this very sound principle, everything said by the commissioners is brought under suspicion, the nature of the charges they made must be examined, and some comments offered as to the degree of truth they may contain.

Certain preliminary propositions might be presented. It should be immediately obvious that had monastic immorality been general, or even fairly common, it would have been well known among a people whose relations with the religious houses had always been intimate. The humorous stories of the kind told by Chaucer — derived by Chaucer from Boccaccio, and by Boccaccio from the oriental fables that began to circulate after the crusades — are beside the point. They were simply within the framework of a convention which nobody took as being more than a convention. For anything like evidence we would have to look elsewhere.

This much may be said: human nature being what it is, we may be sure that there were individual instances of immorality among the monks. But a knowledge of human nature cuts the other way as well: it gives one a conviction of an average of decency and respectability. If saints are few, so are scoundrels. And though it is perfectly true that certain periods are worse than others, it is not permissible to say this of any particular period unless the contention can be supported with real evidence.

The early Protestant Church historian Fuller describes Cromwell's agents as "Men of prying eyes as afterwards they proved of gripple hands . . . men who well understood the message they were sent on, and would not come back without a satisfactory answer to him who sent them, knowing themselves to be no losers thereby." In short, they found out what they were being paid to find out. This is evident from the report sent by Dr. Layton to Cromwell from York, when he was about to begin on St. Mary's Abbey: "Whereat," he writes, "we suppose to find much evil disposition, both in the abbot and the convent, whereof, God willing, I shall certify you in my next letter." Indeed, when the visitators did make a favourable report, they were likely to be suspected by Cromwell or the King of having taken a bribe. Thus when the report was received about the admirable nuns of Catesby, to whom reference has already been made, the Augmentation Office (the department established to receive the monastic revenues), wrote back through its Chancellor to say: "The King's Highness was displeased, saying that it was like that he had received rewards."

The charges that were brought against the religious often turned out to be either vague or preposterous. Who can possibly believe the report made (on the word of one of the disgruntled members of the community) that the monks of any abbey went to the chanting of the Office "as drunk as mice, and played some at cards and some at dice" during Matins? For while it is possible that occasionally a monk arrived in choir the worse for drink, or that the community as a whole was somewhat perfunctory, the chanting of the Office at all calls for a degree of attention that would make cards and dice quite impossible.

As for the vagueness: one of the most frequently used phrases is that of "voluptuous living." This must not be understood in the modern sense. People in those times were habitually addicted to extravagant language. It was of a life spent in "licentious ease" that Sir Thomas More accused himself to his daughter while he looked with her out of the window of his cell on the Carthusian martyrs being tied to their hurdles. Yet he had worn a hair-shirt since youth. If we translate "licentious ease" and "voluptuous living" into "worldly comfort" we shall approximate the meaning intended. Of that much probably many monks might be not too unjustly accused.

The most common specific charge is that of secret vice. It might be as well to remember that it was precisely this charge that the Nazis, when they were trying to discredit the monastic orders in Germany, also used. The obvious must again be insisted on: vice which is secret is exceedingly difficult to discover, though as such an accusation can hardly be disproved, it was very serviceable to Cromwell as well as to Hitler. But if nothing was unearthed along these or other lines, then the monks were accused of collusion, as when Ap Rice wrote to Cromwell of his visit to the Abbey of Bury St. Edmund: "There is a grave suspicion that the abbot and convent had agreed together not to tell anything against themselves, for though report says that the monks live licentiously, still there was never anything less confessed to."

Such charges, it might be noted, rarely if ever appear in the pages of those first attacking the Church in books or pamphlets. It was so in the case of St. German and so also in the case of Fish. Nor do they appear in the writings of the bitter-tongued Tyndale. His favourite gibe is that of the Catholic reliance on good works as against the Lutheran justification by faith alone. "Pope-holiness" is his term for this, regarding which Brewer acutely comments: "If [the old religion] had been in its practice so generally corrupt as it is represented to have been by modern writers, such denunciations were idle."* Gairdner puts his finger

*Modern writers of repute suggest nothing of the sort. Brewer was writing eighty years ago, since which time, largely because of the gathering of the documents made by him and his successors, such notions have been pretty generally abandoned.

on the pith of the matter when he remarks, "The defaming of the monasteries was simply a step towards the confiscation of their endowments."

We happen, however, to have evidence of a very different kind gathered after Cromwell's visitators had made their reports. These were the reports issued by the local commissions appointed to see to the actual closing of the religious houses selected for dissolution. The members of these commissions included country gentlemen who were in a position to know the true state of affairs, and they present a very different picture from that of the haphazard and rapid investigations made by Drs. Leigh and Layton and London and the notary, Ap Rice. In the 376 religious houses that fell within the law passed in 1536 only 22 men and 3 women are listed as of bad repute – out of about 2000 religious.

I have dealt with the charges first because it was on the strength of the *comperta,* or reports, sent by Cromwell's agents that the suppression of the smaller monasteries was decided upon. We hear in Elizabeth's time, but not until then, of a "Black Book," full of monastic enormities, that had been presented to Parliament. As no such book is in existence, and was not even mentioned in Henry's time, we may reasonably suppose that it is entirely mythical. And if its absence is to be accounted for with the conjecture that it was destroyed during Mary's days as incriminating, it is strange (in that case) that the *comperta* were allowed to escape. The truth of the matter would seem to be that a confusion has arisen between these *comperta,* which were sufficiently defamatory, and the "Black Book" of legend. But that even the *comperta* were presented to Parliament seems to be disproved by the preamble of the act of 1536, which indicates that the existence of monastic corruption was accepted on the King's authority who "had knowledge that the premises were true." Of one thing we can be quite sure: if there ever was any "Black Book" it could have been based only on the *comperta,* and these we have.

The Parliament summoned at the beginning of 1536 to deal with the monasteries was more than usually carefully packed. Not only were many of the members of the House of Commons nominated by the government but pains were taken to see that such members of the House of Lords as were likely to give too much trouble were graciously permitted to absent themselves. A typical instance of this was recorded by Richard Hyliard, the secretary of Bishop Tunstall of Durham. While the Bishop was on the road to London he was met by the bearer of a letter from Cromwell. This, after expressing the King's special affection for the Bishop, said that on account of the inclement weather and the difficulty of travel to a man of his age he would probably find the journey too much for him.* When he did not take the hint, he received another letter, this time from the King himself, ordering him to return to his diocese. Things of this sort explain how it happened that the act passed a House of Lords in which the bishops and the abbots greatly outnumbered the temporal peers. So many of the spiritual lords had been excused that they were not able to put up any effective opposition.

In both Houses of Parliament the very appealing argument was used that the suppression of the smaller monasteries would mean that the country would be relieved from the burden of taxation it was finding almost insupportable. The Crown would have its revenues so greatly augmented that never again would there be any need to call upon Parliament for a grant. Not only that, the monastery lands which had hitherto supported a few people in idleness would be broken up and so widely distributed that afterwards such a person as a poor man would not be found in England.

A definite assurance was given that so far from any harm being intended to the institution of monasticism, only its benefit was aimed at. The act not only specifically exempted the larger monasteries but explicitly praised them, contrasting "the vicious, carnal and abominable living" found in the smaller religious houses with "the great, solemn monasteries wherein (thanks be

*He died twenty-four years later at eighty-five.

to God) religion is right well kept and observed." The preamble also asserts that "manifest sin . . . is daily committed among the little and small abbeys, priories and other religious houses . . . where the congregation . . . is under the number of twelve persons." This is not only damnatory of the later procedure of Henry but is patently absurd. For while it might be reasonably said that less than twelve persons are unable to perform the Office with fitting solemnity, there can surely be no relation between morals and numbers. If anything, one would have supposed that in the larger houses (which were also as a rule the richer houses) there were more opportunities for vice should any of the community have been determined to practise it.

The rule finally decided upon was not that the houses lacking enough religious were to be suppressed – for *that* there would have been something to be said – but that the houses with a yearly revenue of less than £200 were to go. For while there may have been some rough approximation between income and numbers, it was far from being close enough to be used as a standard. A house containing twenty monks or nuns might fall under the monetary limit set, whereas a house with eight or even six members might rise above it.

Some of the abbots and bishops – such as were permitted to attend – though having misgivings about what was proposed, allowed themselves to be persuaded that the act would work in the interest of reform. It is common observation how easy it is to assent to a reform that does not touch oneself. The preamble of the act not only seemed to guarantee the continued existence of the larger monasteries but encouraged the idea that they would be strengthened with new subjects, those they would absorb from the smaller houses. It is true that one member of the House of Commons was so blunt as to say, according to Hall, that the houses then being suppressed "were the thorns, but that the great abbots were the putrified old oaks, and they must follow." But even in face of that warning, such spiritual peers as were in attendance were either so subservient or so timorous or so stupid as to accept the act as being, upon the whole, beneficial. We do hear, however, that the bill was hotly debated in the Commons and that in the end the King quelled all opposition by sending for some of the members and informing them that he would have his bill or some of their heads.

The act, like so much that was driven through Parliament at this time, was regarded as permissive rather than mandatory. The King was empowered to suppress all the religious houses whose income fell below £200 (£5,000 in modern values), but he was not obliged to suppress them all, and had, at least for the moment, no intention of doing so. Of the 376 monasteries and convents that fell within the scope of the act, 123 were refounded, restored, or respited.* Henry even founded two or three new houses during the course of that year. Another was founded by him in 1537 with the special purpose of praying for the repose of the soul of Jane Seymour. However precarious their existence proved to be, and may have been felt to be from the start, the application of the statute was not as stringent as the statute itself.

All through this controversy (in so far as there may be said to have been a controversy at all) there was a fatal flaw in the argument. Those who wished to have the monasteries abolished tended to deny the doctrine of Purgatory, as though monasteries existed with no other object in mind than praying for the dead. Those who defended monasteries tended, on the other hand, to base their defence on the need for having prayers for the faithful departed. Even Thomas More wrote in this vein when replying to Simon Fish, though he, of all men in England, best understood the nature of the contemplative life. In all this the main point was often lost sight of: it was quite possible to have a firm belief in Purgatory and in suffrages for the poor souls and yet to think that the monastic endowments for this purpose were excessive and should be somewhat reduced. Put conversely, they could have been reduced, because they were excessive, without

*The number is sometimes given as 31, on the authority of a document cited by Canon Dixon. But Gasquet shows that this applies only to the number spared up to August (*Henry VIII and the English Monasteries*, Vol. II, p. 19 fn.).

any lessening of the obligation that had been attached to them. But the way the central issue was lost in irrelevancies shows how little idea of the real meaning of monasticism then prevailed. There was even, in England and elsewhere, a disposition to attack the Mass itself as though its sole purpose was to deliver souls from Purgatory. At all events we find these "private" Masses already being brought under question, though the orthodox King continued to uphold them. What Henry was not prepared to do was to uphold the sacredness of the contracts that had been made between those now presumed to be in Purgatory but who, while living, had arranged, by means of monastic donations, to secure for themselves the prayers they knew they would need. The King as the Head of the Church decided that the royal necessities were greater than theirs.

In obtaining what he wanted Henry cared nothing for the hardship he inflicted. Theoretically the plan was to transfer dispossessed monks and nuns to other houses, and had reform been seriously intended, this of course would have been done. But few such transferences were made, though many of the larger monasteries had abundant room for new members. The fact is that the share of income made over for their support was utterly inadequate. This being the case, the act of 1536 meant in effect that the religious were ejected and had nowhere to go.

This ejection was brought about in various ways. One was that Cromwell's visitators were armed with injunctions that had deliberately been made severe in the expectation that the religious would find life intolerable and leave of their own accord. This peeps out in the postscript of one of Ap Rice's letters to Cromwell: "I think it best that at their own instant suit [the religious] be dismissed to avoid calumniation and envy. And so compelling them to observe these injunctions ye shall have them all to do shortly." And Chapuys wrote: "It is true that they are not expressly told to go out, but it is clearly given them to understand that they had better do it, for they are going to make a reformation of them so severe and strange that in the end they will go, which is the object the King is aiming at, in order to have better occasion to seize the property without causing the people to murmur." Even those who were willing to do their best in monastic life under excessively strict regulations were discouraged by the large fees demanded by the Crown for permission to keep their houses open, and the bribes that had to be paid, on top of these, to Cromwell and his agents.

Along with the suppressions that were made under the law, there were already being made a few more or less voluntary surrenders. If the statute was not rigorously applied in some instances, in others it was stretched. To any monk or nun who asked to be allowed to leave the religious life, Cromwell gladly gave the necessary permission, along with a dispensation in his capacity as Vicar-General. As hardly anybody did seek this privilege, it was forced on many. All monks and nuns under twenty-four were to be dispensed whether they wanted it or not. This monastic reform was based upon the notion, not of improving the quality but of reducing the quantity.

In the hope of scaring the nuns away, the prurient-minded visitators used to ask them bluntly lewd questions. Fuller notes: "The Papists do heavily complain (how justly God alone knoweth) that a third sort of agents were employed to practice on the chastity of the nuns, to surprise them into wantonness. Some young gallants were on design sent to some convents, with fair faces, flattering tongues, store of gold and good clothes, youth, wit, wantonness and what else might work on the weaker sex." Many of these unhappy women may well have wondered whether it would not be better to take their chances in the world than be subjected to such annoyances in the cloister.

To offset this, a special relaxation of the ordinary rule could be obtained by those who showed themselves co-operative by turning informers or by supporting the King's Supremacy in some striking way. Thus we find a monk of Winchcombe named John Horwood writing to say that he would like to see the words of St. Paul, "*Non est potestas nisi a Deo,*" written on every monk's head. In return he gets a requested reward.

"Thanks," he writes again, "for excusing my getting up for Matins at midnight. The Abbot says that this has given cause to some murmurs and grudging among the convent. The truth is, I do not like the burdens and straightness of religion." Any discontented monk or nun was empowered to lay grievances before the Vicar-General without let or hindrance. The effect on religious discipline can be imagined. These reformers, while imposing with the one hand new regulations virtually impossible of observance, with the other broke down all possibility of carrying out the regulations that had hitherto been obeyed.

Whether Henry knew much about such goings-on is doubtful. He was never a man who enquired very closely into the details of administration. He was told that the monasteries were corrupt, and he believed it, because it suited him to believe it. From what he knew of Cromwell as he had been in Wolsey's service, he probably guessed that some of his methods would not bear examination; well, in that event, he would not examine them. It was enough for Henry that a steady stream of money reached him; he did not realize that much of the proceeds escaped, purloined by his agents. Strange mixture of greed and generosity that he was, he would sometimes stake a manor on a single throw of the dice, or give one away to a cook who had pleased his palate, or (more commonly) for the sake of obtaining ready cash sell an estate at far below its true valuation.

The plight of the nuns was worse than that of the monks. These might eventually hope, if they were priests, to be appointed to a living. But for the ejected nuns there was nothing unless they could find a refuge with relatives or friends. Some of them received a small pension, just enough to keep body and soul together, and it is significant that most of those mentioned in the *comperta* as disedifying were among this number. As with the monks, a good way of getting special consideration was that of delating others or accusing themselves.*

---

*In the case of the nuns, however, against whom even Cromwell's agents did not often bring serious charges, it must be remembered that,

The fact that convents were poor as compared with the houses for monks probably accounts for so many of them being spared as long as they were. They were spared for much the same reason that the friars were spared at this time: they were hardly worth suppressing, and there was fear of arousing popular indignation. Though an instinct of compassion may be too much to imagine of Cromwell, his commissioners had to go warily with regard to the nuns, knowing that charges of moral delinquency against them would seem too absurd for credence.

To some of the ejected monks there were given what were called "capacities," a certificate that they might accept a benefice, if one were offered. While these were, in many instances, a reward for compliance, another motive operated: the sooner these monks obtained jobs, the sooner they would be removed from the pension-list of the Augmentation Office.

Not many such jobs were immediately available, as England was already over-stocked with priests. But that the capacities were worth having is proved by the fact that we now and then hear of their being forged. Not only that, the new situation created what we should call a "racket." There were several instances of clerics (real or bogus) who presented themselves at monasteries and convents as royal commissioners, whereupon they made their visitations, charging the customary fees and extracting what they could in bribes. Pensions also were sold to speculators, usually going for what they would have brought in for two or three years, by religious desperately in need of ready cash. These even passed through several hands, like a negotiable note, until the base traffic was stopped by statute in the next reign. There was no end to the exploitation of the unfortunate religious. Those living at a distance from London often

---

in some instances, of those who are put down as of bad life, reference was being made to a shady past rather than to later misconduct. For ladies of good family, a convent was often a haven of refuge from scandal. But as only women of influential families could obtain this privilege, it may be that sometimes the special treatment they received from the commissioners was due to family "pull" rather than to their being "co-operative" during the enquiry.

had to club together and employ an agent to go to the Augmentation Office in their behalf. Such agents charged a commission and the expenses of their journey, but found that there were fees to pay in London, as the clerks there wanted their little rake-off. And deductions were sometimes made for "loans" to the King. What finally reached the pensionnaires – small though it had been on paper, averaging, in modern values, £80 for a monk and £60 for a nun – might be only half that amount. It is perhaps hardly to be wondered at that Audley, the Lord Chancellor, one of those who had helped in the process, when writing to Cromwell to ask for the abbey of Walden in Kent, put his claim on the ground: "I have sustained great damage and infamy in serving the King's Highness, which this grant shall recompense." The poor fellow found nothing so soothing as a salve of gold.

The Court of Augmentation was headed by our old friend Richard Rich at a salary of £750 a year, or between £15,000 and £18,000 in modern values. On top of that he obtained valuable pickings, among which was the priory of Lighes in Essex. This he should have taken as his territorial title when raised to the peerage in 1547, but as he knew what people who remembered his perjury at More's trial might say, he thought it safer to be known simply as Baron Rich. Altogether apart from the injustice and cruelty involved in the suppression of the monasteries, it was the occasion of a venality perhaps without parallel. Yet Froude thinks that the scoundrels who rode off from the monasteries wearing doublets made out of valuable copes and their dagger-sheathes beaten out of the reliquaries of the saints should be pardoned because of their excessive zeal in God's cause. It seems that the "hot puritan blood" was already spurting in their veins! The dictum may in some ways be preferred to the latitudinarian Macaulay's opinion about the advantages of a reformation put through by men indifferent to religion, but it is even more comical. To these may be added, as another of the curiosities of history, the commendation given by Foxe the martyrologist to Cromwell. Among all his "noble acts and memorable examples and worthy virtues" one rises supreme, "his singular zeal and laborious travail bestowed in restoring the true Church of Christ, and subverting the Synagogue of Antichrist, the abbeys, I mean, and religious houses of friars and monks." One does not know whether to be more indignant or amused.

In this first spoliation some attempt was made to pass on part of the old obligations of the monks to the new proprietors. That the corrodies were usually abolished was perhaps all to the good. What was, however, soon felt as a serious loss to the community was that the monks' practice of hospitality, though theoretically imposed upon the purchasers of the monastic estates, was from the start evaded and before long forgotten. The attempt to fasten such an obligation – which had been part of a religious rule – on a secular owner was probably not taken very seriously; its main use was to make the spoliation a little less obnoxious to the people. At any rate, before 1536 was out we hear constant complaints that hospitality had ceased. The advowsons, the right of patronage to country churches possessed by many monasteries, were transferred, like a fixture in a house, to the new owner, and these were often sold to the highest bidder. Even when a monetary transaction was not involved, it was but natural that the livings should be given only to such men as were pledged to uphold the new order of things. But, if it comes to that, the men in the larger monasteries made little protest. They were, because of their failure to resist at this time, to be easy victims a year or two later.

The returns from this first looting, reckoned as annual income, came to about £32,000. Men still in their middle age well remembered when it would have been enough for all the purposes of government. But that was under the economical Henry VII. His son was to find even this huge augmentation of his resources quite insufficient for his spendthrift habits. Having started on this course, it was inevitable that such a man should find it necessary to continue it to its end.

CHAPTER ELEVEN

"The Most Unhappy Lady in Christendom"

THE Princess Mary far better deserved the title she gave herself than that successfully fastened upon her by Protestant tradition. Any person of education who now uses the term "Bloody Mary" does so with such an intonation that quotation marks are put round it. For unwise though Mary certainly was in many of her actions, she was so far from being cruel that it may be said that, at least in her treatment of known traitors, she was injudiciously merciful. The only bit of personal vindictiveness she showed was towards Cranmer, the man who had divorced her mother. Yet even Cranmer would have been forgiven this, along with his treason towards herself, had he made a recantation of heresy in whose sincerity anybody could believe. As it was, he was not executed until nearly three years after Mary had ascended the throne.

One would have expected Mary to have become hard and bitter as a result of the treatment her mother received, and in which she herself was caught. This of course made her sad, and it steeled her. But though she was her mother's partisan, she was not bitter at all. She wished to give as little offence as possible but tried to hold her own ground in the hope that one day it might be given to her to restore England to Catholic unity. In that task she failed, and died knowing that she had failed. Well might she call herself the most unhappy lady in Christendom.

Her father had been genuinely fond of her when she was a child. We see him exhibiting his wonderful baby to foreign ambassadors, boasting, "By God, this child never cries!" We have a pretty picture of her at two calling Dionysius Memo, one of the court musicians, "Priest! Priest!" until he went to play with her. Henry was so delighted with this, that, taking the little girl into his arms, he declared in Latin to the Venetian ambassador, "By God, that man is a very good and dear fellow, a very dear one; nobody serves me better than he has done." It is a pleasant relief to look back to the Henry of 1518 and the years that immediately followed, still a charming and affectionate young man, who even in the midst of court functions would playfully pull his little daughter's red hair over her dress to show it off.

As she grew older he was proud of her accomplishments and saw to it that she had the best of tutors. We have glimpses of her at four and a half giving a performance on the virginals for some visitors and at nine replying to a complimentary Latin speech with a speech of her own. Henry, who consulted Sir Thomas More regarding the education of his son the Duke of Richmond, consulted him also about Mary. The result was that the Spanish humanist, Jean Luis Vives, was brought to England to draw up a plan of studies for her. While there he wrote his book, *The Instruction of a Christian Woman,* and this the Queen asked Thomas More to have translated, so that it was, in fact, Englished by Richard Hyrde, one of the many able men who served in turn as tutor to More's learned daughters. Though Mary was not as brilliant as her half-sister, Elizabeth, she was very well educated and had special proficiency in music.

Poor Mary could never have been very happy after the treatment her mother received, but she might have escaped her father's animosity had it not been for Anne Boleyn. It is a well-known psychological truth that it is commonly the perpetrator of a wrong who feels more of a grievance than the victim; Anne accordingly hated Mary, all the more so after her disappointment that the child she bore was only a girl. Had it been a boy, Anne would have felt secure herself and known her son would succeed his father as king. But she realized that the English people would disregard Mary's bastardization and put her on the throne before Elizabeth.

The malice Anne showed Mary after Elizabeth's birth was of the meanest kind. She lost no opportunity of making it plain that her baby took precedence over the seventeen-year-old girl, no longer known as the Princess but merely as the Lady Mary. That Mary usually succeeded, with the connivance of those round her, in quietly asserting her own precedence, only enraged Anne further. "She will be my death, or I hers," was a word frequently in the Queen's mouth. Indeed, she talked so openly about having Mary killed at a time when the King was about to go abroad that Lord Rochford had to caution her against being so indiscreet, or so Chapuys reported. He added that when Rochford told his sister that she had better be more careful in what she said, she answered that she did not care but would do it if she were burned or skinned alive. Though the imperial ambassador may have exaggerated, there can be no doubt that Anne was given to saying wild things. Chapuys took them seriously enough to advise Mary, as he had advised Katherine, to guard against being poisoned. He did not put it past Anne – or, for that matter, the King – to murder both women.

There followed a period when Anne, having failed to break the girl's spirit with threats, attempted blandishments. In this she may have been acting under Henry's instructions, for she offered to let Mary walk by her side and to rank immediately after her, on condition that she made a complete submission. As such a submission would have involved a declaration that her mother's marriage was incestuous and that she herself was a bastard, Mary of course contemptuously ignored Anne's advances. She always thought of Anne as Chapuys did, as the Concubine. Never would she admit that her mother had not been truly married to her father. People might, if they pleased, address her as the Lady Mary instead of by her title of Princess;

to her loyal and logical mind Katherine was always, as she signed her letters, Katherine the Queen.

The worst time of all for Mary was when she was sent away under the charge of Anne's aunt, Lady Shelton. We get glimpses of petty meannesses that would have been hard for a servant girl to bear, and yet they had to be borne by a king's daughter. Thus Anne, prompted apparently by nothing except her malignity, wrote to tell Lady Shelton to give Mary "a box on the ear now and then for the cursed bastard she is." Fortunately Lady Clere, Mary's other jailer, was a good-natured woman, and when the Duke of Norfolk complained that she did not treat Mary harshly enough and as a bastard, he got the answer that, even if she was the bastard of a poor gentleman, she was a good girl and, as such, deserving of respect.

Mary's main offence was that she refused to accept her father's Supremacy over the Church. When this was demanded from her she declined and dared to conclude her letter to the King with: "If I agreed to the contrary, I should offend God; in all other things your obedient daughter." When her bastardy had been made statutory Lady Shelton went to her in triumph saying, "If I were in the King's place I would kick you out of doors for your disobedience."

Henry probably would have been willing to leave Mary alone had he not been under Anne's domination. The new Queen, whenever she wanted anything, usually won her way by "playing the mad woman" or throwing a hysterical fit, a feminine device against which Henry, even more than most men, was helpless. But though Henry was emotionally too unstable to resist that sort of thing, he was anything but a fool. So when Anne bribed a soothsayer to "reveal" to the King that she could not conceive another child so long as Katherine and Mary were alive, he was not taken in by the transparent trick. As there were limits to what Henry was prepared to do in the case of his daughter, Anne wrote to Lady Shelton: "My pleasure is that you do not further move the Lady Mary to be toward the King's Grace otherwise than it pleaseth herself. What I have done has been more from charity than from anything the King or I care what road she takes, or whether she will change her purpose, for if I have a son, as I hope shortly, I know what will happen to her, and therefore considering the Word of God to do good to one's enemy, I wish to warn her beforehand, because I have daily experience that the King's wisdom is such as not to esteem her repentance of her rudeness and natural obstinacy when she had no choice."

This letter (so clearly indicative of Anne's shallow and spiteful and rather stupid make-up) was left by Lady Shelton in Mary's oratory, where she knew it would be picked up and (she hoped) read. Mary did read it and copied it out to send to Chapuys; then she left the paper lying as though it had not been disturbed.

Chapuys admired the girl's serene courage then, as on other occasions; but he was more frightened than Mary was. Katherine had it in her power to protect herself against poison by having her food cooked in her own room under her own eye; all that Mary could do was to try and get the cut of meat next to the one her jailer had taken. Her situation was indeed perilous when one of the commissioners her father sent down to have her take the oath recognizing him as Head of the Church could shout at her, "If you were my daughter I would beat you to death and knock your head against the wall until it was soft as an apple."

Henry made a visit to Hatfield while Mary was there, but out of fear of Anne's displeasure – and perhaps to save himself embarrassment, for he was addicted to running away from unpleasant interviews – he took care not to talk with her. It was only when he was leaving that he saw her, and then she was kneeling at a window looking down on him piteously as he was mounting his horse. His heart sufficiently relented for him to take off his cap and wave. With regard to Mary he was of a double mind. Affection, or at least the memory of the affection he had once had for her, stirred in him from time to time; but he was also angry at her obstinacy, all the more so because he was sure that she was covertly receiving support. A typical instance of this, about which Henry never heard, was when Edward Fox, his Almoner, who had been sent to accompany her on her journey to Hatfield rode up to her litter and whispered to her to remain firm. He was very much of a King's man and more inclined to Protestantism than most Englishmen of his time, but he, like everybody else in England, except the little circle round Anne, admired the Lady Mary.

One cannot but admire her courage and constancy, even though one is left a little aghast by her temerity. Thus once when Norfolk was leaving and asked her whether she had any message for the King, she answered, "None except that the Princess of Wales, his daughter, asks for his blessing." When Norfolk replied that he dared not give such a message, she said, "Then go away and leave me alone."

Chapuys, when he saw that he was never going to get Katherine's consent to a rising in her behalf, turned his attention to what he thought Katherine would not oppose – Mary's escape from England. Such an escape, as Chapuys planned it, was not only perfectly feasible but could be carried out with hardly any possibility of failure, once he brought Katherine to agree. Mary was a magnificent rider, as she was to prove eighteen years later when it was her horsemanship that foiled the Duke of Northumberland's coup. Nothing could be easier than to have her met at one of her periods of exercise by armed men, "captured" by them, and taken to the swift galley that would be lying off Greenwich, while heavily armed ships hovered at the Thomas estuary. Once safely in Flanders she could be married to her cousin Reginald Pole – not yet in major orders though his cardinalate was near.

This marriage was one that Mary's mother had always wanted, not so much for its political advantages (though to these she was by no means indifferent) as because of personal reasons. Reginald's mother, Lady Salisbury, had been since her first days in England a close friend. She felt that Mary's marriage to a man of such fine character would be desirable, not only on that account but because it might be considered an act of reparation for the execution by Henry VII of Lady Salisbury's brother, the young Earl of Warwick. Katherine all through her life felt that her troubles were, in some obscure way, due to that crime.

Had Mary been married to this true Plantagenet in her youth, when she must be presumed to have been capable of bearing children, the whole history of England might well have taken an entirely different course. It was not to be: Katherine did not wish to countenance even so much of an overt act against her husband as Mary's escape. She knew that Mary would almost certainly get safely away, as everybody would connive at it; but she feared that the escape might be the signal for rebellion. Not only was she loyal to Henry but her gentle heart dreaded the thought of bloodshed. The Emperor was also against any rising, as he feared that, if it took place, he would be drawn into backing it, if only formally and for honour's sake. So he discouraged Chapuys' clever plans and they came to nothing.

Plans of this sort were not discussed without Cromwell's getting some wind of them. Henry was therefore at pains to keep mother and daughter apart. When on February 12, 1535, Katherine wrote to her "special friend," Chapuys, asking him to request the King to permit Mary, who was at that time ill, to stay with her at Kimbolton, though a kind of consent was given, it was never actually carried into effect. Katherine had sent the assurance: "There is no need for anyone to nurse her but myself; I will put her in my own bed in my own chamber and watch her when needful," but Henry suspected that, even if Mary's illness were genuine, it might provide an opportunity for some plotting. It was, however, very hard on Mary and her mother. The fact that there were some men on the Council who were saying that it would be a blessing if Providence removed Mary made all the doctors reluctant to prescribe for her. They knew that if she died they would be sure to be believed to have poisoned her. So the most that was done for Mary was to let her go near Kimbolton where she could receive visits from her mother's Spanish physician and apothecary.

The last chance of a rebellion in England with help from abroad came and passed in the autumn of 1535. That August, Charles had been victorious in his campaign in North Africa and had taken Goletta. When Chapuys reported to Henry and Cromwell what had happened he noted sardonically that, while stammering out their insincere congratulations, they looked "like dogs that had tumbled out of a window." They realized that, now that the Emperor was free, he could, if he wished, have the deprivation against Henry enforced. Henry also realized that, even without the Emperor, Katherine was capable of raising a rebellion. He told his council: "The Lady Katherine is a proud, stubborn woman of very high courage. If she took it into her head to take her daughter's part, she could quite easily take the field, muster a great army, and wage against me a war as fierce as any her mother Isabella ever waged in Spain." But he counted upon this not happening; he knew that Katherine could do it, he also knew that she would not. Nor did he think it likely that the cautious Charles would involve himself in English affairs. At that moment the Emperor was, in fact, showing himself inclined to seek an English alliance. Nothing was ever to be looked for from him except fair words.

The danger was, nevertheless, considered great enough for the attainder of both Katherine and Mary to be talked about in the Council. If it was not followed through, this was partly because Katherine was known to be in failing health, and death was expected to remove her before long. But it is hard to imagine any circumstances in which Henry would have ventured to risk a bill of attainder against Katherine in Parliament, or (worse still) a public trial. There would have been no holding back the nobles or the people from rebellion had that been attempted. The only feasible way of getting rid of Katherine, unless natural death came, was by murder. This was why the thought of poison, or the assassin's dagger at night, haunted the dreams of Chapuys.

Mary's immediate danger sprang from the danger in which

Katherine stood. After Katherine's death, the menace, though not entirely removed, was not so pressing. On the other hand, she lacked her mother's moral support. As Katherine was in her grave – and Anne too – the question of the divorce had become academic; Mary therefore decided to submit, to recognize her father as Head of the Church, and to do anything else that was required of her.

Probably she would never have submitted had it been a question of recognizing Anne, but Mary's new stepmother was an entirely different kind of person, not only unaffectedly kind but beautifully tactful. Queen Jane took the Lady Mary's hand in hers and made her leave the room at her side, disavowing her own precedence. After the harshness Mary had suffered, she could no longer resist. She signed the document with which she was presented, without looking at the contents, as though to emphasize the mere formality of the act. It was written on what she had signed that she was "most humbly prostrate at the feet of your most excellent Majesty"; that she declared her mother's marriage "by God's law and man's law incestuous and unlawful"; and that she acknowledged her father as Head of the Church in England. Therefore she "utterly refused the Bishop of Rome's pretended authority."

Chapuys, her mother's friend and her own friend, had always advised capitulation if it proved to be really necessary. He saw that it could no longer be avoided. To the Emperor he wrote: "After the Princess had signed the document, she was most dejected, but I relieved her of every doubt, even of conscience, assuring her that the Pope would not only not impute to her any blame, but would hold it rightly done. If she let this opportunity slip, there was no remedy in the world for her." There could be no doubt that he had judged the situation accurately; further resistance was useless.

It was not enough for Henry that Mary had signed the paper; he wanted to be sure of her "sincerity." He was not contented at having made her yield to force; hers was to be a whole-hearted conviction. From time to time he would question her further, and from time to time she had to add to her humiliation with a lie. His cold little eyes shot their sharp gimlets at her; the suspicious little mouth pursed up. But he had to be content with an assurance in which he never really believed. He used to tell her that he hated nothing so much as dissemblers. Why, he would never dissemble, even with foreign ambassadors, however much his councillors urged him to do so! She must remember never to dissemble with him.

It was hard for a woman of her honesty to live such a life, but she held on, not out of fear for herself but because there was no way of telling whether, even yet, she might not become Queen and bring England back to Catholic unity. There was so much to shock and grieve her, if it was only to see her father carelessly flaunting on his finger the famous ruby known as the "Great Regal" that had been filched from the shrine of St. Thomas of Canterbury. No wonder the French ambassador, Marillac, wrote to tell his King on June 3, 1542, that she had said: "While my father lives I shall be only the Lady Mary, the most unhappy lady in Christendom."

CHAPTER TWELVE

The Fall of Anne

It was during the early months of his imprisonment, when Sir Thomas More was allowed to walk with his visitors in the gardens of the Tower, that one day he turned to his daughter Margaret and asked her how the Queen was, meaning of course Anne Boleyn.

"In faith, father," Margaret answered, "never better."

"Never better, Meg," he returned. "Alas! Meg. Alas! it pitieth me to remember into what misery, poor soul, she shall shortly come."

That prophecy did not pretend to be supernatural. More was making a shrewd inference from what he knew of Henry's capricious character. He also knew that Anne was the kind of shrill vixenish person who would soon grate on any man's nerves, and that she had enemies who were waiting to strike the moment this was safe.

During the long years when she had been waiting for Henry to get his divorce, Anne had frequently upbraided him for delay, goading him on to still greater efforts. She was, Chapuys had reported, "growing impatient, complaining that she was wasting her time and youth to no purpose." Henry had always resented her shrewishness, though before marriage he was too besotted to object openly. Even an intelligence less acute than More's would have seen that Anne was creating a fund of grudges in Henry's slow secretive mind for which she would one day have to pay.

Only a few months after the wedding to Anne, Henry, who

appears to have been quite faithful during the long "engagement," began to dally with other women. When she made a fuss about this, she was roughly told that she must learn to close her eyes as her betters had done. Who these favourites were we do not know, except that Jane Seymour was not among them. There was one in the summer of 1533, another in the spring following Elizabeth's birth, and still another early the following year. To divert the King, Anne tried to interest him in his old hobby of theology and, when that did not prove sufficiently fascinating, she deliberately threw her cousin, Madge Shelton, at his head, on the principle that Madge would be less dangerous to her than one who might set herself up as a serious rival.

Noting the state of affairs, people began to turn against her. She had never really had any friends, nothing but a party who had pushed her forward to gain their own ends. Norfolk, though he was her uncle, considered that she was acting injudiciously and tried to tell her so. She replied to him in terms, he said, that one would not use to a dog. His own language was not very refined and he was heard muttering something about *une grande putaine* when he left the room where she was. Even her rapscallion brother, George Rochford, a man as bold and brilliant as he was corrupt, was afraid that she had over-reached herself, antagonizing everybody by her insolence. Rochford's wife, who was on bad terms with her husband, was an open enemy. Anne's aunt, Lady William Howard, and her uncle, Sir Edward Boleyn, had gone over to the party closing in against her. Even her old flame, the Earl of Northumberland, had joined the opposition, though he was a man too spineless to be much of a danger. Wherever Anne looked she saw nothing but eyes that were watching for her fall. Aware of what was happening, she told Henry in the spring of 1534 that she was pregnant again. The lie was not very useful, as at best it could serve for only a few weeks. It is the gauge of her desperation that she used it.

As early as February, 1535, we know that Henry was talking about the possibility of divorcing her. But when he consulted canonists on this point, they informed him that a divorce from

Anne would mean that he would have to take Katherine back. Rather than eat that humble pie he determined to endure Anne. But he did so grimly, hating her for having put him in this predicament. When later in 1535 Anne really did become pregnant, all thoughts of getting rid of her were, for the moment, put away: she might this time bear a son.

When she failed again, and the project of a divorce was revived, the Emperor sent rather surprising instructions to Chapuys. These, dated March 28, 1536, told him: "If the sentence about the [new] divorce be executed that the King may forsake the Concubine, he may marry somebody else, while it is clear that from the said Concubine he can have no progeny that can hereafter dispute the right of the Princess [Mary] to the succession." He indicated also that he would promote Henry's reconciliation with Rome only if this would mean substantial political advantage to himself. Otherwise he preferred that Henry should stick to Anne. Chapuys was therefore ordered to treat with her and form an alliance with her. If the decision was appallingly cynical, so were a good many of the principles upon which people were acting. The Emperor's instructions came too late; it had already been settled that Anne was to be destroyed.

Anne had always thought of Katherine as her greatest danger. She never ceased being afraid that Henry would go back to her. So it seemed to her the best of good news when word came that on January 8, 1536, Katherine had died at Kimbolton. Or if this was not the very best thing that could happen — for that would be the birth of a son — it could be taken as an augury of that happy event.

Chapuys had been given permission to visit Katherine. Henry had told him, "She won't live long," so a visit did not matter. And Katherine had greeted him as the loyal friend he had always been, saying, "I can now die in your arms; not abandoned, like one of the beasts." She did not die while he was there, but he never saw her again after this visit with the long, intimate conversations he had with her, sitting on her bed.

She made a noble end. On the morning of her death, shortly after midnight, her confessor, Jorge de Ateca, the Spanish Bishop of Llandaff, seeing death's approach, had offered to say Mass for her in her room at once. She would not permit this; he had to wait until the canonical hour. She was confessed and received Communion, and she died. A day or two before her death, she wrote to Henry as "My most dear lord, king, and husband," a very moving letter, in which she put him "in remembrance with a few words of the health and safeguard of [his] soul"; conveyed her full pardon; commended Mary to him; asked marriage portions for her ladies-in-waiting and the payment to her servants of the wages due them "and a year more, lest they be unprovided for." She concluded, "Lastly, I make this vow, that mine eyes desire you above all other things."*

Chapuys suspected poison, and it is true that there were some suspicious circumstances. But the fact that Katherine's Spanish doctor, De la Sá, and her confessor were not allowed to leave England may be explained on the ground that the King did not wish them to carry abroad any further accounts of the harsh treatment Katherine had received. Henry himself lent some colour to the idea of Anne's attempting the use of poison by exclaiming, very shortly afterwards, "The Duke [of Richmond] and his sister, the Lady Mary, might thank God for having escaped the hands of that poisonous wretch who had conspired their death!" This sort of thing, however, may be safely dismissed. The slow poisons in which everybody believed in those days are mythical. Moreover poison of any kind could have been administered to Katherine only by De la Sá himself, which is unthinkable. Finally, the condition of Katherine's heart at the post mortem examination — black and with a growth attached — probably indicates cancer. That her death was expected proves no more than that she was known to be very ill; that she survived as long as she did is surprising.

---

*Gairdner in his *English Church in the Sixteenth Century* (p. 167) questions the authenticity of this letter; it is, however, generally accepted by historians.

When the news reached the court Henry unabashedly rejoiced. "God be praised!" he said, "Now the old harridan is dead, there is no fear of war." Instead of putting on mourning, he dressed in yellow, from his hat down to his shoes, and so did Anne. Little Elizabeth was brought to court and, with the child in his arms, Henry went round the room in the highest spirits exhibiting her to everybody. That evening they had the gayest of balls at Greenwich.

If Anne rejoiced at the disappearance of the woman she had displaced, but whom she had continued to fear as a rival – "Now I am Queen, indeed!" she exclaimed – Henry was relieved for political rather than personal reasons, though, because of her refusal to accede to his demands, he had come to feel a hatred for the woman he had once loved. The English ambassadors to France were instructed to drop a hint to Francis that, as there was now no issue between Henry and the Emperor, the French had better close with the English proposals while there was time.

Chapuys himself proceeded to take advantage of the new situation. In February he sounded Cromwell, suggesting that Henry now submit to the Pope and declare Mary legitimate. The Emperor would help the King straighten out his affairs with the Holy See. In return Henry was to help Charles against the Turk and form an offensive and defensive alliance. Cromwell appeared to be receptive, but may have thought that too much was being asked. He answered that it might be best to begin the negotiations with some minor matter before going on to the principal question at issue. It seems to have been in reply to this letter that the Emperor instructed Chapuys to cultivate Anne and give her whatever backing was in his power. She was to be preferred to a third wife who might bear Henry a legitimate son. Chapuys was, after all, bound by his instructions. The Emperor, though he had acted correctly with regard to his aunt, and though he believed her to have been poisoned, was not going to make further trouble. Katherine had been a nuisance to him during life, now her death set his political hands free.

The joy of the Boleyns was a little premature, as was soon apparent. If Anne bore a son she would be saved; not otherwise. Katherine's death had put her in an imminent danger she was not intelligent enough to see; Henry could now divorce his second wife without having to go back to his first. On the same day that Katherine was buried in Peterborough Abbey (now its cathedral), January 29, Anne was brought to bed. She was delivered of a still-born boy.

For the mishap she bitterly blamed her uncle, Norfolk. He had, it seems, not broken to her gently enough the news that the King had been thrown from his horse; and the shock had brought on the miscarriage. People, however, had thought she had taken the news of Henry's mishap, which turned out to be trifling, very calmly. But of course in her panic she had to blame somebody.

What had happened to her was much worse than bearing a live daughter; it is just possible that that might have given her a reprieve. Henry gazed down stonily at her as she lay weeping in her bed and said, "I will talk to you later." Later that day he confided to his intimates that he had "made this marriage seduced by witchcraft and for this reason considered it null; and that this was evident because God did not permit them to have any male issue, and that he believed he might take another wife."

Nothing was done for the moment except that Anne was left in a miserable isolation. How completely out of favour she was was proved when on April 23, St. George's Day, there was an election for a Knight of the Garter. Then Anne's brother, Lord Rochford, who had been counting on this honour, was passed over and Sir Nicholas Carew chosen instead. The Knights had taken their cue from the King.

At that moment Cromwell felt that he, too, was slipping from power. He had carried through Parliament the act for the suppression of the smaller (and less affluent) monasteries, and with this his usefulness appeared to be at an end. When the Boleyns fell, all the new men would fall with them, Cromwell hardest of all. There would be an aristocratic restoration, with Norfolk and Gardiner at the head of affairs. Cromwell saw that he had to find some means of immediately ingratiating himself with the King.

He proved himself fully equal to the emergency. The most signal service he could render to Henry was to provide means for getting rid of Anne. His private secret service cost him a pretty penny but was worth all that it cost; he now set his spies to work on the Queen. It was his life or hers.

Nothing was more easy than to "frame" her. Though one may accept as an abstract proposition the possibility that she may have accepted a young and vigorous lover to beget the son that the obese and diseased King could not provide, there is sufficient evidence against it in the birth, a year and a half later, of the future Edward VI. Anne was, however, very indiscreet. She loved admiration and encouraged gallant speeches from the courtiers. Bits of talk were overheard by Cromwell's spies; they were enough to give him a handle against her. In his business-like, dispassionate way he arranged for her destruction.

Henry already had at hand a new wife with whom to displace Anne. He may have seen her in the days when, as a young girl, she had been one of Katherine's ladies-in-waiting. But as she was not much to look at, he probably did not notice her then, and had paid no attention to her until, in the September of 1535, he had stayed with her father, a Wiltshire squire named Sir John Seymour. His daughter Jane was a kittenish blonde, gentle in manner (which was a relief after the strident Anne), and with a primness which the King took to indicate virtue.

Since the new year he had been making advances, but she had held him off, returning a purse of gold and a letter unopened. Those who had witnessed what had happened in Anne's case knew that this was the best tactics. Jane had clever and ambitious brothers, and they advised her, as did Sir Nicholas Carew and Sir Thomas Elyot, Henry's former ambassador to Charles V and the author of *The Boke Called the Governour,* on no account to yield to his solicitations. Elyot at least, let us hope, spoke with moral considerations in mind; the others probably did not. Coached by them, Jane made high-flown speeches that greatly impressed the King. Yet, despite the cynical view of Chapuys, she seems to have been a virtuous, if also a rather stupid, young woman. To her credit it must be said that, as a partisan of her former mistress, Katherine, she had never regarded Anne as Henry's legitimate wife. She felt no qualms about ousting the Queen.

Cromwell's evidence was gathered in dead secrecy. It was mainly obtained from Mark Smeaton, a lute-player at the court, one who was likely to be more easily terrified than the other young men who were marked down. He was privately arrested by Cromwell and privately subjected to torture, and he confessed to enough for Cromwell's purpose. Even before this, on April 24, a special commission had been appointed to enquire into the Queen's misdemeanors, when they should be brought to light.

On May Day there was a tournament at Greenwich, and at this Lord Rochford and Sir Henry Norris were the chief challengers, the obese King, no longer fit for this furious exercise, sitting in the gallery with Anne by his side.

He watched and applauded, as though nothing were on his mind. But as he rode home Henry called Norris to him and told him that he was accused of adultery with the Queen. Greatly shocked, Norris denied everything, but was put under arrest. The next day he was lodged in the Tower with Rochford (who was accused of incest with his sister) and four knights, Francis Weston, Thomas Wyatt, Richard Page, and William Brereton, who were charged with adultery. The next day the Queen herself was arrested.

As what followed is one of the most shocking episodes in history — the execution of a wife by her husband — some explanation, which may also be a partial extenuation, may be offered. It must be conceded that a queen who commits adultery is not only guilty of a private sin but of a public crime; she may palm off a child by a lover as the legitimate heir. It may therefore be argued that hers, as the very highest kind of treason, should be made liable to the most severe of punishments. Such at all events is the theory which, however cold-blooded and horrifying, is hardly controvertible in logic.

Whether Henry really believed in Anne's guilt it is difficult to say. He wanted to believe in it and, as his mind was naturally suspicious, it could not have been hard to convince him. Had he merely wished to get rid of her a divorce would have been a simple matter, and that was obtained as well. But before the grounds on which a divorce could be given by the resourceful Cranmer were chosen, the adultery charges had already been made. Henry made up his mind to exact the penalty in full—ostensibly because of his wife's unfaithfulness but really to settle scores for all the years in which Anne had ridden him so pitilessly.

London openly rejoiced in her downfall. The people of England had always bluntly called her the King's whore, and many of them suspected her of being Katherine's murderess. They crowded out on the banks of the Thames and went out on the river in boats to get a good view of "Nan Bullen" as she was taken in her barge, in full daylight, to the Tower. But their opinions had never had the slightest effect, except that now they gave Henry further justification for ridding himself of a liability. He blamed Anne for his unpopularity, and certainly one of the most popular things he ever did was what he was doing now. So sure were the officials of the result that they did not bother to pack the grand jury, nor did they attend the hearing. It was all a foregone conclusion.

Henry's personal conduct, however, gave scandal. Even those who rejoiced at Anne's misfortune could not but feel some shock. For though it was given out that the King was overwhelmed with grief, Chapuys commented that he had never seen a man who wore his horns more pleasantly. All London could not fail to observe that, for a man reputedly so downcast, the King seemed to be astonishingly merry. Very much in evidence was the King's barge as it passed several times during the day and often at night, with its lanterns glowing on the water and with musicians playing; and everybody knew whom he was visiting. It may be true, as Pollard, Henry's chief contemporary defender, remarks, that Henry was every inch a King; it cannot be doubted that Pollard is right in admitting that Henry was no gentleman. His coarseness and vulgarity and the colossal insensitiveness of his egotism were never more evident than now. Though England was more than ready to welcome a new queen, it wished that the King was behaving in more seemly style. The very courtiers who devised new amusements for him, could not refrain from whispers of contempt.

There was still worse unseemliness of which England at that time knew nothing. Cranmer, terrified for his own life now that his patroness had fallen, wrote to Henry a letter which some people have taken to be a gallant defence of Anne but which seems to me one of the most despicable acts of his life. For what he says in one breath, he takes back in the next. I cannot see that it is anything else but a complete betrayal.*

The first half of this letter, written on May 3 from Lambeth, where Cromwell had ordered Cranmer to stay, without trying to see the King, was little but canting commonplace: Henry was to accept everything at God's hands "as well things displeasant as pleasant." Nor was he to consider that his honour had been touched, "but her honour to be clean disparaged." The Archbishop had never had a better opinion of a woman than he had had of her, "which maketh me to think that she should not be culpable. And again, I think your Highness would not have gone so far, except she had been surely culpable."

Later he elaborated on this. He hopes she will be found

*This letter is (in condensation) in *Letters and Papers,* Vol. X, pp. 333–334, but the full text is in Froude. It is also in an anthology of English prose in the World's Classics, where it is presumably included because the editor admired it. Well, it is in its way a wonderful performance.

innocent. "And if she be found culpable, considering your Grace's goodness to her, and from what condition your Grace of your only mere goodness took her, and set the crown upon her head, I repute him not your Grace's faithful servant and subject, nor true unto the realm, that would not desire the offence without mercy to be punished, to the example of all other." The Archbishop says he had loved her because of the love he thought her to have for the Gospel; but if she be proved guilty, the more one loves the Gospel, the more one must hate her. "For there never was creature in our time that so much slandered the Gospel." He suggests that God has sent her this punishment "for that she feignedly hath professed the Gospel in her mouth, and not in heart and deed." How anybody – and here we have to stretch the line from Froude to Miss Edith Sitwell – can think that a brave letter instead of a base one is beyond my comprehension. The only kind of extenuation possible is that Cranmer was so prompt to disavow his patroness, lest by any identification of her with the cause of the "Gospel," that cause should suffer. He took pains to remind the King that his royal favour to the Gospel "was not led by affection unto her, but by zeal unto the truth."

Worse, if possible, was still to come from Cranmer. He was sent to interview Anne in the Tower and in his gentle wheedling way managed to extract from her, not a confession of guilt (for that she never made) but something that could be used against her. Again there may have been some extenuation. Cranmer was in Cromwell's power, as would be indicated by the yearly grant of £40 Cromwell had been receiving from the Archbishop – one may presume for holding his tongue about Mrs. Cranmer. And Cranmer may have been assured that no harm was intended the Queen and have hoped that, by talking with her, he would find some means of helping her. Any promise he gave may have been given in good faith; she was allowed to understand that, if only she was amenable, she would be allowed to retire to Antwerp. So if there was any betrayal on the part of Cranmer, he also may himself have been betrayed. He was not the manager of this affair but Cromwell, and Cromwell saw that, to save his own neck, Anne must be sent to the block.

At first Anne did not seem to have any idea as to the gravity of her position. She was lodged in the royal apartments in the Tower where she had slept, as custom dictated, the night before her coronation. She was given high-born ladies as her attendants, though these were of course really jailers, and she ordered them about with all her old arrogance. She also displayed her characteristic levity and lack of discretion, using several expressions which were made to implicate several of the men charged with being her lovers. Rochford, however, was mainly brought down by his estranged wife. Wyatt and Page managed to exculpate themselves.

Anne's trial was the usual judicial farce. The panel of peers before whom she appeared included a number of her avowed enemies, though, as to that, the government would have found it well-nigh impossible to bring her before any impartial tribunal. Norfolk her uncle presided over the proceedings, perhaps not without some secret pleasure. But Anne's father, the contemptible Earl of Wiltshire, in order to prove his loyalty came forward with offers to serve on the commission, though even Henry would have had delicacy enough to excuse him.*

Before such peers as could be gathered, Anne became at last aware of her extreme danger. She defended herself with coolness and ability, and had the counsel appointed for her – a special concession in a treason trial – really tried to serve her, they could have raised such difficulties that the prosecution might have been forced to content itself with a divorce. But of course her counsel did not dare appear too strenuous in her behalf, instead they virtually acquiesced in a sentence which was predetermined.

Some of the things of which Anne was accused are so ridiculous and so beside the point as to reveal the weakness of the

*Perhaps also to let it be known (what was the truth) that he had often been alarmed at Anne's reckless courses. Rochford, her brother, had also sometimes warned her, though he had much of her temperament.

Crown's case. She was accused of having made fun of the King's clothes, and even of his poetry. If she had ever done this, she showed herself a poor literary critic, but it had nothing to do with the charge of adultery. She was accused of most improbable promiscuity, and of having in each instance solicited her lover. Each was alleged to have consented reluctantly. Moreover, some specific instances of her misconduct were indicated as having occurred shortly before or shortly after the birth of her still-born son. As though all this were not, on the face of it, sufficiently unlikely, she was charged with incest with her own brother – the "proof" being that she had been alone with him in a room for several hours!

Rochford when he was brought to his trial defended himself with such cleverness that bets were being laid in court, two to one, that he would be acquitted. An acquittal of this sort had occurred in 1533 when Lord Dacre had been charged with treason, delated by his enemy, Percy; the same thing might happen again. There was, however, this difference: Dacre had friends among the peers, whereas George Boleyn only had enemies. Knowing this, he knew that he was foredoomed. Therefore when a question was put to him in writing, as there was no wish to ask it in open court, he defiantly read it aloud. It asked whether his sister, the Queen, had ever told him that the King was sexually impotent.* If Rochford was not lost before, he was lost after letting that shameful imputation against Henry be known. But Boleyn meant to get this little scrap of revenge.

Henry for his part also showed spite, and spite of a much more malignant sort. One would have supposed that it would have been enough to get rid of Anne by cutting off her head. But no, he had also to divorce her, so that she could die in the knowledge that her daughter Elizabeth had been declared illegitimate and therefore could not succeed to the throne. It is, however, doubtful whether Anne now cared much; she understood that, legitimate or not under statute, Mary would be preferred by the overwhelming mass of the English people. She

*That is what it came to; of course this expression was not used.

had little or no affection for the child who, by having the wrong sex, was a bitter disappointment and had contributed to her downfall. She did not ask to see her baby before she died. Elizabeth later would never speak of her mother.

Anne's conduct in prison continued to alternate between a hectic piety and her accustomed frivolity. According to one account, which is questionable, she knelt before Lady Kingston, the wife of the Constable, and asked her to go to the Lady Mary and beg her forgiveness. She certainly asked that the Blessed Sacrament be placed in a little room opening out of the one she occupied. She was calm then, but at other times she talked wildly and went off into fits of shrill laughter. Sir William Richmond could not make it out at all and said afterwards that he had never seen anybody who seemed so glad to die, though he had had the smiling Sir Thomas More in his charge.

On May 17 the five men, Rochford and Norris and Brereton and Weston and Smeaton were executed. When Smeaton repeated his confession on the scaffold Anne was shocked and said that she feared his soul would be damned for such a lie. As he was not a "gentleman" and therefore should have been executed at Tyburn by hanging and disembowelling, the suspicion is created that a deal had been made with him by which he might purchase the swift death of the axe by saying what was required. Something like this was to happen in the case of Cromwell four years later. But whatever Smeaton may have said, the others would not confess, except that Rochford, after the verdict of the jury had been brought in, asked to be allowed to change his plea to guilty. It was obviously a move to protect his property from confiscation by the Crown.

Anne had been sentenced to burning or beheading at the King's pleasure. When the beheading was graciously decided upon, she obtained a further grace which meant a further delay; she requested to have her head cut off with a sword, so an expert had to be sent for from Calais. She put her hands round her long, thin neck and asked Sir William Kingston whether the stroke would hurt. He assured her that she would feel no pain at all, "it is so subtle." Yet when she was brought out into the courtyard of the Tower on the morning of May 19, dressed for death in a night robe of damask and a red damask skirt, she kept nervously looking round the scaffold to see the sword. The executioner kept it hidden under a pile of straw until she had laid herself, blindfolded, on the block.

She had made, if it was reported correctly, a good speech a few minutes before. It was expected of all those who died at the Tower (or even at Tyburn) that they accept their death "meekly," making a last obeisance to the sacred law even if they did not admit their guilt. Anne said: "Good Christian people, I am come hither to die; for according to the law, and by the law I am judged to die, and therefore I will speak nothing against it. I come hither to accuse no man, nor to speak anything of that whereof I am accused and condemned to die. But I pray God save the King, and send him long to reign over you; for a gentler and more merciful prince was there never; and to me he was ever a good, a gentle, and a sovereign lord. And if any person will meddle in my cause, I require them to judge the best. And thus I take my leave of the world, and of you all; and I heartily desire you all to pray for me."

Chapuys, who had disliked and despised her, nevertheless appears to have been inclined to believe her innocent, writing, "The lady who had charge of her had sent to tell me in great secrecy that the Concubine, before and after receiving the Sacrament, affirmed on the damnation of her soul that she had never been unfaithful to the King." History is willing to accept that judgement, though it further blackens the infamous Cromwell. Nor can Henry altogether escape infamy, for, if he believed in Anne's guilt, it was because it suited him to do so. So far from being overwhelmed by discovering it, he was obviously glad that he had a pretext for getting rid of her. She died unmourned, unless it was by her father and Cranmer, and their emotions were mainly relief that they had not been involved in her ruin. Cranmer had protected himself by betraying her, and Thomas

Boleyn was highly endowed with every instinct necessary for survival.

Cranmer performed another signal service to Henry by divorcing him from Anne before her execution. This was specially shameful as coming from him, as he was the man who two years earlier had announced her marriage (though made before Katherine's divorce) to be valid. Now he complaisantly reversed his decision.

Too much has been made of the illogicality of punishing Anne for an adultery she could not have committed without being married. For as she had been counted as the King's wife any son she had borne would have had to be presumed the King's heir. Had the charges against her been well founded she would have deserved death.

The grounds of the divorce were never published. But they emerged and did no honour to the King. Pressure was brought to bear on Northumberland to declare that he had been engaged to Anne, so that there might be a plea of a precontract. But Northumberland took an oath before the Archbishops of Canterbury and York and a group of nobles, which included the Duke of Norfolk, that this precontract had never existed. There is some reason to suspect him of perjury, as the admission might have made him liable to a charge of treason for concealing a fact that should have been revealed before Henry married Anne. But at the time he dared not make such a declaration, and now there was nothing for it but to make emphatic denials. That easy way out for Henry was therefore blocked.

Chapuys discovered the true reason for the divorce Cranmer now pronounced, though even without Chapuys' testimony the reason might have been inferred. What he wrote to Granvelle was: "The marriage between the Concubine and the King was invalid, he having carnally known the said Concubine's sister. . . . It would have been more honourable to have alleged that she had been previously married [Chapuys is referring to a precontract with Northumberland], but God has been pleased to reveal still greater abominations, which is the more inexcusable as ignorance could not have been alleged either of the law or the fact."

How could Henry use his affair with Mary Boleyn as the grounds for a divorce from Anne? His ingenuity (or Cranmer's) was quite equal to it. Henry's dispensation to marry Anne, after he had established an affinity with her through Mary, had been obtained from the Pope in 1528, at which time the King was confidently counting upon obtaining his divorce from Katherine from the Holy See. But since his marriage to Anne on January 25, 1533, it had been made law in England that no appeals should be made to Rome. Therefore all dispensations from Rome could be considered as of no effect, and it could be argued that he had never been married to Anne. Monstrously unjust as the proceedings were they are at least legally justifiable.

Henry was now forty-five and had for children only the bastard Duke of Richmond and two bastardized daughters. Yet he seemed little disturbed, in spite of all his fine talk since 1525 about his anxiety regarding the succession, though now he was ageing and ailing. Before long he had no heir at all. Young Richmond, who had attended Anne's execution, died before the year was out of the tuberculosis that had carried off Henry VII and was to carry off Edward VI.

Even before Anne's execution – in fact as soon as it was known that she was under arrest – the Emperor proposed the Infanta of Portugal as Henry's next wife, offering a dowery of 400,000 ducats, or the young widow the Duchess of Milan (who was to be proposed again later). Francis I, for his part, was anxious that Henry marry a French princess, though he was not definite about any particular person. What counted in diplomacy was that Henry of England was in the marriage market again.

Henry's own view of the matter was that he was a man unlucky enough to have contracted, of course in innocence and good faith, two unlawful marriages. But he had proved his faithfulness to God by divorcing both wives. That being the case, God would be sure to reward him with a son. But he did not need the help of Charles or Francis in selecting a wife; he had her already picked out. On the day after Anne's execution he was betrothed to Jane Seymour. Ten days later they were married.

This time, however, he took the precaution of safeguarding the succession by statute. God would no doubt send him a son, but in case God did not, Parliament empowered the King to bequeath the Crown by personal will. Such a designated successor should enjoy all the rights after his decease, "in as large and ample manner as the lawful heirs of his body would have done." This was an unheard of departure in English law and one, as time was to show, that the English people would not accept.

The King was dutifully thanked by Parliament for his new marriage, and with some sincerity. Thomas Boleyn lived until 1539, but he had never counted a great deal; what the country had feared was the possibility of Anne's governing, helped by her brother, in the name of the little Elizabeth. Mary was considered, for the time being, the true claimant, but everybody hoped that Jane would bear Henry a son.

CHAPTER THIRTEEN

The Pilgrimage of Grace

Now that Katherine and Anne were dead the road was open for a reconciliation with Rome. Many who had loved and admired Katherine and had believed her in the right were almost as much relieved at her removal from the scene as was the King himself, though for very different reasons. Even had Anne managed, after this, to remain in Henry's good graces, easy terms could have been reached with Paul III. The Holy See was willing to let bygones be bygones. The Pope let it be known that he was willing to close the quarrel, if Henry made an advance, which was of course in itself an advance made by the Pope.

Henry ignored this offer, though not without misgivings. He feared that to reject it outright would be at the same time to close the door upon the possibility of friendship with the Emperor. Were this to become known, Francis, who had been in a more or less suppliant attitude with regard to Henry's favour – out of fear that he would make an imperial alliance – would now find it much less necessary to offer concessions to England.

Yet Henry did refuse the chance of reconciliation with the Holy See. Partly this was due to his vanity; having taken up a position, he was disinclined to change it. But other considerations weighed perhaps still more heavily. His need for money was as great as ever, even after he had suppressed the lesser monasteries. It might be demanded of him that he restore stolen goods, and certainly further spoliation would be impossible if he returned to the Roman obedience. He saw clearly that he could never obtain nearly as much by taxation as he could by looting the Church. But perhaps what operated most strongly of all against the project of reconciliation was that four months after Anne's execution the nearest approach to a rebellion that Henry experienced occurred. It greatly frightened him, so much that he wished to avoid giving any appearance of being frightened. As he was well aware that any favourable response he made the papal overtures would be regarded as weakness, his obstinacy and pride forbade him to do other than reject them.*

It was, in fact, very hard to get anywhere with Henry. For example, just a month before Anne's fall, when Chapuys approached him on behalf of the Emperor, Henry had said that he was not a child to be whipped first and caressed afterwards. He was an injured man, and as such he must have a written letter of apology from the Emperor. He added (and perhaps really believed) that if it had not been for his support, Charles would never have been elected. All the while he spoke Chapuys noticed how Henry's excitement revealed itself by the way he drummed on his knee with his finger. In the same way, on only one condition would he have been willing at this time to have returned to the Roman obedience – it was if Paul III would reverse the decision on the divorce given by Clement VII. The most ignoble of passions – vanity, fear, and greed – combined to block a road that seemed for a moment to be open.

Cromwell himself, who cared nothing about religion one way or the other, was somewhat inclined at this time to stop the loot of the monasteries and to favour the return of England to the unity of Christendom. In this he was actuated only by political considerations, for he wondered whether the risks involved by

---

*This is no conjecture. Nobody was in a better position to know the true state of affairs than Stephen Gardiner. Addressing the assembled court in Mary's reign on December 2, 1554, he said: "When the tumult was in the north, in the time of King Henry VIII, I am sure the King was determined to have given over the supremacy again to the Pope: but the hour was not then come, and therefore it went not forward, lest some would have said that he did it for fear."

schism were not too great to be incurred. Henry had, it is true, come through safely so far, but if ever Charles and Francis should decide to unite to enforce the decree of deprivation, Henry would be lost. Indeed, Henry would be ruined, even if Charles should act alone. All that the Emperor would have to do was to send a small invading force—and Cromwell guessed that Chapuys was constantly advising this—for the country to burst into flame. The only possible allies that England could obtain were in Germany or Denmark, and they were too far away to be of any use except as an annoyance to the Emperor. Moreover, their terms were unacceptable: Henry would have to declare himself a Lutheran. His present situation—neither a Protestant nor (in the Pope's sense) a Catholic—was decidedly dangerous.

Cromwell's personal situation, however, was also dangerous. He had, it is true, saved himself from one peril by bringing Anne Boleyn to her doom. But with the advent of Jane Seymour, her brothers had gained an ascendancy over Henry. Moreover, should their sister bear a son, they would be its natural guardians and, after Henry's death, rule England in the infant's name. They did not wish to hamper their future policy, or lose the profits they expected, by a reconciliation with Rome. Faced with this new situation, in which the Seymours were backed by most of the new men, Cromwell had no choice except to acquiesce, against his better judgement, in a continuation of the schism and the looting of the Church.

Just at this point events occurred which enabled Henry to regard the remaining monasteries as hotbeds of disaffection and to provide himself with an excuse, lacking under the law, to proceed to further spoliation. For whether or not the risings which occurred during the autumn of 1536 were instigated by the monks, they were certainly in favour of the monasteries. The religious houses against which no vice could be alleged could now be charged with treason.

The very name, the Pilgrimage of Grace, indicates that it was not really a rebellion at all but a demonstration. Nor do the clergy seem to have been its prime movers, though many joined it, or were pressed into it, after it had occurred. It was rather a spontaneous protest, made by thousands of the common people. And it failed because it had no leaders, or only such leaders as those of the gentry whom the mob compelled to take command. But still more it failed because of its reluctance to use force, the only argument to which Henry would have listened.

The causes of the commotion were by no means all religious, though religion was the mainspring of what happened. There was dissatisfaction over taxation which, though not very onerous now, people had been assured would not be necessary after the lesser monasteries had been seized by the Crown. There was also a dislike for the Statute of Wills and Uses, which the King had at last forced through Parliament for the restriction of powers of bequest. In addition there were rumours (erroneous, but which seemed to be well founded) that the King intended to confiscate all Church plate and to leave parish churches only chalices of tin. What was not an issue was the King's supremacy over the Church; it was raised later but apparently as an afterthought. The grievances that operated in the beginning were more immediate and local.

In the two counties affected – Yorkshire and Lincolnshire – there were a very large number of religious houses that came within the operation of the act passed earlier in the year – 53 in the one county and 37 in the other, or about a quarter of all the houses in England with an income of less than £200 a year. The temper of the people and of the monks themselves was rising. When on September 28, 1536, the royal commissioners went to Hexham in Northumberland to take over its priory, the canons refused to surrender. They all stood in arms on the walls and called down, "We be twenty brethren in this house, and we shall die all, ere that ye shall have the house." The next day the canons were joined by sixty armed men of their tenantry, so the commissioners decided that it would be more prudent to withdraw. Later those canons, along with other monks who were considered refractory, were by Henry's personal orders hanged under martial law. But for the moment they and their property were saved.

There was, in spite of this isolated incident, no rising just then in Yorkshire, only wide-spread murmuring. The rebellion, if it can be called one, broke out in Lincolnshire – at the time of the Hexham affair but without anybody in Lincolnshire having so much as heard about it. Only two men were killed, one of them the Chancellor of the diocese, the other Dr. Leigh's cook, who had made himself specially obnoxious in the closing of monasteries. Except for these exceptions, it was an orderly though an angry assembly. Most of the men went indeed with arms in their hands, but their purpose was only to lay their grievances before the King, in the too simple faith that he would redress their wrongs once he was informed of them.

In a petition they asked that the holidays of the Church (some of which had been abolished by its new Head) be observed as before; they asked also that the suppressed monasteries be restored, except the ones the King had taken "for his pleasure only" (a significant concession); that there be no more taxes unless these were needed because of a war; and that the new bishops be deprived. Cranmer was specially mentioned as among those suspected of heresy, and Cromwell, as the chief engineer of what was being done, and Rich as the chancellor of the Augmentation Office. At the same time these Lincoln men protested their perfect loyalty.

Henry's reply, when it arrived at Lincoln on October 11, was in its way superb. One must give a reluctant admiration to the vigour of its language. The King went at once to the question of his councillors, denying that their appointment could be anybody's business but his own. He followed this up with: "How presumptuous then are ye, the rude commons of one shire, and that one of the most brute and beastly in the whole realm and of least experience, to find fault with your prince for the electing of his councillors and prelates, and to take upon you, contrary to God's law and man's law, to rule your prince." As for the monasteries, their suppression had been by act of Parliament, "and where ye allege that the service of God is much thereby diminished, the truth is the contrary; for there are no houses suppressed where God was well served, but where most vice, mischief and abomination of living was used." He even denied that the hospitality of the monasteries had been a public relief. "Now what unkindness and unnaturality may we impute to you and all our subjects that be of that mind that had rather an unthrifty sort of vicious persons should enjoy such possessions, profits and emoluments as grow of the said houses to the maintenance of their unthrifty life than we, your natural prince, sovereign lord and king, who doth and hath spent more in your defence of his own than six times they were worth." It was of course impossible for the men at Lincoln to meet such blanket assertions and denials, though they knew them to be untrue; they had supposed the King would accept what they had said, as falling within everybody's knowledge. When he did not, they were at a loss what to say. As for the King's wars, though a great deal of money had been spent on them, practically all of this had been raised by taxation and was not paid for out of Henry's personal resources. And it was a question whether any of these wars, except the campaigns against the invading Scots (the least costly of all) had been necessary to the defence of the realm.

The gentry from the beginning had been lukewarm in the cause, and when the King's letter arrived they were so filled with fear that they read it out to the people with some of the more truculent bits omitted, so as not to infuriate the mob. A canon who was looking over the shoulder of Thomas Mayne the reader called out that "the letter was falsely read," so that Mayne was threatened with death. Indeed two hundred of the infuriated commons decided to kill all the gentry, who were then meeting in the cathedral, and would have done so had they not slipped out by another door. The upshot was that the next day, October 13, the gentlemen rode off to meet the Duke of Suffolk to discuss terms of surrender. Yet Suffolk had so small a force that, if the insurgents had only attacked, the Duke would have been entirely wiped out. But now, paralysed by the defection of their reluctant leaders, they disbanded without having struck a blow. The following year they were punished with the execution of forty-six men, among whom were two abbots and ten priests.

What followed in Yorkshire was almost as inept. This was the true Pilgrimage of Grace and it would have succeeded had it not been for the monstrous perfidy of the King. For while it may be allowed that Henry had given no promise of pardon to the Lincolnshire men and was under no more than a general obligation to be merciful to those who had caused such little trouble, in the case of the men of Yorkshire definite pledges were given but were not honoured. The excuse that may perhaps be found for the savage executions in Lincolnshire is that the feeble fizzle of fire in that county served to light a bonfire elsewhere. And what happened in the low-lying lands between the estuary of the Humber and the Wash, though terrible, was far less than what happened further north. Henry had threatened that, if the Lincolnshire men did not yield, his forces would "burn, spoil and destroy goods, wives and children"; so he probably considered himself merciful that he hanged less than fifty rebels. In Yorkshire it was a different story because Yorkshire could have toppled Henry from the throne, had it only pressed its advantage.

Yet what happened there proved in the end to be only Lincolnshire on a somewhat larger scale, this though the Yorkshire leaders included some of the men whom Chapuys had counted on in 1534 and 1535. Several of these were in favour of a much bolder course of action than the one followed, but chance gave the supreme command to a man of a different type; and he ruined everything.

This man was Robert Aske, a lawyer practising in London, who happened to be in Yorkshire only because he was on a vacation. On his way home, on reaching the Lincolnshire side of the Trent, he was forced to take the Pilgrims' oath and to act as leader of the 4000 men in the locality. He organized them so well and impressed himself so much upon them that before long he found himself at the head of 60,000 of the Pilgrims, who gave him the title of the "Great Captain," one that mightily pleased his vanity. But of course he remained a lawyer, thinking always of words rather than deeds and believing that his skill in negotiation would obtain all that was needed. He was not a traitor, though some Catholic historians, disgusted with his mismanagement of affairs, have called him one. But he was weak, being too trusting, too simple, and too confident of his own powers. Henry, quickly recognizing this weakness, played upon it, to Aske's undoing and that of his followers.

That he was susceptible to Henry's charm is not surprising. Even the cynical Chapuys felt that charm, though he was proof against it. Sir Thomas More felt it, and was saved only because of his adhesion to principle. But other men – Cranmer for instance – did what they were told not merely because they were in awe of the kingly office but because they were enchanted by the man Henry. To come into that majestic presence, to experience its overwhelming force, and then to find a hearty affability, and a humorous raciness of talk, almost invariably meant complete, instant, and permanent captivation. The King had started with the advantage of a veneration so extreme that we hear of the Lincolnshire men taking off their hats when the royal letter arrived, as though it were some sacred thing. How could men like these expect to rebel successfully? As Lord Darcy said when he was waiting execution, "If I had seen my sovereign Lord in the field, and I had seen his Grace come against us, I would have lighted from my horse and taken my sword by the point and yielded it into his Grace's hands." And if that was true of the soldierly Darcy, it can be imagined how incapable were his followers of anything more violent than a respectful presentation of grievances.

In Yorkshire, because of having more capable leadership, the requests made to the King were more specific than those that had come from Lincolnshire, though they were along the same lines. The dissolution of the lesser monasteries was still the main grievance. But now other articles appeared – heretical books were to be destroyed, and among these was listed St. German's work; the Lady Mary was to be declared legitimate, which implied a recognition of the King's first marriage; and the spiritual authority of the Pope was to be restored. The Pilgrims' oath read: "That they should enter into this Pilgrimage of Grace for the love of God, the preservation of the King's person and issue, the purifying of the nobility, and expulsing of all villein blood and evil counsellors, and for no particular profit to themselves, nor to do displeasure to any, nor to slay nor murder any for envy, but to put away all fears and take afore them the cross of Christ, His faith, and the restitution of the Church, the suppression of heretics and their opinions." The religious nature of the Pilgrimage was further emphasized by their marching under the banners of the Five Wounds and of St. Cuthbert.

The Pilgrims could have swept everything before them had they acted with decision. At Doncaster alone they had a force of 35,000 men, many of them well mounted, and whatever Aske's merits may have been as a military commander, in Lords Neville, Scrope, Latimer, Lumley, and Darcy, with Sir Robert Constable the most notable of many knights, they had officers of the kind under which Englishmen were accustomed to serve. The King had no standing army with which to oppose them and the 8000 men Norfolk had hastily levied were, for the most part, in sympathy with the Pilgrims' cause.

So, for that matter, were most of the officers in command of the royal army. The Marquis of Exeter and the Earl of Shrewsbury were among the nobles who had only recently been treating with Chapuys. The Duke of Norfolk himself, though anything but averse to getting his share of the monastic loot, was a bitter enemy of Cromwell's and had complete contempt for all newfangled notions in religion. Knowing his men to be disaffected and incapable of meeting the Pilgrims in pitched battle, he saw that his only chance was to negotiate — to negotiate and to betray.

Aske and the lords of the north were apprehensive that at any moment England would be invaded by Scots coming to their aid. There would be the excuse that this was done in the Catholic cause, but to accept such an alliance was unthinkable to patriotic minds. The instant there was a foray across the border, the Pilgrims would have to drop everything else to repell it. With the Scots at their backs the Pilgrims could not give undivided attention to what was before them. Instead of at once attacking Norfolk, as he should have done, Aske agreed to negotiate.

The Pilgrims' requests were laid before the Duke at Doncaster on December 6. A Parliament was to be held in the north for the redressing of grievances. Meanwhile all the Pilgrims were to be unconditionally pardoned. On the 9th of the same month this was granted under the Great Seal and signed by the King at Richmond. Yet Henry, so far from being gracious about it, could not forbear sending a letter written in the same tone as the one he had used to the men of Lincolnshire: he was an upholder of the faith of Christ; they were showing themselves unkind and unnatural to "their most rightful King." As for the Church of England, "whereof we be the Supreme Head on earth, we have done nothing so onerous and chargeable to them, as many of our predecessors have done, on much lesser grounds." The monasteries were again accused of "abominable life"; if any of the property of the monks had been taken, it was for "defence against foreign enemies." Never had a king of England introduced so many "wholesome, commodious and beneficial acts for the commonwealth." They were but "brutes and inexpert folk." And they were asked, "What king hath given his subjects more general and freer pardons?" Henry concluded: "Wherefore, we let all you our said subjects again wit, that were it not our princely heart cannot reckon this your shameful insurrection, and most ingrate and unnatural rebellion, to be done of malice or rancor, but rather by a lightness of mind given in manner by a naughty nature to communalty, and a wondrous sudden surreption of gentlemen, we must needs have executed another manner of punishment."

A wigging of this sort had worked wonders before, and Henry counted upon it working again, as it did. But now there was a definite promise of pardon, not merely a boast from the King as to how merciful he was. This promise was trusted, and nothing should have been trusted less. As Mr. Fisher remarks with the blistering sarcasm of a mild man: "The king, in whom good faith was not an article of honour, viewed the capitulation at Doncaster as a blot upon his scutcheon. To grant a free pardon and a free parliament at the call of armed rebels, who disputed his policy and challenged his prerogative, was a confession of weakness which extreme necessity might justify, but which the workings of a punctilious conscience might be trusted to repair."*

It is rather amusing to observe the working of that royal conscience. When Norfolk first proposed the betrayal of the Pilgrims, the King did not take it with a very good grace, for as usual he was deceiving himself even more than he was deceiving others. Henry as a matter of fact instructed Norfolk to go away for six or seven days, as though he had gone south for a consultation, and though the promise of pardon was (as we have seen) instantly issued, instructions were given that it should not be immediately promulgated. If a few days of delay were gained, it might never have to be promulgated at all. But in spite of the slightly shocked tone Henry assumed, it must be remembered that Norfolk had written to him, "In the end you said you would esteem no promise that you should make to the rebels, nor think your honor touched in the breach and violation of the same." In other words, the Duke had to remind Henry that, though he (Norfolk) was willing to be an instrument of perfidy, the perfidy did not originate with him. It was always as well to get little matters of this sort straight with Henry.

The King had by now taken Aske's measure. He was well known in London legal circles as a man without guile; therefore guile should catch him. Katherine of Aragon had to the end of her life believed that Henry was a fundamentally good man who had unluckily fallen under the influence of bad advisers. Aske now thought of Henry in similar terms. When he was invited to London under safe-conduct to lay the grievances of the Pilgrims – of the people – before the King in person, he imagined

* *The History of England*, p. 413. By permission of Longmans Greene & Co.

that everything had been won. Completely ignorant of the devious depths of Henry's true character, he went, suspecting nothing less than treachery.

Henry when he received Aske promised everything that anybody could want. Not only would there be a Parliament in York but the Queen should be crowned there, and the elections to the House of Commons would be made without any attempt to control the choice of members. The King turned on the vain, rather clever (and therefore all the more defenceless) young lawyer all the batteries of his charming affability, loading him not only with promises but presents. Aske returned to the Pilgrims in the north perfectly sure that the royal word would be honoured and that the evil courses of the past five years were ended. By way of completing what he had done, he assured Lord Darcy and Sir Robert Constable that they could safely accept the King's invitation to court.

All this time Cromwell had kept completely in the background; he knew himself too hated to appear in the business. In fact, one reason why the Duke of Norfolk had exercised himself so vigorously at this time was to regain an ascendancy that had been for some time in partial eclipse. Cromwell's idea was to keep the Duke, and also Stephen Gardiner, as far from court as possible. But Norfolk was at least a soldier, which Cromwell was not—though in his chequered career he seems to have served as one in Italy, doubtless in the commissariat department; and now Norfolk's special talents were to be brought into play. What he had so far demonstrated was his aptitude for butchery, as after the Evil May Day of 1517 and the devastation of the near-lying parts of France in the campaign of 1522. In 1536 his aristocratic name and his bluff way of swearing "By God's Body!" seemed a guarantee of good faith. He was trusted, as Henry was trusted.

Alas, there is no scoundrel so dangerous as one who veils his misdeeds behind his bonhomie, except of course the scoundrel who makes simultaneous parade of his affability and his piety. Henry's piety was genuine, so was his geniality; but one can see how he held both on tap. Hardly ever did he turn on both taps at once; hardly ever were both completely turned off. But this was one time when he screwed them tight and, assisted most ably by Norfolk, exhibited the most appalling cruelty.

The chance they had counted upon came soon enough, and (one cannot but suspect) was cleverly engineered by them. Though the Pilgrims had been astonishingly orderly, it was inevitable that among so large a number of angry men some violent acts should have occurred. When Aske left them to go to London they were suspicious, remembering what had happened in Lincolnshire.* Rumours were spread among them – one may suspect by Cromwell's *agents provacateurs* – that ships were bringing artillery to Hull, that the Scarborough fortifications were being strengthened, that new taxes were about to be levied. Though some of these rumours may have been false, it was true that (whether by chance or design) the tax-gatherers got busy again, to the irritation of the people; it was also a fact, verifiable by all, that a royal letter had reached the Mayor of Hull calling upon him to disarm the Pilgrims there.

In that atmosphere disturbances that were very advantageous to the royal purposes inevitably occurred. There was a man of twenty-eight, Sir Francis Bigod by name, who precipitated them. That he had been employed, while still only a youth, by Wolsey and afterwards by Cromwell should be borne in mind. It was this man, Bigod, who suggested to an unguarded enthusiast named John Hallam that he should seize Hull while Bigod himself besieged Scarborough.

Aske was in consternation over this new outbreak and did his best to suppress it. It was in fact one of his aides, Sir Ralph Ellerker, who took the surrender of Bigod on January 19, 1537, at Beverly. But of course this loyal action did not save Ellerker, or even the *agent provacateur* Bigod; they were both hanged later. The modern technique is to hurry such men out of the

*But so far, of course, the King had been most careful not to exact any punishment of the Lincolnshire men. The Yorkshiremen had first to be lulled into trustfulness.

country; in the sixteenth century a still safer method was used: after they had performed the service required of them, they were hurried out of the world.

Henry now had an excuse for not keeping his word, though we know from the letters that had passed between him and the Duke of Norfolk that he had never had any intention of keeping it. He was, however, in the position he had looked for – that of being able to charge that the treaty had been broken by the other party and that he was thereby released. He took full advantage of the situation.

Martial law was at once proclaimed. And as by now the Pilgrims had disbanded, trusting in their King's word, Norfolk received his instructions: he was to hang men freely, not too closely enquiring into their personal guilt, as a warning to others.

This was a commission right up Norfolk's alley. His father had fought on the wrong side at Bosworth but had afterwards redeemed himself (and regained his forfeited dukedom) by the victory of Flodden. His son was a right soldierly hangman. England had never known anything that had even begun to approach what he did, under personal instructions from a king who was rather disappointed that his agent did not do even more.

Norfolk, though without much real intelligence (he had boundless craftiness) had a kind of ferocious wit.* Perhaps one should call it humour, for he compelled the relatives and friends of the "rebels" to serve on the jury at their trials. He wrote pleasantly to Cromwell – who had now crawled out into the daylight again – "I dare well to put divers on the quests [of whom] some

*The English are sometimes credited with having a wit over-subtle, or is it a humour that is over-subtle? Neither quality was exhibited by that son of Sir William Kingston, Sir Anthony, who in Edward's reign, while suppressing the Cornish rising, visited the Mayor of Bodmin. After dinner he asked to see the gallows on which he had to hang some rebels. When he was shown it by the Mayor, whose guest at dinner he had been, he said, "Then get up, because it is for you." English wit and humour surely redeemed themselves from the accusation of over-subtlety on that occasion. And so also with the Duke of Norfolk's sense of humour; his wit manifested itself mainly by swearing by God's Body.

have married with the Lord Darcy's daughters and some with Sir Robert Constable's." He continues that his object was "to put the best friends these men have upon their inquests [meaning juries], to prove their affection whether they will serve his Majesty truly and frankly in this matter, or else to serve their friends, and if they will not find [bring in a verdict of guilty] then they may have thanks according to their cankered hearts." Regarding another trial he wrote to Cromwell, with whom he was in momentary alliance, "I will appoint such that I shall have no more doubt of than of myself." The packing of juries was sufficiently monstrous; what can be thought of compelling friends and relatives to serve on them – and to bring in a verdict of guilty – in order to save their own lives?

When Aske was invited to go to the King he was requested to write out his own account of what had happened; this came in very handy later. Perhaps it was a little indiscreet of Aske to say that "it was thought" that the divorce Cranmer had given the King from Katherine was unlawful, though he did not positively commit himself to this. What is more to the immediate point is what he had to say about the opinions prevailing in the north, and which, for that matter, prevailed everywhere. The abbeys, he said, "give great alms to poor men and serve God." Many of these abbeys, he pointed out, were in wild places, "where the people are rude of condition and not well taught of the law of God. And when the said abbeys stood the said people not only had worldly refreshing in their beds, but also spiritual refuge both by the ghostly living of them and also by spiritual information and preaching." The suppression of the abbeys, he says, meant the dispossession of their tenants, as well as the lack of hospitality for travellers, "for never was in these parts denied either horse meat or man's meat, so that the people were greatly refreshed by the said abbeys, where now they have no such succor." Furthermore, he said, "The abbeys were one of the beauties of this realm to all men and strangers passing through the same. Also all gentlemen [were] succored in their needs, with their many young sons there assisted, and in nunneries their daughters brought up in virtue. . . . And such abbeys as were near the danger of sea banks, were great maintainers of sea walls and dykes, maintainers and builders of bridges [and] such other things for the commonwealth." Does it need to be argued when 40,000 men in Lincolnshire and an even greater number in Yorkshire and the adjoining counties rose to prevent the suppression of the monasteries that the monks were held in great local esteem? Even if they were not all that they might have been – and which of us is that? – weight should be given to the fact that the people round them were so incensed at the treatment they were getting as to do a thing unprecedented in Henry VIII's reign: they had taken up arms.

That they had not used these arms did not protect them from a charge of treason or from wholesale executions. The King waited until things had quieted down before he acted, for by the time the little adventure of Bigod occurred, most of the Pilgrims had dispersed to their homes, believing that the King would honour his promises. The King's troops were now able to march down on men caught completely by surprise.

For ordinary offenders martial law was used, as there were too many of them to bring to trial; only the leaders were reserved for the packed juries. Nothing like it had ever been known in England. It was the King himself who wrote to Norfolk: "You shall in any wise cause such dreadful execution to be done upon a good number of the inhabitants of every town, village and hamlet, that have offended in this rebellion, as well by hanging them up in trees, as by the quartering of them and the setting of their heads and quarters in every town, great and small, and in all such other places, as they may be a fearful spectacle that would practice any like matter: which we require you to do, without pity or respect, according to our formal letter." This meant that every hamlet, however small, should have its gibbet, if even one man from that place (and there was always at least one) had been on the Pilgrimage. Queen Jane begged for mercy but begged in vain. Henry was determined to take this opportunity of striking such terror as to make the thought of rebellion an impossibility again. Never would he have so good a chance of cowing his subjects.

Norfolk carried out his instructions with gusto. But when the more compassionate Earl of Sussex was touched by the plea of one old man to the effect that he had served in the wars against the Scots and so wrote to Henry suggesting that he be spared, the answer came: "Considering that he hath so often received our wages and would nevertheless at the last be thus corrupted against us, we think him for an example more worthy to suffer, than the rest that had not . . . received benefit of us." The royal egotist completely overlooked the fact that this poor old fellow had rendered him service; his soldier's pittance made him all the more guilty!

Whenever possible these men were hanged in chains, so that their rotting bodies could dangle indefinitely. And if a woman were caught taking down her husband or son or brother for decent burial, she too was liable to be hanged. Norfolk had to write to Henry to excuse himself for not using chains in every case; it was impossible to find enough chains for the purpose, so he hoped the King would pardon him for falling back upon ropes.

Norfolk could urge in his own extenuation that never had so many men been put to death at one time. How many these were we can only guess – as no precise record was kept of what was done. But there were probably several thousands of them.* Not much enquiry was made as to guilt; it was presumed that every able-bodied man had been out with the Pilgrims. The only reason why every man in Yorkshire (not to mention those of the adjoining counties of Lancashire, Cumberland, Westmore-

*In his *History of England,* Froude estimates about 200, adding "the severity was not excessive." Later, in his *Divorce of Katherine of Aragon,* he admits that his first estimate was too low and raises the figure to "less than three hundred." The letters that passed between Norfolk and the King make it clear, however, that the executions were on a very much larger scale. It would seem safe to multiply Froude's higher estimate by ten.

land, Durham, and Northumberland) was not hanged was that it was not to the King's interest to make a complete depopulation. All that was necessary was to strike terror, and in this he thoroughly succeeded.

If all this seems ferociously cruel, it is necessary for the modern man to be just in considering it. There is this much to be said in extenuation: hanging was the punishment for every felony, and it has been estimated – probably with no very great exaggeration – that in the thirty-eight years of Henry's reign seventy-two thousand people suffered at the gallows. Public susceptibilities were so indurated that, in order to make a special effect and give a sharp enough warning to possible misdoers, hangings had to be on a large scale. For ordinary conspiracy (or what was alleged to be such) Tyburn or Tower Hill sufficed. But in the case of what could be called a rebellion, where a large number of people were implicated, a large number had to be hanged. It was argued then – as it can still be argued in the case of the murderers our society executes – that executions are merciful, if not to the miscreants themselves, then at least to the public at large. Finally, Henry was aware that he had lived for some years in danger of a real rebellion. Now he could prevent all further danger, once and for all, by the liberal use of the rope. If any innocent people happened to be hanged, they could console themselves in their last moments, that in their deaths they were serving the sacred cause of law and order.

One wonders, however, whether such philosophical reflections crossed the poor wretches' minds. It is heart-warming to recall Lord Darcy's words at his trial when, knowing himself doomed, he said to Cromwell's face: "Cromwell, it is thou who art the very original and chief causer of this rebellion and mischief, and art likewise causer of the apprehension of us that be noble men, and dost earnestly travail to bring us to one end and to strike off our heads, and I trust that . . . though thou wouldst procure all the noblemen's heads within the realm to be stricken off, yet shall there one head remain that shall strike off thine head." It was not exactly a prophecy: Darcy knew his own class, and that the very lords who sat on the tribunal that condemned him hated Cromwell and would, in the end, exact their revenge.

Darcy was a grizzled old soldier who in his youth had served as a volunteer under Ferdinand and Isabella at the siege of Granada. He suffered decapitation on Tower Hill, the privilege of his noble blood. Robert Aske and most of the other leaders were tried at York on May 9, 1537. Norfolk took pains to see that upon the jury were John Aske — Robert Aske's brother — and men who had married daughters of Lord Darcy and Sir Robert Constable, presumably to see that the accused got a fair trial. The charges against them were that they had conspired "to deprive the King of his dignity, title, name, and royal state, namely that of being on earth the Supreme Head of the English Church." In addition they had committed the offence of trying to force the King to summon a Parliament. Finally they were held guilty of having repeated their offence after having been graciously pardoned. As the pardon could not be denied, it was turned into an aggravation of the offence.

Aske was hanged in chains at York because, as Henry said, it was there that he had been "in his greatest and most frantic glory." Constable, who had been for vigorous action and who could have led the Pilgrimage to success had his advice been followed, suffered at Hull. Among the others hanged at various places were Abbot Sedbar of Jervaulx; William Thirsk, the former Abbot of Fountains; several priors and a number of priests. But most of the nobles got off, among them Lord Latimer, a Neville, and the second husband of that Katherine Parr who was to be the King's sixth wife. They were able to plead, with varying degrees of truth, as did Edward Lee, the Archbishop of York, that they had been forced to take part in the Pilgrimage of Grace. But then nobody was guilty of anything, unless it was Bigod of treachery and Aske of a foolish vanity and a still more foolish simplicity.

Henry all through these months had been thoroughly scared, in spite of all his bluster. For this he had reason, as he was well aware that, at any rate in Yorkshire, a capable leader might appear at any moment. Moreover, the Emperor Charles, though he had held his hand so long, might think this too good an opportunity to miss for landing a force to stiffen Catholic resistance. His aid would have been welcome, whatever the Pilgrims felt about the Scots. The leader of this contingent could have published the Pope's bull of deprivation, thus freeing the Pilgrims from the sense of guilt they felt even in doing so much as march out in arms. Best of all would have been the appearance at this time of Cardinal Pole, Henry's cousin, as papal legate to England.

As usual Rome acted too late. Pole could not be persuaded to accept the red hat until the end of 1536 and by the time he was selected as legate the rebellion had collapsed. He reached Flanders only to find that the Regent would not admit him; nor would Francis permit him to remain in France. After a short and useless stay in neutral territory he had to return to Rome, lucky at having escaped assassination or kidnapping. Even in Rome he was obliged, after this, to protect himself with a bodyguard. It was a depressing spectacle seeing all those in the right fumbling as to their course of action, while those in the wrong were decisive, if only in their use of the axe and the rope.

We find here another item in the long series of delays: the delayed decision regarding Katherine's marriage, the giving of belated orders (and of then holding them in suspense), of bulls drawn up (but not to be executed). All of this sprang from the Papacy's tolerance but was taken as nothing but an exhibition of weakness. That the Pope wished to avoid extreme measures was supposed by Henry to mean that the Pope feared him, and anything done against him, however moderate it might be, was regarded as a sign of profound malice.

It had been so with the book which Reginald Pole had written at Henry's own request and which arrived in England a few days after Anne Boleyn's execution. Pole had towards Henry a great goodwill and wrote to Tunstall: "If God would give his Grace to taste but one tear of pure penance . . . all the pleasure and comfort that ever I had from childhood or the whole world could give, were not to be compared with the sweetness thereof." Unluckily Pole had taken seriously Henry's insistence that he be perfectly candid, with the result that he so infuriated the King as to drive him in the direction opposite the one to which Pole had hoped to guide him. One must admit, too, that the *De Unitate Ecclesiae* was written in a high-flown stilted style, displaying a pedantic learning and giving the impression that the writer was trying at all costs to appear learned. Pole was a man completely devoid of ambition, utterly disinterested, but he had his little literary vanity. One seeks in vain in his pages for anything like Thomas More's simplicity and homespun humour. Though what Pole wrote was sound, his manner made it the reverse of effective polemics.

Henry was furious with his cousin over this book, even though what Pole had sent him was intended only for his own eye. What Reginald thought of as a friendly admonition, Henry took to be a vicious attack. As he could not lay his hands upon Pole – though Sir Thomas Wyatt was instructed to arrange for his murder and the Regent of the Low Countries was offered the pay of 4000 soldiers for ten months as a return for Pole's extradition, and a price of 50,000 crowns was put upon his head – the King was already thinking of revenging himself upon Pole's mother and brothers. Lady Salisbury, who had written at Henry's dictation asking that her son visit her (an invitation she knew he would ignore), now wrote, again at Henry's dictation, a letter of expostulation. Privately she and the rest of the Poles approved of his conduct, but they had good reason to be alarmed.

So little did Reginald Pole wish to give offence to Henry that he did his best to refuse the cardinalate that Paul III was pressing upon him. He knew that this honour would be sure to be taken as a proof that he had passed over completely to the enemy camp, and so consented to accept it only under obedience. Thomas Starkey, a man who had been with him abroad and was now one of the royal chaplains, urged him to decline, saying: "No one will receive so much hurt by it as yourself," and

Tunstall and Stokesley wrote him a joint letter in which they told him: "For the vain glory of a red hat you would make yourself an instrument of his malice, who would stir up rebellion in the realm." Pole's answer was that, if the King would return to the Church, he would be glad to resign his cardinalate and become a hermit. But with the very best of motives, he had, in fact, succeeded in doing the Catholic Church in England a poor service.

The main error of judgement, however, was not Pole's but Paul III's. The tone of Pole's book, one of elaborate and learned sarcasm – such that Cardinal Contarini advised against it – would not have mattered very much had it reached Henry a year sooner, though it still would have failed to persuade him of his errors. But Paul III by appointing Pole as Papal Legate to England did something worse than useless, as it was done after the Pilgrimage of Grace, not just before. Pole, knowing Henry as he did, foresaw what would happen and wrote to the Pope: "The case is very possible that the King, in order to appease the discontent of his subjects, may promise to redress their grievances, without any design of doing so; and, when the danger is over, may proceed at different times, and on several occasions, to punish the leaders with death." He went on to advise, "If the nation on this account should desist from further thought of relief, or want some means to pursue it, some proper person should be appointed to keep up their resolution, and a sufficient fund allowed for that purpose." It was all of no avail; by the time the Papacy had swung into action, it was too late. All that Paul III had succeeded in doing was to infuriate Henry further, and to make him inflict a more fearful punishment than would perhaps otherwise have been exacted.

As though the failure of the Pilgrimage of Grace were not enough, Henry's position was further consolidated when at last he got what he regarded as the most signal proof of God's approval of his actions; on October 12, 1537, Queen Jane gave birth to a son, the future Edward VI. He was given his name because he was born on the vigil of the feast of St. Edward the Confessor, but with a desire to compliment, at the same time, the elder of the Seymour brothers. Henry grieved as deeply as it was in his nature to grieve when, twelve days later, the child's mother died. For the repose of her soul he ordered the singing of twelve hundred Masses and founded a monastery, though he was in the midst of destroying religious houses. Yet his grief was much less than his joy and triumph. There could be no question of this boy's legitimacy: he would be the founder of a royal line of kings.

Henry had always been fond of young children. It had been so with Mary during her first years; it had been so with Elizabeth, until he had further revenged himself on Anne by bastardizing her; it was so now with little Edward. Sir Richard Cromwell* wrote to his uncle, that the King spent whole days with the Prince, "Dallying with him in his arms for a long space, and holding him to the window to the sight and great comfort of all the people."

The birth of this boy greatly increased Henry's self-esteem. This was vast already, but, until now, there was one dark question recurring in his conscience: could he have been right in the way he had treated Katherine? Had he been right, would not Anne have borne him a son? It was usually possible for him to reassure himself: no son had been born of either marriage because both were incestuous; nevertheless, doubts did flicker sometimes across his mind. But now that Jane had borne him this boy he saw it all plain: though God in His inscrutable wisdom may delay the reward of virtue, He does not fail to send it in the end. The rebellion itself could now be looked upon as providential: never again would any of his subjects be so "unnatural and unkind" as to rise. There was only one way for the Pope to make peace with him – that of admitting his predecessor's error. Instead the pestiferous monks had instigated rebellion against him, and the Pope had tried to stir up further trouble by

*Richard Cromwell's real name was Williams, but he took his uncle's name. He was the great-grandfather of Oliver Cromwell.

appointing Reginald Pole as legate to England. Well, he would let the Pope and the whole world see who was supreme. Until now Henry had been, in his own estimation, moderate in his treatment of the monasteries, those nests of sedition. From this moment he might lay all his scruples aside and go on roughshod to complete the work he had begun.

CHAPTER FOURTEEN

Church in Subjection

MEANWHILE pacification of another sort, though using somewhat similar methods, had been going on in Wales under the direction of Rowland Lee, who was appointed Bishop of Lichfield in 1534. He was a cleric very much after Froude's own heart and is described by that historian in the gusto of his approval as "fitter for harness than a bishop's robes, for a court of justice than a court of theology; more at home at the head of his troopers, chasing cattle-stealers in the gorges of Llangollen, than hunting heretics to the stake, or chasing formulas in the arduous files of controversy." As he managed to hang about five thousand men, it is clear that he did his work of pacification well.

The chief offence of the Welsh was that they wished, like the Irish, to retain their tribal customs and privileges. Yet in all likelihood many things happened in their wild country that would not have been tolerated elsewhere. To put these down called for the kind of heavy hand that Bishop Lee was more than willing to use. As he wrote to Cromwell, shortly after Henry had given so signal a manifestation of his justice upon the Pilgrims of Grace, "If we should do nothing but as the common law will, these things so far out of order will never be redressed." In other words, law and order could be established only by a disregard of law. By such methods the Welsh were incorporated into the English political system.

Cromwell had by now come out of the obscurity with which

for a time he found it prudent to cover himself. Hardly had he pulled off his brilliant coup against Anne Boleyn, just at the moment when only something of this sort could have saved him from the coalition forming against him, than the troubles in Lincolnshire and Yorkshire began. In both counties there was loud execration of his name, with Cranmer and Audley and Rich as minor figures of public detestation. Until the Pilgrimage of Grace had been completely suppressed, it was not safe for Cromwell to appear as the director of affairs.

Now there was work for him to do. The rising had given the King a new pretext against the monasteries. Until then he had been empowered under the law to suppress only the smaller religious houses, though of course the law could always be stretched so as to force a "voluntary surrender" for moral delinquencies in a particular case. This method was now used in a larger way. It was not necessary to bring even the usual flimsy charges of viciousness of life; the most strictly regulated monasteries, especially those in the infected parts of the north, could be accused of having given aid and comfort to the rebels.

How well based such charges are it is usually not easy to say. But it is probable enough that all the monasteries had sympathy with the Pilgrimage of Grace and that some of them – if not as corporations, then in the persons of individual members – gave practical expression to such sympathy. The law of treason was so interpreted as to permit the seizure of many of the richest of abbeys, including those of Barlings, Jervaulx, Whalley, Kirkstead, and Bridlington. The Abbot of Furness was obliged to sign a surrender of the abbey to the king under a threat of attainder, and the Abbot of Holm Cultram escaped only by dying before the arrival of the commission sent to try him. Even so his abbey did not escape; Cromwell appointed a new abbot, one who he knew would make no difficulty about doing anything that he was told. The principle of attainder was used as late as 1539 for the seizure of monastic property. It was by this principle that the abbeys of Glastonbury and Colchester and Reading were destroyed.

Such procedure was monstrous. A private person, convicted after trial for treason or attainted by Parliament, had all his personal property confiscated. But an abbot did not own his abbey; he could not be said to own it any more than the youngest member of the community really owned it. Whatever wide powers of administration the abbot may have had, everything was vested in the group as a whole, and their corporate rights could not be affected by anything done by an individual member. Nevertheless these rights were ignored, so that without the passage of any new law against the monastic system it was eventually entirely eradicated. Only after the spoliation had been completed, was a law passed declaring that all that the monks had owned now belonged to the King.

If relatively few houses were suppressed under attainder, this was due to a number of reasons. One was that it was easier and more expeditious to persuade the monks to make a surrender on their own initiative, as this called for nothing more than a few signatures on a paper, than to wait until Parliament was sitting and go through the elaborate performance of drawing up a bill and having it voted upon. Nor was it always necessary even to threaten attainder. In many cases it was discovered that the larger and richer monasteries which, in the act of 1536, had been explicitly described as those in which "thanks be to God, religion is right well kept and observed" were corrupt after all. Cromwell in his capacity of King's vicar-general could reform them out of existence.

But there was another reason for not doing much against the monasteries just then. A good many of the smaller monasteries had still to be suppressed; they could not all be dealt with at once, great as was Cromwell's dispatch. From these a considerable amount of loot had come in, with a larger amount still to come. The python was gorged but had not yet digested his meal. Henry was therefore content to have established the principle that attainder could be used against the monasteries and then to follow the matter up at leisure. He may not yet have quite made up his mind as to whether he was going to make a clean sweep of the religious houses. But we can see that a process had begun which it would have been difficult to arrest, even had Henry wished to do so. His personal expenditures were increasing more rapidly than his augmented income, and he was continually being egged on by those who had not yet obtained a share of the loot commensurate with what they believed to be their deserts.

The costs of governmental administration were also steadily mounting and on top of everything else there was a general rise in the cost of living. This was in part due to the influx of precious metals from the New World, and though it affected England later than some other countries, it happened eventually and inevitably everywhere that, with the greater amount of gold and silver currency put in circulation, higher prices were charged for rents and all commodities. Professor Tawney on page 198 of his *Agrarian Problem of the Sixteenth Century* gives a table which shows that whereas from 1410 prices had remained stable for a full hundred years, except for tending to drop slightly, in the second half of the sixteenth century prices doubled for such staples as wheat and peas, barley, beef, mutton, and pork. Without attempting anything like a detailed analysis, for which I have neither space nor competence, it does not call for a professional economist to perceive that the various disturbances in the economic order were bound to be disadvantageous to the people as a whole, however much those may have profited who were in a position to exploit the new situation.

The enclosures had been to the advantage of the landowners, though not to the peasantry; and now in the space of less than four years the entire monastic wealth – at least a fifth and possibly a fourth of the manorial holdings of the country – by passing into new hands, shook the structure of society to its foundations. Had only a tenth of the wealth of the country been involved, the economic revolution would have been serious enough. But when the spoliation was on a much wider scale, with the endowments of the bishoprics left uncertain, the sudden and violent disturbance of the immemorial social balance can hardly be measured.

Out of the loot the King got much less than he expected, even on the basis of paper valuations; and the true value of these was diminishing because the general rise in prices had, as yet, hardly affected the sale of land, or rents. It was on the basis of valuations that had long been stationary, and were now obsolete, that the King often had to dispose of monastic estates in order to obtain sorely needed ready cash, so that they went for much less than they should have fetched. To crown everything, the very fact that so much land was thrown at once on the market tended to depress the standard price, too low though this already was.

The Crown of course extracted what it could and, when no favour was looked for from the purchasers, they usually had to pay what looked like a fair price. But that even the lands that went at the highest prices were bargains is clear from the fact that land speculators instantly appeared, the Greshams being notable as such. And, perhaps even more significant, we find syndicates being formed by London tradesmen who, unable to operate individually on a large scale, made substantial profits very quickly by operating as a group.

Many of the courtiers got estates for a nominal price or advantageous exchange or outright gift. Greedy though Henry was, he was also lavish at times in his generosity. And when he was lavish to one man, another who considered himself equally deserving of some reward was able to point to the precedent of previous lavishness to justify his own demand. Men of this sort sometimes obtained from a dozen to thirty monastic estates, though of course of varying size and value, and of the estates so obtained it was usual for them to do as the King did and to dispose of some of the holdings for cash. It thus came about that in a remarkably short time the greater part of the monastic estates had been widely distributed, many within a few years passing through several hands. When Henry felt, as he sometimes did, a bit rueful about the way the wealth of the Church was melting away, Cromwell was able to assure him that the possession of what he held was all the more secure because so many other people in the country were implicated with him and had the very best of reasons for giving their support to what was going on.

Cromwell was an able business man as well as an astute politician. But in politics he was interested, as are all men of his kind, only in the immediate advantage to be gained. If he had any inkling as to what the eventual result of this redistribution of property was going to be, he kept it to himself. But probably he never imagined that the outcome would be vastly different from what he had promised. While the King was making himself wealthy and powerful a new landed class was being created, one that, when it had consolidated itself and grown conscious of its powers, would take the real government away from the King. The death warrant of Charles I was being signed during the years of the monastic spoliation.

The immediate effect seemed to be an enhancement of the King's authority. Yet by acting through Parliament, so as to throw upon it so great a share of responsibility for his own misdeeds, Henry inevitably gave Parliament enlarged powers, or powers that would eventually be enlarged. At the moment he was often obliged to terrify Parliament before it consented to be an instrument of his will. But in doing so he created in Parliament an obscure desire for revenge and revealed to it its capacity for eventually exercising a control over the Crown somewhat analogous to the control the Crown was then exercising over Parliament. If we leap over the centuries to look at parliamentary government as we now know it – a cabinet responsible to an elected House of Commons, with the House of Lords shorn of all real power, and the King no more than a decorative figurehead – it is permissible to think that the outcome has, after all, been good. Yet even to that picture there is another side: it can hardly be denied that parliamentary institutions, even under the best of democracies, are often subtly directed by combinations of wealth. These combinations, and the influence they have been able to exert – all that we understand by what is called the capitalist system — if not originating at this time, got their chance of control because of the economic upheavals of the sixteenth century. We may hopefully believe that this flaw in our society will eventually fade away and that we shall realize an economic democracy; but that has not happened yet, and if it ever happens, it will owe nothing to Henry VIII. What he did, or allowed to be done, was something quite contrary to the object he had in mind. This was the emergence of a landed aristocracy so strong that the English King became its servant. Just as there is something to be said in favor of an oligarchy of squires as compared with an oligarchy of industrialists and bankers, so there is also something to be said in favour of the monarchy, as it existed as an ideal during the Middle Ages, as against an oligarchy of squires. But whatever the reader's personal preference may be with regard to political and economic systems, there can be no question that what eventuated was something very different from what Henry desired.*

If the King failed of his ultimate aim, so he was continually being hoodwinked and cheated by his agents. Nothing was easier than for the men on the spot to purloin some of the valuables of a monastery. Bribery, which had been practised under Wolsey's suppression of monasteries and during the application of the act of 1536, became possible on a wider scale when there were no longer any statutory limitations as to the suppression. Now that the larger houses were being dealt with, much bigger sums could be extracted than had been paid by the religious houses with an income of less than £200 a year. We find two abbeys — those of Allaband and Pollesloe — each paying £400 to be allowed to continue. And though other payments were as low as

---

*Perhaps I should make my own position clear. When I became an American citizen I swore allegiance to the American constitution, though without thinking it perfect. I believe that political democracy, if it is to survive, must be implemented by economic democracy. I am equally opposed to communism and capitalism, and in particular I reject the current notion that capitalism is somehow necessary to the successful functioning of democracy.

£20 for this privilege, something between a hundred and two hundred pounds seems to have been what was usually paid. We must conclude that the King took what he could get, bearing in mind the financial resources of the house, but also allowing the complaisance and co-operation of the community to affect the matter.*

In addition to what the King received there were presents privately made to Cromwell and his agents. To take only Cromwell in this regard, and him only to the extent of a few typical instances, we find him writing for a loan of £40 to the superior of a house.** The conditions for repayment were so very peculiar that we may be sure that only euphemistically is it to be called a loan. To the Prior of St. Faith's he intimates that a reward would be acceptable. He dunned the Abbot of Leicester for £40 and the Abbot of Muchelney for the same amount, though he had already received £100 from the same source. The same large personal bribe came from the Abbess of Shaftesbury, the Abbot of Cerne, and the Abbot of Rewley. The Abbot of Pipwell writes that he will "do all that a poor man can to gratify your Lordship," and offers £200. The Abbot of Peterborough indicates that he will make it worth Cromwell's while to allow his abbey to remain unmolested, and the Abbot of Colchester was ready with no less than £2,000. So large a bribe got the abbey spared until 1539, though in that year it went under and its Abbot was hanged.

In addition to these money gifts there were gifts of another sort that were clearly intended to soften Cromwell's heart — Irish hawks for this famous sportsman, geldings, fish, game, and even apples and cheese. The community, especially when it was a community of women, usually also promised their prayers, however little store the Vicar-General set on such intangibles. It was unlucky for the good nuns when they could offer nothing better. The dishonesty was so flagrant that in Queen Elizabeth's time

*Gasquet gives a list of such payments in an appendix to the second volume of his *Henry VIII and the English Monasteries*.

**The record of this transaction is in Merriman's *Cromwell*, Vol. II, p. 49.

an enquiry was instituted, and the information it gathered, though incomplete, proved shocking venality.

Cromwell's visitators were equally corrupt, but had to exercise some circumspection. They were ecclesiastical adventurers of no good repute and they were always spying upon and complaining against one another. All of them were in Cromwell's power and at least subject to a kind of blackmail. While taking bribes secretly from the religious, they tried at the same time to bribe Cromwell. Thus we find Dr. Layton offering £100 for the office of chancellor to the diocese of Salisbury, and though he did not obtain this, he was made Dean of York. So little did these men trust one another that we actually have Ap Rice writing to Cromwell to say that he is in danger of his life from Dr. Leigh's rufflers. And in the end it was Dr. Leigh who was put on the track of Dr. London and succeeded in having him convicted of perjury and cast into prison, where he died.

London's is a specially instructive case. For he was really a "Pope's man" and had been induced to serve on the commission mainly as a way of getting out of trouble a nephew who had spoken some rash words against the King's supremacy. London believed, as many people did, that the breach with the Papacy was only temporary, but once having entered Cromwell's service, there was, for such men, no way of getting out of it, until, after years of base service, they were rewarded with a deanery or a prebendary's stall. It is of course utterly impossible to believe men of this type, even when they happen to be speaking the truth.

Not only must the minor bribes taken by Cromwell's agents and the larger bribes he was in the position of extracting, be added to the cost of the spoliation, we must take into account an immense amount of petty pilfering that went on among the attendants attached to the train of the commissioners. There was so much available that they could not see how this little ring or that curiously chased chalice would be missed. And what was not purloined could be purchased for a song at the mock auctions held every time a monastery was dissolved. And then, after all the bells had been melted and the lead stripped from the roof and thrown into huge cauldrons lighted with the carvings of the rood-screen and choir-stalls, the people of the locality would descend to carry off anything that was left — the stained glass from the windows, the doors and hinges and locks. The walls of the monastery, the pillars of its chapel, the very stones of the tombs were regarded as a quarry that anybody might use. Even those who grieved at the expulsion of the monks, saw no reason why they should not take what the despoilers had not thought it worth their while to cart away.

When set beside other elements in the devastation, the wanton vandalism regarding books seems hardly worth mentioning. Yet it meant an incalculable loss. Countless beautifully illuminated volumes that would now be priceless were looked upon as so much waste paper. Who would ever want again one of those enormous tomes used in choir? Or that quaint and crabbed chronicle? Or a copy of Duns Scotus? A lazy monk might have spent a year in making such a book; it now went for a few pence to the junk-dealers who followed like jackals in the wake of Drs. Layton and London and Leigh, and from their hands it passed to those who needed something for the wrapping up of parcels. Those who did suspect that these things might have a mild antiquarian interest were often able to buy a whole library for forty shillings. Little Edward VI when he saw one of the "bare ruined choirs in which the sweet birds sang," asked naïvely, when he was told of the iniquity of the monks, "Then why did not my father punish the offenders and put better men into such goodly buildings?"

Even setting on one side losses of an extent at which one can hardly guess, the full extent of the plunder can never be estimated correctly. We have only the figures of the Court of Augmentation, and these are far from complete regarding details. But if the yearly value of the rents of the monastic manors be put as somewhere between £150,000 and £200,000, of that amount Henry got much less than he expected. Gasquet gives on pages 534–535 of his second volume a summary of the accounts of the Court of Augmentation, and though these do not correspond in all respects with the later researches made by Dr. Savine, they may be taken as at least roughly accurate. The total receipts paid in between 1536 and 1547 were £1,338,442.9.2½, which should be multiplied by twenty-five to get an idea of what this means in modern values. The total expenditures left a balance of not much over a hundred thousand pounds. To break these disbursements down a little, the King derived from the monastic lands in rents a little over £415,000. The sales of the lands brought in another £855,752. Other large items are those of £26,000 odd from the sale of vestments, lead, and bell-metal, and about £22,000 deducted as forced loans to the King from such religious as received pensions.

When we turn to the other side of the ledger it is instructive to note that the entire amount of the pensions came to only about half as much again as the pensionnaires were obliged to return, though to this perhaps should be added part of the item of £25,000 paid out in annuities. The King received £274,086.19.8¾ for the expenses of the royal household, another £23,000 for the household of Prince Edward, and over £61,000 for the royal palaces. About £600,000 went on the upkeep of the army and navy, such as these were, and another £64,000 on fortifications. The King took for himself over £11,000 worth of plate and gave away in presents well over £14,000 worth. The separate accounts of the Jewel House make no mention of precious stones, and indicate only that portion of the plate that was melted down. This comes to slightly under £80,000. The largest disbursement here was a sum of £42,000 given to the King.

These figures are so incomplete that perhaps all we can treat with any confidence are those relating to the amount received from the monastic lands in rentals and that fetched by the sale of those which were disposed of. If these two items be added together and divided by eleven for the last eleven years of Henry's reign, we can see that the King did not get on an average much more than £100,000 a year. It was a large amount, twice as much as an economical English government of the period would have found necessary for all its normal needs, but it was a disappointment. Henry should have obtained nearly twice as much.*

The outright gifts, according to Dr. Savine's figures, were not very numerous, about seventy in all. But there were another 188 properties listed for which it is not stated for what consideration they were allowed to slip out of the King's possession, and probably most of these were gifts. Moreover of the 1300 properties which went by sale or exchange or a combination of sale and exchange, probably few brought in their full value. What emerges at the end is the fact that, while the King was indeed enriched, he was jockeyed out of a large proportion of the proceeds. Of this he used about half on what might be called public purposes, the other half he squandered on his pleasures.

Henry had made large, if somewhat vague, promises as to what he would do in the way of endowing chairs at universities and in founding nineteen new bishoprics. Six of these bishoprics were, in fact, founded, most of which are still in existence. But the endowment for these did not come out of the sums indicated but from the revenues of monastic lands left for the support of the dioceses. It was easy to turn an abbey into a cathedral and its monks into the cathedral chapter. Taxation, the need for which was supposed to have ended with the suppression of the monasteries, was not noticeably reduced. The building of ships for the navy and the improvement of ordnance had always been something of a hobby with Henry; he was now able to indulge it. But most of this outlay was not really necessary and would never have occurred had not the King suddenly found so much extra money available. In short, just as he was swindled in the gathering of the money, of what reached his hands he wasted a great deal.

*Probably at least three times as much, if real, as against nominal values, be considered. The real value of the expropriated property was, of course, obtained, but by the new rich and the speculators, not by the King.

Those who profited most were the new men, and some of the members of the older aristocracy too, who bought lands on easy terms or who had lands given them. So also did the speculators who shrewdly calculated that the value of the lands would soon go up. Though it is not necessary to claim that the old monastic landlords bore lightly on their tenants, for of this we have no statistical proof and we know that, at least in some cases, they were keen on getting all that they could out of their lands, we also know that one of the charges against the monasteries is that they mismanaged their estates. This usually meant that they had neglected to make them yield all that might be extracted in the way of rents. Their respect for tradition inclined them not to disturb those who paid by custom a rent that was by this time far too low. Under brisker and more business-like management it was believed that this state of affairs could be altered.

Altered it was. And the change was felt by the estimated forty to eighty thousand people who had been tenants or employed by the monasteries in one capacity or another. Most of the servants found new masters, and some may even have benefited by the change; but the tenants soon groaned under the rack-rents of the new lay owners, and with the sudden bounding upwards of rents the spiral of the cost of living lifted itself still higher. Those who had grumbled in the past about the greed of the Church, now found how much greater was the greed of the secular exploiters.

Those of the ejected monks and nuns who received pensions were given – as a rule – only barely enough to support life. But as the amount of these pensions was sometimes a good deal more than adequate, we must conclude that their fortunate recipients were those who had rendered some such service as that of accusing their superiors or their communities of a mode of life that gave an excuse to Cromwell to close the house. An almost equally sure way of getting a pension was for a monk or a nun to make a self-accusation, for the names of these are nearly always found on the pension rolls.

The friars, when they had to be dealt with, as they usually possessed no estates at all, were turned adrift with a suit of clothes and a few shillings. How poor they were is indicated at Norwich, where there were four houses of friars. When their property was seized it was valued at forty-nine shillings — apart, of course, from the friaries themselves. The suppression of these houses was obviously not dictated by greed but was necessary because of the policy that had been adopted. Whatever oaths the friars had given to Hilsey and Browne, they were part of an international organization directed by generals stationed abroad, whereas the monks and nuns (the majority of whom belonged to one or other of the branches of the Benedictines) were autonomous and therefore isolated.

In contrast to the treatment given the friars, some of the wealthier abbots and abbesses were handsomely provided for. In several instances they received pensions of a hundred or two hundred pounds, and even more, and were assigned a house to live in. This was because they could be (or at least were) approached as though they enjoyed the personal ownership of the monastic estates. Then if they yielded gracefully or, better still, helped in persuading other abbots to yield, they were rewarded according to what was considered their deserts, but also with due relation to the value of the property they had made over to the Crown. Similarly many of the "good" — that is, the co-operative — monks were given benefices as a recognition of their compliance, but also because the bestowal of a benefice relieved the Court of Augmentation of paying a pension. Such monks, even when they had to be pensioned at first, were beneficed as soon as possible. With such inducements held out by Cromwell, it is hardly to be wondered at that he found so many religious willing to render the kind of service he required.

A few of the abbots were created bishops. Among these were Kitchen, who was appointed to Llandaff; Salcott of Bangor; More of Colchester; Rugg of Norwich; Holbeach of Rochester; Chambers of Peterborough; Barlow of St. David's; Bush of Bristol; and Parfew of St. Asaph. The two friars who had been such useful instruments in dealing with the mendicant orders were also suitably compensated. These were Hilsey, the Provincial of the Dominicans, who preceded Holbeach at Rochester, where he succeeded Fisher; and George Browne, the Prior of the London Augustinians, who as Archbishop of Dublin did his best in the reign of Henry and Edward to get the Irish to accept the changes in religion. He was hated by the Irish and did not make himself any better loved by publicly burning Ireland's most precious relic, the staff of St. Patrick.

The case of Robert Holgate is typical of men of this sort. He was the head of the Gilbertine Order (the only religious order to be founded by an Englishman). He was made Bishop of Llandaff in 1537, where he preceded Kitchen, as recognition for what he had accomplished in bringing about the surrender of the twenty-four Gilbertine houses. In 1545 he became Archbishop of York; during Edward's reign he married; under Mary he was imprisoned and recanted. He died as a Catholic. None of these men had any distinction except that of being useful tools in the carrying out of the monastic suppression.

Henry had started out as the reformer of an institution which he regarded as being, in itself, admirable. But his disapproval of monks increased as his financial needs mounted. Yet though he came, in effect, to assert that all monks were corrupt, he never said that the ideal of monasticism was false. Whatever he may have thought of chastity, as it applied to himself, he stringently enforced, or attempted to enforce, clerical celibacy. He also approved of obedience, though he came to believe that it should be rendered only to the King. Poverty one must suppose he did disapprove of, as he made the lack of possessions the grounds for his first attack.

There was, however, no obvious reason why he could not have incorporated monasticism into his new Church. That it answers a deep human need – if one must put it that way – is shown by the fact that religious orders have flourished in our own time in Anglicanism. Surreptitiously indeed it began to appear there again as early as the seventeenth century, though only to wither away in the spiritual desert encountered later. If Henry suppressed the monasteries it was out of naked avarice and because of the avarice of the men round him.

We have no reason to suppose that the monks showed a much greater reluctance to conform to the Henrician settlement of religion than did the secular clergy. Only the Carthusians and the Observant Friars have, as orders, a good record in this matter. The overwhelming mass of priests, secular and religious, took the oath of supremacy. Of these some may have had mental reservations, but the majority seem to have had no more scruples about this than other people. No great enthusiasm for the Pope existed, and this was not the first or last time that political considerations had outweighed religious convictions. These men were Englishmen first and Catholics second, and the first article in their faith was the duty of loyalty to the King. The only real reason that the monasteries were suppressed was that Henry needed money in greater and greater quantities, and this was obtainable most easily and in the largest amount from this source. Henry was pushed much further by his own extravagant habits than he had ever intended to go. The necessity of securing support for what had been thought of at first as a mere modification and adjustment of monasticism ended in the total extinction of that institution.

If further proof is needed of this it is found in the profanation of the shrines. Some of these were immensely wealthy; in fact that of St. Thomas of Canterbury was reputed to be the richest in all Europe. For the destruction of this shrine Henry discovered the excuse that Thomas à Becket was not a saint but a traitor, indeed a heretic, because he had resisted royal authority. His body was therefore exhumed, subjected to a trial and then, it would seem, burned.

In other cases — those of the hardly less celebrated shrines of St. Swithin's at Winchester, St. Cuthbert's at Durham, and Our Lady of Walsingham — another pretext had to be found. It was readily to hand: they were the occasion of popular superstition; it was therefore to the glory of God that Henry should suppress them and pocket their treasures.

It is possible, of course, that a degree of superstition did exist in some minds. Yet as Gasquet shows, the manuals of instruction and devotion of the time make it clear that the people of England must have understood perfectly well the Catholic doctrine on the veneration of images. In any event a charge of superstition comes with all the less grace from a man like Henry who was given to consulting soothsayers. In happier days he had made his pilgrimages to Walsingham and had been in the habit of sending a yearly offering to the shrine of St. Thomas. But now, when he thought of the jewels and the gold in those places, he decided that the live King could put them to much better use than the dead saint.

It was noticed that the zeal of Cromwell's commissioners against superstition was in direct proportion to the value of the treasures of the shrine. Of course they did not lay this down openly as a guiding principle, but now and then they let it out that it would be as well to destroy some shrine not worth the trouble of looting, so as to prevent people saying that they were actuated solely by greed. Thus Pollard, the man in charge of the sacrilege at Winchester, after listing in a letter to Cromwell the precious things there, concluded, that after he had completed that job: "We intend, both at Hyde and St. Mary's, to sweep away all the rotten bones that be called relics; which we may not omit lest it be thought we care more for the treasure than for avoiding the abomination of idolatry."

It is interesting to record what happened with regard to one set of "rotten bones." At the end of 1539 Dr. Leigh went to despoil the tomb of St. Cuthbert. After taking all the valuable adornments, his men came at last to the coffin. It was strongly bound in iron and had to be broken open with a sledge-hammer. There they found the saint lying after eight hundred and fifty-two years, his body quite incorrupt. The man who had burst the coffin open found, however, that he had broken one of St.

Cuthbert's legs and was dismayed. Dr. Leigh went up to see what had happened and in his turn called in Dr. Henley, the assistant commissioner, and Henley, disbelieving the story, went up to look for himself. Not knowing quite what to do, they left the saint's body in the sacristy until the King's pleasure should be known. While waiting for this, the monks of the yet undissolved cathedral priory took up the body and buried it again in secret.

The amount of precious metals stripped from these shrines was immense and was duly listed in the accounts, except for what was purloined. But no attempt was made to give the number or value of the gems taken, as these were handed over to the King for his personal use. The Great Regal Ruby of Canterbury, a gift from Louis VII of France in 1179, was soon smouldering on Henry's finger; there was at least no superstition about that. While one may perhaps credit the King with some degree of sincerity about his divorce suit, or even in his assertion of the royal supremacy, with regard to the looting of the shrines and the monasteries (but especially the shrines) the mind simply refuses to yield him more than the extenuation which may be accorded one who is besotted with the passions that override judgement. And here the ruling passion was the ugliest that can be found—a crude greed.

Henry was still uneasy about the succession. Mary was now bastardized and so was Elizabeth. The heir was a sickly little boy who would be completely in the hands of his uncles when Henry died, and the King's health was far from good, with what may have been a syphilitic sore on his leg giving him increasing trouble. Doubts could not but cross his mind as to whether the rule of the Seymours would be accepted by the older aristocracy. It was even possible that the right of the Tudor dynasty would be challenged. He therefore decided to strike at all posssible claimants, and to sweep away what was left of the Plantagenets. This accorded not only with what he considered sound policy but with his appetite for revenge against Reginald Pole.

Lord Montague, the Cardinal's brother, and Henry Courtenay, the Marquis of Exeter (a descendant of Edward IV), were both executed on December 9, 1538, and with them, for good measure, Sir Edward Neville. Sir Geoffrey Pole was spared, as the King hoped to get something out of him, and the miserable man did give evidence that was useful, for which he lived in lifelong remorse. Exeter's son, young Edward Courtenay, was sent, for safe-keeping, to the Tower, from which he emerged in Mary's reign only to indulge in such dissipations that she rejected him as a possible husband. Margaret Pole, the Countess of Salisbury, was attainted with her sons but reserved for later punishment.

Montague was accused of having said that he approved of what his brother the Cardinal was doing and that he wished "for a change of this world, without meaning any hurt to the King." It also came out that he read Sir Thomas More's books. Sir Geoffrey Pole testified that his brother and Exeter and Neville did not like the dissolution of the monasteries, and Montague had been heard to say that he hoped that the Cardinal would marry the Lady Mary.* He had also said, "In times past kings' words had been believed, but nowadays they be used [to deceive]. Wherefore if the Commons do rise again they will trust no fair promises nor words." Flimsy as all this may seem, even less often sufficed to send a man to the block.

Henry in past years had been accustomed to say that Lady Salisbury was the saintliest woman in England. Now he considered her saintliness as too much in the mode of that of Fisher and More. If strict legalities were to be observed, she was the rightful queen of England. For Edward IV's children had once been declared illegitimate by a diocesan court, and she was the daughter of Edward's brother, the Duke of Clarence. Though she would never have dreamed of asserting any such claim, she

*Such a possibility remained until Mary, as queen, decided against it. Pole, though a cardinal, was not yet a priest, though even had he been one, the Pope could have dispensed him from his vow of celibacy and no doubt would have done so to consolidate a Catholic monarchy in England. A later pope dispensed a Jesuit cardinal when he succeeded to the Crown of Poland.

would have been glad to see her son Reginald marry Henry's daughter Mary; and Reginald, had he wished to organize a party, might have had a following as against the little Edward. But mere possibilities of this sort obviously do not constitute treason, and the only evidence that Cromwell could unearth against Lady Salisbury was a tunic that was discovered in her house. This had embroidered upon it the arms of England surrounded by a wreath of pansies and marigolds. The pansies, it was alleged, represented the Poles and the marigolds, Mary. For further damnation this tunic also bore the emblem of the Five Wounds and was therefore supposed to prove her ladyship's sympathy with the Pilgrimage of Grace. That she did sympathize with the objects of that demonstration may be safely inferred, but this did not necessarily mean that she approved of that demonstration being made, still less that treason was intended.

How weak was the case against her is shown by the fact that she was merely kept in custody until May 28, 1541, and not executed until then, though long before that, at Cromwell's orders, the tomb she had prepared for herself in Christchurch Priory, with magnificent carvings by Pietro Torregiano, was smashed. When word came to Cardinal Pole of what had been done – and it was to spite him* that Henry had had Lady Salisbury's head struck off – he said: "Hitherto I thought God had given me the grace to be the son of one of the best and most honourable ladies in England, and I gloried in that fact and thanked God for it. Now, however, He has honored me still more and increased my debt of gratitude to Him, for He has made me the son of a martyr. For her constancy in the Catholic faith the King has caused her to be publicly beheaded, in spite of her seventy years. Blessed and thanked be God for ever!" She is now venerated by the Church as Blessed Margaret Pole.

*A pretext was found in the fact that shortly before this there had been a new attempt in Yorkshire to organize a rising. Its weakness is indicated sufficiently by the fact that no man of prominence was implicated, and Lady Salisbury knew nothing whatever about it. Only one man of title suffered, Sir John Neville of Chevet, and he only on a charge of not revealing what he knew. Yet over sixty men, including twenty-five priests, according to Chapuys, were hanged.

More than a year before the Countess of Salisbury went to the block and the conspirators of Yorkshire to the gallows, the suppression of the monasteries had been completed with the surrender on March 25, 1540, of Waltham Abbey, a foundation of Harold, the last of the Saxon kings. But what is of greater importance was the forcible seizure at the end of the previous year of the great abbeys of Reading, Colchester, and Glastonbury and the execution of their abbots for not being sufficiently compliant to the King's demands. They had all three taken the oath of supremacy, but more was required of them when, on April 28, 1539, Parliament passed a statute affirming that "Whereas sundry abbots, priors, abbesses and prioresses and other ecclesiastical governors . . . have of their own free and voluntary minds, good wills and assents, without constraint, co-action or compulsion of any manner of persons . . . given and granted . . . all their said monasteries to our sovereign lord, be it enacted that all such monasteries are dissolved . . . and all their property vested in the King." Most superiors had, it is true, bowed to the inevitable and had put up no resistance, as this was their only chance of obtaining some conpensating preferment. Few had the courage of the Abbess of Ambresbury who had said simply: "If the King's Highness command me to go from this house I will gladly go, though I beg my bread, and as for the pension, I care for none." But now as three abbots were at last putting up a useless fight, they were marked down for death.

It is instructive to note Cromwell's memoranda about these matters. He was always jotting down such things, mere details in a life crowded with far more pressing concerns. Many of such notes are, of course, harmless enough, but among them we find these: "*Item* to see that the evidence be well sorted and the indictments well drawn against the said abbots and their accomplices. *Item* the Abbot of Reading to be sent down and tried and executed at Reading with his complices. *Item* the Abbot of Glaston to be tried at Glaston, and also executed there with his complices." Mr. Pickthorn, the author of two recent valuable monographs on Tudor government, has what seems to me a highly disingenuous explanation of this: it is that Cromwell did not mean that their condemnation was assured in advance but merely that he *supposed* they would be found guilty and executed. This does not accord with what we know of Cromwell's methods, and is contradicted by his arrangement to have the evidence "well sorted." There can be no doubt that he had decided, before the three abbots were brought to trial, that they were to die.

Dr. Layton, Cromwell's commissioner, wrote to him: "The Abbot of Glastonbury appeareth neither then nor now to have known God, nor his prince, nor any part of a good Christian man's religion." As the Abbot could not be charged with refusing an oath which he had taken (surely with a bad conscience) he was arraigned, with two of his monks, for robbing the monastery church. It is not unlikely that he had concealed some valuables – we do not know what – which he knew the commissioners would have confiscated. But who today will blame him for hiding some part of the abbey's property from the abbey's robbers? According to the very explicit terms of the statute passed earlier that year, the King's title to such property existed in what had already been voluntarily surrendered; and in these cases the surrender had not yet occurred.

The pleas availed nothing. Richard Whiting of Glastonbury, with two of his monks, was dragged to the top of Tor Hill, facing the abbey which, according to tradition, had been founded by Joseph of Arimathea, and there hanged. Even Froude was horrified at the thought of "the bleak hill-top on the dreary November day, the gallows, and the infirm old man guilty of nothing which he can understand to be a crime." On the very same day (November 15, 1539) Abbot Cook of Reading was hanged at the gateway of his abbey with two of his monks. Dying, he proclaimed his fidelity to the Holy See. About the same time the Abbot of Colchester was hanged, he too at the gateway of his abbey. After that no religious house dared to offer the slightest opposition to the Vicar-General of the Supreme Head of the Church in England.

CHAPTER FIFTEEN

"The King's Doctrine"

LOOKING back upon what happened during the years 1531 to 1540 one is amazed at the way so many people, even to the end, clung to the belief that what was going on in England was merely a passing quarrel between the King and the Pope. Yet in this we are being wise after the event; to the men of the time there seemed firm grounds for hope. It was generally believed, as Katherine had believed, that Henry was a good man misled. First Anne was blamed, then Cromwell and Cranmer, but especially Cromwell. But as on several occasions their influence appeared to be on the wane, people comforted themselves by believing that it would terminate in their sudden and complete eclipse. Though bishops of the "New Learning" were appointed, the two most outspoken of them – Latimer and Shaxton – resigned in 1539, after which the hierarchy was as a whole orthodox, except on the point of the royal supremacy.

The King took his title of Defender of the Faith seriously. So far from feeling under any obligation to resign it because of having broken with the Holy See, it was his pride to demonstrate that he was more Catholic than the Pope. If in the years that followed the schism people were frequently puzzled about religion, most of them found a term that justified their own professed beliefs: it was "the King's Doctrine."

Henry was, in fact, equally opposed to what are now called the Reformation and the Counter-Reformation. Certainly anything contradictory to Catholic doctrine (except as regards the Pope's authority) was more violently reprobated by him than it was even by the majority of those who remained within Catholic unity. Nevertheless he was opening the door to the Reformation in England and ensuring its success elsewhere. Without England's adhesion to the anti-papal side, what we now understand by Protestantism could not possibly have maintained its gains. Yet Henry, while undermining the authority of the Papacy, really believed that he could provide a still more solid basis for orthodoxy in the authority of the Crown.

Actually of course he laid no foundation at all and was merely destructive. But that was not his intention, any more than it was his intention to create a new class of landowners who could wrest control from the monarchy. His intentions, however, should be allowed for, even when we see his failure and why he was bound to fail. His religion was not Anglicanism, not even high-Anglicanism, but Henricianism, a specialized and artificial product. High-Anglicanism is poles apart from his system, and consists of nothing more than a small group quite at variance with the Protestant Anglicanism in which it finds itself. Even in this respect Henry has created nothing but confusion.

This confusion may be discerned in his religious regime even from the outset. Despite his orthodoxy he was not above using heretics when this suited his purpose, if only to give trouble to the Church while he was pursuing some little plan of his own. It was so in the case of Simon Fish who was allowed to return to England, according to Foxe the martyrologist, with a safe-conduct from the King. It was so also with Robert Barnes who, having recanted his heresy in 1526, went to Antwerp in 1528 but was invited back by Cromwell in 1531. It was thought that he might be of service in persuading the Lutheran divines to give their approval to Henry's divorce from Katherine. Later he helped to negotiate the marriage to Anne of Cleves. He was burned in the end, for the heretic he was, but only after his usefulness was over and he was showing new truculence. But if there were theological conferences with German Lutherans and at the same time (and again later) an attempt at a political alliance with them, nothing was accomplished because Henry could not stomach Lutheranism or the Lutherans Henricianism, which they regarded as in some ways more objectionable than the old religion itself.

The first move in this direction came quite early, when an adventurer named Jurgen Wullenberger came into power in Lubeck and aimed at creating a federation of Protestant municipalities, by which means he hoped to dominate Denmark and Norway. When in August, 1533, some ships of Lubeck anchored in Rye harbor, their crews were arrested as pirates but through their leader, Marc Meyer, managed to persuade Henry that Lubeck might be useful to him. Meyer was made a knight and sent on his way, and Henry was inspired with the fantastic ambition of obtaining, by the favour of Lubeck, the crown of Denmark, or of at least appointing a king who would be subsidiary to himself. The Lubeckers promised him support of his marriage to Anne Boleyn and therefore, of course, their backing, for what it was worth, against the Pope, on the basis of this extracting a loan of 50,000 gulden. That in effect was the end of this absurd little deal. It brought about also the end of Wullenberger a little later, for Christian of Holstein became King of Denmark, and Wullenberger was overthrown and paid for his political ambitions on the scaffold. As Henry was repaid his gulden, he at least lost nothing, even if he had gained nothing.

A scheme of this sort, even had it been successful, could not have served any purpose except that of annoying the Emperor. In continuation of the same idea, though on a larger scale, Henry in January, 1536, sent over a number of divines to Wittenberg to see if they could not reach a political and theological understanding with the Lutheran princes. Among these emissaries was the Nicholas Heath who in 1559 was deprived of the archbishopric of York he had obtained under Mary and who was publicly twitted by Queen Elizabeth with having been one of those most active in upholding her father. He was the "orthodox" member of the English commission to Wittenberg, certainly far more so than Robert Barnes, who was with him, or even than Edward Fox, a decent enough man but a straddler.

Not even the famous English gift for compromise availed at this time. Indeed, it was the Germans who did most of the compromising. In deference to Henry, whom they wished to secure as an ally, they passed over the Mass and communion in two kinds for the laity, the marriage of priests and (as Henry was still posing as being the reformer of monasticism) the vows taken by monks and nuns. They could not quite abandon the characteristic Lutheran tenet of justification by faith alone, but they attempted to phrase it so ambiguously as to make it capable of interpretation in a Catholic sense. The articles, discovered in 1905 in the archives at Weimar, were drawn up by Melancthon, but were approved of by Luther in advance, though they have little of his belligerent spirit.

The English commissioners also accepted the articles, but only tentatively and on condition that Henry accepted them too. This, however, he refused to do, much to his credit as a theologian. He smelled heresy in them, and with heresy he was determined to have nothing to do. All that eventuated were the Ten Articles of 1536.

These Ten Articles have often been described as indicating greater Protestant leanings than Henry subsequently permitted himself. It is true that they are less unequivocal than the Six Articles which replaced them three years later. They also employ some of the phraseology that had been adopted at Wittenberg, after debate and compromise, by the Henrician and the Lutheran theologians. But that is really the most that can be said; they are Catholic, so far as they go, and assert no heresy.

On the contrary they declare that the rule of faith is the canon of Scripture, which of course was a divergence from the Lutherans, as they reject part of that canon. Common ground was found in the acceptance of the Apostle's, the Nicene, and the Athanasian creeds. But again there is a concession at the expense of the Lutherans in the recognition of the authority of the Fathers of the Church and the four early councils, for this authority the Lutherans had rejected.

It may be thought that by mentioning only three sacraments these articles implied that there *were* only three. And probably there was in this some wish not to bang the door in the face of the German divines, but to leave it open a few inches with a view to future negotiations. But the three sacraments mentioned – those of Baptism, Penance, and the Eucharist – appear correctly enough as those "necessary for salvation." Holy Orders, Matrimony, Confirmation, and Extreme Unction are not "necessary" in just this sense, great as is the grace that they convey. And here the Henrician definitions are explicit: the doctrine of the Eucharist is fully and accurately stated, and Penance is defined as having three parts – auricular confession, contrition with a firm purpose of amendment, and satisfaction. This and the further explanations given were at variance with the Lutheran position. Only those very imperfectly informed as to Catholic teaching (and this includes most of the historians who have written on the subject) can discover any Protestant tinge in the Ten Articles. That they were adopted instead of the Wittenberg compromise was due to the strong orthodoxy of the English King.

In 1537 the so-called "Bishops' Book" appeared. Its first draft, owing to Cranmer's influence, insinuated as much heresy as Cranmer dared venture upon. Henry disapproved and Cranmer wrote to Cromwell that he would not be "a picker of quarrels with his Grace's book," for that was what it was after Henry had done with it. Cranmer therefore merely offered suggestions, subject of course "to his Grace's censure and judgment." He declares further, "I refer all my annotations to his Grace's most exact judgment." Its official title was *The Godly and Pious Institution of a Christian Man* but was popularly known as the "Bishops' Book." In it the four sacraments that were not mentioned in the Ten Articles were defined, quite accurately, and though the "Romish doctrine" of Purgatory is in a fashion denied (as that might give some justification for the continuance of the monasteries whose suppression had begun), it was nevertheless declared that prayers for the departed souls are praiseworthy and the existence of Purgatory was implicitly and explicitly affirmed.

Even if some straddling can be discovered on this point, here too Henry's foot leans heavily to the orthodox side.

Though a conference with the Lutherans was renewed in London during the summer of 1538, compromise was again found impossible. The royal injunctions about worship issued by Cromwell on the last day of September were orthodox, though a tendency to slight "ceremonies" was capable of being taken as favouring the "New Learning." But I suppose that I need hardly point out that there are ceremonies *and* ceremonies; those that are a part of the Liturgy of the Church were not questioned.

As though to emphasize his unshakeable orthodoxy, the King in the following November staged a wonderful show by trying in person a man named John Nicholson, who also passed under the name of Lambert. There had been a number of heretics burned under Henry during his schismatic period, but this was made a very special occasion. Nicholson had been examined by Cranmer, Shaxton, and Latimer (all secretly heretics themselves) but had appealed to the King, so before the King he was brought.

Nicholson was a brave man. Not only had he denied the efficacy of praying to the saints (which Henry, after having despoiled their shrines, might have allowed to pass) but also the Real Presence, a doctrine to which Henry was genuinely devoted. So the King clothed himself in white from head to foot—white being the colour of the Holy Ghost—and sat on his throne in Westminster Hall, surrounded by a number of bishops, to hear what Nicholson had to say for himself.

The poor fellow had let it out that he had been hiding under an assumed name. This in itself was taken as presumptive evidence of guilt, as Henry always boasted that he could not bear anything that wore the slightest tinge of deceit. He expected other people to practise his own perfect candor, his honest bluffness. Yet so little had Nicholson really tried to conceal himself that he had not been able to refrain from parading his eccentric opinions in public places; but that he had used the alias of Lambert went against him. Nevertheless, he was given a fair trial, as was always true of trials for heresy as compared with those for treason. And he was given every chance to recant gracefully in face of the arguments put up by seven bishops in succession. Among these was Cranmer himself. And then Henry questioned the man in his most magisterial style. In the end they got him so confused that, without recanting, he threw himself on the King's mercy. The stern answer was, "Then thou must die." And die he did at the stake at Smithfield.

On the other side was John Forest, for whom was reserved the distinction of suffering for both heresy and treason. Under the statute of 1535 that had sent More and Fisher to the block and the Carthusians to the gallows, a simple charge of the treason of denying the King's title as Head of the Church sufficed. But Henry now discovered that heresy was also involved in upholding the spiritual authority of the Pope. He maintained of course that, whether or not other monarchs asserted their rights, each was supreme, under the law of God, over the Church in his own dominions; he looked upon himself as loyal to a standard of orthodoxy that other kings were culpably neglecting.

If other heretics were not treated like Friar Forest, this was due to Henry's clemency. But this was a special case of which a special example should be made. John Forest belonged to the Observants of Greenwich, once Katherine's (and Henry's) favourite religious order. He had been Katherine's confessor, and the King had showed him such attentions as sending him delicacies from his own table. People at large might have some shadow of excuse for their errors, but never those to whom Henry had gone out of his way to be kind. To these the King attributed personal malice and was bitterly vindictive. So the friar was condemned to expiate his dual crime by being hanged and burned simultaneously.

This could only be done in chains, as the fire lighted under the victim would have burned through a rope. Therefore in a kind of iron cradle he was dangled over a fire, and for the giving of a further dramatic touch, the faggots were the broken bits of a wooden statue of a saint formerly venerated in Wales. It was that of St. Darvel Gadarn.*

This ceremony took place on May 22, 1538. Bishop Latimer was appointed to preach the sermon, and in accepting the commission wrote to Cromwell: "If it be your pleasure, as it is, that I shall play the fool after my accustomed manner when Forest shall suffer, I would wish my stage stood near unto Forest." He wished to convert him. "Such," he explained, "is my foolishness."

In spite of Latimer's implied admission that he was something of a clown — as to which we have other evidence — it should in fairness be added that he had an admirably racy and colloquial style, full of salt and humour, and was the most honest of the "advanced" men in England. But on this occasion, however much Latimer may have impressed the crowd with his popular oratory, it had no effect on Forest. As Stow relates, "When the Bishop asked him in what state he would die in, the friar with a loud voice answered that if an angel should come down from heaven and teach him any other doctrine than he had received and believed in his youth he would not believe him." He added that Latimer seven years earlier would not have dared, for his life, to make such a sermon. So they swung him over the fire in the chains and, comments Hall, "So impatiently he took his death as never any man that put his trust in God." In spite of that squirming, the Church has beatified him. Like the rest of the martyrs he could have saved his life. As early as 1534, when he was first imprisoned, his friend Queen Katherine had written to him saying that she did not doubt his willingness to die for Christ.

The men who gave most valuable support to the Henrician revolution in religion were not those of most pronounced re-

*"Gadarn" means powerful in Welsh. If the Welsh really believed, as was alleged, that this saint was so powerful as to be able to take souls out of hell, they must have been badly instructed in their religion. One may surmise rather that this was only a deliberate hyperbole, a fashion of speaking not literally believed.

forming tendencies but the divines of otherwise orthodox beliefs who accepted the royal supremacy. Men like Latimer and Shaxton were, upon the whole, rather an embarrassment, and resigned in 1539 after the promulgation of the Six Articles. If the arch-heretic Cranmer did not resign, this was only because he was prepared to swallow any decision the King made; he, though well known to be riddled with heresy, officially professed orthodoxy on the essential point of Henricianism – undeviating submission to the Crown – than which nothing could be more orthodox.

The arguments for the Henrician position were put forth in two books, one rather feeble, the other rather powerful. Pole in his *De Unitate Ecclesiae* found what was written by Richard Sampson, the Bishop of Chicester, a ridiculous performance and raked it through and through. It opened with what appear to be a number of old sermons by this wheel-horse of the King's civil and ecclesiastical service, platitudes about the love of God and the love of one's neighbour, all leading to the conclusion that this love could be most practically shown by submission to the royal authority: "Whatever the King says and commands, that say and do." He at least demonstrated his own adherence to this principle by the way he adhered to his bishopric through Edward's reign, with its further changes in religion, safely into Mary's, when Catholicism was restored.

Stephen Gardiner was a man of a much larger calibre. He had worked strenuously for Henry's divorce from Katherine of Aragon, but afterwards led what resistance was offered in Parliament to the religious revolution. This, however, he accepted as soon as it became law, on the ground that "an act of Parliament discharges his conscience and that of the King's subjects." It was the argument elaborated in his *De Vera Obedientia;* if the King gave commands contrary to the law of God, it was he and not his subjects who would be held responsible. The subject's duty was to obey. It must be said to Gardiner's credit, however, that under Edward, he resisted the policy introduced in the young King's name and, for this, was deprived of his see and imprisoned. It is also to his credit that Henry, believing that he would take the same line as Warham, passed him over in favour of Cranmer at Warham's death, when nominating a new archbishop of Canterbury. And in Mary's reign he not only took the lead in bringing England back to Catholic unity but died repentant, saying with almost his last breath, "I have denied like Peter, but I have not wept like Peter." That he mourned his lack of tears is the measure of his sorrow.

His book of 1535 was an able performance. It sought to find justification for the King's title as Head of the Church in England. And probably Gardiner sincerely believed, as did most of the other bishops, that as the breach with Rome had occurred, the best that could be done under the circumstances was to uphold the Supremacy and use it as a barrier against heresy. If they resisted the King, so Gardiner and the other Henricians thought, they would be swept away and the King would fall into the hands of bishops of the new school. The orthodox men could save more by surrendering on some points, and they managed to persuade themselves that heresy could be more decisively dealt with by the King than by the ecclesiastical authorities. Wolsey had been lax in this respect, as none knew better than the man who had been Wolsey's secretary.

This was not of course the whole story, but it is at least part of it, and it offers some extenuation for men like Gardiner and Edmund Bonner. He too stood firm in orthodoxy under Edward VI and was deprived and imprisoned, as happened to him again under Elizabeth. When in Mary's time he was reproached by an accused heretic for having written against the Pope when Henry was on the throne, he candidly admitted the charge, saying, "My lord of Winchester [Gardiner] . . . did write a book against the Pope's Holiness, and I also did write a preface before the same book, tending to the same effect. And thus did we, because of the perilous world that then was: for then it was made treason by the laws of this realm to maintain the Pope's authority, and a great danger it was to be suspected a favourer of the see of Rome; and therefore fear compelled us to bear with the time, for otherwise there had been no way but one." If it was an honest man who made that confession, it cannot be said that either Bonner or Gardiner were heroic, and there are times in human affairs when nothing less than heroism is enough. The best that can be said for the Henrician bishops is that they prevented what was bad from becoming worse. Yet had they been willing to be less prudent and more courageous, by opposing a united front to the King, he would not have dared to proceed against them. Those ready to lose their lives are those who, even in this world, save them.

The laity, except for the aristocracy, can hardly be blamed, as they had no voice in anything. The election of members to the House of Commons was made by a very small group, and these hardly did more than ratify the nominations made by the Council, just as the members, after election, were subject to a pressure hardly to be resisted. The only means open to the populace at large for making itself felt was by insurrection, and they could not rise because their possible leaders had either gone over to the other side or were too disunited for effective action. Pot-house orations accomplished nothing at all. When the people did make their protest in Lincolnshire and Yorkshire – what happened in 1536 was no more than a protest, though a protest in arms – they were given a punishment that could never be forgotten.

There can be no doubt that this mass of simple, ignorant, and inarticulate men disapproved of what was happening. What may remain open to doubt is whether they disapproved enough. The probability is that they disapproved with only half of their minds; with the other half they disapproved of themselves, in the sense of feeling a sense of guilt for having risen at all, in however mild and moderate a way. Yet even had they felt more strongly than they did, they would still have been helpless without the kind of decisive captaincy they lacked.

One is forced to the conclusion that though the English people were, upon the whole, sound, they were also soft and slack. It was easy to confuse them with false promises and facile explanations. We must not think of them as living in a modern democracy where the sources of information are, at least to some extent, open to all, and where discussion is free. The nearest approach they had to a newspaper was an official proclamation, the nearest approach to a public meeting was a sermon; and as the preachers were instructed by the government as to what they were to say the people could be deluded at every turn. At the beginning of the troubles nobody understood what was happening, except that the King was asking the Pope for a divorce. When after several years he failed to get it from the Pope and proceeded to take matters into his own hands, the people could have had no idea as to where this was going to end. Nor did the clergy know. It is very much a question as to whether the King himself knew, or that adroit manager of the affair, Thomas Cromwell.

In the very year that the partial suppression of the monasteries was decided upon the Ten Articles were issued, an assurance that, whatever might be done to the Pope's authority in England, England was going to remain Catholic. Parish life was not affected by the destruction of the monasteries, as the monks did not serve parishes. The advowsons, or the right of appointment possessed by some of the abbeys, were taken over by the new lay owners, so that no change was noticed. Except for the abolition of a few popular holidays and an occasional sermon denouncing the enormities of the Bishop of Rome, everything went on pretty much as before. Times were getting hard; prices were rising; taxes had not been reduced as had been promised. But England seemed to be as Catholic without the Pope – perhaps even more so – as it had been under the Pope. People might grumble, but few had much capacity for definitely linking cause with effect.

With the publication in 1539 of the Six Articles, any misgivings a Catholic mind might have had were set at rest. The Whip of Six Strings, as it was called by those who did not like it, even imposed a stringency of discipline greater than had existed previously. Where infraction of the ecclesiastical code had been punished (if at all) only by the Church, some infractions of this sort were now made civil offences. A man was actually hanged in London for eating meat on a Friday. And further to obliterate the familiar distinction between what was commanded by the Church and what was commanded by the law of God, clerical celibacy was declared to be part of the divine law. Not only was the denial of transubstantiation made punishable by death (that was the case under already existing statutes) but any one who spoke against or in practice departed from any of the other five articles – regarding Communion in one kind for the laity, clerical celibacy, monastic vows, private Masses, or auricular confession – should, for the first offence, be fined and imprisoned and, for the second, suffer death. This was being more Catholic than the Pope with a vengeance.

The Six Articles were too severe to be enforced except sporadically, but fear was struck, and under it Cranmer hurriedly sent Mrs. Cranmer back to Germany. Cromwell said to him: "His Majesty will never give credit against you, whatsoever is laid to your charge; but let me or any other of the Council be complained of, His Grace will most seriously chide and fall out with us." He added, perhaps as a broad hint, "Therefore you are most happy if you can keep you in this estate." However, a man was fairly safe who could write to the King as Cranmer did, "This is mine opinion and sentence at present, which nevertheless I do not temerariously define, but refer the judgement thereof wholly unto your Majesty." He was the one man upon whose obsequiousness Henry could entirely depend; it was enough to make him swallow without visible pain the royal orthodoxy that so disgusted him.

Henry's devotion to the central question – the Real Presence – never faltered. He was growing so enormously fat, and had such a painful sore on his leg, that he could kneel only with great difficulty. When it was reasonably suggested that he might receive Holy Communion sitting in his chair, he answered, "If I could throw myself down, not only on the ground but under the ground, I should not then think that I gave enough honor to the Holy Sacrament."

A word should be said regarding the King's attitude towards publication of the Bible in the vernacular; Henry remained perfectly orthodox, yet he was so careless that he allowed himself to be hoodwinked. After Tyndale's translation of the New Testament had been burned in St. Paul's churchyard in 1526, the question was discussed whether another translation should not be published under authority. This was eventually decided against, but only "considering the malignity of the present time." An assurance was given that, after heresy had been extirpated, and corrupt translations discovered and destroyed, "His Highness intended to provide that the Holy Scripture should be by great, learned and Catholic persons translated into the English tongue."

It is not necessary to tell any Catholic reader that the Church has never been opposed to the Bible being read in the vernacular, so long as proper safeguards are taken and an accurate text provided. But as it is possible that even some Catholic readers associate the first English version of the Scriptures with the name of Wycliffe, or may even imagine that, as a matter of historic fact, the demand for the Bible was due to the spread of Protestantism, a few brief remarks should be offered on the point. Translations of the Bible had been made prior to Wycliffe and others since his time. We have seen how Sir Thomas More wrote explicitly: "I myself have seen and can show you Bibles, fair and old, written in English, which have been known and seen by the bishop of the diocese, and left in the hands of laymen and women, whom he knew to be good and Catholic people who used the books with devotion and soberness." But such translations were in manuscript, and therefore so expensive that only rich men or college or monastic libraries could possess copies. Not until the invention of printing was it possible to circulate any book widely.

Why then, it may be asked, was not a book of this immense

importance printed before this? Of the eighty books published by Caxton, why was not the Bible one?* The answer is simple, or rather there are several answers. One is that nearly everybody who could read at all could read Latin, and these were content with the Vulgate. But another reason is that it was far from easy to find a translator equal to so stupendous a task, for though any one of several men would have been willing to undertake it, nobody was found who was considered by the English bishops to have the learning that might make them feel safe in entrusting it to his hands. It was for this reason that Tyndale, when Tunstall refused to back him because his orthodoxy was already under suspicion, went abroad and produced a translation which, both in its renderings of key words and in the notes (mostly taken from Luther's version) was not only misleading but designed to mislead. That Tyndale proved that he had remarkable literary powers is beside the point: they made him only the more dangerous. What was wanted was not only a good writer but a good scholar, and not only a good scholar but one free from all taint of heresy.

By the purely accidental circumstance that this first printed (and therefore best known) version of the Bible was condemned, a vague association was established in the popular mind between Protestantism, or the New Learning as it was sometimes called, and the Bible, where none actually existed. And in the turmoil that followed Henry's breach with Rome, there was so much to attend to that the crying need for an accurate English rendering of the Scriptures tended to be neglected.

The need nevertheless remained and was admitted in theory even by those who most doubted whether it was advisable to allow such a book to be indiscriminately circulated at that particular time. It was this admitted need, and the fact that it had not been supplied, that gave Cranmer his chance.

He could not of course introduce Tyndale's version into England, or the continuation of it made by Coverdale, the man who

*And Caxton had died in 1491. Since then hundreds of books had been printed in England — but no English Bible!

had tried to work with Tyndale but who had not been able to endure his nasty temper. For though Henry had said of Tyndale's *Obedience of a Christian Man,* where the Fascist formula was contained: "One King, one law in the realm; no class of men exempt from the temporal sword; no law except the law of the land," "This book is for me and all kings to read," he would certainly have burned Tyndale if could he have got hold of him. This Henry tried to do, even to the extent of begging the Emperor to deliver him up. For the man was a manifest heretic and had added to his offence by denying Henry's right to marry Anne Boleyn. In the eyes of the King the Tyndale translation of the New Testament was quite unacceptable.

The Tyndale-Coverdale version was, however, just what Cranmer wanted. Something may be allowed to Cranmer's admiration for its style, for what Cranmer could do with the English language was proved by his Prayer Book, when it was produced in Edward's reign, and in Henry's by an achievement as great on a smaller scale, his Litany. How to get round the King's objection, both to Tyndale personally and to his heresy, was a problem. Cranmer himself could not undertake to translate the Bible, even had his learning been sufficient. For one thing he lacked sufficient time, and the book had to be got out quickly, if it was to serve his purpose. For another thing, Cranmer excelled only in the short passage of prose. He was an engraver of cameos not a sculptor on the heroic scale. If it ever crossed his mind to translate the Bible he soon dropped the idea.

Instead he brought out a disguised edition of Tyndale and Coverdale, eliminating all the obnoxious notes (which it would have been fatal to include), and using a toned-down version of the text made by John Rogers. But as Rogers' name would have betrayed the plot, the book was put out as a translation made by an entirely fictitious Thomas Matthew. This became the official English Bible and was licensed by the King, who was completely taken in, and it remained such until, after some protests were made, it was further revised and reissued as the Bishops' Bible.

This action of Cranmer is only one of many which revealed that, obsequious though he was to the King, he was always watching for a chance surreptitiously to advance the Protestant cause. He knew that he had to move most circumspectly, but if he was deferential to the King to the last degree, this was not merely because to be so was part of his nature and part of his religion, but also because he saw that it was only by following this policy that he had any chance at all. If men like Gardiner and Bonner fell in with Henry's views in the hope of keeping him orthodox, Cranmer fell in with them in the hope of pushing him at least a few further inches away from Catholicism, yet always looking for some sudden change in events that would make possible a good deal more than that. In this matter of the Bible he was not taking a great deal of risk; if his deceit were discovered, it was capable of being explained as an oversight or a fault committed by a subordinate. He could say that he himself had been imposed on.

The trick was so successful that Cromwell – Cranmer apparently was this time not involved – authorized in 1539 the publication of what is known as Taverner's Bible, edited by Richard Taverner with an introduction in which Protestantism was insinuated – a denial of the priesthood, the reduction of the sacraments to outward signs, with the Eucharist no more than a symbol, and so forth. It is a wonder that Taverner himself escaped with nothing worse than an imprisonment in the Tower. His edition served to justify the charges that, soon after its publication, were brought against Cromwell (but not, it should be observed, against Cranmer) of favouring heresy.

In 1542 all the editions of the Bible except those definitely authorized by the King were prohibited. At the same time an act was passed which declared that though his Majesty had permitted the Bible to be read in English by his subjects, as all kinds of people were taking it upon themselves to be expositors of the Scriptures, their use should be strictly limited to those capable of profiting from it. No person under the degree of yeoman might possess a copy to read to himself. Nor should any woman, unless she were of the gentry, read it. Rustics and journeymen and apprentices and children were to be content to learn about the Bible from the heads of their families.

Such an act of Parliament was of course ineffective. But though it was foolish to try and exercise control in this way, the principle of control was sound. It could be exercised only by an orthodox priesthood. Yet where the control should have started was with a more careful scrutiny of the English Bibles that were allowed to appear. As this was not done the habit of text-chopping and the vagaries of private and irresponsible interpretation produced so much heresy that it was soon hardly possible to check it. Cranmer had very artfully accomplished almost all that he had wanted to do.

Cranmer himself escaped, but only narrowly. After the fall of Cromwell he was in a most dangerous position. And when, as the result of Cromwell's removal, men like Gardiner obtained more influence over Henry's mind, Cranmer came very close to his own fall.

For that matter, even while Cromwell was still at the head of affairs, Cranmer had one rather narrow shave. Henry had asked him to write out for his private eye his criticisms of the Six Articles. This Cranmer did, aware that the King was often willing to argue with people without rancour, so long as they would, if necessary, in the end confess themselves overcome by his learning. But on the way to the palace, the boat in which Ralph Morice, Cranmer's secretary, was travelling, taking with him Cranmer's annotations, was capsized by a bear swimming in the river. The bearward rescued the manuscript, but seeing what it contained, refused to surrender it and, being himself a strong Catholic, carried it to the Council as damning evidence against the Archbishop. Cranmer, however, had been forewarned, so when the bearward appeared, he got a severe wigging from Cromwell for his officiousness, and Cranmer was saved from his enemies on the Council.

In 1543, or thereabouts, the question of Cranmer's orthodoxy again came up. His own prebendaries of Canterbury laid complaints against him for heresy. But the only result was that Henry, when he next met the Archbishop, made a joke of the matter, saying to Cranmer, "O my chaplain, now I know who is the greatest heretic in Kent!" As he gave Cranmer the paper in which the accusations were listed and told him that he might himself appoint the examiners and the judges, the Archbishop was naturally not only acquitted, but those who had accused him were obliged to ask his pardon.

There was a still more extraordinary instance of Henry's determination to protect a man whom he must have known to be a heretic but who offset this with a complete submission of all his opinions to the Head of the Church in England. The Catholic members of the Council had gone to the King saying: "He and all his learned men have so infected the whole realm with their unsavory doctrine that three parts of the people are abominable heretics." That was a gross exaggeration, for heresy had as yet infected only a few people, but it was true enough that the inroads of false doctrine were causing alarm. Henry agreed that the Archbishop should be put under arrest, but that same night gave Cranmer a ring telling him that when the Council committed him to the Tower, "Then appeal you from them unto our person, and give to them this ring by which they shall well understand that I have taken your cause into my hands from them."

The next day Cranmer was summoned at eight in the morning and kept waiting ignominiously at the door among the lackeys. But Morice hurried to Dr. Butts* who let Henry know what was happening, and when Cranmer was at last admitted to the Council chamber and was charged with being a heretic, he produced the ring, to the consternation of everyone there. Lord Russell, a time-server whose heart had never been in the plot against Cranmer, exclaimed, "Did I not tell you, my lords, what would come of this matter? I knew right well that the King would never permit my Lord of Canterbury to be imprisoned, unless it were for high treason." When the Council later went to the King he

---

* The appearance of Dr. Butts places this incident as before 1545, as in that year the doctor died.

stormed at them in his grandest manner: "I would you would well understand that I account my Lord of Canterbury as faithful a man towards me as ever was prelate in this realm." When Norfolk tried to explain that they intended only to send the Archbishop to the Tower so that he might emerge with all the greater glory after an acquittal, Henry was a little mollified, but said, "Well, I pray you use not my friend so. . . . There remaineth malice among you one to another; let it be avoided out of hand, I would advise you." After which, says Morice, nobody ever dared molest Cranmer again.

It came to this in his case, but in his case alone: so useful was he as a servant to Henry that he might believe as he please. He might hold, for example, as he did, regarding the Real Presence: "Figuratively [Christ] is the bread and wine, and spiritually He is in them that worthily eat and drink the bread and wine; but really, carnally, and corporally He is only in heaven" – a view worse than Lutheran, as it was Zwinglian. So long as Cranmer "officially" maintained the King's doctrine, nothing else mattered. This was something he was most careful to do.

Stubbs in one of many entertaining passages in his lectures has described Henry as wishing to be, "with regard to the Church of England, the pope, the whole pope, and something more than the pope." Yet Henry must have been aware that there could be no guarantee as to the orthodoxy of his successors. He must even have realized that after his death the Church would be ruled, like a state department, in the name of his young son by men who were already heretics at heart. One can therefore only conclude that, while priding himself upon his personal orthodoxy, he cared little about orthodoxy as such. The King's doctrine during Henry's reign remained Catholic, except in relation to the Papacy; but it is clear that Henry regarded the King's authority as of vastly greater importance than the doctrine itself.

CHAPTER SIXTEEN

The Fall of Cromwell

JUST after Henry had married Jane Seymour in May, 1536, Cromwell, discussing the matter with Chapuys, with whom he had a queer sort of friendship, assured him that the King, whatever had happened in the past, now intended to live chastely. As he spoke Cromwell, so Chapuys noticed, put his hand over his mouth to hide a grin. Nevertheless, Henry did, so far as we know, prove a faithful husband to Jane and, after her death, indulged in no affairs. He sincerely mourned her and arranged to be buried by her side.

If he remained a widower as long as he did, however, it was mainly because he thought that, when marrying again, it would be as well to make a diplomatic alliance. He let it be known that he would be pleased to bestow his hand on Mary of Guise, and he was distinctly annoyed when Francis I married her instead to James V of Scotland, Henry's nephew. But he still thought of a French marriage and suggested that a bevy of the most eligible high-born French ladies be sent to Calais so that he might have a chance to inspect them. When the eyebrows of the French Ambassador went up at this proposal and he said that they were not to be trotted out like so many hackneys — so could not the King send somebody to the French court to look over the field? — Henry retorted, "By God, I trust no one but myself! The thing touches me too near. I wish to see them and know them some time before deciding."

Charles for his part was not slow in dangling marriage possibilities before Henry, as he had done the moment he had heard of Anne Boleyn's fall. He suggested again the widowed Duchess of Milan, whose previous marriage was certified to have been merely nominal, and who was reputed to be a great beauty. As a husband for Mary he proposed at the same time Don Loys, the Infante of Portugal, an arrangement that would make the alliance doubly sure. The Duchess, however, had a mind of her own and is reported to have remarked that she would not mind marrying the King of England if she had two heads on her shoulders. And Henry was stubborn about Mary's bastardization, as to remove it might look like an admission that he had been really married to her mother. The upshot was that Charles and Francis eventually dropped Henry and drew together, making first, through the mediation of the Pope, a ten years' truce in June, 1538, and eighteen months later an alliance. This meant that Henry, if he wished a diplomatic marriage, would have to look elsewhere.

Cromwell had from time to time since 1533 flirted diplomatically with the German Lutheran states. But the bar to a German marriage was that the German Princes of the Smalcaldic League were as firmly set in their Lutheranism (at least for political purposes) as Henry was in his own brand of Catholicism. The efforts made in 1535 and again in 1538 for a religious rapprochement, with a political object in view, had failed. The only other lady who seemed eligible was Anne, the sister of the Duke of Cleves. He had not definitely gone over to the Protestant camp, but his maintenance of friendly relations with the Protestant princes of the Empire meant, it was hoped, that Henry would eventually be able to reach an understanding with them and yet escape accepting their obnoxious theology. The Duke of Cleves, though not a very important personage, might in this way be useful to him; Henry even expressed the pious hope that, with the Duke as an intermediary, he might help to compose the religious dissensions in Germany. But of course in all this he was not foregoing remarriage as a means of obtaining another male heir. The life of the sickly Edward was too frail a thread upon which to hang his dynasty.

Cromwell undertook to manage the affair, and promoted it so actively as to bring about his own downfall. He assured Henry that Anne of Cleves outshone the Duchess of Milan as the sun outshines the moon,* and to prove this he sent over Holbein with a commission to paint Anne's portrait.

This portrait we have, and if Henry was satisfied with the looks of the lady as she was depicted, he must have been easily satisfied. But if it is true that the portrait flattered her, discreetly removing Anne's pockmarks and imparting a bloom to her complexion, Henry had some right to feel that he had been badly used. Anne was decidedly plain and, as it came out later, ungainly and uncouth. Yet, if we may judge from the Holbein painting, she was not much below the average of Henry's wives in this respect, and we can all sympathize with Bishop Stubbs's comment on "the deadly-lively sort of ladies whose portraits are, if not a justification, at least a colorable occasion for understanding the readiness with which he put them away." This does not explain, however, why he chose them in the first instance, for all of them, with the exception of Anne of Cleves, were evidently to his taste at the time he married them. In this case he was startled and horrified at what he found he had let himself in for.

Those who had been sent to escort Anne to England – four hundred gentlemen, with the Earl of Southampton at their head – were dismayed at what they saw, though they had had nothing to do with the selection. Here was their future queen, a woman absolutely devoid of all accomplishments, who could neither sing nor play on any musical instrument, and was awkward at dancing. Moreover, she knew no language except German, not even much of the lingua franca of colloquial Latin with which she could have talked to Henry while she was learning a little English. During the fifteen days she had to wait at Calais for the weather to clear, Southampton taught her to play cards, to give

*They had to ignore the fact that Anne was twice as old as the Duchess. She would have had to be beautiful indeed to offset that.

her some means of amusing the King. And to make the best of a bad situation he wrote to Henry praising her appearance. Yet he and all the members of Anne's escort felt sure the bridegroom would be far from pleased with the thirty-four-year-old bride they were bringing him. She was, they could see, quiet and simple and kind and sensible, but they feared that the King would not consider this enough. One of her few redeeming features was that, though her appetite was enormous, she was, for a German, moderate in her use of beer.

That her clothes were dowdy, or looked so on her, was perhaps something that could be rectified later. But they knew that this would make a bad initial impression. To make that impression worse was the appearance of her ladies-in-waiting. Regarding this the French Ambassador reported to his court that they were "dressed so heavily and unbecomingly that they would be thought ugly, even if they were beautiful." Southampton and those with him were certain that the King was in for a terrific shock.

Henry was now nearly fifty, yet he had been so worked up by the accounts that had reached him of Anne's charms, that he hurried down to Rochester to meet her, so great was his romantic impatience. But just what everybody feared would happen did happen; he was so "marvellously astonished and abashed" at the sight of her that he felt at once "a discontentment and disliking of her person." After a few moments he could stand it no longer and left in an ominous silence. He had "busied not to speak with her twenty words." To Sir Anthony Browne he said glumly, "Say what they will, she is nothing so fair as has been reported." To others he said even worse.

Cromwell tried to bring Henry round by suggesting that Anne had "a queenly manner," and other people tried to soothe him regarding her lack of accomplishments by telling him that in Germany they take it "for rebuke and an occasion of lightness that great ladies should be learned or have any knowledge of music." Such mild recommendations weighed little against Henry's strong repugnance.

His meeting with her was on January 1, 1540, and the marriage had been arranged for the 6th. There was still one desperate chance that he might escape: a bare possibility that a precontract could be established between Anne and the Duke of Lorraine. When it was shown that Lorraine had signed a complete discharge, Henry could only groan and ask, "Is there then no remedy, but that I must needs, against my will, put my neck into this yoke?"

Remedy there was none. The Emperor and Francis had, on the very day of Anne's arrival in England, signed, through their envoys, a pact in Paris. At that of all moments Henry dared not give what would be a mortal affront, not only to the Duke of Cleves himself but to all the German princes whom he hoped to win to an alliance through this marriage. While dressing himself on his wedding morning Henry said to Cromwell, "My lord, if it were not to satisfy the world and my realm, I would not do what I must do this day for none earthly thing." Into the yoke the unwilling head went.

The morning after the marriage Henry confided further to Cromwell about his "Flanders Mare": "Surely, my lord, I liked her not well before, but now I like her much worse." It was noted, as Stow records, that from that time the King "was in a manner weary of his life."

The situation was now really serious. Cromwell knew that, as the marriage had been part of his policy and had not brought any tangible diplomatic profit, he was himself in considerable danger. It was obvious that Henry was already seized by a new fit of superstition; he was beginning to convince himself that his unconquerable repugnance to Anne was a sign that God was displeased with him. In perfect innocence of course he had made another of his matrimonial errors and had entangled himself in a marriage that was no marriage.

This time it seems likely that there really was no marriage. For as Cromwell said to Wriothesley on June 7, "The King loves not the Queen, nor ever has from the beginning; insomuch as I think assuredly she is as yet as good a maid as when she came to England." To which Wriothesley returned, "For God's sake devise how his Grace may be relieved by one way or the other." Cromwell merely shrugged his shoulders and asked, "But what and how?"

A divorce might be a solution, but apart from the danger of making Henry appear ridiculous, it was also sure to make enemies of the German princes. And how the Pope would laugh! And what a sardonic grin would come from the long-chinned Emperor! England would be left friendless in the world just when it needed friends most. Cromwell had hoped at first that Henry would come to like his wife a bit after marriage; when he saw that there was no chance of that, he was obliged, as foreign minister, to point out to the King the perils of repudiating Anne.

Henry's resentment was mounting. If Cromwell, who had got him into this position, would not get him out of it, there were others who might — the clever Mr. Wriothesley, for instance. He had begun to whisper to the King that he did not believe that a German alliance was of much value. If that were so, why not cut the knot, wipe the slate clean, and make a new beginning? Henry was, in his slow, secretive way, reaching the point of exasperation at which he would explode and take a savage revenge.

Cromwell, whether he knew it or not, had been on very uncertain ground for some time. He had maintained himself by being useful to the King. Now his usefulness appeared to be over: he had thoroughly subdued all the bishops as the King's Vicar-General; he had despoiled in March the last of the great abbeys, that of Waltham. But his foreign policy, which he had never been able to play with Wolsey's masterly skill, had reached the dismal eventuation of the Cleves marriage. His enemies — and he had no friends, except perhaps Cranmer — thought their chance had come. Sir William Paulet assured them, "The King calleth him villain, knave, bobs him about the head, and thrusts him out of the privy chamber." If only a little of this was true,

Cromwell's enemies knew that they could safely gather to the attack.

The courtiers understood the position of the officials they all detested. The King looked upon their unpopularity as, up to a certain point, enhancing their value by making them directly dependent upon him, for they had no powerful class to stand behind them and give them support. This meant that, except for those who were actively supported by the King, they were weaker even than the clergy. The courtiers knew that it was Henry's way to conceal his dislike of any man he had determined to ruin and to smile upon him as affably as ever while laying a trap.

The nobles constituted a closed corporation, although within it there were animosities. But this time the new men would be in full accord with the older aristocracy; the Seymours and the Howards would work as one. And among the officials it was always a case of each man playing his own hand, working with his eye on the job of the man above him. Wriothesley and Audley and Rich owed their advancement to Cromwell; this would not prevent them from joining the pack that was noiselessly closing in.

The clergy, too, would be with them, and the timid Cranmer would not dare to say a word but would think only of saving his own neck. If the nobles had scores to settle with Cromwell for the treason trials of their friends – for when they had turned in their verdicts of guilty this was only because they could not help themselves – the bishops had had much to suffer at the hands of this vulgar layman who had been set above them. Now Cromwell's enemies on the Council could and did discreetly drop into the King's ears – which at that moment were very receptive – things that beautifully accorded with the suspicions that, in Henry's case, were so easily to be aroused. They understood the King very well, and they had gauged the situation correctly.

Henry nevertheless remained for some time very hesitant.

It was not part of his make-up ever to be grateful; rather he considered that those whom he had appointed to high place should be grateful to him. But he was still not sure whether Cromwell's unpopularity was not going to be as useful to him as it had been in the past; he reckoned it a bad sign when a member of the official class was not heartily disliked. Moreover, he could see no man in those round him equal to Cromwell in ability. Gardiner perhaps, but Gardiner was a cleric, and the day when a cleric was put in command in England was over. Norfolk? Well, the Duke was serviceable but hardly more. Edward Seymour was more of a soldier than a statesman, and his brother, the loud-swearing, jovial Thomas, was only a boon companion. Audley, Paget, Paulet, Wriothesley, Rich – none of them were anywhere near the efficient Cromwell as a manager of Parliament. It was now packed with his men, ready to do his (and therefore the King's) bidding.

Cromwell proved his parliamentary ability when the new Parliament met by putting through a bill suppressing that immensely rich order of chivalry, the Knights of St. John.* As they had become an anachronism, there was no special outcry against their spoliation. And on top of all this Cromwell enforced a subsidy of four shillings in the pound from the clergy and a tax of four-fifteenths from the temporality. It was all carried through so smoothly and swiftly that those not in the inmost circle of all came to believe that once again Cromwell had redeemed himself. On April 11 he was created Earl of Essex, the day after Marillac the French Ambassador had written to Francis: "If he remains in his former credit and authority, it will only be because he is very assiduous in affairs."

Cromwell remained assiduous to the end, but so did his enemies. As usual with Henry there was a long period of weaving and wavering, and though the earldom conferred in April may

*Some years later these knights, alone among the religious, except those whom Cromwell had taken it upon him to dispense, were freed from their vows of celibacy.

have been merely a means of masking the King's intentions, it would seem to reflect at least a passing mood of approval. It was taken by the world as a sign that Cromwell was, after all, to be retained in power – perhaps to go even higher.

The new Earl apparently thought so too. He was enjoying his new rank and felt himself safe. When the blow fell it caught him completely off his guard. On June 10 – significantly three days after the conversation with Wriothesley in which Cromwell had said he did not know how to get the King released from his marriage – he had attended a sitting of the House of Lords in the morning and in the afternoon went to the palace of Westminster to a meeting of the Privy Council. At the stroke of three, a carefully prearranged moment, the Duke of Norfolk rose in his place and said, "My Lord of Essex, I arrest you of high treason."

The Lieutenant of the Tower was waiting outside the door of the council chamber. He entered with a couple of his halberdiers to take Cromwell prisoner. The accused man had jumped to his feet and in an outburst of passion he flung his cap to the floor, shouting, "This then, is my guerdon for the service I have done! On your consciences, I ask you, am I a traitor?" But when he looked at the hard malignant faces he saw that his doom was already decided, so he added more quietly, "If the King my master believes so ill of me, let him make quick work and not leave me to languish in prison."

Norfolk strode up to him and tore the St. George from his neck. The Earl of Southampton, who pretended to be his friend, stripped off the Garter. Then the prisoner was led to a side door where a barge was waiting, and he was conducted at once to the Tower. The people of London had no suspicion as to what had happened until late that afternoon they saw Sir Thomas Cheyney, the Treasurer of the Household, and two guards entering Cromwell's house.

His papers were seized in the hope of finding something that might be used to prove treason. Nothing was found except what showed, what was already well known, that he had been working hand-in-glove with heretics. The inventory of his personal effects turned out to be less than had been expected – only about £7,000 in money, with rather more than that in plate. This included, as Marillac wrote, "Many crosses, chalices, mitres, vases and other spoils of the Church." These were immediately carried to the royal treasury, a clear indication that the King had no intention of restoring them. If the money and other articles did not amount to the immense sum pictured by popular imagination, it was still very great, about £350,000 in modern values. The abbatial mitres, and possibly also some of the Church plate, had been kept not so much out of greed as because Cromwell was a connoisseur of *objets de vertu*. None of this, however, takes into account the estates he had been given by the Crown, or the estates he had bought on very easy terms, or the buildings he had put up. Cromwell had made himself very rich. If he was not as rich as people had supposed, this was partly because he had maintained an expensive private secret service. It must be added that, though he was in all conscience greedy enough, he preferred power to money.

All sorts of charges were brought against him. Some were well based, others were ridiculous. He was even accused of having plotted to marry the Lady Mary. His son had married Jane Seymour's sister, the widow of Sir Anthony Ughtred, and perhaps this was why this youth, harmless almost to the point of idiocy, was exempted from the effects of the attainder passed against his father.* But Mary was a different story; even as one technically bastardized, she was still considered as being potentially a valuable pawn in the diplomatic game.

Much more to the point was what Paulet said about him just before his fall, and which was said again afterwards: "He is the greatest briber [accepter of bribes] in England. The King has six times as much revenues as any of his noble progenitors ever had, and all is consumed and gone to naught by means of my

*Sir Richard Cromwell, his nephew, was also spared.

Lord Privy Seal, who ravens all that he can get." This, though true enough, bore still more heavily on Henry than on Cromwell himself. It was the King's extravagance that was at fault.

For this reason there was no mention in the act of attainder about the amount of money that had run through Henry's fingers during Cromwell's administration. So also with those unjustly put to death by Cromwell; it was done always at the King's instance. But there was mention of his acceptance of bribes and of his extortion, though apparently what was regarded as an offence of equal magnitude was that "being thus enriched, he had held the nobles in disdain." Yet there was hardly treason in any of this, nor "in disturbing the faith of the King's subjects on the nature of the Eucharist and other articles of the Christian faith." For doing so, as for having "granted licenses to persons detected or openly defamed of heresy to teach and preach," he should have been made subject to the laws against heresy rather than to treason. But of course a charge of heresy would have permitted Cromwell to escape by recantation, and it was settled that he should die.

One of the articles in his attainder seems to have referred to Cranmer, for in it Cromwell is said, when complaints had been made against particular heretics and heresies, to have "terribly rebuked their accusers." It was certainly what he had done in the case of the bearward who tried to give proofs to the Council of the Archbishop's dissent from the Six Articles. The result had been that "the King's good subjects had been in fear to detect the said heretics and heresies."

Cromwell had undoubtedly protected Dr. Barnes, but Henry had used Barnes when it had suited his book. It was utterly incredible that the accused man had ever said, when upholding Barnes's preaching: "If the King should turn from it, yet would I not turn; and if the King did turn, and all his people, I would fight in the field with my sword in my hand, against him and all others; and if I live a year or two, it will not lie in the King's power to let [prevent] it if he would." Nobody knew better than Cromwell that he held power, as Wolsey had held power, only by the King's favour, and that he could be destroyed whenever the King chose. Nevertheless, if treason be given the wide meaning it had at this time, and be made to include things done to the grave detriment of the realm, nobody was more deeply stained with treason than Cromwell. Whatever deficiency there was in legal correctness, Cromwell unquestionably deserved his fate.

Cranmer, realizing his own extreme danger, wrote to the King a letter in a similar vein to the one he had written upon the fall of his patroness, Anne Boleyn. Froude discovers courage in this; I can see only terror. Whatever is said in Cromwell's defence is put up only to be thrown down. What each letter conveys to the King is that Cranmer is glad that the true nature of the accused had at last come to light (though of course the discovery pains him), and an assurance that he, Cranmer, is in no way implicated. "I heard yesterday in your Grace's Council," Cranmer wrote on June 14, "that the Earl of Essex is a traitor; yet who can be more sorrowful and amazed that he should be a traitor against your Majesty – he who loved your Majesty, as I ever thought, no less than God – he who studied always to set forwards whatever was your Majesty's will and pleasure – he that was such a servant, in my judgement, in wisdom, diligence, faithfulness, and experience as no prince in this realm ever had – he that was so vigilant to preserve your Majesty from all treasons, that few could be so secretly conceived but he detected the same in the beginning! – I loved him as my friend, for so I took him to be; but I chiefly loved him for the love which I thought I saw him bear ever towards your Grace, singularly shown above all others. But now, if he be a traitor, I am sorry that ever I loved or trusted him; and I am very glad that his treason is discovered in time; but yet again, I am very sorrowful; for who shall your Grace trust hereafter, if you may not trust him? Alas! I lament your Grace's chance therein. I wot not whom your Grace may trust." I leave it to the reader's judgement whether that is a brave defence or a cowardly betrayal.

Cromwell was not given any trial but was condemned by attainder, a method that seems (and is) monstrous, unless it be used to give statutory force to a verdict previously reached by a court of justice. It is often said, a little inaccurately, that Cromwell had himself introduced this method of dispatching victims, as being surer and swifter than a trial. What he had actually done was to use attainders so freely that what was not his invention came to be closely associated with his name. It was therefore something fitting that he should now be condemned in this way.

A bill of attainder had the advantage of implicating Parliament – and in a sense the whole nation – in what was done. It had, however (or might have), one drawback: Parliament might vote it out. It was because of this imminent possibility in the case of Sir Thomas More early in 1534 that Cromwell himself had advised the King to drop that name from the bill. There was not the slightest danger of this happening now. Though the House of Commons had been largely picked by Cromwell's own hand – so that he was able to write to Henry, "I and your dedicate Councillors be about to bring all things to pass that your Grace never had more tractable Parliament" – his own nominees voted against him, along with the men whose careers he had made possible. Rich – since 1536 the Speaker of the Commons – Audley and Wriothesley without any trace of compunction voted his death. The bill passed on June 29, less than three weeks after Cromwell's arrest. By it he was declared to be both traitor and heretic,* and, as such, liable to the kind of execution that Father John Forest had suffered a couple of years previously.

He was not executed at once but kept waiting a month. The reason for this was that Henry still had an important service for Cromwell to perform. Cromwell quite understood that only by performing it to the fullest satisfaction could he escape hanging at Tyburn or burning at Smithfield. In other words, he was to purchase the merciful death of the axe by giving written evidence

*Parliament had no competence in this matter, as under the law the trials of heretics were in the hands of the ordinaries. But heresy was of course thrown in merely for good measure.

in support of the suit for divorce Henry had decided to bring against Anne of Cleves. Cromwell had tried to shrug the matter off in conversation with Wriothesley on June 7 by saying that he did not see what could be done about it. Very well, he should be the one to do it now.

Henry had talked to others of his courtiers about his disgust with his bride from Germany, but to none of them so freely or explicitly as he had done to Cromwell. That the King could speak of his wife (or any woman) in the gross terms he used with his fallen minister does him little credit, but that he had done so was fortunate for him, as it established (if this evidence is to be believed) the nullity of the Cleves marriage on the ground that it was never actually consummated because of Henry's repugnance to the person of his bride. Cromwell in the Tower was taken over the ground again and was asked all kinds of most intimate questions regarding what the King had told him, and to all of them he gave the kind of answers that he knew the King required. But they were probably substantially accurate. He signed the long document, "Thomas Cromwell, Shearman," to emphasize his degradation, and then further degraded himself voluntarily with the famous postscript, "Mercy! Mercy! Mercy!"

Anne might have contested (truthfully or not) the statements made by Cromwell. Like a sensible woman she did nothing of the kind, but did all she could to facilitate her divorce. She was rewarded with an income of £4,000 a year, a couple of manors, each with a fine house and a spacious park, and the title of the King's Sister. This would give her precedence over all the ladies of England except the King's children and the Queen, when Henry should marry again. On July 9 convocation declared the marriage invalid and three days later this was ratified by Parliament.* The condition imposed on Anne that she remain in England — nobody wanted her to go off to Germany bearing tales — was placidly accepted by her. She could not have had

* This act was one of many such obsolete statutes whose repeal was voted in Parliament 400 years later, on June 4, 1948. One wonders why.

half so comfortable a life in Cleves as in her "brother's" realm, where she was free to marry, should she come across anybody with sufficient hardihood. She settled down to enjoy herself and remained on such good terms with Henry that several times there were rumours that he intended to take her back. It was in England that she lived for the rest of his reign, seeing him marry two more wives, conforming herself to whatever was required in religion, and dying the year before Elizabeth came to the throne. So far from there being any need to be sorry for Anne of Cleves, she may be called quite the luckiest of the women Henry married.

On July 28 Cromwell was led out to die. Those who had known him in the height of his power were surprised when he whined so abjectly for mercy. They thought that he would show more stoicism. Though they hated him they believed he had more iron in his nature. Cromwell, however, may have hoped that he would be spared; he knew that Henry would sometimes respond to a sufficiently abject appeal, that he liked the feeling of being "clement" to those who acknowledged themselves in the wrong. He may also have counted upon some such vacillation of the King's mind as he had witnessed in the case of Wolsey. Henry had regretted the loss of the services of so able a man, and Cromwell, though not of Wolsey's abilities, was the ablest man then at the King's disposition.

At the end he made a speech which, according to Foxe the martyrologist, who places the Hammer of the Monks, "the subverter of the synagogue of Antichrist," among his heroes, was most edifyingly Protestant, and even tender in its piety. Another version makes him say: "I die in the Catholic faith, not doubting in any article of my faith. . . . I confess, that like as God, by His holy Spirit, doth instruct us in truth, so the devil is ready to seduce us – and I have been seduced." Though Reginald Pole was inclined to doubt whether he really did repent, and though it is true that the Vicar-General of the Head of the Church in England had tended to further the Protestant cause, so far as he dared, we know (what Pole did not know) that Cromwell had left money for Masses to be said for the repose of his soul, so we may infer that the destruction of the monasteries and the favouring of such men as Cranmer and Barnes were based solely on political considerations. It seems more charitable to believe that, when faced with the ultimate reality, Thomas Cromwell did utter something like an act of contrition on the scaffold.

The block was, even as he experienced it, more merciful than the stake or the disembowelling at the gallows; but the headsman – according to Hall, "a ragged and miserly butcher, who very ungoodly performed his office" – bungled his job, perhaps because he was new in it or nervous or drunk. A number of blows were necessary to remove the round Cromwellian head from its short, thick neck. Like Anne Boleyn, he died unlamented, but he was not a man wantonly cruel, and his private morals had (at least from the time that he appears in history) been exemplary. Something may be accorded to him on this score, but he was greedy and corrupt and nobody had ever applied more ruthlessly the Machiavellian maxims. Though not a man of genius, but rather a perfect example of the difference between the efficient man and the inspired man, his work remained. He had created the Henrician Church and therefore had laid the foundations of the Protestant Church of England as by law established.

Two days after his execution there were six others. Henry with fine impartiality burned to death at Smithfield Dr. Barnes and Thomas Garret and William Jerome (all three of them priests) for heresy and sent to the same place three other priests to be hanged for treason. Two of them, Thomas Abell and Richard Featherstone, had been in Katherine of Aragon's service, the one as her chaplain, the other as tutor to the Princess Mary. The third man was Dr. Edward Powell. Like Abell he had been in the Tower since 1534. He was dragged to Smithfield on the same hurdle with Barnes.

All six men deserve more than a bare mention of their names at this place, but one of them, Robert Barnes, must have a few further words as his execution accentuated Cromwell's downfall and was a victory for Stephen Gardiner. Barnes, it will be remembered, had been prior of the Augustinian friars at Cambridge when he was thirty, at which time he had been convicted of heresy and had recanted. He was later used by Henry to try to persuade the Lutheran divines to approve of his divorce from Katherine of Aragon and in 1535 was one of the commissioners sent to Wittenberg to reach, if possible, a compromise with the German theologians. His real offence now was that he had been one of those used by Cromwell to negotiate the marriage with Anne of Cleves. Cromwell had rewarded him by making him a prebendary, but Barnes was so injudicious as to attack the orthodox Gardiner in a scurrilous sermon delivered at Paul's Cross on the first Sunday in Lent, February 15, 1540. When Gardiner demanded a discussion before indifferent judges Barnes found it prudent to confess himself confuted by the Bishop's arguments. However, when (like Garret and Jerome) he was ordered to preach a recantation sermon during Holy Week, he (again like the others) did so in a way considered so unsatisfactory that all three of them were committed to the Tower.

This was an embarrassment to Cromwell, who was aware that he was in some danger, even though he did not realize how great it was. He and Gardiner met on March 30 and after what seemed a friendly conversation lasting four hours, were thought to have patched up their differences. Their reconciliation must have been less complete than appeared on the surface, for a few days later there was some talk of appointing Tunstall, the strictly orthodox Bishop of Durham, the King's Vicar-General in place of Cromwell. Though shortly after Cromwell was created Earl of Essex his fate, if not yet determined upon, was already inevitable.

Barnes and his fellow-Protestants died as one of the consequences of Cromwell's fall; the Catholic martyrs apparently were dragged out to death at the same time for no other reason than that Henry wished to demonstrate that an orthodox reaction was not going to mean any lessening of his claims to spiritual supremacy. As Marillac, the French Ambassador, wrote to his King, it was a "strange spectacle." He commented further: "Of the iniquity of the system no further evidence is needed than these executions. . . . It is no easy thing to keep a people in revolt against the Holy See, and the authority of the Church, and yet free from the infection of the new doctrine — or, on the other hand, if they remain orthodox, to prevent them from looking with attachment to the Papacy."

The shrewd Marillac was right: it could be brought about in the end by only one way — that of teaching the English people to hate Catholicism as well as the pope.

CHAPTER SEVENTEEN

Cross Currents

THE last years of Henry's reign, those that follow the fall of Cromwell, seem, when compared with what had gone before, almost an anticlimax. Important events happened, and yet they appear to be scantly significant. The Scottish invasion of England and the English invasions of Scotland were routine affairs, and bore no results. The last war with France was, if possible, even less glorious than those that had preceded it in 1513 and 1522–1523. The one really decisive event was the one that did not happen, but that many people more than half expected would happen: this of course was a reconciliation with the Holy See.

With the fall of Cromwell it looked for a while as though a strong Catholic reaction were about to set in. It was not that Henry himself became more orthodox, for orthodox he had never ceased to be; it was that the forces which had been secretly working for further religious changes were now blocked. Cranmer was indeed left as primate, but without Cromwell's protection he dared not make the smallest move in the direction of Protestantism. Things remained in a state of precarious equilibrium. When in 1545 the Archbishop produced his masterpiece, his Litany, though it contained the verse (since deleted), "From the tyranny of the Bishop of Rome and all his detestable enormities, good Lord, deliver us," it also contained petitions thoroughly Catholic in sentiment – invocations to the Virgin, the saints, patriarchs, apostles, and martyrs. Though by that time Cranmer had regained his influence with the King, he recognized that Henry would tolerate no heresy.

During the second half of 1540, and the months following, there seemed to be some chance of England's restoration to Catholic unity. Now was the moment – one of many that occurred, but perhaps the best – for bringing this about. Cromwell was gone, and he could be conveniently blamed for everything. And though the seizure of the monastic lands (now complete) was a barrier to reconciliation with Rome, it was not an insuperable one. That this was so was proved not long afterwards in Mary's reign, when an arrangement was reached with the Holy See that the new possessors of those lands were not to be disturbed.*

Perhaps even Henry's title as Head of the Church could have been left to him, had an explanation been given that it was to be understood as extending only to temporalities, not differing in essence, though perhaps slightly more extended in scope, than the lordship which English kings had been accustomed to exercise over the Church during the Middle Ages. In other words, something along the lines of the concordat made between Francis I and the Holy See, and with perhaps even better terms for Henry than Francis obtained, was perfectly feasible.

The factor that really prevented any such arrangement being

---

*The possession of these lands by the new owners operated of course as a deterring fear, though I do not believe that it was designed by Cromwell, as Mr. Belloc so confidently asserts, as a means of preventing reunion. But the fear largely accounts for Elizabeth's being steered, against her private inclination, in a Protestant direction. And when in James II England again had a Catholic King, he published in 1686 a sermon by one of his chaplains, the Benedictine Philip Ellis, declaring in the name of his order that no claim would ever be made for any of the land formerly belonging to it. For that matter, as late as 1826 the vicars apostolic of England took it upon themselves publicly to disavow any right to the property of "the Established Church in England." The matter still rests upon individual consciences, as was shown by the action of the nephew and heir of Lord Lothian, a recent British ambassador to the United States, when of his own free will he made a restoration of property that had been seized from the monks by his ancestors in Henry's reign. Queen Mary made a serious political mistake when she insisted on restoring £60,000 a year, what was by that time left to the Crown of the monastic loot. Her delicate conscience must be commended, but it would have been wiser to have accepted the Bull of Julius III to the letter, so as not to make other owners of former monastic property nervous.

reached was Henry's obstinacy, one of the marks of his immature mind. He demanded, as a preliminary to all discussion, that Paul III should admit that Clement VII had made a mistaken decision regarding the divorce from Katherine. With this went a steadily increasing sense of his self-importance. His deprivation had been attempted and had failed, and this left him with an additional grievance against the Papacy. Everybody had wronged and betrayed him; he now intended to show the world that he could stand alone. And he meant to prove that he was a better guardian of the Faith in England than any pope or bishop had been. Though from time to time he felt some qualms and was, right to the end, at moments half inclined to close the quarrel, his inclination for this was never strong enough, or was always stifled by some consideration that made that particular time seem inopportune. Therefore all conciliatory moves failed, though hope was never quite abandoned.

Those hopes rose very high when, on August 8, 1540, thirty days after Henry had divorced Anne of Cleves,* he married again, and this time took as bride Catherine Howard. It was a marriage promoted by Stephen Gardiner, the Bishop of Winchester, the ablest man now left and the ecclesiastical leader of the Catholic party.

In marrying Anne of Cleves Henry imagined that he was doing something that would be diplomatically useful. It had turned out to have little or no political value, and the King was so disgusted with the bride he had received that he would not even think of making such a marriage again. This time he would select an Englishwoman of high rank, whose charms he could discover for himself before putting his head into the yoke. Catherine, who, like Anne Boleyn, was a niece of the Duke of

*It would probably be a little rash to say that Rome would have recognized this divorce and the validity of the new marriage. But in face of the evidence presented to Convocation, and the declaration made by Convocation, it would appear likely that no difficulty would have been raised by the Pope. At any rate there were none of the political complications that had existed in the case of Katherine of Aragon.

Norfolk, was young and daintily built and dark, a sufficiently strong contrast to the big blonde German *Hausfrau* of whom he had just rid himself. Though the painting of her in the National Portrait Gallery hardly shows her as beautiful, Catherine was at least good looking as compared with the Flanders Mare. In marrying her the fat, senile Henry felt that he had recaptured his youth.

The Howards now came into the ascendancy, though without quite eclipsing the Seymours. For even if Catherine bore a son, Edward would remain the heir to the throne; only in the event of the little Prince's death would the aristocratic Howards be able to eject the Seymours from their position as expectant governors of England in their nephew's name. Even so, the marriage represented a triumph for the aristocracy of England. The Duke of Norfolk had always been regarded as a focal point round which they might rally.

The Howards were also, rather oddly, looked upon as the leaders — on its secular side — of the Catholic party. They had no definite religious convictions — any more than their parvenu connections the Boleyns — but in much the same way as the Boleyns had been thought of as being in favour of religious change, the Howards, and nobles of their type, were thought of as being in favour of preventing religious changes being carried any further. The Duke's most memorable contribution to theological controversy was a boast that he had never read the Bible. It was scarcely sufficient to make him the champion of the Catholic cause. Nevertheless, this time-serving politician, of little talent but of ruthless cruelty and perfidy, was looked upon as the man who, through the new Queen, might help in bringing England back into communion with Rome.

Religiously, however, England remained in much the same condition as before, with a capricious tyranny continuing. It was on May 28, 1541 — less than a year after Henry had married in Catherine the hope of the Catholics — that the Countess of Salisbury was at last led out, at the age of seventy, to die at the block. On the other side of the ledger was the burning of an eighteen-year-old lad named Richard Mekins for maintaining consubstantiation.

He was one of the victims of the Six Articles which, when they were enforced, were far more stringent than the old statutes against heresy. He was prepared to abjure, but his abjuration was not accepted. Edmund Bonner, since 1539 Bishop of London, though he could not save him, treated him with the kindest consideration, as Mekins confessed at Smithfield. But he at least knew why he was condemned and was sincerely repentant. Lady Salisbury never was told even of what it was she was charged. But of course she knew: her real offence was that of being Cardinal Pole's mother and of being resolute in her Catholic loyalty.

These events were soon forgotten in the scandal that overwhelmed the Queen.

Of all his wives the only one who had ever really loved Henry was Katherine of Aragon. Of all his wives the one who loved him least was Catherine Howard. But what counts in the story is that Henry loved *her*. There was not here the kind of half-insane passion he had felt for Anne Boleyn, for the time for that sort of thing was long past. But there was a doting on his part for the girl, which, when seen in an old man, covers all beholders with embarrassment and contempt. It would have been felt to be almost obscene had it not been so ridiculous. And Henry was so entirely bemused that, in the vast ignorance of women which is one of his chief characteristics, he was greatly taken with her "maidenly manner."

His awakening was really cruel.

In June the King and his young Queen made a state visit to the North, accompanied in their slow progress by four or five thousand people. Everywhere Henry and Catherine were received with adulation, and in several places ceremonies of pardon were staged for those who had been implicated, however slightly and unwillingly (in the case of the gentry), in the Pilgrimage of Grace. As there could now be no doubt in anybody's mind as to the King's power to put down any rebellion, and a vivid memory remained of how savage repression had been, Henry could afford to extract profit from a display of his clemency.

No man in the world could be more affable than Henry when he chose, and he was, in fact, feeling very mellow just then. Though there were every now and then fierce pangs from the sore on his leg, and these made him roar with rage, he was, except at such times, in the best of humours. This was his Indian Summer, and he basked in it, luxuriating in the love he was receiving (as he supposed) from Catherine. His only disappointment was that his nephew, the young King James V of Scotland, refused to fall into the trap prepared for him and excused himself from meeting Henry at York.

In the absence of the royal pair the enemies of the Howards had been busy. The Seymours cared no more for religion than the Duke of Norfolk did, but they stood in much the same relation to the new things as Norfolk did to the old. Though Catherine had shown no sign as yet of producing a child, she might still do so, prematurely old though the King was, and a son would enhance her position and that of her family. Should the sickly little Prince of Wales die, it would mean the total eclipse of the new, the "advanced" men. Accordingly they conspired to destroy her, just as, before the end, they succeeded in destroying the Duke himself and the Duke's heir.

They were too wary to come out openly against Catherine, lest their plot should go awry. They therefore chose as their instrument a man who could not be suspected of having any personal animosities or personal ambitions, but one whose position was now very insecure and who would leap at this chance of re-establishing himself. This was Thomas Cranmer, the Archbishop of Canterbury, whose further qualification for the work he was to undertake was that he had several times proved a master hand at betraying people, always of course with sorrow visible on his gentle face.

Cranmer need not be suspected of being particularly anxious to get Catherine Howard removed as an obstacle to further religious reform. In that regard Cranmer had discovered that she was quite null. Nor was there anything much to be feared from the Howard family, for they had in fifteen months done nothing except sit tight, holding on to what they had got out of the loot of the monasteries. If there was any religious consideration in Cranmer's mind, it was only the possibility that, in bringing Catherine down, the Catholic Gardiner might be brought down at the same time. He had promoted this marriage, in somewhat the same way that Cromwell had promoted the King's marriage to Anne of Cleves. There was a difference of course: for where Henry loathed Anne, he was enamoured of Catherine. But his recoil might, for that very reason, be all the greater; the plan was at least worth trying.

In all this there was a tangle of motives. The one openly professed was that of zeal for the "Gospel," of which Gardiner was a notorious enemy. Cranmer knew that Gardiner would be delighted to be able to convict him of heresy and he fancied, perhaps not without reason, that mingled with the concern for orthodoxy the Bishop of Winchester had always shown was a smarting sense of disappointment that he had not been made archbishop of Canterbury. Here was a wonderful opportunity for striking at him through the Queen.

The royal couple were gone long enough to allow full investigations to be made. The first clues as to Catherine's conduct before marriage may have come to light by chance. However that may be, they were promptly followed up. Further informers were sought out and spies put to work, Cranmer, who had had contacts in the past with Cromwell's secret service, being useful in getting hold of its former agents. By the time Henry and his bride were back at Hampton Court the mine was ready to be touched off.

On All Saints' Day, November 1, the King and Queen attended Mass, as they did every day, and Henry made one of his frequent Communions, Catherine receiving the Host by his side. Following Mass he ordered the celebrant, his chaplain, John Longland, Bishop of Lincoln, to intone a *Te Deum* in thanksgiving for the pleasant life the King was having with his modest and maidenly wife. That day they were allowed to remain undisturbed. Indecent haste might be inadvisable; on the other hand, those who had been gathering their information might be considered negligent in duty if they waited too long. Besides, if they did not present their information, it might reach the King from unauthorized sources. News of this explosive sort had to be handled carefully but also without delay.

The very next morning, the Day of the Dead, when Henry was again at Mass, Cranmer slipped into the chapel and put a paper into his hand. Just what was written on it we do not know, but we can be sure of its gist: "It has been proved that the Queen is guilty of wantonness." Cranmer could be very terse on occasion, as the collects of the *Book of Common Prayer* attest, and though at other times he was rambling and long winded, profuse of sighs and protestations and abasements before the King's Grace, we may suppose that he reserved his tearful condolences and his assurances that afflictions are a sign that one is specially loved by God, to another place and occasion. A note that had to shatter King Henry's pious meditations had to be brief; the details could be supplied later.

When Henry was given these details, he broke down and cried. He was magnificent in his self-pity, "regretting his ill-luck in meeting with such ill-conditioned wives." Then he would rage against the Council, blaming them for what had happened, so that they trembled for their lives. At one moment he refused to believe a word against Catherine; at the next he was calling for a sword that he might himself cut off her head. One must pity the poor old fellow, and yet one cannot but feel contempt for his astonishing lack of dignity. Usually, whatever happened, he displayed that. It was an exhibition of mingled sentimentality, senility, and egotism, all quite unabashed.

The proofs against Catherine were clear. Her offences stretched over several years, beginning, when she was still a child, with her relations with her spinet-teacher, a young man named

Manox. In this case there was probably no more than what we sometimes hear of other adolescents who are unfortunate enough to fall in with a pervert for a teacher. The dowager Duchess of Norfolk, Catherine's grandmother, in whose house she had been brought up, surprised them one day and gave the girl a whipping and at once dismissed Manox.

From that point, however, Catherine rapidly progressed. Though it is not necessary to produce the evidence in all its nastiness here, it must be said that a youth named Francis Dereham, who was a page in the household, used to steal late at night into the large bedroom Catherine shared with several other girls, bringing them cakes and wine. But much more than that happened; it was testified by the informer John Lascelles, whose sister had been a kind of governess in the Howard mansion, that Catherine had him in bed with her "an hundred nights."

There may have been some exaggerations, but after all due discounts were made, what remained as ascertained fact was damning. Catherine had had more beatings from her grandmother, and Dereham had found it advisable to take refuge in Ireland. At the time Lord William Howard, Catherine's uncle, was disposed to make light of the matter as being no more than a little skylarking. But now he and the dowager Duchess were arrested and condemned to perpetual imprisonment for having failed to report what they knew about a girl who seems to have been rather promiscuous. They were, however, released before long.

Catherine's part in this might have been passed over had it rested there. It should have been possible to treat these things as due to the inexperience and folly of youth and to consider that Catherine was much less responsible for her early wantonness than those who had seduced her, or even less culpable than her grandmother and uncle, who had failed to exercise a discipline sufficiently strict. Henry, of course, would not have taken her back after what had been discovered, but he was at first disposed to do no more than divorce her on the basis of a precontract with Dereham. This young man, however, when put to the torture would not admit the precontract. The most that could be obtained from him was the admission of the brag: "An the King were dead I am sure I might marry her."

Cranmer was now brought in to see what he could do. As he had shown with the Nun of Kent and Anne Boleyn, he was an adept at wheedling things out of women. This time he did not succeed, doubtless because Catherine would not trust the man who had contrived her ruin. She would not believe that if she admitted the existence of a precontract, her life would be spared; but after first refusing to admit anything at all, in face of the evidence she finally sobbed an acknowledgement of premarital misconduct. Perhaps she imagined that, as she had not been sent to the Tower but was merely being kept in the former Bridgettine monastery of Syon, extreme measures were not intended.

As no precontract could be established, no other legal grounds for divorce were possible. It would seem that this time the King lacked the convincing feeling that had come over him in his other three divorces that he was not married. At all events, that idea was dropped and it was decided to charge high treason instead. Further enquiries had been made and these indicated that the Queen had lived loosely not only before but since her marriage.

These charges seem on the face of them rather improbable. It is hardly to be believed that Catherine, with the memory still fresh in her mind of her cousin Anne Boleyn's fate, would have dared to misbehave herself in a court that was always buzzing with malicious gossip. What she may have done, though — and it was quite enough — was to amuse herself in flirtation with lively young men. The King was old, with an obese body eaten up with various diseases, just the kind of person who, for all his toughness, might die at any moment. Catherine might well have pictured herself as a widow free to pick a new husband very soon; in the meanwhile she could keep a few amorous swains in tow by giving to each a kind of promise, not at all seriously meant, that he should be her "next." But to wish for the King's death was high treason; even to speak of the King's death could be interpreted as such a wish. On this ground, she and her lovers were undoubtedly liable to be declared guilty, under the law as it stood.

One of these young men was the same Francis Dereham who had been Catherine's lover before her marriage to Henry. It was the height of imprudence to allow him to come anywhere near her. For if her past were ever discovered it was inevitable that people would conclude that, as Dereham was still round, adultery was being committed. As though that were not enough, she had been at least very indiscreet with Thomas Culpepper, one of Henry's favourites, a man to whom he had given a monastic estate and who often slept in a room adjoining the King's. He had taken advantage of this intimacy to make love to the Queen, though to what lengths they went must be uncertain.

One of the letters she had written to him was found, and it appeared to be incriminating. Moreover it was learned that Lady Rochford, Anne Boleyn's sister-in-law, kept guard on staircases while the Queen and Culpepper met late at night. The worst could be (and of course was) deduced from all this, especially because Culpepper, in his office of gentleman of the royal bedchamber, had accompanied Henry and Catherine during their recent progress of the North.

Manox was spared as, after all, what could be charged against him was not of the same degree of turpitude, and though he had been Catherine's initiator into vice, what he had done was long before her marriage. Nor would Dereham have suffered had he not been as indiscreet as the Queen herself by accepting employment at the court. At his trial he attempted to justify himself on the ground of the precontract he had formerly denied. This came too late; he was being charged with adultery with the Queen, and such adultery was high treason.

Nor did Culpepper's* declaration at his trial do him any good. He said that, though he had loved the Queen and she him, "Up to this hour no wrong has passed between us." He confessed that

*Catherine's mother was a Jocosa Culpepper, so he and Catherine would seem to have been cousins.

he had hoped to make her his wife, before the King chose her. He also confessed that he had written her a letter and had received one from her. That was all, he said, "on his honor as a gentleman."

That he was a gentleman was no doubt the reason he was spared the barbarities of being hanged and then disembowelled while still alive, though according to routine this sentence was passed upon him. It was delivered by the Duke of Norfolk, Catherine's uncle. He was in such danger himself that he could extricate himself only by some such signal service. He emphatically condemned "the abominable deeds" and "repeated treasons" of his niece. But while Culpepper was merely beheaded, Dereham suffered the extremity of punishment for treason.

Lady Rochford was sentenced to the block. Whether or not Catherine was actually guilty of all of which she had been charged, the corrupt older woman had done her best to make it possible, in the case of Culpepper, by staying on guard to give warning.

The two women were escorted from Syon House to the Tower by the Duke of Suffolk. When they disembarked Catherine was shown the external marks of respect to which a queen was entitled, for, unlike Anne Boleyn, she was to die still Queen of England. But, unlike her cousin, she did not ask for a swordsman; instead she had the block brought to her apartment that she might practise placing her head on it.

A few days later, on the morning of February 13, 1542, she was led out to die. Her uncle the Duke of Norfolk was among the official witnesses; so also was her cousin the Earl of Surrey, the famous poet. It was necessary for the Howards to disassociate themselves in the most public way from her conduct. Indeed the Duke had approved the proceedings taken against his own mother for failing to report Catherine's misconduct in girlhood. As Marillac reported, "Such is the custom of this country, that it is right for those who are related in blood to maintain that attitude and to go against their nature, in order that they may thus show they have no part in their relations' crimes."

Catherine made the usual short speech from the scaffold. She confessed that she loved Culpepper, but declared that she had not wronged the King. Then asking those present to pray for the repose of her soul, she knelt down and the headsman struck her head off. After this had been done, Lady Rochford was brought to the block "in a kind of frenzy," so Chapuys reported. It was in this way that this wicked woman died.

The King after his own frenzy had quieted down, himself directed most of what happened. But when the necessary arrangements had been completed, he went off to a country place, accompanied only by musicians and entertainers, in whose society he sought to distract himself. After Catherine's death, so Norfolk told Marillac, the King could not speak of her without weeping. Hearing of this, Francis I, who was much more of an expert in *l'amour* than Henry had ever been, wrote him a sympathetic letter, asking him not to be too downcast over "the lightness of a woman." The gallant Frenchman kept to himself any opinions he may have had as to the propriety of a husband's executing his own wife.

Chapuys was openly cynical, as was commonly true of that clever observer of Henry's conduct. If, he said, the King was really plunged in grief, it must be because he was like the woman who mourned her tenth husband more than all his predecessors, though they had all been good men. The reason was that she had previously been able to console herself at the time of death with the thought that she had her next husband already picked out. That tenth time she mourned so much, because she had not provided herself with a man in reserve. So it was, Chapuys thought, with the much-married Henry.

One wonders whether it ever crossed the King's mind that, where women were concerned, he was a fool. Extremely able in every other way, he was grotesquely foolish in all his private affairs. From the time that he had failed to see that in Katherine he had of wives the pearl paragon, he had gone on to one disaster after another. Even his marriage with Jane Seymour, though it had brought him a son, had got him too much under the influence of his Seymour brothers-in-law. But probably he felt no sense of inadequacy, unless it was that he admitted to himself that he was getting too old for marriage, too old for a young wife, too old to beget another child.

That the possibility of another marriage was not put out of his mind is amply demonstrated by the fact that he had Parliament pass a law which made not only a queen's adultery treason but also the unrevealed misconduct of a queen before her marriage. This law was the occasion of some not very seemly jests among the people; they naturally wondered why a man who posed as such an authority on the subject of virginity in 1529 (from experience gained in 1509) should, fourteen years afterwards, when he had in the meanwhile married three more times, have failed to find out that his fifth wife was not a virgin. Henry was far from being without a sense of humour, but it was of a not very subtle kind and it was quite blind when it came to a perception of anything ridiculous about himself. He soon rebounded from whatever grief he felt – it was rage and outrage rather than grief – and consoled himself with savage remarks on the false nature of women and with eating and drinking more heavily than ever.

Henry had failed in his efforts to persuade his nephew James V of Scotland to meet him at York during the summer of 1541. James had a shrewd idea of what would be said and he had no wish to hear it from the lips of his overpowering uncle. Already Sir Ralph Sadler, Henry's emissary, had tried to detach the King of Scots from the Roman obedience, but had been told: "By my troth there are two laws, the spiritual and the temporal. The cure of the one pertaineth to the Pope's holiness and the spirituality; the other to the King's power and the temporality. And for my part I trust I shall do my duty to God in the discharge of such things as pertain to the temporal power within my office and rule in this realm. But as for the spiritual law, in good faith we take no regard thereof, but commit that to the Pope's holiness, and the other ministers of the Kirk within our realm." It was a perfect statement of the principles that had guided all the monarchies of Christendom until the advent of Henry.

Though religious conditions were not all that they should have been in Scotland, they were not nearly so bad as has been represented. Most of the bishops and abbots we hear of as having children raised these families before they accepted priesthood, often deferred until relatively late in life so as not to make them guilty of any breach of the vow of celibacy.* The system of lay commendatory abbots was not a good one, but it was tolerated by the Pope as a means of avoiding worse evils. It was a way of making provision for scholars and statesmen as well as for royal bastards. At least some of these abbots seriously interested themselves in the abbeys over which they nominally ruled, and from which they drew their incomes. Even when they were negligent, it involved only the diversion of a part of ecclesiastical revenues to lay uses, as contrasted with the outright confiscation adopted in England.

So also with the bishops. Cardinal Beaton, the Archbishop of St. Andrews, and his brother, the Archbishop of Glasgow, were not the best-living of men; they had previously been lay commendatory abbots, raising families without undue scandal, but ceasing their irregular connections when advanced to the episcopate. What they had done was to be preferred to Cardinal Wolsey's uncanonical wife or the surreptitious Mrs. Cranmer. At any rate Scotland remained strongly Catholic, except for a small group of nobles who gazed longingly at the plunder of the Church that had been perpetrated on the other side of the border.

Scotland had, or believed it had, very good reasons for dis-

---

*Hay Fleming, in his *Lectures on the Reformation in Scotland* (appendix) discovers that there were 600 clerical bastards in Scotland during the years 1530 to 1560. That number is of course high, but it does not prove a general corruption of clerical morals. Fleming takes the word "Dominus" before a man's name as indicating that he was a priest. But others besides priests were entitled to the same appellation. Probably only relatively few of these bastards were children of priests, though undoubtedly many of the fathers became priests later, under the system which has already been pointed out.

trusting England, fearing lest it be swallowed up by its larger, more populous, and richer neighbor. It was the tradition of Scottish nationalism to maintain an alliance with France as the only means of preserving Scottish independence. The result was that the words "English" and "heretic" became almost synonymous. The relations between Church and State were good, the two institutions existing side by side with their functions clearly defined. Neither King nor people wished to disturb them. Instead they had come to think of a strong Church as an additional guarantee against the English enemy.

Unfortunately the French connection was a source of weakness as well as of strength to Scotland. For the French had a way of egging on the Scots to attack England, even at times when this was not in the Scottish interest, though it must be said the Scots usually needed little urging to make a foray across the border, whereupon the English would retaliate in kind. On the other hand, the Scots often had real grievances against England in which they could not interest the French, though upon the whole the French alliance was of considerable advantage to them.

In 1542 Henry began to put fresh pressure upon his nephew. He was demanding that the two countries sign a pact of perpetual peace and undertake to give mutual aid against all temporal and spiritual enemies. This of course meant that the Scots were to renounce their alliance and, if called upon, join Henry against the French and the papal authority. Under no circumstances could James have accepted his uncle's terms, which in effect meant submission to the suzerainty of the English Crown, but he had less inclination than ever to do so because on August 24, 1542, Sir Robert Bowes had gone into Scotland with four or five hundred men and had been overwhelmed at the battle of Hadden Rig. It was a trifling incident, of hardly more importance than a hundred other things of the kind, but Henry decided that his honour had been outraged and so, in October of the same year, sent the Duke of Norfolk northwards to avenge him with a full-scale invasion.

Henry announced war in his grandest manner. He was not going to criticize his father for having married one of his daughters to a king of Scotland, but he "must lament and be sorry it took no better effect." Sir Robert Bowes had invaded Scotland merely to obtain just redress for an injury; now the injury was all on the English side. "The present war," Henry said, "hath not proceeded of any demand of our right of superiority, which the kings of Scotland have always acknowledged by homage and fealty to our progenitors; but it hath been provoked and occasioned upon present matter of displeasure, present injury, present wrong." He plumed himself on his generosity for not having attacked Scotland during his nephew's minority, but James's ingratitude was more than he could endure. Henry crowned his effrontery by claiming that King James was one "whom we in his youth and tender age preserved and maintained from the great danger of others." The whole of the long proclamation is full of Henry's monstrous self-righteousness.

The campaign that was designed to teach the unnatural James a lesson was a fiasco. Norfolk's supplies began to run short during the march of the army from York to Newcastle; and from Newcastle to Berwick it moved so slowly that, by then, its supplies were almost exhausted, especially with regard to the beer without which Englishmen refused to serve. A few villages just over the border were burned, and that was all. Henry was furious that so much time and money had been spent in doing no more than was often done in a border raid by a handful of men.

If James V had been wise he would have sat back and laughed at his uncle's discomfiture. Instead, he decided that this was the right time to deliver a counterstroke. Flodden, at which twenty-nine years earlier his own father had fallen, was forgotten and only the Scottish prowess at Hadden Rig remembered. James accordingly sent 18,000 men into Cumberland.

Opposing the Scots that November 14 at Solway Moss were only two thousand hastily mustered English yeomen, but added to them was the superb light cavalry of the dales. Their charge sent one part of the Scottish forces reeling back, and among the rest panic broke out. They began to retreat, crying out that the Duke's army – which was thirty miles away – was upon them. And as darkness started to fall, the tide was in flood behind them. Confused and disheartened, they left five thousand of their horses in the treacherous bogs, and those who tried to escape to Scotland were drowned in numbers far greater than those who fell before the English spears. It was, in fact, one of the least bloody battles ever fought, for the English lost only seven men killed and the Scots only twenty. But when the English commander sent a list of his prisoners to Henry, on it were the names of two earls, five other lords, and five hundred knights and lairds, among whom was James's favourite, Sir Oliver Stanley.

The defeat was so complete and disgraceful that James V survived it only a few weeks. Lying on his death-bed he was told that his wife, Mary of Guise, had given birth to a daughter. The story is that when he heard the news he exclaimed bitterly, "The devil go with it; it will end as it began: it came with a lass and it will pass with a lass." At midnight December 14 he died.

His daughter born six days earlier was to be famous in history as Mary Queen of Scots. Her son, James's grandson, was to be king of England and Scotland, of England James I, of Scotland James VI. In the union of the two crowns, the wise policy of Henry VII, whose results had been aspersed by Henry VIII, justified itself after all.

CHAPTER EIGHTEEN

Even to This an End

HENRY now had what looked like a free hand with regard to Scotland. And it must be said that his plans, in so far as they followed the lines of his father's policy — the union of the two countries under one crown — were sound. But he spoiled everything by overshooting his mark. It was not enough for him to try and arrange a marriage between his son Edward — now five — and James's little baby daughter who became Queen of Scots when she was a week old; he had to couple this with an assertion of the suzerainty of the English kings over Scotland, thus enraging all its people.

Of the noble prisoners who had fallen into Henry's hands at the battle of Solway Moss ten were won over by various promises and some more tangible considerations; after which they were allowed to return home pledged to work in the English interest. Not only that, the regent, Lord Arran, who was appointed to conduct Scottish affairs, agreed to support the English designs. There was to be a despoiling of the monasteries according to the Cromwellian model, though of course Henry regarded himself as being the protector of orthodoxy for Scotland, as he had been for England. This brand of orthodoxy envisaged Scotland's breach with the Papacy.

The opposition was instant and violent. As its leader was the patriotic Cardinal Beaton, Henry began to plot to have him murdered or abducted and sent to England for safe-keeping. Arran did in fact manage to keep the Cardinal in prison for a short time, but then, yielding to popular clamour, he released Beaton and came to an arrangement with him under which the man who was already papal legate also became chancellor of Scotland.

Because of this the Treaty of Greenwich, signed on July 1, 1543, became so much waste-paper. Indeed it was the signing of this treaty that roused the Scots to fury, so that Arran and the English party in Scotland had hastily to disavow what they had done. Arran was the head of the Hamilton family, and in 1548 he received the French dukedom of Chatêlherault; playing a devious part in Scottish politics far into the reign of Queen Elizabeth, he always set his own interest above that of his religion and his country. Beaton, on the other hand, whatever his faults and limitations may have been, consistently adhered to a policy both Catholic and national. He paid for this by being removed, though not just yet, by assassination, which, according to one's cast of mind, may be regarded as the "Godly act" John Knox called it or a dastardly crime. So long as he lived the Scottish liberties and the ancient faith of the country were safe.

Somewhat to everybody's surprise Henry married again for the sixth time on June 12, 1543, after having been a widower for nearly a year. Again he took one of his subjects to wife, but this time he married sensibly — a woman indeed twenty years younger than himself, but not so young as to make the marriage absurd. Catherine Parr was of a sedate habit, and had already been a widow twice and was to marry, as her fourth husband, a few weeks after the King's death, Henry's brother-in-law, the Thomas Seymour she would have married in 1543, had she been permitted this. Chapuys considered her even less handsome than Anne of Cleves, but this would not seem to be so, judging from her portrait; at all events it was not so in Henry's estimation.

Only a widow would be likely to consent to marry the King in face of the law passed after Catherine Howard's execution, and even then only a widow too respectable to be suspected of any previous flightiness. She risked something on other grounds, perhaps, for she had more than a leaning towards heresy, but even that her discretion was able to deal with. In her Henry found a good wife, a kind and sensible home-body of a woman, who looked after his creature comforts and humoured him. If she was not very exciting, that was not what he wanted any more. That she was about as unlike Catherine Howard as it was possible for anybody to be was sufficient recommendation. The clue to Henry's matrimonial adventures would really seem to be that each time he chose a wife quite different from the last—a somewhat crude and naïve way of looking for the right woman.* It never crossed his mind that he might not be the right man for anybody.

Nor did it cross his mind that this third Catherine of his was not very sound in her religious beliefs. Or perhaps he considered it enough of a guarantee that her second husband, only recently dead, Lord Latimer, had been implicated in the Pilgrimage of Grace. That fact, though it had made him liable to the penalties for treason (if any of the Pilgrims were really traitors), showed at least that he must be orthodox. Henry overlooked the fact that her brother William Parr,** on whom he bestowed this year the earldom of Essex (Cromwell's old title), was as slippery a politician as one could wish to find, and perhaps this should not be remembered against Catherine. And as yet there was no reason to suspect him at this time of positive heresy, for politicians were, of all people, the ones most careful not to offend in so unimportant a matter as religion. As for his sister, Henry was not disposed to enquire too closely into the workings of the inner springs of character, so long as subservience was shown.

*Anne of Cleves does not count, as Henry never saw her until five days before their wedding, and his choice was no longer free. But though he did not select her because she was different from her predecessor, he certainly picked in the one who immediately replaced her, a wife who in age, build, cast of mind, colouring, and character was an almost startling contrast. So also when he replaced Catherine Howard with another Catherine.

**He was one of the leading conspirators behind Lady Jane Grey when an attempt was made to put her on the throne in place of Henry's daughter, Mary. Mary spared him, being always reluctant to shed blood, but perhaps also in grateful memory of his good-natured sister.

Did he hope that this sixth wife of his would bear him a son? It is impossible to say with any certainty, and after his failure in this respect with the youthful Catherine Howard, he must have had at least some reason for doubting whether he was any longer capable of begetting children. For that matter, the question written in French and handed to Lord Rochford at his trial points to at least a partial failure in potency as early as 1536. But we know that it was not complete then, and it may not have been complete even in 1543.* Henry's vanity was, however, so inordinate that it is not impossible that, flickering in the depths of his abysmal pride, was the hope of proving his virility by fathering a son by a wife whose previous husbands had not been able to manage this. Catherine was not much over thirty, and was fully capable of bearing children, as she showed in her fourth marriage in 1547.

One thinks of the lady with kindness and also with some admiration for her ability to manage a husband by now all but unmanageable. She was of a gentle and affectionate disposition, and she, like Jane Seymour before her, took pity on the ill-used Lady Mary. Her father, it is true, had received her back into a kind of favour, but he still bore resentment. As people told him that men spoke of her and to her as though she were a nun, he put it to a brutal test, telling Sir Francis Bryan, a man whose character is indicated by his nickname of the "Vicar of Hell," to try her at a masked ball with bawdy talk. Bryan was received in such a way as to leave no doubt in his (or this precious father's) mind that Mary was all that she was said to be.

With Mary the new Queen corresponded in Latin, but this was mainly a kindness on the erudite Mary's side, as it helped to improve her stepmother's literary style. Yet the Queen did all she could for the neglected girl, and her delicacy was shown when Chapuys, at last leaving his long embassy in England, went to say good-bye to her. Queen Catherine suggested that they might want to talk in private, something that Henry would

* The "facts of life," as they are called, have been dwelt upon a good deal in this book. May I be excused from further exposition?

not have permitted, and least of all just then. Mary was equally obliging to the Queen; she declined the offer, so that the farewells were said in Catherine's presence. By that time Mary had no secret messages to send her cousin Charles, the Emperor.

Though the King had unwittingly married a heretic, he took some special pains to demonstrate his orthodoxy again. He did so both by word and deed, theory and practice, a book and some burnings.

The book, which had been in preparation for several years, and which appeared at last in May, 1543, under the title of *A Necessary Doctrine and Erudition for Any Christian Man; set forth by the King's Majesty of England*, became popularly known as the "King's Book" to distinguish it from its predecessor of 1537, the "Bishops' Book," which was intended to be merely provisional. It was a performance so thoroughly Catholic that, in Mary's time, Cardinal Pole, Archbishop of Canterbury and Papal Legate, ordered chapters of it to be read from the pulpit pending the preparation of a volume of homilies. Especially was *A Necessary Doctrine* clear and correct on the Sacraments, most of all in its elaborate exposition of the Eucharist. Because the whole thing was so well written, some have attributed it to Cranmer, or at least the long preface on faith.

To do so is to make Cranmer out an even greater hypocrite than he was. He customarily gave an equivocal assent to propositions he did not believe, if the King was behind them, but he avoided, if possible, any positive statement contrary to his own secret convictions. Moreover, Cranmer was not the only English bishop who could write well, and his forte lay in the single sentence, the collect, not in exposition. In all the more extended pieces of his writing we find him ragged and diffuse. He may have touched up the style of the King's Book, but one cannot believe that he was the actual author even of its preface. There is explicitly stated the Catholic view of faith: "That faith alone justifies and suffices for salvation cannot be affirmed without great danger and scandal for souls; for it is manifestly contrary to Scripture, which says: *Justificatur homo ex operibus et non ex fide tantum.* If the ancient authors sometimes used the expression, *sola fides justificat,* they oppose it to the Judaical doctrine of justification by the works of the Law, but they did not at all intend to exclude the works of faith." It was a decisive rejection of the Lutheran doctrine.

What Cranmer's real views were regarding the hierarchy upon which the administration of the sacraments depends, is clear from the answer he gave to the question circulated among the bishops about this time, when he said that no more grace is conferred on the ecclesiastical than on the civil office; that all ecclesiastical functions flow from the prince as much as do those that are civil; that though there "be divers comely ceremonies and solemnities used," these are for seemliness and not of necessity; that though a bishop may make a priest, so may "princes and governors also." He added: "To be a bishop or a priest needeth no consecration, by the Scripture; for the election or appointing thereunto is sufficient. If it so fortuned that all the bishops and priests of a region were dead, and that the word of God should remain there unpreached, the King of that region should make bishops and priests to supply the same." Could anything cut more radically under the whole concept of the priesthood and the sacramental system than this view of the Archbishop of Canterbury? Nothing could be less Catholic; nothing could be less Henrician. Nothing, for that matter, could be farther away from the official doctrine of the present Church of England.

If anybody should have been burned as a heretic it was this man who had several times found people guilty of views which he privately entertained. The three heretics who were burned at Windsor on July 28, 1543, all held opinions in one respect or another similar to Cranmer's. The priest Pearson had attacked the Catholic sacramental doctrine. Filmer the tailor (it is curious how much heresy was found among men of this trade) asserted that the Eucharist was no more than a sign. And Testwood, the third victim, had disparaged relics and the invocation of saints.

(This, one might have imagined, would have made him acceptable to Henry; but the King of course declared himself opposed only to *superstition* in this regard – the superstition, presumably, of thinking that shrines should be allowed to possess their treasures.) The only difference between these men and Cranmer was that they advanced heresy in a crude and offensive fashion, whereas he was always a scholar and a gentleman. It is easy to see that those who had to suffer the fire, as these did, were the people who attracted attention to themselves by an irreverent manner, while those who took the precaution of picking their words carefully were passed unnoticed by those whose duty it was to enforce the Six Articles. So long as a heretic did not make himself objectionable he was reasonably safe. Cranmer, so far from being objectionable, secured immunity by his unfailing obsequiousness towards the King.

The most celebrated of these cases of burnings is one that occurred within a few months of Henry's death, showing that he never faltered in his orthodoxy. It obtained its celebrity not only because of the social position of the lady who suffered but because she herself wrote a long account of the matter which Foxe used with great effect in his *Acts and Monuments.* This was Anne Askew, the wife of a Lincolnshire squire named Kyme. She was arraigned at the Guildhall, along with Shaxton, formerly bishop of Salisbury, John Hadlam, a tailor – another tailor! – and Nicholas White. They were all four condemned for holding Zwinglian views (those of Cranmer) on the Sacrament of the Altar. Shaxton and White were persuaded to recant by Bishop Bonner, and this saved them, though it had not saved the poor boy Richard Mekins a couple of years earlier. But Anne Askew and the valiant tailor stood firm.

One must admire this brave but rather blunt woman. She told Shaxton to his face that it would be better for him had he never been born. And she endured the rack with heroic fortitude. The Lieutenant of the Tower, sickened by the torture he was called upon to inflict, desisted – so that Wriothesley (now lord chancellor in succession to Audley) and Sir Richard Rich (a future lord chancellor) took over the rack themselves and turned it with their own hands. It did no good. Anne Askew would not recant, and when lifted off the rack – in what condition may be imagined! – sat on the floor two whole hours arguing with them.*

She was burned at Smithfield on July 16, 1546. With her suffered Hadlam and a priest named Hemsley and a John Lascelles who may have been the informer against Catherine Howard. The preacher appointed for the occasion was none other than the Bishop Shaxton who had been condemned with Anne, but whose courage had failed. Anne kept interrupting his sermon, and gave a wonderful exhibition of truculent bravery and resolution. Cranmer, even though he did not preside over the court that sentenced these people, abetted their execution. These were things carried out when he was the primate of Henry's Church.

Anne Askew's case was much talked about. There was another case of heresy which would have been the most startling of sensations had it not been hushed up. It was when the Queen, Catherine Parr, was in danger. Skilful as she usually was in managing Henry, she ventured upon religious argument with him and made him so angry that, without letting her know what was being done, he directed that articles charging her with heresy be drawn up by Gardiner and Wriothesley, the man who had distinguished himself a few years earlier by desecrating the shrine of St. Swithin. This indictment the King signed.

Catherine was warned, however, as to what was afoot. She was so terrified that she became hysterical and worked herself into such a state that Henry had to go to her to see what was the matter. By then she had recovered her wits and very adroitly contrived to let him know that, if she had argued about religion with him, it was not because she for one instant imagined that she could instruct him; it was only "to pass away the time and pain of his infirmity." The explanation completely mollified him.

*It has been suggested that these distinguished gentlemen acted as manipulators of the rack with the intention of applying the torture lightly, using it to frighten rather than hurt. But as Anne had to be carried to the stake in a chair, she must have been severely racked by them.

"Is it even so, sweetheart?" he exclaimed. "Then we are perfect friends again."

When Wriothesley arrived later in the day with a guard to arrest her, Henry carried his huge bulk down the garden walk to meet them, calling the Chancellor a fool and a knave. He seemed to have forgotten that everything had been done exactly according to his own instructions. So long as submission to his royal person was complete, that was all that mattered.

Foreign politics, fortunately for Henry, had become considerably simplified. Wolsey had played that game with a masterly hand, often, one cannot but think, for no other purpose than to show off his dexterity, and hardly ever with any more solid gain than that of having impressed himself and the King upon European consciousness. After the break with Rome the only factor that had ever given much of a pattern to Wolsey's manoeuverings — England's support of the Papacy as a temporal power — vanished. And because of the divorce of Katherine of Aragon, Henry was no longer in the position of being able to play off Francis and the Emperor against one another, but was obliged to rely on the dubious friendship of the French. By the end of 1539 he had lost even that much, because of Cromwell's mistake of looking for allies among the Lutheran princes. Yet this policy, because of the insult subsequently given to the Duke of Cleves, came to nothing. Henry had to extract what consolation he could from the reflection that such allies were in a geographical position in which their only value to him could be that they might be an annoyance on the flank of the Emperor; they could give him no aid in any war. Moreover, after 1543, his Scottish policy had resulted in the estrangement of the French, the traditional allies of the Scots. Accordingly, when at last the chance occurred of winning back Charles's political friendship, it was taken.

It was all very different from the old days of Wolsey's bewilderingly clever sleight of hand. For Henry no longer was much interested in continental adventures which were now seen to be chimerical. Yet with the Scots to the north and the French just across the Channel an ally was needed for moral support. Henry's real achievements had been all at home: he had made himself Head of the Church and he had destroyed the monasteries. He now had to settle down and give what remained of his life to holding his own. No longer could there be any serious hope of invading France or of putting the crown of the Valois on his own head; it was now merely a question of repelling a possible invasion by the French in support of a new thrust from Scotland.

Nevertheless, though the alliance with Charles was more a defensive precaution than anything else, the arrangement made in 1543 was that, in the following year, the Emperor and Henry should invade France simultaneously, each at the head of 42,000 men, of whom 7000 were to be cavalry. England's military weakness was, however, indicated by a request (the significance of which was not lost on the Emperor) that a force of a thousand Spanish harquebusiers be supplied to patrol the Scottish border. Really, if Henry, after all the gun-metal he had secured from the melting down of thousands of great monastery bells, was so short even of small-arms, and if, after his victory of Solway Moss, he still had occasion to fear the Scots, he was not likely to be of much use in a full-scale war.

Nor was he. Yet his main weakness was not in men or ordnance but that, in spite of all the plunder taken from the Church, he was short of money. As this had somehow to be raised, he was forced to various ruinous expedients. That the forced loan of 10 per cent in 1542 was made an outright gift the next year, when Parliament absolved the King from repaying his debt, did not greatly matter, except that it made people wonder how it could be that, after the seizure of the wealth of the monasteries, there should be any need to tax them so soon. For that forced loan (and the dispensation for its repayment) was only a small part of the financial burden of the war. A graduated income tax was introduced, as well as a tax on jewels and plate, and levies on "corporations, brotherhoods, fraternities and communalities" – the last of which eventuated in their extinction.

England so swarmed with associations that combined religious with beneficent and convivial purposes — of which the most important were the trade guilds — that virtually everybody belonged to at least one of them. As these groups, though composed of people of the middle or lower ranks of society, were often wealthy and had what were for those times large reserve funds, the Crown thought it but right that they should help pay for the war. In Edward's time, under the rule of his Seymour uncles, what remained of these funds were, for the most part, appropriated outright — generally on the pretext that they were being put to superstitious uses, meaning that chantry priests were maintained out of them for the saying of Masses for the repose of the souls of deceased members.

Even in Henry's time such endowments were not greatly respected, for in the same session of Parliament that legislated against heretical books, there was passed an act empowering the King to dissolve chantries, hospitals, and free chapels. Among the institutions that went down were the four hospitals of London, but because Henry afterwards partially restored St. Bartholomew's, his memory is held in grateful memory there as the founder, his statue being the first object that greets the eye of the visitor. It was so in the next reign with the destruction of the grammar-schools,* of which the country was full. The few that were spared are known to this day as "King Edward the Sixth Grammar Schools," as though they had been established by him!

Such proceedings were not only flagrantly unjust but socially ruinous. For there were many private associations for the keeping of bridges and dykes in repair — obligations that had also often been freely undertaken by the monasteries. Now with the suppression of the monasteries, followed by the looting of the various benefit societies, as their social services could not be

*The term grammar-school at that time meant primarily a school in which Latin (and sometimes Greek) grammar was taught. Though the study of the humanities began at an early age at this time, such schools approximated more closely to what are called high-schools in modern America than to our grade schools.

allowed to lapse, these had to be undertaken by the Crown. It meant in effect that the King, in order to get his hands on the reserve funds that had been slowly accumulating – sometimes for centuries – was saddling himself with mortgages upon the royal revenues, hoping that at some future date he would be able to pay them off. Though in part these obligations were eventually met, its immediate result was that all repair work was suspended, except what was absolutely unavoidable. The result was that the mass of ordinary people not only had to pay, as individuals, heavy taxes, but that they also lost a large part of what had been built up for group protection.

The network of such associations was so closely knit that it was hardly possible to touch this or that of their varied functions without affecting them all, or without doing some injury even to people who were not actually members of the associations. For example, the chantry priest was commonly also the village schoolmaster. Therefore when the chantry fell, the school also had to be closed, with disastrous results to popular education.

Higher education also suffered. The attendance at the universities began to drop off alarmingly, now that men had little inducement to offer themselves to a priesthood whose future seemed so uncertain. Where twenty years earlier there had been an excess of clerics, now there threatened to become a shortage. The state of the universities – the vast majority of whose students had been those intending to accept orders in the Church or young monks sent there by their monasteries – was running down so rapidly that plans were drawn up for confiscating their endowments as being no longer necessary. The colleges, already discouraged by the small number of students they were getting, became paralysed with fear, expecting the abolishing blow to fall. It was just barely averted.

Nor was this all. To meet the exigencies of the war, a great many of the monastic estates that were still held by the King were hastily sold. Such selling under pressure was usually a sacrifice made by the Crown. Hitherto the annual revenues of these monastic manors were so large as to provide the King with an income which, if never really commensurate with his increasing extravagance, at least went a long way towards meeting the expenses of his government, even after huge deductions for his private use. The wholesale mortgaging or outright disposal of these lands and buildings was simply the cashing of investments, a ruinous living upon capital. It was for this reason that, by the time Henry died, two thirds of the monastic property seized by him had been alienated. He remained indeed still very wealthy, yet was often in difficulties because of the expenditures in which he was involving himself. Henry VII, with far less resources at his command, had by frugal management set aside a vast financial reserve; Henry VIII was a prodigal son who wasted his substance not only in riotous living but, still more, on gaudy, unnecessary, and fruitless wars.

Financial mismanagement of this kind, as everybody knows, proceeds in a geometrical rather than an arithmetical proportion. Disaster had to be staved off by all kinds of expedients, some of them ill-judged and others shifty. The debasing of the coinage,* both in silver and gold, was one of these, and it can only be regarded as a swindling of his subjects by the King. It was to this disgraceful end that had come the most gigantic instance of loot in history. The people suffered, and yet the King did not greatly benefit because his expenses rose more rapidly than his augmented revenues. The only group that really profited was that of the new landed gentry; an oligarchy was already in process of formation that would further impoverish the peasantry and would eventually lord it over the King himself.

The course of the war, to wage which Henry had been obliged to resort to so many ignominious or ignoble devices, should now be briefly indicated.

*On the progressive debasement of the coinage from 1542 see the *Cambridge Modern History*, Vol. II, p. 470. In 1542 the gold coinage was 23 carats fine with one carat of alloy, with a silver coinage of 10 ounces pure silver to 2 ounces of alloy. In 1545 the gold coinage was down to 22 carats and in 1546 to 20. The silver coinage by that time, had an alloy of three-fifths — that is 4 ounces to 6 where four years before it had been 10 to 2!

There need have been no war at all with Scotland (after Solway Moss) had Henry not aroused suspicions by creating an English party in that country and – worse – kindled the fiercest sort of resentment by publicly asserting his suzerainty. Had he been content with a treaty for the marriage of Prince Edward and the little Queen Mary, that would have served sufficiently well as a treaty of alliance, though of course as the actual marriage could not take place for another fourteen years, the arrangement could have been regarded as no more than tentative. But just because it was tentative it would have been less objectionable, even in the eyes of such Scots who most disliked the idea of an English king as consort for their queen. Henry made the Treaty of Greenwich unacceptable to Scottish patriots from the start by claims dictated solely by his vanity and against which political realism should have warned him.

Realism was, however, perhaps the quality Henry had always most conspicuously lacked. It was this lack that had allowed him to be hoodwinked by his crafty father-in-law, Ferdinand of Aragon; it was this that had led him to follow the divagations of Wolsey's foreign policy; it was this that had been the origin of all those fantastic scruples of conscience that assailed him whenever he wished to get rid of a wife; it was this that had made him fail to see what would be the effect of his repudiation of the Pope's authority and his seizure of the monastic lands; and it was lack of realism that now, after over thirty years' experience of politics, left him still politically immature. Preferring, as always, what may be called a glittering shadow to the solid substance, he once again plunged England into an expensive war from which nothing whatever could be derived.

It began on a fairly modest scale with the sending in July, 1543, of a small force to Flanders under the command of Sir John Wallop. That it accomplished nothing in particular, except the taking of a part in the siege of Landrécies, did not much matter; it was meant to be only a beginning, a preliminary to the great invasion planned for the following year.

As before this occurred Henry decided that it would be well

to deal with the Scots as they deserved, he sent in May an army across the border under Edward Seymour, the Earl of Hertford, a good soldier. Hertford advised the seizing and fortification of Leith, as this was the key to the Forth, but Henry, impatient to get on with his larger schemes elsewhere, considered that a swift campaign of devastation would bring the Scots to their senses. This was very thoroughly carried out, and included not only the burning of all farms and cornfields in the path of the raiders but the wasting of Edinburgh and Leith and the putting of Holyrood to the torch. But though this was done from Leith, where a sea-borne English army had been landed, it was not intended to result in the holding of any part of Scotland and was, after all, only a border raid on a large scale. The sole result was that of further embittering the Scots and confirming the leadership of Cardinal Beaton.

The northern border, however, might now be considered secure. So on July 14, 1544, Henry crossed the Channel to Calais where his great army was waiting for him. And it must be said that though he was much too fat to sit on a horse for long, and his legs too swollen and ulcerated to endure armour, he showed a flaring-up of his old energy. He was extremely testy because of the pain he was in, and yet this game of war could at times make him forget his agony. But this time, as he could not prance about on a stallion, as in the days of his furious jousts in the tilting-yard, he confined his attention mainly to the invention or improvement of military gadgets. He had always been interested in the designing of ships and in bettering the cumberous ordnance of the time; now he was fascinated by new toys – portable boats and ovens and a waggon that contained a mill which ground corn by a force generated by the movement of the waggon wheels. Henry was, in truth, a very versatile man who, in other circumstances, in which he would not have scattered all his talents, might have proved himself remarkable in any one of a dozen different departments.

It proved to be beyond the King's powers of invention to discover a means of imparting much mobility to the English army. Yet the country was left so wide open, while Francis was turning his attention to the far more serious threat of the imperial forces, that Henry should have been able to take all Picardy without difficulty. The only real success he had – and this was not permanent – was the capture on September 14 of Boulogne. Could it have been held, it would have provided another bridge-head besides Calais, and probably would have led to the taking of a long strip of the French coast, something that it would not have been easy to wrest out of English hands. But Boulogne was never to be of any higher value than a flashy bauble for Henry; when peace was at last signed in 1546 he undertook to restore it to France at the end of eight years. Then the ransom which Francis was to pay was not to be regarded as reparations but as the clearing-up of pensions long in arrears.

The fact is that Henry was not merely without an army capable of withstanding the full force of the French, should Francis ever trouble to exert himself, but that Henry lacked sufficient money to conduct a war of this kind. "I am at my wit's end," wrote Wriothesley, the Lord Chancellor, to Paget, in November, 1545, "how we shall possibly shift for the next three months." The enormous sum of £1,300,000 (over £30,000,000 in modern values) had already been spent, just about the total amount received from the monastic loot. Even with the forced sales of monastic estates at bargain prices, to meet immediate needs, loans had to be raised at a ruinous interest. It was therefore only prudent to withdraw at that time, when it could be made to appear that the English had covered themselves with glory and before Henry's bankrupt condition was exposed to the world.

The war at sea was equally inconclusive. It was only with luck that the English were saved from a disaster in July, 1545. For when their fleet encountered the French, with their twenty-five galleys, they could not manoeuvre for lack of wind and lost the *Mary Rose* – one of their few "great" ships, which keeled over when attempting too close a turn – and nearly lost Henry's pride and joy, the *Great Harry*. The advantage shifted only with the change of wind, when the more mobile galleys were outclassed by the weight of the English ships of the line. Even so, Lord Lisle, the English admiral (son of our old friend Edmund Dudley and the future Duke of Northumberland) felt it advisable to keep within the narrow waters of the Solent, though the French landed on the Isle of Wight in an effort to smoke him out. As that failed, they eventually withdrew, with no decision having been reached.

It was a somewhat similar story with regard to the manoeuverings off the Sussex coast the following month, when occurred what is dignified with the title of the Battle of Shoreham. England has achieved many resounding victories both on land and sea in the course of her history, and to these my English blood can still thrill. But I confess to finding not much satisfaction in anything that happened in Henry's wars, except for Flodden in 1513. Here in an engagement in the Channel the English managed to hold off D'Annebault's galleys and ships, and had a slight advantage. As the French withdrew under cover of darkness, a victory could be boasted.

A claim, however, perhaps can be made for Henry that, because he was under the necessity of building up more of a fleet than any of his predecessors needed, he should be regarded as the founder of the British navy. If so, he never did very much with it, and, despite his great opportunities, he consistently neglected to exploit the possibilities open to England on the sea. Even trade was as yet so little adventurous that English merchantmen rarely went farther than the Scheldt, Bordeaux, or, at most, the Gulf of Biscay. Commerce with the Baltic was carried on almost exclusively in German keels and with the Mediterranean by the enterprising Venetians or Genoese.

There is one possible word of excuse for Henry's lack of success in this war, and Henry said it very loudly: Charles had deserted him at a time when concerted effort would have brought France to her knees. But Charles's objects in the war had never been the same as Henry's; it was enough for the Emperor to display just sufficient force against Francis as would obtain a free hand in Germany. But by making an alliance with England, he had been obliged to declare war on Scotland. This he did not want to do for a number of reasons, one being that the war between England and Scotland had something of a religious character, and it put the Emperor in a false position to seem to be supporting the anti-papal Henry while trying to control anti-papists in his own dominions. He felt this anomaly all the more keenly because it resulted in a cessation of trade between Scotland and Flanders.

It was somewhat to Henry's credit that when Francis first tried to detach him from the alliance with Charles, he held to it. This, however, was not so much out of loyalty to his ally as because he could not hope to gain what he was after except with his ally's help. The Emperor from the beginning had limited objectives, and as soon as these had been achieved, he left Henry in the lurch. If that was not very handsome of him, it must be remembered that everybody concerned was acting only to get what he could; Henry could hardly expect the nephew of Katherine of Aragon to put himself out for the ex-uncle's advantage. But of course the Peace of Crespy, signed between Francis and Charles on September 18, 1544, was looked upon by Henry as pure treachery. Having at that very moment captured Boulogne, and wishing to keep it — very absurdly he declared it was more valuable to him than Paris itself — there was no way out of the war for him just then. So it dragged on for another two years in desultory fashion between England on the one side and France and Scotland on the other.

It is amusing to observe in all this the rather clumsy diplomacy conducted by Henry. After having tried to impress the Emperor with his orthodoxy (while the Emperor was his ally), no sooner had the alliance fallen apart than he tried again, as he could find allies nowhere else, to make the German Lutherans believe that there was no essential difference between himself and them. The only real point of contact, as the Germans saw clearly, was in the opposition to the Pope. But as Henry was still manifestly more Catholic than the Pope, this attempt at a rapprochement broke down like those that had preceded it. Henry could not give the Lutheran princes any military aid, nor did he have any money at his disposal, as during the early years of his reign. Though they might be of some little use to him, he could be of none whatever to them; so on every ground his overtures were declined. Henry had to plough on heavily alone.

The war with Scotland still brought no very definite results. It was mainly a matter of raiding, and this sort of thing was sporadic, though on a small scale, even during what were officially times of peace. On February 27, 1545, Sir Ralph Evers was defeated at Ancrum Moor – no great achievement on the part of the Scots but at least a proof that they could defend themselves. It was punished in September of the same year when the Earl of Hertford again invaded Scotland in force, fighting nothing that could be described as a battle but inflicting a devastation almost as great as that of the previous year. He burned and laid waste in a truly heroic way, destroying four large towns, five others of a smaller size, two hundred and forty-two villages, sixteen castles, seven monasteries, and three hospitals. The farms burned were of course without number. By the time he had finished, most of the south of Scotland had been ravaged.

Meanwhile Henry had been building up an English party among the Scottish nobility. His chosen instrument, this time, was Matthew Stewart, Earl of Lennox, a young man who was to prove himself a most shifty politician. By way of cementing the alliance Henry married him on June 6, 1544, to his niece Lady Margaret Douglas, the daughter Margaret Tudor and her second husband, Archibald Douglas, Earl of Angus. They were to be the parents of the ill-fated and ill-famed Lord Darnley.

This man Stewart was closely related to Mary Stuart, and was therefore bribed by Henry's undertaking to recognize him as next in succession to the Scottish throne. He was also to be appointed governor of Scotland as soon as it had fallen into Henry's hands, or rather had been delivered to Henry by the Scottish "fifth column."

The scheme failed. Lennox was of no more use than Arran

had proved to be. Though there were other Scottish nobles willing to betray their country, there was as yet not nearly enough disaffection from the Catholic religion to make any concerted movement possible against Cardinal Beaton. He stood in the mind of the people at once for the Catholic cause and for national independence. Virtually the entire country was behind him.

Nevertheless, there was heresy there as elsewhere, and heretics were people for whom the orthodox Henry could often find a use. As early as 1527 Patrick Hamilton, whose grandfather had married a sister of King James III, and who was endowed, like so many other young aristocrats, with an abbey *in commendam*, having turned Lutheran, was burned at St. Andrew's. The more recent execution (on March 2, 1546) of George Wishart,* also at St. Andrew's, was (on the following May 29) avenged with one of those bloody deeds that are so common in Scottish history. At dawn that day a band of conspirators succeeded in making their way into St. Andrew's Castle, and there they stabbed Cardinal Beaton to death. Whether or not Henry was directly implicated in this murder, there had been plenty of assurances of reward and protection to anyone who carried it out. The assassination was so greatly to Henry's advantage that he made no pretence of not being overjoyed. Scotland, he thought, now that Cardinal Beaton had gone, would be a plum ripe for the picking.

Though it may be said that Henry's leading policy with regard to Scotland was sound in general conception, however often it was spoiled by his vanity and soiled by corruption, pillage, and murder, even that much cannot be granted to his policy in Ireland. It can be touched upon, however, only briefly here, as it was of not much significance when set beside what was happening elsewhere. Had the policy of conciliation, initiated by Richard II and to some extent followed by Henry VII and even

*George Wishart may be the same man as the one who appears simply as "Wishart" and who had not long before gone to Hereford with an offer to raise Fife for the English, if he were furnished with the necessary funds.

by his son, during the early years of his reign, been consistently followed, a real union with Ireland might have been effected, in which event England would have escaped what is the darkest stain on its history.

But England, if the truth be told, had never been seriously interested in Ireland until the Reformation. It was considered a papal fief, with its "lordship," but not its kingship, held by the kings of England under the pope. Even this much might be called a legal fiction of very questionable legality, and certainly English power in Ireland extended no further than the rather indeterminate boundaries of the "Pale." Because of the English lack of interest, English authority tended to grow feeble.

At the same time there was so ready a commingling of the English and Irish that it is clear that, just as the Irish charmed the English in their midst to the acceptance of the Irish mode of life, so the English could have probably eventually won the Irish everywhere to an acceptance of the technical "lordship" of the English king. It would have had to come about gradually and with delicate regard to Irish susceptibilities, but a conciliatory policy, had it been persisted in, might have worked wonders. It was the only policy that stood any chance of success.

Henry VIII instead did two offensive things, or rather three. In 1541 he proclaimed himself king of Ireland; he insisted that the Irish recognize him as Head of the Church; and he proceeded to despoil such Irish monasteries as he could reach. The first of these changes might possibly have been accepted, had that been all – though even this is doubtful, as it was too sudden and drastic. But what the Irish violently recoiled against was Henry's anti-papal policy.

Nevertheless, the official classes in Ireland, as in England, showed some willingness to fall into line. In 1539 the archbishops of Tuam and Cashel, and eight other bishops, meeting at the summons of George Browne, the Augustinian agent of Cromwell's who since 1536 had been archbishop of Dublin, took the oath of supremacy, and this was eventually accepted by twenty-two out of thirty Irish bishops. As of those twenty-two several were men who had been appointed by the Pope in disregard of Henry's wishes, it is evident that the resistance of the hierarchy in Ireland to the religious innovation was not, at the outset, very much greater than that put up by the English bishops. No doctrinal changes, other than that relating to the authority of the Holy See, were involved. And, as in England, the monasteries suppressed made a voluntary surrender – at the point of the gun. Also as in England, the thing was put through by giving the Irish magnates a share in the plunder.

To all this there was strong popular resentment, but after the fall of the Geraldines in 1535 no effective leader appeared. Had Silken Thomas been backed the English could easily have been thrown into the sea. That this did not happen was due to fatal Irish rivalries but also – and perhaps even more so – because at that date no very active opposition to the English presence had developed. That it did develop was largely due to Henry and his daughter Elizabeth.

Rather belatedly a kind of reversion was made to the older policy, to the extent of giving a few more Irish chieftains earldoms and knighthoods. But this was of slight effect, as was the attempt to buy their support by giving them also a share in the monastic loot. Even these partakers in the fat of sacrilege had qualms of conscience and could not stifle their awareness of being Irishmen and Catholics. As for the mass of the people – according to English standards, wild, unruly and barbarous – they felt an attachment to their Irishry which, until then, many of them had not known they possessed. And when their religion was touched, they came, before the century was out, to discover under the blows of persecution, for what it was their race and culture really stood. That the English government's lamentable failure in Ireland must be laid at the door of the policy initiated by Henry VIII. Once again he had revealed his lack of political realism.

Meanwhile a struggle had been going on between the Duke of Norfolk, or rather the Howard family, and the Seymours. The

Howards were semi-royal, whereas the Seymours, though not exactly parvenus, and even boasting a drop or two of royal blood (like a good many other people in England), had been merely country squires, with no higher expectation than that of knighthood, when Henry cast his eyes on their sister. In their interests they definitely counted with the "new" men, and therefore inevitably had jealousy of that older aristocracy of which the Duke of Norfolk was now the leader.

The Duke was a useful enough man, especially when some ruthless butchery had to be done, but useful as well on an embassy which needed to be headed by a great name yet on which the real management of affairs could be attended to by brighter brains. He had served Henry loyally, even during those years when the Nevilles and Courtenays and Poles were only waiting a word from the ill-treated Queen Katherine to break into open rebellion. Under Cromwell Norfolk retained a high place on the Council but was as often as possible sent on some distant mission so as to keep him away from the King. Especially was this so after the Seymours had appeared on the scene, with their sister as queen and their nephew as heir to the throne.

During the eighteen months when Catherine Howard was queen, her uncle regained his ascendancy, but when Catherine was discovered to be a baggage the Duke was in such danger that he could extricate himself only by loud expressions of disapproval of all that his niece had done, and even of the negligent conduct of his mother and brother. He not only saved himself but was even in a position to give his support, a little later, to the unsuccessful attempt to ruin the credit of Cranmer. Yet he was himself a man marked down for ultimate destruction. It was not safe for the Seymours to have a man of his wealth and lineage round, for should the young Prince die their influence would immediately disappear. In fact, even if the Prince outlived his father and became king, a contest for control would be sure to develop between the greater nobles, led by the Howards, and the younger, more aggressive, less blue-blooded men.

It should be noted that from 1522 to 1542 almost every important military command was given to Howard. He did not show himself nearly equal to his father; nevertheless, he was considered the man who would normally take charge of an English army. But after 1542 this command passed to Edward Seymour who was not only better at burning farms than the Duke but had real soldierly qualities. By that time he had hardly passed his middle thirties, whereas Norfolk, though still very tough, was almost seventy.

He showed a wonderful capacity to survive – even in the physical sense. He lived to be eighty-one, which in a period when premature senility overtook so many people is itself remarkable. Still more remarkable was his ability to surmount the political dangers that threatened every man in his position. He was, however, beginning to run down, and his heir was Henry Howard, the Earl of Surrey, a man even younger than the Seymours and with an ability greater than their own.

This young man had borne himself bravely in the French wars and had before that, while still in his middle teens, been mentioned as a possible husband for the Princess Mary, before her statutory bastardization. In 1541, he was made a Knight of the Garter and Steward of Cambridge University. He was all too obviously destined to have a career even more illustrious than that of his father. The old Duke Thomas, as he might die at any time, could perhaps be fairly safely disregarded; but the new Duke Henry was likely to have a force and a following that would be a danger to the Seymours.

It is this man who is now remembered as being, with the possible exception of his friend and cousin Sir Thomas Wyatt, the best English poet of the time. But though of so good a poet good brains may be confidently presumed, it does not follow that a good poet will have good judgement. At all events, Surrey, in spite of all his brilliance, showed little of that quality. In 1539 he was called "the most foolish proud boy that is in England." In 1543 he had been arrested – not for the first time – for creating a disturbance in London, a midnight frolic in which he had broken people's windows with stone bows and shot pellets among the prostitutes parading the river bank. He was of course soon released; the playfulness of a young noble had to be condoned.*

What was not condoned was something that happened, or was alleged to have happened, three years later. He had quartered upon his arms those of King Edward the Confessor (an eccentricity in heraldry which one would have supposed would have been merely laughed at), and this was interpreted as a claim to be in the royal succession. A further charge was that he had conspired to make his sister, the widow of the young Duke of Richmond, the King's mistress.

It is not easy to see how the accusation about the widowed Duchess of Richmond – who, by the bye, was Henry's daughter-in-law – could be twisted into treason, even if true. Surrey met it by pointing out that he was not on such good terms with his sister as to make it likely that he would try to secure this honour for her. Of even greater flimsiness was the fact that he had in his service an Italian clown who had formerly been employed by Cardinal Pole. But there seems to have been some truth in the charge about the armorial bearings, though only a faulty heraldry could have considered them as really those of Edward the Confessor. He hit the nail squarely, if with characteristic arrogance, on the head when he said, upon being condemned to death: "I know that the King wants to get rid of the noble blood around him and to employ none but low people."

His sister, Richmond's widow, had borne witness against him that he had expressed hatred of the "new men" (the Seymours) who, he said, "when the King was dead should smart for it." But she did her best to protect her father, and Norfolk himself did his best to save himself by denouncing his son and by making over his property to the Crown. These unhandsome ruses succeeded to the extent of getting his execution deferred. It turned out to be an indefinite reprieve.

---

*When two years previously Lord Dacre (of the south) had been hanged for murdering a gamekeeper, the nobility considered it an outrage that a man of his rank should have to suffer.

Fourteen years earlier he had given a friendly warning to Sir Thomas More that the wrath of the prince is death, and had got the smiling answer, "The only difference is that I shall die today and you tomorrow." Actually, however, there were in 1534 twenty years of life still in store for him. He lived on until the accession of Queen Mary, when he was at last released to enjoy whatever satisfactions such a life as his can find. The Duke was saved only by the fact that a few hours before the time set for his execution, the King died. The gifted and unguarded Earl of Surrey went to the block on January 19, 1547.

The old King's life had almost run its course. The great athlete had long been a mass of obese putrefaction, groaning from the pain in his leg and getting more and more savage every day. Four men were needed to lift his ponderous body from his chair and four to put him to bed. Yet he could at moments exercise his famous charm, and, whatever his faults, one could not but feel that he was a great man in ruins. It is worth remembering that Cardinal Pole could say that "the greatest enemy I had in the world was the King whom I loved above all other men," and called him the greatest king England had ever had.

During the last years of his life not much could be expected of him, except such outbursts as in the furious suspicion that struck the Howards down. Yet as late as the end of 1545, hardly more than a year from his death, he gave a wonderful, and apparently quite impromptu, exhibition of his force and capacity when he delivered in Parliament one of his best speeches. Always he had a majestic presence and, even when he canted most unblushingly, he must be said to have shown a majestic intelligence. Yet in this last recorded speech of his there was scarcely a single touch of cant, but what seems to be sincerity, grandly phrased. Sir John Mason, who has left one of the accounts of what Henry said, tells us that "He spoke so sententiously, so kingly, so rather fatherly" that his audience was deeply affected, perhaps all the more so as those present had not expected the King to speak at all.

This speech is worth quoting here: "I hear that the special foundation of our religion, being charity between man and man, is so refrigerate as there was never more dissension and lack of love between man and man, the occasion whereof are opinions only and names devised for the continuing of the same. Some are called Papists, some Lutherans, and some Anabaptists; names devised of the devil, and yet not fully without ground, for the severing of one man's heart by conceit of opinion from the other. For the remedy whereof, I desire, first, every man of himself to travail first for his own amendment. Secondly, I exhort the bishops and clergy, who are noted to be the salt and lamps of the world, by amending their divisions, to give example to the rest, and to agree especially in their teaching – which, seeing there is but one truth and verity, they may easily do, calling therein for the aid of God. Finally, I exhort the nobles and lay fee not to receive the grace of God in vain; and albeit, by the instinct of God, the Scriptures have been permitted them in the English tongue, yet not to take upon them the judgment and exposition of the same, but reverendly and humbly, with fear and dread, to receive and use the knowledge which it hath pleased God to show unto them, and in any doubt to resort unto the learned, or at best the higher powers. I am very sorry to know and hear how unreverendly that precious jewel the Word of God is disputed, rhymed, sung and jangled in every alehouse and tavern. This kind of man is depraved, and that kind of man; this ceremony and that ceremony. Of this I am sure, that charity was never so faint among you; and God Himself, amongst Christians, was never less reverenced, honored and served. Therefore, as I said before, be in charity with one another, like brother and brother. . . . Then may I justly rejoice that thus long I have lived to see this day, and you, by verity, conscience and charity between yourselves, may in this point, as you be in divers others, accounted among the rest of the world as blessed men."

This speech was delivered on Christmas Eve, 1545; yet that it was not intended to inaugurate anything like religious toleration was proved by the execution less than seven months later of Anne Askew. But of course the real significance of the speech is its admission that the situation was getting out of hand, and that, in spite of all efforts to control the use of the Bible, it was being used as an arsenal of texts by every eccentric – in short, that the inevitable disintegration of Protestantism had already begun. It should also have been obvious (though of course nothing was less so to Henry) that the door to religious dissension had been opened by his own hand. It was being discovered that it was not possible to maintain orthodoxy except under the authority of the pope. When a notorious heretic like Cranmer was primate of England, and behind him stood the Seymours and their gang, all waiting for the King's departure to initiate new and more radical changes in religion, Henricianism was already doomed.

Froude chooses to represent religious conditions in such a way as to suggest that the King had, from the beginning, followed the temper of his people, going along with them (but always slightly behind), and that he had now reached the conclusion that the time was ripe for completing the Reformation in England. According to this theory Henry was only waiting for a propitious moment, now imminent, for introducing a fully rounded Cranmerian Protestantism.

Nothing could be further from the truth. Though heresy was spreading rapidly, even now, thirteen years after the breach with Rome and nearly thirty years after the breaking of the storm in Germany, English heretics were still few, and nearly all of them were to be found in London or those seaports through which there was contact with Germany. These few heretics could have been entirely rooted out had Henry addressed himself to this steadily instead of by fits and starts. As it was, the heretics – except for a handful of rash people who insisted on thrusting themselves into public notice – bided their time. And in the key position was Cranmer, Archbishop of Canterbury and arch-heretic, safe in his subservience, and with an understanding with the men who would soon be taking control.

Most revolutions are carried much further than they were

originally intended to go. It was so at all events in the case of Luther. But Henry was in every fibre of his being conservative; nobody had less taste for change than he. Even when he threw over the Pope it was with the plea that he was freeing England from a "usurpation" and reverting to an ancient order of things. Yet in all other respects he was determined to keep England orthodox, to make it, if possible, more orthodox than it had ever been before.

The two contradictory stories we have as to what was in his mind during his last days must both be regarded with some scepticism. One, given out by Nicholas Sanders in the reign of Elizabeth, is that he was meditating reconciliation with Rome but was held back from this by advisers who feared that it would mean the restoration of the seized monastic property. This is the likelier of the conflicting traditions. At any rate Gardiner, who was close to the King, says that Henry, after the fall of Anne Boleyn, and again after the fall of Cromwell, and finally in his last illness, had some such idea. On the other hand Foxe relates on the authority of Morice, Cranmer's secretary, that the King was thinking of turning the Mass into something like the Communion Service it became in the later Anglican *Book of Common Prayer*. This would seem to be contradicted by everything we know of Henry's personal devotion to the Mass and the pains he took several times to see that the full Catholic doctrine of the Eucharist was clearly and accurately stated. What is probable enough is that Cranmer, who never ceased his attempts to edge Henry away from the central fact of the Mass, felt at moments that he might succeed. In speaking confidentially to his secretary, Cranmer may have unduly enlarged upon these hopes; or Morice himself, hearing about all this at second hand, may himself have done so. In the end Henry evaded the issue by leaving everything exactly as it had been at the time of the schism.

This is fully borne out by his will, which was dated December 30, 1546, less than a month before his death. There he officially styles himself: "King of England, France and Ireland, Defender of the Faith, and on earth immediately under God the Supreme

Head of the Church of England." But he invokes the Blessed Virgin and all the saints to pray for him so long as he lives and at the time of his passing from this world, "that we may the sooner attain everlasting life after our departure out of this transitory life, which we both hope and claim by Christ's passion and word." Further to emphasize his belief in Purgatory and the Mass, he left ample provision for the establishment of an altar by his tomb at Windsor, where he wished "the bones and body of our true and loving wife Queen Jane be also put," and there daily Masses were to be said perpetually, "while the world shall endure." Whatever passing doubts may have crossed his mind, it was now too late to do anything; the responsibility had to be passed on to those who came after him. Officially he died what he had been for thirteen years, an anti-papal Catholic.

In 1536 an act of Parliament had given him the right to bequeath the Crown if necessary. The true heir was, of course, little Prince Edward, now a boy of nine. Under the King's will, should Edward die without issue, the Crown was to descend to the Lady Mary and her heirs, next to the Lady Elizabeth and her heirs, though both were by statute illegitimate. The Scottish line, descending from Henry's elder sister, Margaret, which should have inherited after Henry's daughter, Mary, was completely ruled out. In its place was put, after Elizabeth, the daughters of Henry's sister Mary by Charles Brandon, Duke of Suffolk. It left the door open, however, to the possibility of the union of the English and Scottish crowns by the marriage of Edward to the infant Mary Queen of Scots.

Henry lay in the great bed of the palace of Whitehall, which he had stolen from the archdiocese of York upon the fall of Wolsey. The members of Parliament had just gone home, which was a convenience to the inner circle of the Council which meant to take charge. While the King stertorously breathed his way towards death, Edward Seymour the Earl of Hertford, and Lord Wriothesley the Chancellor, and Lord Paget the Comptroller of the King's household were conferring together as to what they would do; one of the things they had in mind was to set aside some of the provisions of the will. They wished that Henry would hurry up and die.

One of them asked whether he wished that Cranmer come. He seems to have agreed, though he was probably too far gone to care, or perhaps even to understand what was said. At any rate Cranmer was sent for from his house at Croyden and rode through the night at full gallop. Henry may have made a confession; he assuredly would have done so had he been able to speak. But as we hear only of Cranmer kneeling by his bed and holding his hand, there probably was no more than a pressure on the palm in answer to the Archbishop's questions. Cranmer would have given him absolution, little as he believed in the sacramental value of what he did. He was a priest, and he knew that this would console the dying man. Then there came a thick indistinct whisper which was thought to be an invocation of Our Lady of Walsingham, and all was over.

All, that is, except the bringing of little Prince Edward, the new King, from Hatfield to the Tower for safe-keeping. Until that had been done, the death of Henry was kept a profound secret. Edward was crowned by Cranmer after Mass, with the ancient Catholic ritual. The Seymours and the new men – Cranmer among them – now had the boy safely in their hands, and could proceed to what was not possible before, the Protestant Reformation.

Bibliography

Acton, Lord, *Lectures on Modern History*, London, 1912.

——— "Wolsey and the Divorce of Henry VIII," in *Historical Essays and Studies* (pp. 1–64), London, 1926.

Allen, J. W., *A History of Political Thought in the Sixteenth Century*, New York, 1928.

Allen, P. S., *Opus Epistolarum Des. Erasmi Roterodami* (continued by H. M. Allen and H. W. Garrod), 10 vols. to date. Oxford, 1906– .

Armstrong, E., *Charles V*, London, 1902.

Ashley, Sir W. J., *The Economic Organization of England*, London and New York, 1935.

——— *An Introduction to English Economic History and Theory*, 4 vols., London, 1888–92.

Bacon, Sir Francis, *Life of Henry VII*, London, 1622.

Bagwell, *Ireland Under the Tudors*, Vol. I, London, 1885.

Baskerville, G., "The Dispossessed Religious after the Suppression of the Monasteries," in *Essays in History Presented to Richard Lane Poole*, Oxford, 1927.

Belloc, Hilaire, *A History of England*, Vols. III and IV, London, 1931.

——— *A Shorter History of England*, New York, 1934.

——— *Wolsey*, Philadelphia and London, 1930.

——— *Cranmer*, Philadelphia and London, 1931.

——— *How the Reformation Happened*, London, 1928.

Besant, Sir W., *London in the Time of the Tudors*, London, 1904.

Brewer, J. S., *The Reign of Henry VIII*, 2 vols., London, 1884.

——— *English Studies*, London, 1881.

Bridgett, T. E., C.SS.R., *The Life of Blessed Thomas More*, London, 1891.

——— *The Life of Blessed John Fisher*, London, 1888.

Burnet, Gilbert, *History of the Reformation* (Pocock's edition), 7 vols., Oxford, 1865.

Busch, Wilhelm, *England Under the Tudors* (Vol. I: *King Henry VII*), Translated by A. M. Todd, London, 1895.

Cambridge Modern History (Vol. II: *The Reformation*), New York and Cambridge, 1894.

Camm, Bede, O.S.B. (editor), *The English Martyrs*, Cambridge and St. Louis, 1929.

——— *Lives of the English Martyrs*, first series, 2 vols., London, 1904.

Campbell, Lord, *Lives of the Lord Chancellors*, fifth edition, London, 1868.

Cardinal, Edward V., *Cardinal Lorenzo Campeggio*, Boston, 1935.

Cavendish, George, *The Life and Death of Cardinal Wolsey,* Temple Classics.

Chamberlin, F. C., *The Private Character of Henry VIII,* London, 1932.

Chambers, R. W., *Thomas More,* London, 1935.

Cheney, E. P., *Social Changes in England in the Sixteenth Century,* Boston, 1895.

Constant, G., *The Reformation in England, I: The English Schism (1509–1547),* translated by R. E. Scantlebury, New York, 1934.

Crabites, Pierre, *Clement VII and Henry VIII,* London, 1936.

Creighton, M., *Cardinal Wolsey,* London, 1895.

Demaus, R., *Latimer,* London, 1881.

——— *Tyndale,* London, 1886.

Dictionary of National Biography.

Dixon, R. W., *History of the Church of England,* Vols. I and II, London, 1878, 1881.

Dodd, M. H., and R., *Pilgrimage of Grace,* 2 vols., London, 1915.

Ellis, Sir Henry, *Original Letters, Illustrative of English History,* 3 vols., London, 1825.

Eyre, Edward (editor), *European Civilization* (Vol. IV: *The Reformation*), Oxford, 1936.

Fanfani, Amintore, *Catholicism, Protestantism, and Capitalism,* London, 1935.

Fisher, H. A. L., *The History of England from the Accession of Henry VII to the Death of Henry VIII* (Vol. V of *The Political History of England*), London and New York, 1906.

Floyer, J. K., *Studies in the History of English Church Endowments,* London, 1917.

Foxe, John, *Acts and Monuments,* edited by J. Pratt, 8 vols., 1853–1870.

Friedmann, Paul, *Anne Boleyn,* 2 vols., London, 1884.

Froude, James Anthony, *The Reign of Henry VIII,* 3 vols., Everyman Edition.

——— *The Divorce of Catherine of Aragon,* second edition, London, 1891.

Fuller, Thomas, *The Church History of Britain, from the Birth of Jesus Christ until the year MDCXLVIII,* edited by J. S. Brewer, 6 vols., Oxford, 1845.

Gairdner, James, *The English Church in the Sixteenth Century, from the Accession of Henry VIII to the Death of Mary,* London, 1904.

——— *Lollardy and the Reformation in England,* 4 vols., London, 1908–1913.

——— "Mary and Anne Boleyn," *English Historical Review,* Vol. VII (1898), pp. 53–60.

——— "The Age of Anne Boleyn," *English Historical Review,* Vol. X (1895), p. 104.

——— "New Lights on the Divorce of Henry VIII," *English Historical Review,* Vol. X (1896), pp. 674–702.

Gardiner, Stephen, *Letters*, edited by J. A. Muller, London, 1933.
——— *Obedience in Church and State: Three Political Tracts*, edited by P. Janelle, Cambridge, 1930.
Garvin, Katherine (editor), *The Great Tudors*, New York, 1935.
Gasquet, Cardinal, *Cardinal Pole and his Early Friends*, London, 1927.
——— *The Eve of the Reformation*, London, 1913.
——— *Henry VIII and the English Monasteries*, 2 vols., London, 1899.
——— *English Monastic Life*, London, 1924.
Gee, H., and Hardy, W. H., *Documents Illustrative of English Church History*, London, 1896.
Hackett, Francis, *Henry the Eighth*, New York, 1929.
——— *Francis the First: First Gentleman of France*, New York, 1934.
Haile, Martin, *The Life of Reginald Pole*, New York, 1910.
Hall, Edward, *Chronicle* (the Whibley edition in 2 vols.), London and Edinburgh, 1904.
Harpsfield, Nicholas, *The Life and Death of Sir Thomas More*, edited by Dr. Elsie V. Hitchcock for the Early English Text Society, 1932.
——— *A Treatise on the Pretended Divorce Between Henry VIII and Catherine of Aragon* (Pocock edition), London, 1878.
Henry VIII, King, *Songs, Ballads and Instrumental Pieces by King Henry VIII*, coll. and arr. by Lady Mary Trefusis, Roxburghe Club, 1912.
——— *Assertio Septem Sacramentorum* (see below).
——— *Defence of the Seven Sacraments* (Latin text and English translation, edited by the Rev. Louis O'Donovan), New York, 1908.
——— *Love Letters of Henry VIII to Anne Boleyn*, London, 1933.
——— *A Necessary Doctrine and Erudition for Any Christian Man*, London, 1932.
Herbert of Cherbury, Lord, *The Life and Reign of King Henry the Eighth* (reprint from Kennet's folio edition of 1719), London, 1872.
Herkless, J., *Cardinal Beaton, Priest and Politician*, Edinburgh, 1891.
Holinshed, Raphael, *Chronicles*, 6 vols., London, 1807–1808.
Hume, Martin A. S., *The Wives of Henry VIII*, New York, 1905.
Innes, A. D., *England Under the Tudors*, edition revised by J. M. Henderson, London, 1932.
Jenkyns, H., *The Remains of Thomas Cranmer*, 4 vols., Oxford, 1833.
Kennedy, W. P.McC., *Studies in Tudor History*, London, 1916.
Letters, Despatches and State Papers relating to the Negotiations Between England and Spain, preserved in the Archives at Simancas, Vienna, Brussels and elsewhere, edited by G. A. Bergenroth, Don Pascual de Gayangos, and M. A. S. Hume, Vols. I to VIII, London, 1866–1904.
Letters and Papers, Foreign and Domestic, Henry VIII, edited by J. S. Brewer (Vols. 1 to 4), J. Gairdner (Vols. 5 to 13), and J. Gairdner and R. H. Brodie (Vols. 14 to 21), with *Addenda*, His Majesty's Stationery Office, 1864–1932.
Liljegren, S. B., *The Fall of the Monasteries and the Social Changes in England leading up to the great Revolution*, London, 1924.

Lingard, John, *History of England* (the Belloc edition), Vols. IV and V, New York, 1912.

Lipson, E., *An Introduction to the Economic History of England,* Vol. I, London, 1915.

Lodge, E., and Chamberlain, S. (editors), *Portraits of Illustrious Personages of the Court of Henry VIII,* London, 1828.

Lupton, J. H., *Life of Dean Colet,* London, 1886.

——— *Colet's Influence on the Reformation,* London, 1887.

Maitland, F. W., *Roman Canon Law in the Church of England,* London, 1898.

Maitland, S. R., *Essays on Subjects Connected with the Reformation,* London, 1849.

Marti, Oscar A., *Economic Causes of the Reformation in England,* London, 1929.

Mathew, David, and Mathew, Gervase, O.P., *The Reformation and the Contemplative Life,* New York, 1934.

Mathew, David, *Catholicism in England, 1535–1935,* London, 1936.

Mattingley, Garret, *Catherine of Aragon,* Boston, 1941.

Maynard, Theodore, *Humanist As Hero: The Life of Sir Thomas More.* New York, 1947.

Merriman, Roger Bigelow, *Life and Letters of Thomas Cromwell,* 2 vols., Oxford, 1902.

More, Sir Thomas, *English Works,* edited by William Rastell, London, 1557.

——— *English Works,* edited by W. E. Campbell. To date only Vols. I and II have been published, London, 1927, 1931.

——— *Apology,* edited by A. I. Taft, Early English Text Society, 1930.

——— *Utopia,* translated by Ralph Robinson, Everyman Edition.

——— *The Correspondence of Sir Thomas More,* edited by Elizabeth Frances Rogers, Princeton, 1947.

Muller, J. A., *Stephen Gardiner and the Tudor Reaction,* London, 1926.

Mumby, Frank A., *The Youth of Henry VIII: A Narrative in Contemporary Letters,* London, 1913.

Murray, R. H., *The Political Consequences of the Reformation. Studies in Sixteenth Century Political Thought,* London, 1926.

Nichols, F. M., *Epistles of Erasmus,* 3 vols., London, 1901–1917.

O'Brien, J., *An Essay on the Economic Effects of the Reformation,* London, 1923.

Oppenheim, H., *A History of the Administration of the Royal Navy and of the Merchant Shipping in Relation to the Navy, 1506–1660,* London, 1897.

Pastor, Ludwig von, *The History of the Popes,* Vols. IX and X, translated and edited by Ralph Francis Kerr, St. Louis, 1923.

Pickthorn, Kenneth, *Tudor Government,* 2 vols., Cambridge, 1934.

Pocock, N., *Records of the Reformation,* 2 vols., Oxford, 1870.

Pollard, A. F., *Henry VIII,* London, 1913.

——— *The Reign of King Henry VII from Contemporary Sources,* 3 vols., London and New York, 1914.

——— *Thomas Cranmer,* New York and London, 1906.

——— *Wolsey,* second impression. London and New York, 1929.

——— *The History of England from the Accession of Edward VI to the Death of Elizabeth* (Vol. VI of *The Political History of England*), London and New York, 1910.

Power, Eileen, *Medieval English Nunneries,* Cambridge, 1922.

Prescott, H. F. M., *A Spanish Tudor: The Life of "Bloody Mary,"* New York, 1940.

Read, Conyers, *The Tudors,* New York, 1936.

——— *Bibliography of British History, Tudor Period, 1485–1603,* Oxford, 1933.

Rogers, Elizabeth Frances, *The Correspondence of Sir Thomas More,* Princeton, 1947.

Rogers, J. E. Thorold, *The History of Agriculture and Prices,* Vol. IV, Oxford, 1882.

Roper, William, *Life of Sir Thomas More,* edited by Elsie V. Hitchcock, Early English Text Society edition, 1935.

Routh, E. M. A., *Sir Thomas More and His Friends,* Oxford, 1934.

Sanders, Nicolas, *De Origine et Progressu Scismatis Anglicani,* Cologne, 1585. (Translated by David Lewis, London, 1877.)

Savine, A., *English Monasteries on the Eve of the Dissolution,* Oxford, 1909.

Seebohm, F., *The Oxford Reformers of 1498,* London, 1896.

Smith, H. Maynard, *Henry VIII and the Reformation,* New York, 1949.

Smith, Preserved, *The Age of the Reformation,* London, 1922.

Snape, R. H., *English Monastic Finances,* Cambridge, 1926.

Spelman, Sir Henry, *The History of Sacrilege,* edited by C. F. Warren, London, 1895.

Stapleton, Thomas, *The Life and Illustrious Martyrdom of Thomas More,* London, 1928. (Translation by Monsignor P. E. Hallett of the life of More in *Tres Thomas,* Cologne, 1612.)

State Papers During the Reign of Henry VIII, 11 vols., His Majesty's Stationery Office, 1830–1852.

Stow, John, *Annales,* London, 1615.

Strickland, Agnes, *Lives of the Queens of England,* Vols. II and III, London, 1851.

Strype, John, *Annals of the Reformation,* 4 vols., London, 1709–1731.

——— *Ecclesiastical Memorials Relating Chiefly to Religion and the Reformation of It,* 2 vols., London, 1711–1733.

——— *Memorials of the Most Reverend Father in God, Thomas Cranmer,* 3 vols., London, 1694.

Stubbs, William, *Lectures on Medieval and Modern History,* Oxford, 1886.

Taunton, E. L., *Thomas Wolsey, Legate and Reformer,* London, 1902.

Tawney, R. H., *The Agrarian Problem in the Sixteenth Century,* London and New York, 1912.

——— *Religion and the Rise of Capitalism,* London, 1926.

Thompson, A. Hamilton, *English Monasteries,* second edition, Cambridge, 1922.

——— *The English Clergy and Their Organization in the Later Middle Ages,* Oxford, 1948.

Thompson, J. W., *Economic and Social History of Europe in the Later Middle Ages, 1300–1530,* New York, 1931.

Thurston, Herbert, S.J., "The Canon Law of the Divorce," *English Historical Review,* Vol. XIX (1904), pp. 632–645.

——— "Clement VII, Campeggio and the Divorce," *American Catholic Quarterly Review,* Vol. XXIX (1904), pp. 288–306.

Tudor Tracts, 1532–1588, with an introduction by A. F. Pollard, Westminster, 1903.

State Papers and Manuscripts relating to English Affairs, existing in the Archives and Collections of Venice, edited by R. Brown. Vols. II–V, His Majesty's Stationery Office, 1667–1873.

Weber, Max, *The Protestant Ethic and Spirit of Catholicism,* translated by Talcott Parsons, London, 1930.

White, Beatrice, *Mary Tudor,* New York, 1935.

Williams, C. H., *The Making of the Tudor Despotism,* rev. ed., London, 1935.

Wood, Anthony à, *Athenae Oxoniensis,* 5 vols., London, 1813–1820.

Wordsworth, Christopher, *Ecclesiastical Biography,* Vol. II, London, 1818.

Wright, Thomas, *Three Chapters of Letters relating to the Suppression of the Monasteries,* Camden Society, 1843.

Wriothesley, Sir Thomas, *Chronicle,* edited by W. D. Hamilton, Camden Society, 1875.

Index